WHAT DID I DO?

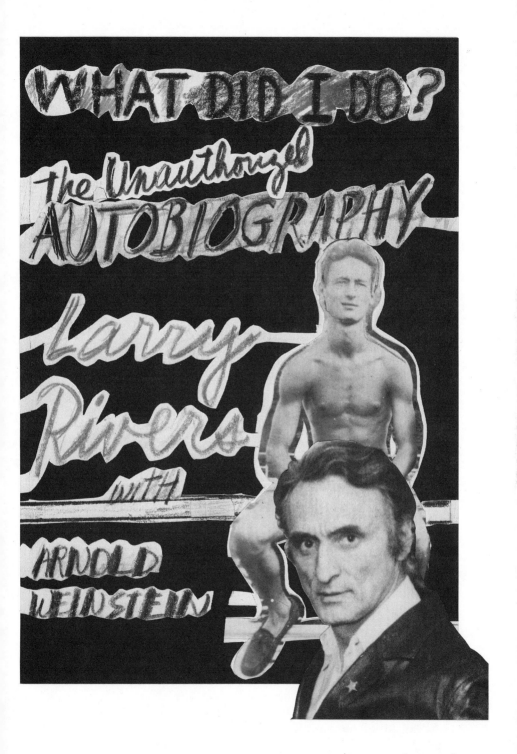

WHAT DID I DO?

the Unauthorized
AUTOBIOGRAPHY

Larry
Rivers

with

ARNOLD
WEINSTEIN

Aaron Asher Books
📖 HarperCollins*Publishers*

Color plates follow p. 182 and p. 374.
Acknowledgments and Illustration Credits follow p. 493.

WHAT DID I DO?: THE UNAUTHORIZED AUTOBIOGRAPHY. Copyright © 1992
by Larry Rivers and Arnold Weinstein. All rights reserved. Printed in
the United States of America. No part of this book may be used or
reproduced in any manner whatsoever without written permission except
in the case of brief quotations embodied in critical articles and reviews.
For information address HarperCollins Publishers, Inc., 10 East 53rd Street,
New York, NY 10022.

HarperCollins books may be purchased for educational, business, or sales
promotional use. For information, please write: Special Markets
Department, HarperCollins Publishers, Inc., 10 East 53rd Street,
New York, NY 10022.

FIRST EDITION

DESIGNED BY JOEL AVIROM

Library of Congress Cataloging-in-Publication Data

Rivers, Larry, 1923–
    What did I do? : the unauthorized autobiography of Larry Rivers, with Arnold
Weinstein.—1st ed.
        p. cm.
    ISBN 0-06-019007-8
    1. Rivers, Larry, 1923–   .   2. Artists—United States—
Biography. 3. Saxophonists—United States—Biography. I. Weinstein,
Arnold. II. Title.
NX512.R58A2 1992   92-52554
700'.92—dc20
[B]

92 93 94 95 96 CW 10 9 8 7 6 5 4 3 2 1

For Barbara Probst Solomon

Larry Rivers '92

PREFACE

The cover of this book, titled *What Did I Do?*, tells you that inside you will find an autobiography of Larry Rivers. The cover, which I put together, also contains a photo collage of myself, one of my "Vocabulary Lesson" paintings from the 1960s, and finally a mysterious "with Arnold Weinstein." What does "with Arnold Weinstein" mean?

Arnold has been a friend of mine since we were in our early twenties. We have lived together, slept in the same bed, gone to the same parties, poetry readings, plays, concerts, know all the same people, most of whom appear in this book. Arnold came to my painting studios often, showed up at my exhibitions, and read my reviews. I read his early poems, went to see productions of his plays, laughed at his jokes. I knew the three women he married, he probably fucked both my wives. What can I say? He's an old pal.

It took two years for Arnold and me to find our sea legs (he was a sailor once). In February 1991, in New York, I switched from a half day of art, half day of writing and working with Arnold, to an all-day routine of writing. Starting in May, in a quiet barn, having removed ourselves to my place in Southampton, we worked for seven months all day and many nights until twelve or one o'clock in the morning, weekends and holidays. Nothing broke that routine except phone calls, dinner invitations, unanticipated delights, and six or seven other things too boring to admit.

I handwrote everything you will read. In order to pluck from these scribbles and cross-outs on curling paper, I would read to Arnold across a thirty-inch table where he sat punching my words into a computer. If Arnold didn't understand what I read to him, he would say, "What do you mean?" Some of my lines, after being sifted through Arnold's bean, got such an ovation of raucous laughter, which always caused Arnold to cough, making the laughter and good feelings more catching, that I would swoop back to the page with great gusto. Sometimes he would frown; he didn't think certain subjects were important enough to deliver yet again to the reader. Arnold encouraged me and agreed that using words from my youthful "street" years would ring true to the way I was then. I didn't want to rewrite those days from the more mellow vantage point of today. Familiar with some of the events of my life, he'd suggest slipping in another point of view, an embellishment that often served to enrich my account. If he felt my words weren't expressing exactly what I meant, we'd discuss what I was after (and there were lots of discussions), and many times he'd come up with a word or try changing the sentence. If I liked it I used it, or used his idea but put it into words I found comfortable and was happy to have the reader take as my own. There were arguments. There was a give-and-take between us that existed before this very special two years, and carried us through them. We always looked forward to our meetings. The writing quite naturally became part of an ongoing verbal dissection of every imaginable subject, influenced by where we were in the book.

I praise Arnold for not only providing me with a one-man audience but for being able to attend seriously to my long story, my sex life and its dysfunctions, my art, my complaints and imagined neglect, my ballsy nature, my having the final say in all our aesthetic arguments. I not only praise him, I am curious to know how he managed to keep awake. No one could be that interesting. Arnold answers, "Well, I liked my reflection in the computer screen, and the barn where we wrote was mine between midnight and ten in the morning."

LARRY RIVERS

WHAT DID I DO?

Parris Island

That hot August noon in 1945 when the A-bomb was dropped on Hiroshima, I was a twenty-year-old saxophone player on a gig with the Johnny Morris Big Band, staying a few miles from the Parris Island Marine camp in South Carolina. I already had a wife and two kids, one hers, one ours. I left them on Crescent Avenue in the Bronx when I went out on tour with the band. As I sat on a dinky hotel veranda overlooking a rolling lawn, I opened the *New York Times* and drew the band's attention to the headlines. A cheer went up for our side.

The A-bomb update came in the midst of our going over the previous night's festivities, consisting of our band's first participation in a military event—the marine officers' graduation ball. These newly commissioned officers in their bright Hall of Montezuma dress uniforms did not know that the bomb was transforming them into peacetime officers.

Also at the ball was a matching number of local southern belles whose long gauzy gowns dusted the wide pine boards of the enormous space. The *Times* headline mingles with two upright bustling files of marine lieutenants and southern party girls. They are stretched along balconies on either side of the room; two narrow metal staircases lead down to the wide dance floor. Not to our band's jump tunes, but to the marine band's processional version of "The Halls of Montezuma," the young crew-cut marines walk down one of the staircases, the curious, lively belles the other. Finishing their descent, they approach each other. I watch; they meet, they stop, the marine tells her his name, she tells him hers; he formally places his arm around her, together they glide toward the other dancers and begin their evening.

Would it have been better if they had been given a choice? The French surrealist writer Lautréamont said, "On the day you decide to marry, the first stranger that crosses your path would make as good a match as any well-thought-out choice."

When all the marines and their assigned dates had floated out to the main dance floor, the marine band retreated noiselessly back to the barracks. Then the Johnny Morris band swung into action and took on the responsibility for the fox trotting, lindy hopping, and trucking the night away.

I played baritone sax in that seventeen-piece swinging bebop band. A good two thirds of our group smoked pot at some point every day. A good third smoked it all day long. Our leader and elder, Johnny Morris, disapproved, thinking one of us would get busted by a southern sheriff who would send the whole band to jail and throw away the keys, and our itinerant musical family would suffer shame and unemployment.

Johnny Morris, alias Gianni Morisi, was a survivor of the big band era's final gasp. His story begins without him.

On Artie Shaw's recording of "Begin the Beguine," a tenor sax solo, more a syncopated melody than a jazz chorus, spawned the career of one Tony Pastor. After sales of a few million Artie Shaw records featuring that revered tenor solo, Tony Pastor tried the path of an independent contractor; he broke away from Artie Shaw to form his own band. The drummer Tony Pastor chose for his new band was Johnny Morris, a pudgy forty-year-old getting pudgier. He never stopped moving his head, his eyes, or his hands, whether he had drumsticks in them or not.

Johnny was very funny on the drums, and fast and furious in the Buddy Rich tradition. Johnny's new boss made a record featuring him on a "specialty number" called "Paradiddle Joe" (a paradiddle is a drum rhythm), and the record became a best-seller. And Johnny Morris, now known as Paradiddle Joe, taking a cue from Tony, also took the path of the independent contractor. And Johnny hired me.

In those days I had no feeling about success other than blowing my horn, getting better at it, and getting high. I was influenced by the best of the bebop musicians. I talked like them, drank what they drank, smoked what they smoked, and occasionally injected into my veins the dope they took. For a while, in spite of my prohibitions against fancy clothes, I sported a peaked beret with a pompom on top simply because I once saw Dizzy Gillespie wearing one. I thought all of it would help me play as "good" as they did. I certainly played a lot, often with some of them, but behind my upbeat behavior was the sense that I had a lot to learn. Working for Johnny Morris, I noticed his ambition. He had had the thrill of playing. Now he wanted the thrill of leading a band.

For me, it was enough to be able to swing, to be in the presence of an admiring crowd and perhaps a groupie who might sleep with you because you sounded like Lester Young or Charlie Parker. I loved playing the latest arrangements of unknown composers in the avant-garde of unimportant big band writing, or jamming with an alto man who played a million notes a minute, or a trumpet man hired for "lip" whose horn could fill a dance hall a block long. The only thing I complained about was that I wasn't born a Negro.

Cherry Point

The week before the graduation gig, the war still going full speed, we were flown down by the marines to play at their Cherry Point, North Carolina, boot camp. A fat transport plane took us there. We sat on a long hard bench, without cushions, against the aluminum siding running the length of the plane. To distract ourselves, some of us began a systematic search for drugs. First stop, first aid kit. We discovered a whole gross of morphine tubes. The top of each two-inch tube consisted of a hypodermic needle with a wide bore, the quicker to exit the tube and enter you.

The substance meant to relieve the pain of soldiers wounded in battle suddenly began to mix with the blood of a bunch of young musicians wounded by life's travails. We were elated. Our discovery and ingenuity, even more than the prospect of getting high, delighted us. We dropped our pants or rolled up our sleeves and skin-popped the not too controlled substance. Within twenty-five minutes of takeoff we were in a state of affectionate quietude— except for the sound of retching caused by the drug.

We landed a little late and were rushed to an outdoor stage where five thousand marines in green fatigues tilting beer bottles into their mouths were waiting for us. Not only were some of us still high on government-issued opiates, we were northerners in the South; we were musicians, longhairs, long-jacketed sissies among warriors; we were Jews and Catholics and liberals and all manner of Mediterranean draft dodgers, on the verge of appearing before an entire contingent of the Rednecks of America. It was a strained moment.

Arc

Actually, I wasn't a draft dodger. In 1942 I enlisted in the U.S. Army Air Corps. Enlisted?
   I enlisted.
   Was it patriotism?
   I wanted to go. Maybe love of country, maybe because a lot of guys my age were doing it. My father was a socialist, so it's hard to imagine I inherited any patriotic blood from him. Just about everyone else in the neighborhood was a Communist. It's even harder to think I got nationalistic feedback there. Enlisting wasn't a Jewish thing either; I was not joining to liberate the concentration camps. Few Jews knew for certain what was going on in Nazi Germany. The Japanese did bomb Pearl Harbor. I guess joining up was some kind of patriotic reaction to that, as well as to the conjecture of my

uncle Benny, family pimp and foreign affairs expert, that Hirohito
had personally raped Nanking.

Hitler, Hirohito, Uncle Benny, my sudden surge of national-
ism, whatever, I did don the khaki and did not wait for the draft to
take me away. Don't forget, it took me out of my parents' home
and the Bronx.

I went for my physical. I managed to keep the medical exam-
iners from spotting my shaky left hand, a neurological problem I'd
had since I was twelve years old. It was identified as an intention
tremor by the doctors my parents took me to. For one of the neurological recruitment tests I had to shut my eyes and arc my index
fingers above my head so that the tips touched. I'm not sure how I
managed to hide my tremor, but my great desire to join the air
force guided my fingers in their trajectory to an impressive landing.
They touched and held steady.

At the time I volunteered I chose the air force over the other
armed services. The air force was youth and adventure, without
mud. The air force was of recent vintage, and at seventeen, so was
I. The air force had an image that came across as modern in newspapers, magazines, and movies.

For reasons I can't explain I was attracted to representations of
the new. Certainly new social and sexual attitudes, and from jazz
and big bands, new sounds. And even if the final result looked silly,
new dress styles. I see now how natural it was for me, later on in
music, and even later in art, to be attracted to something I had
never heard of—the avant-garde.

I made it into the air force. But at Fort Dix, in New Jersey, the
air force was very much on the ground. We marched and sang
"Nothing can stop the Army Air Corps," we ran, we shouldered
arms; we got flu shots, tetanus shots, typhoid shots, shots for tsetse
fly and crocodile bites; we took blood tests, reading tests, and apti-
tude tests, and were interviewed by Freudian bearded noncoms
screening for homosexual tendencies ("Do you have any homosexual tendencies?"). Despite my customary sincerity I quickly reas-
sessed my normal and innocent experiment with my little pal
Heshie and decided that a truthful answer might be a bad beginning
for my Air Corps career. But mainly we trudged back and forth
from barracks to bulletin boards looking to see whether we were
assigned to a training school—or to action.

At night there was more trudging back and forth, to the can-
teen, the movie, or the central communication board. I made it

over to a corrugated band shell where a seventeen-piece all-white swing band played a lot of Count Basie stock arrangements, exact replicas of the Count's hit records "One O'Clock Jump," "Moten Swing," and "Jumping at the Woodside," all featuring great sax solos by Lester Young. Unfortunately, his solos were not written into the arrangements. Still, there were good jazz and non-jazz musicians in the band. I never missed an opportunity to listen or to go backstage and talk shop. On the third evening there was an empty chair in the sax section; the tenor player was doing a ten-day stretch in the stockade for improvising on a weekend pass.

Seventy-two hours earlier, I had left my family with a big fare-well, all the relatives crying, "Why are you going? Who told you to volunteer? Don't go! Don't go!" Suddenly I'm back home. I didn't telephone. We had no phone.

"What are you doing here?" say my mother and father now that they're used to my absence.

"Where's my sax? I've been inducted into the band."

Pro

Now I'm playing tenor saxophone with the Air Corps Swing Band in Fort Dix, New Jersey, the Ellis Island of the armed forces. On the first tune of the first night I come in two beats before I'm supposed to with a loud low note. By the end of the evening, the aesthetic consensus is "Room for improvement," followed by the drummer's aside to the trombonist, "Wait till he finds out what he really has to do."

From 7:30 to 9:30 p.m. I think I'm a star playing for recruits whose fate in a few days will be pinned to a bulletin board. Next morning, 5:00 a.m., I'm woken up by the pup that wakes the bugler up. I am ordered to get out with the band and circle the base playing marching versions of tunes like "The Music Goes Round and Round," "Three Little Fishes" (boop boop dittum dottum wot-tamchu), Tommy Dorsey's theme song, "I'm Getting Sentimental over You," and the unavoidable, inevitable, ever popular sing-along version of "We live in fame and go down in flame, / Nothing can stop the Army Air Corps." We blow the new recruits out of bed and onto the drill field for 5:30 a.m. calisthenics and marching practice. So cold is it that vapor billows from my horn, which I have to play wearing woolen gloves.

"Larry had the attitude of living for every second because he might not make it to thirty-five years of age due to a neurological condition that made his left hand shake. Going to war was an experience he did not want to miss. He had an interest in danger that accounts for some of his high living and for his drugs. Mama used to take Larry with his shaky hand to the doctor from the time he was a little boy of ten. Larry used to practice for hours at a time, he was always very, very serious when he put his mind to anything. That's why, though we didn't mention it when he went off to war, it was kind of peaceful around the house."

Thus spake Goldie.

Thus looked Goldie.

9

My musical military debut was over in about ten happy days. Then I was sent to winter in the flatlands of Sioux Falls, South Dakota, where forty degrees below zero was not rare. Wearing earphones instead of earmuffs didn't help. I was training to be a radio and telegraph operator. As a reward for being graduated among the top ten percent in my class I was sent to summer in Boca Raton, Florida, for radar training. In the winter I get sent to an ice box, in the summer I am shipped to a boiler room. Between frying and freezing, the glory of the modern Air Corps began to fizz fast.

In Boca Raton I was being prepared for the European front and a role in the tail of a B-17 bomber. Every day instructors in khaki showed us films of German fighter planes and the artillery fire we could expect from them. Silently I saw my early death.

When it came time to go overseas my naturally shaky hand began to attract attention. On the rifle range my fellow PFCs put a noticeable amount of space between themselves and me whenever I aimed at a target. My second day on the range, as I lay on my stomach, a smart-looking six-foot-two captain stands over me.

"Put your gun down. What's wrong with your hand, soldier? Are you nervous?" He sends me to see the company doctor.

I was again given the neurological fingertip test. This time I missed miserably. It's possible that I didn't try as hard. After field vision and numerous other tests it was determined I had the symptoms of multiple sclerosis, obviously brought on by my military service. Three weeks later I was given an honorable medical discharge. On the way out, between the air force field and the free world, I walked through a turnstile where a woman at a window sat chewing gum in front of a typewriter. With a duffel bag over my shoulder masking a smile of relief at walking away from death, I heard this woman ask me, "Do you want to put in for a pension?"

On the basis of answering yes to that routine question, I received a pension for the rest of my life. The country was still at war, and Congress was climbing all over itself trying to prove how much it wanted to do for the boys coming home. My allotment was $210 a month. I enrolled in the Juilliard music school, receiving an additional $65 a month for studying under what was then called Public Law 16, a law whose stated purpose was to prepare the veteran for the moneymaking process, despite his serious handicap.

At Juilliard I worked hard preparing to become a serious composer, not exactly a sure way to beat the economy. When a swing band offered me a chair left vacant by a baritone player dragged off to war, I quit Juilliard, and now here I was in Cherry Point, N.C., playing for the marines with the Johnny Morris Big Band.

Jane Wrigley

In our makeshift dressing room we were trying to be casual about getting ready to go on, fingering our horns, playing a few bebop licks, flexing our overly relaxed chops. Jane Wrigley, our "chick singer," a tall dark-haired feast perhaps nineteen or twenty years old, was taping her tits a little higher than where their natural weight laid them on her chest.

On our one-night stands we used to travel from one town to another, one dance to another, in a caravan of four station wagons. Jane would sit between the driver and me on these long trips deep into the night after our gig. We would fall asleep as we were talking, and no matter what positions our bodies innocently took during the night, my twenty-year-old sensory apparatus in operating mode kept me conscious of her. After one of these nights of low-grade erection that left me with a severe case of blue balls, I made a date to meet her in her room in our hotel. Tubby Phillips, alias Philip Puzzalusa, our short Sicilian bass player, got the hot news, probably from my own lips, and in half an hour the whole band knew.

One by one the guys began dropping into my room. What was I building, wasting my time on an idiot chick, choosing the pursuit of sex over the fun of hanging out with the guys and pot and music practice and hip music talk and note-for-note humming of entire Lester Young sax solos? Harvey "The Tiger" Leonard, our piano man and psychoanalyst, warned me of the damage to the band's collective ego. He suggested I get a shrink as soon as possible.

"Have you ever examined this weird urge of yours?"

"What weird urge of mine?"

"This urge of yours to destroy the family."

"Which family?"

"The Johnny Morris Big Band family!"

By the time I left my room to go up to hers, I wondered whether the long-awaited thrill was worth it. I never found out; nothing happened. Forgive me.

11

She was really attractive, with beautiful breasts and long legs, a southern girl with a southern accent that itself gave me a hard-on. She was not very sure of herself, always sweet, asking if she could get us a soda, carry the music, somebody's coat. She was almost never spoken to; no one ever talked to her about her singing. She didn't count. She wasn't Billie Holiday and she didn't play an instrument! Jane was not one of the boys. It was 1945. But that night back in Cherry Hill the band began to play. To our opening musical blast, with a Kabuki shuffle, Jane Wrigley in her gown tight to her ankles walked out from the wings of the stage towards five thousand marines. Instead of cheering and whooping and whistling, they fell quiet as she stood in front of the microphone swaying rhythmically, waiting for us to finish her intro. Ms. Wrigley was ready. Five foot ten inches poured into a velvet gown with only two narrow straps to keep ten thousand eyes from experiencing the miraculous rise of those taped breasts.

Even before she began singing, the hush became a sudden tidal wave of sound. Not only did Jane Wrigley arouse them, they were aroused by their own outbursts, thrashing and lurching and jerking their beer bottles off and catching the trajectory in their mouths.

It began to get tighter and tighter around the stand. This is definitely *not* a concert. Is our chanteuse an asset or a liability? Is Harvey the Tiger right? Looking like a modern dance company, the military police in their white helmets run along the edge of the stage clubbing back the uncontrollables who are trying to mount it.

The marines' reaction took all of us by frightening surprise— except for Paradiddle Joe, who knew exactly what he was doing the day he hired Jane Wrigley.

Three hours later we boarded another military plane. By then we were a very sober musical troupe scouring medicine chests for relief from wounds sustained at the battle of Cherry Hill.

Stopover

When the band got back to New York, I had three or four days free. Before leaving again by station wagon caravan for Maine, our next gig, I went up to our apartment in the Bronx. My wife, Augusta, and our kids and her mother, Berdie Burger, were there.

Augusta says we met at a party where I was playing saxophone, but I remember meeting her at a large dance hall attached to a temple at 167th Street on the Grand Concourse. It was 1944. I'm

not sure why women with a full blouse of flesh slow me down, but I pointed her out to my two experienced pals, a piano player named Hy Nabors, who at nineteen sported a hook nose, a pirate's moustache, and a club foot, and Sy Mandelbaum, a blue-eyed saxophonist sharpie with a cock already sucked by a homosexual actor in the Borscht Belt the summer before.

Augusta was in a soft white dress a little below the knees. She had shapely legs on high heels. She wore a turquoise snood, a net placed on the head to catch the curled-up bottom of the hair. Until that evening I didn't think I liked snoods. I remember thinking them slightly "low class." But if women dress to attract male attention, she succeeded with at least one. I'm not sure we even danced. I got her address and telephone number. I was quite excited. She kept putting her hand up to her mouth when I made her laugh. I imagined she had lots of sexual experience, which attracted and repelled me.

Florence

My sexual experience, thus far, consisted of fucking a girl named Florence when I was sixteen. She was the short, fat, somewhat retarded friend of my father's youngest brother, Uncle Benny, just four years older than I. We were in his apartment. He told her to take me into the bedroom and "do it." She undressed and led me to the bed, placed me on top of her big breasts, belly, and wide thighs, and through the entire squirm she questioned me about how I was doing in high school. My uncle had the good taste to remain in the kitchen. Ungrateful little snipe that I was, I soon went to her on my own. She had no phone, so I had to chance catching her in and her mother out. Even after we had begun having sex, each time I managed to be alone with her I had to start all over again. I'd bring flowers, food, and a cheap article of clothing, and *still* I had to sweat to convince her I liked her for herself before she agreed to go over to her cot, lie back, and spread her legs. Flo, wherever you are, please forgive me for all of this.

For me, at the time, there was something screwy about a girl who allowed me and three or four of my friends to fuck her. She never acted as if it was really happening, even when the fellows sat in a semicircle with cocks out jerking off.

Am I saying that if five women sat on my cock or masturbated in front of me, they'd have a perfect right to categorize me as retarded? Was Florence just having a good time, unconcerned about what her "company" thought of her, and was this too much for me to swallow about labeling her a dumbbell because I was an ordinary boy trapped in the cruel double standard of the time? Florence wasn't retarded because she was having sex with half a dozen men in a row. She was retarded before she was used by men for sexual satisfaction. Maybe "slow" is a better description of her responses. She missed connections between one idea and another and never understood what anyone was talking about. Today I look down on young men who treat any woman the way I was capable of treating Florence. Gang bangs should be against the law.

My uncle remained uninformed about these evenings with Flo, as I was uninformed about evenings when *my* friends showed up on *their* own in her apartment. The apartment had a strong odor of her cunt. It penetrated her closet, where I would sometimes be scrunched up spying on the arrival and subsequent activities of my treacherous friends.

The finale with Flo was on a New Year's Eve. A couple of my cousins, some friends, and I took her riding in a car for half the night, stopping at a few bars, finally winding up in some apartment where my going first, which was customary and seemed correct for my role as producer, was challenged. I was forced to toss a coin. I chose tails, trying to be funny. I lost and one of the cousins went first.

Engagement

I began seeing Augusta on weekends. I remember a pretty silly idea of "seduction" on my part. For about three weeks I never tried to kiss her. This was probably about not being rejected but had the effect of making her wonder whether she was sexually attractive to me. Finally, on the couch in her living room, outside the bedroom where her mother slept with a slightly perceptible snore, we did it. Of course, fully clothed. Of course, I came in two seconds. And in those days when I came, sex was over.

The next night we again made our way to the couch, drunk. Our sexual tussle over, we fell asleep, me unzipped, cock out, and Augusta with her dress up to her face. Berdie, either on a routine urination or simply having heard our erotic groans, came out of her bedroom to investigate. She put her hand on my back gently, shaking me, pointing to the light outside the window.

One morning Augusta called me from her job as secretary.

"I'm pregnant."

My mother suggested I get married and use this pregnancy as a way to "settle down." Marriage for me had another logic, nothing to do with settling down, starting a mature life, raising a family. If we got married I could at last fuck Augusta without her clothes.

Nuptials

The wedding took place in my house on Mace Avenue in the North Bronx, six flights up the rear where my childhood days were spent.

Everybody sing. "It wasn't much like Paradise / but 'midst the dirt and all / there sat the sweetest maiden / one whom I fondly call / my yiddishe Mama" made the party.

I always thought we were poor. All those fights over money! Was my father going to give my mother twenty-five dollars for the week's expenses or a big thirty? And many more such small but

*My yiddishe Mama
(and Papa)*

great economic differences that twice resulted in his belting her in the lip she was giving him. But poverty is relative. Considering where Augusta and her mother could be found on the money ladder, we, the Grossbergs, were well off. However, don't get carried away. It was a small wedding. What made it a reception was Mom removing the plastic covers from the Alexander's French Provincial furniture. My square cousins came, and all my aunts and uncles, who spoke either Yiddish or Henglish. Berdie's sister arrived with three fifty-year-old spit curls on her forehead and her gigantic children.

My friends arrived, the ubiquitous Hy and Sy and the rest of the guys, and became a band five minutes later and filled the apartment with the sounds of modern jazz. To emphasize our coolness, we puffed a joint in the bathroom. I began playing with them.

Augusta wore a gray dress with pink trimmings and a little gray hat with a veil. She was already bordering on juicy, as it took us a

few months to make up our minds about getting married. At the
wedding she was in her fourth or fifth month. My cousin Al, alias
Abe Kores, to prove his fondness for me, snuck up behind Augusta
as she was watching me play, put his hands squarely on her tits,
and squeezed them.

Called to join my parents in the wedding march, I put my horn
down. The rabbi was standing between the windows in the living
room. Over his left shoulder was our Van Gogh print. The wedding
march turned into "You Can Depend on Me," a Lester Young tune
we were all crazy about. A small chuppah (a kind of ritual marriage
umbrella) was held up, and Sy never stopped blowing choruses
until the rabbi, about to pronounce us man and wife, shushed him.

Germs

Augusta had a serious phobia about germs. It made her and everyone around her unhappy. You couldn't lean over a pot of food.
Germs might dislodge themselves from your forehead or face and
fall into the soup or pot roast. She would pull you away from the
stove. When she used a public phone, she never got closer than
nine inches from the mouthpiece and she never allowed the receiver to touch her ear. At home she had more control over the
phone's hygiene, and when she thought she wasn't being watched,
she would swab it with peroxide. When she had to take a bill from
a cashier, she nipped it between the second and third finger and let
it float into her opened pocketbook with as little handling as possible. Coins were too dirty and distressful to deal with. She grabbed
them, closed her eyes, dumped them into her bag, and made believe it didn't happen. After we were married and she was no longer
shy about asking, I had to take a serious bath, something I was
never serious about, with lots of sudsing and soaking, before we
could join genitals.

Augusta followed those little invisible fascinating creatures
everywhere they went. From her point of view they were out to get
her. To Augusta it was not funny. Nor was it to me.

The choices we make we call our character. And what do I
understand about myself by having chosen to marry Augusta? This:
that fucking Augusta in the nude proved to be more important than
the drag of dealing with her germ phobia. And then there was the
logic that no marriage certificate, or if you prefer, license, could
keep me home or from whatever destiny had in store for me.

Joseph

When we first met there was a little boy living with Augusta and her mother. He was about three and a half years old and his name was Joseph. Augusta told me he was an orphan, a ward of the city: feeding, clothing, and roofing him brought her and Berdie twenty dollars a week from the New York City foster child program. Joseph smelled nice, a dark serious kid with long legs. I soon found out that little Joseph was not a ward of the city but an illegitimate son of Augusta's.

At seventeen Augusta got pregnant as a result of a serious love affair with a neighborhood Italian. For seven and a half months she was able to conceal her pregnancy from her parents. At that swelling point she was forced to tell Berdie. In order to keep Sydney, her father, in the dark about her condition, she went to "visit relatives" in Florida at the end of the school year, in late June. Baby Burger —as his name appeared on his birth certificate—was born in the middle of August. When Augusta returned to the Bronx in September, Sydney told her to put the child up for adoption: under no circumstances was he going to have "that bastard" under his roof. Without giving up her rights as Joe's mother, Augusta put him in

Berdie and Joseph

an orphanage, visiting him with Berdie every weekend. When the
orphanage closed down Sydney relented, and in the still of the
night Joseph began to live with his "family." The frost of Sydney's
opinion about having an illegitimate child in the house finally
melted when Joseph, despite the usual brush-off, jumped onto his
grandfather's lap and planted a long kiss on his bald pate. By now
having been sufficiently impressed and depressed by Augusta's previous sexual experiences, I think if it wasn't love I felt, it was what
most men think is love—jealousy! To possess in the present, miraculously ridding the loved one of her terrible but thrilling past. Because I asked, I had to listen to Augusta tell about being fucked in
a hearse by an Italian boyfriend, and when he finished, by one of
his friends. This always induced a hard-on and a depression.

The Tiger Gives Up

The Johnny Morris band was waiting in New York until our three-
week engagement in Maine began. Our pianist, Harvey the Tiger,
assembled us all in the McAlpin Hotel lobby and introduced us to
a cat who looked like a psychiatrist. He was in fact a psychiatrist, a
certain Dr. Zygmund Birnbaum. He sat modestly smoking an eight-
inch Havana cigar. The Tiger paced on the thick carpet, sweat
pouring down the ample furrows of his prematurely balding head,
pushing his Dickensian lenses rhythmically from the tip of his
pointy nose to the bridge.

"Fellas, after two months of touring with you guys up and down
the East Coast from New York to fucking Florida and back, one-
night stands, blowing our brains out risking our fucking lives for a
bunch of rednecks, smoking lots of grass, staying up three nights in
a row, I realize I must take a break."

"Tiger," Johnny Morris said, "Maine is going to be different.
We're gonna be in one place for three weeks. We'll work on a lot of
new music! And if we draw crowds, we'll get an extra week! You
gonna really go to sleep every night?"

Dr. Birnbaum stood up. "Fellas, the fact is the Tiger's burnt
out. He should go for a short stint in the Klezmer rest home with a
stack of old Lester records and lots of therapy to distract him."

"Aw, Tiger."

The Tiger would have none of it. With Dr. Birnbaum at his
side, he made his way through the revolving door out into the
boiling afternoon.

19

We needed a piano player. Jack Freilicher, alias Jack Fry, a lively and dependable jazz musician, was recruited at my suggestion and after a brief audition—"Do you or don't you get high?"—was hired without playing a note. He didn't play his first note with the Johnny Morris Big Band till opening night in Old Orchard Beach.

Commitment

Not long after Tiger gave his farewell address, I began getting ready for Maine and what I thought Maine was going to be about. First I bought a few boxes of baritone sax reeds, then I dropped off my horn at Charles Ponte to be checked out for leaks, maybe a new pad or two. Knowing I was going to do lots of writing for the band, I stopped at Manny's for music paper and fat-point pens. Though I thought there'd be no time for things like swimming or beach fun, as we were going to concentrate on rehearsals of new music, I chose a bathing suit for myself at Macy's, even got some socks and a long-sleeved shirt.

By now Augusta looked as if she was attached to an air hose. The basketball in her stomach as well as all her other distortions increased my sexual interest. Women's bodies after the sixth month feel different. It's taken me a few decades and three pregnant women for a theory to evolve: Men accept the obvious problems connected with having children because the heightened thrill of sex with their inflated mates manufactures a natural tranquilizer affecting the areas of the brain that produce anxiety. This tranquilizer continues to flow until the woman brings breast feeding to a halt. Even after the child is born, male anxieties about the immediate future are lessened.

Ars Musica

Before I leave with the band for Maine, Augusta is telling me she doesn't want to be left alone in New York.

I tell her she has a mother.

After a few discussions that strongly resemble arguments, I ask her if she wants to be invited to Maine. She makes it clear only one solution exists. I must give up my position as baritone saxophonist in the Johnny Morris Big Band.

"The more you play, the better you sound. Look, if I'm not blowing, who am I? No one!"

Fingers clenched, fists buried in her billowing hips, Augusta presents me with an alternative.

"You can get a job in New York. What's the difference where you play your sax?"

"It's hard to get a job as a baritone player. And the Johnny Morris band plays music I like! And it gives me a chance to write music. It's not easy to find a job like that."

I let a minute go by, I try to unheat the situation. I move toward her. "I'll be back."

She moves away. "Don't."

She doesn't mention our singer Jane Wrigley, here, now. She mentioned Jane the day before. During a calming cup of tea.

"How's Jane Wrigley doing?"

"She's okay."

"Do the crowds like her?"

"Some crowds. The marines liked her. She went over very big."

"I'll bet she went over *very big*." Sullen silence. "Does she have a boyfriend?" Curled lip. "Do you like her looks?"

"She's attractive. Why do you want to know if I like her looks?"

"What does she do after the band stops playing? You're not fooling me, Larry, I know you're interested in her."

"I'm interested in playing my fucking saxophone. And that's why I'm with the Johnny Morris band, and that's why I'm going to Maine. The more you play the better you sound. I'm a saxophone player. If I'm not blowing I'm no one."

Weird Gigs

I never was sure, as we continued growling and acting very disappointed in each other, whether what I was saying gave Augusta a true picture of my ongoing identity crisis.

My steady employment playing with the Johnny Morris band was due partly to luck and some talent, and without doubt to the fact that many ace baritone players were fingering instruments of war. In periods of unemployment I visited "the floor," as we called the Musicians Local 802 hiring hall, looking for a job. To be seen could turn out to be heard.

Age is a great and ancient social binder, so it was natural, in that gigantic crush of musicians looking for work, to stand around with my contemporaries; they were called "dopers" by the entrenched, bow-tied club-date specialists who literally had at the tip of their tongues and fingers every song that was ever written, *and* in the correct key!

Though powerless to dispense club dates, the dopers had the power of youth, looks, exuberance, suicidal tendencies, and the PR edge on being hotshot jazzbos. Though white-skinned, we had black heart. We played for less money, having fewer options. We would go anywhere to blow. This, along with our silly hair and wild clothes, induced many a club-date contractor to hire us for weird and sometimes dangerous gigs. Which I gladly took. And I don't necessarily mean some supper club with a maître d' leading you to your candle-lit table; nor do I even mean your smoke-filled stripper joint where a recently paroled bouncer pushes you to the bar and says, "What's your pleasure?" I'm talking ethnic neighborhood social clubs.

Once I had a job for a month with a Greek band. I had a special function playing popular tunes of the day, old favorites dotted with my own personalized bebop licks. I was the American wing of the band. The elders who ran the show felt obliged to provide contemporary American music so that their children, not knowing the Hellenic dances, could still swing and sway in the same space with the rest of the family. Before that Greek club date, it never crossed my mind that I played American music.

Trucking

On those impecunious occasions when I couldn't even find weird, dangerous gigs, I worked in my father's S.B.S. trucking business. At the zenith of his success, during the war, when even if you slept for a living you could make money, he had two trucks. What did S.B.S. stand for? Those were the letters painted on the side of the first truck my father bought secondhand. He didn't know what the initials stood for, nor will anyone ever know. He kept S.B.S. to save the expense of a sign painter redoing the letters. My father had no identity problem.

I had an identity problem.

Working for my father required pushing a hand truck along the sidewalks and streets of the garment center. I always acted as if I worked for him because he needed extra help during the season and it only incidentally afforded me a few bucks. My position embarrassed me. What was a swinging saxophonist doing pushing a hand truck? My father's business could have done without me.

Giving and accepting money was not familiar behavior for either of us. My father came from a European small-town barter society, whatever else it was. He gave me money I could use. What did I have that *he* could use? There was no way of fighting that ethic.

Pushing my truck down the streets of the garment center became hazardous. If I spotted a hand-truck pusher I knew from the 802 union floor, I would quickly move from sidewalk to street, avoiding an imminent face-to-face. To pull off this switch required very special handling. Parking in the garment center even in those days was impossible; there were almost no spaces between the big trucks at the curb for me to roll my hand truck into the street. If I got stranded on the sidewalk I would enter some lobby, truck and all, to avoid the confrontation. Once, an elevator starter said, "Listen, sharpie, use the service entrance around the corner," just as Jeffrey Allen, alto sax, was pushing his truck past the glass doors. I hid my head in the truck and fumbled in its empty bottom.

When I pushed a hand truck for my father, I hid my head. When I played my saxophone I stood up, and looked for a bright light and a microphone.

V-J Day

I finished packing for Maine in silence. As I was going out the door of the apartment with my horn and valise, Augusta raised a heavy wooden coat hanger and brought it down fiercely across my back, shoulder, and neck.

No one punches a pregnant woman. I struck her with my fist in the center of her back, knowing full well it was a painful blow.

During the whole melodrama our voices were raised. My punch raised hers to a scream. I was so angry I didn't even know or care what might happen. Sobbing, she sank into a chair. I went through the door, took the subway to Fiftieth and Broadway.

Out in the street I looked at the crowd and what was going on. I realized that we had been arguing all day long, all V-J Day long. As best I could with my two heavy arm stretchers, fighting my way through a mob that kept congratulating me for ending the war, I arrived at the Ambassador Hotel. The band's station wagons were at the curb being packed. Tubby Phillips greeted me. Martin Dane, alias Mario Dione, the road manager, gave me a visual frisk to see if I was high. I wasn't. That green tint in my complexion was depression.

23

We were leaving.

Again we squeezed it all into four Ford station wagons, the luggage, the instruments, the bandstands, the band. In one of those vehicles, in the front seat, between the driver and me, was Jane Wrigley, this time in a light summer dress.

Our caravan got under way the evening of V-J day, August 14, 1945. The streets were filled with happy, energetic drunks, sailors, soldiers, cops, et al., embracing, kissing, and trying to open the doors of our cars to embrace and kiss us—a celebration we had to forgo. We didn't dare open the doors or windows; even if we could throw the marijuana away in time, the fumes would send us to jail.

We finally escaped the citywide traffic jam and got on the road toward New England. A half hour out on the highway one of the cars in the caravan lost the car in front of it, not that we knew the way in the first place. Our navigator, Martin Dane, busy reaching for the variety of pot being smoked, wasn't navigating. It took two hours for the procession to reassemble. Finally we arrived at Old Orchard Beach, Maine. The six-hour drive from New York had taken us twelve.

Old Orchard Beach

Maine is known for lobsters and moose and lachrymose Edmund Muskie and Rockefeller's Bar Harbor and George Bush's Kennebunkport, and as the working retreat of the poets Robert Lowell, Elizabeth Bishop, and Kenneth Koch, and Fairfield Porter painted there, and Alex Katz and Neil Welliver still do, and Buckminster Fuller did his geodesic stuff in that geographic area. Wilhelm Reich began his American medical practice in Maine (though it and his life ended in a federal prison elsewhere). There were summer and winter homes of the most interesting kinds of social fauna, including Bette Davis, plus Indians suing the state and winning land, money, and concessions.

With our luck, the Johnny Morris band ended up in Old Orchard Beach, New England's Coney Island, a downscale seaside resort whose economy revolved around the Ferris wheel and the loop-the-loop in the center of town. Old Orchard Beach's Tunnel of Love was a serious place; couples went in single and came out engaged. On the backs of the brightly lacquered merry-go-round horses, midst the hurdy-gurdy melodies, rode the tourists' only hope for a hot time in Old Orchard town. Yankees, reputedly nononsense sexless penny pinchers, still had to waste some of their time, as well as some of their money.

Into this scene rolled the Johnny Morris jump and bebop caravan. I staggered bowlegged out of the car, so afflicted that I looked as if I'd arrived on horseback from Montana. Next came Jane stuffing her chaste tits back into her summer dress. Johnny Morris, his feet hanging out the door of the car, still sitting on the seat, took one last swig of Jack Daniel's. As our other cars opened their doors, twelve hours of accumulated reefer fumes billowed out and stoned tourists fortunate enough to be within a ten-foot periphery.

Cold Water Casino

On the shore of the darkest waters lapping our country, Old Orchard Beach featured fresh seafood. A long wharf poked pretty far out over a frigid ocean that all of us found impossible to enter even at hot high noon in the middle of August. The wooden wharf ended at a giant dance hall known as the casino—Cold Water Casino, I called it. Here we were going to play six nights a week for one month.

Shortly before we went onstage each night, Johnny Morris would stagger into the band room, roll his eyes, liver his lips, and with the drumsticks he always carried play a paradiddle fanfare to his question, "What time does the balloon go up?" I'm still not sure what he meant, but chances are it had something to do with getting high.

It wasn't easy for us to get a constant supply of marijuana up there. We found a "hip" black "cat" out of Atlanta, Georgia, who lived in Portland and loved the way we jammed Ellington's "A Train." In gratitude he offered to make the run to Boston and bring us back some first-class grass. We pooled our resources and laid the result on our admirer. As he waved goodbye he winked warmly and in a soft voice sang Ellington's "Do Nothin' Till You Hear from Me." We still haven't heard from him.

One time a female postgraduate at the Boston Conservatory of Music came slumming by. We were particularly inspired that night, and she was impressed by the band's innovations. This hip Florence Nightingale came backstage and by way of congratulations dispensed the cure for which there is no known disease. A whole Prince Albert Tobacco can full of hashish, enough for an army of bedouins, lasted us two days and one night.

Finding speed, at the time known innocently as "uppers," was no problem. Benzedrine was totally legal and went by the name of Benzedrex, an antihistamine. It came in a handy inhaler. Directions: Break inhaler, drop Benzedrine-drenched filter in Coca-Cola, and swallow.

Our leader scorned our practices, preferring the straight bourbon he kept in the little warehouse in his room. Johnny Morris, Jr., age nine, had been schooled by us to concoct our refreshment. When the band and the nights were steaming and the sweat oozed out as we played, little Johnny would pass the Coca-Cola. He would hand the preparation to the end trombone player, who'd give it to the player beside him, who in turn would give it to the trumpet player and so on, until those who partook were restored, and ready for a couple of nights of no sleep. It took us about half an hour to become oblivious to the sult of those August nights and ready to blow our music of the spheres. The balloon had gone up. We were ready to entertain.

And entertainment it was, as much as it was music. Our private perception of ourselves was that we were a group of musicians devoted to raising the musical consciousness of the public to our own avant-garde level. Actually, we were the bebop version of Spike Jones, a popular novelty band of the time. Spike's mad sidemen blew whistles and Bronx cheer bladders, shot pistols, sounded gongs, and wore masks and wigs; in his famous "Führer's Face" number, his entire band donned Hitler moustaches.

I considered it morally disgraceful and aesthetically unprincipled to go for commercial success at the expense of my beautiful ideals. If I tried to reach the romantic high place and didn't make it, I could be applauded for the attempt. But it depressed me to watch a man walk out on the stage and smear himself with feces, thinking the audience's applause would nullify his olfactory sense. What goes on in his nose if nobody laughs or claps? Nothing goes on in his nose. He smells shit.

That's how complicated my thoughts were in those days—a product of my youth, my Benzedrine inhaler, and the dregs of the Prince Albert can.

The house lights would lower and the tiny bulbs in Johnny Morris's wire brushes would start blinking. His drums would light up like a movie marquee, flashing his name on the bass drum. Even Johnny Morris himself lit up thanks to an electric bow tie.

That was only the light show. For the music show, we would apply all the imagination and innovation in our young bebop souls to unfurling a repertory of songs like "One Meat Ball," "Knock Knock, Who's There" ("Matzos!" "Matzos who?" "Time matzos on!" or "Marmalade!" "Marmalade who?" "That's what Papa wants to know!"). And of course the perennial "Paradiddle Joe."

A popular song of the time was "Sam, You Made the Pants Too Long," which Maestro Morris considered too highbrow; he commissioned me, the poet of the band, to take it down a peg or two by changing it to "Sam, You Made the Putz Too Long." Johnny was asking me to lower my standards! It was an aesthetic dilemma. I didn't lose much sleep over it. Benzedrine kept me awake that week anyway. My deliberation finally ended. Let's face it, changing "pants" to "putz" was not going to do much damage to the Cause. My first chance to sell out! This was a big moment in my development. I had something to sell!

There were some numbers in the band's book that were really good, numbers we wrote to express where the best of our musical abilities lay. The entertainment numbers were concessions to the warp and woof of bread and butter. But what makes it all the more poignant and difficult is the fact that some of the dumb ditty numbers called for instrumental solos, and these were uncontrolled, and no one including the bandleader demanded anything except what the musician wanted to blow. So Mike Shane, our lead trumpet player, could stand up in the middle of "One Meat Ball" when we had just got done shouting the silly words and blow a fantastic solo that totally ignored everything about the song except the chordal structure underneath it.

Crustacean

I also connect Old Orchard Beach with the first time I ate shrimp. I took one bite of the pink little thing, and soon I was trying lobster, crab, crayfish, clams, mussels, and finally even—bacon!

Religious prohibition was not the reason for my family's scorn of the pig, so we said. We simply thought the pig was a lowlife animal. My family was more superstitious than I like to admit. And there was, as always, the Italian question, their Neapolitan pork stores with small rock-hard salamis and vast mortadellas with islets of pig fat, and pig snouts and hogs' balls tied in cotton string dangling in the windows. We laughed at it all and pretended to vomit. Who could eat that stuff? The Italians! Yeh. Naturally. They could eat anything. Plus a lot of Jewish puss! What about my wife? Her too! Italians!

My father was a closet pork eater. When I was sixteen years old I worked after school in his business, on the truck. On Saturdays, no less, he would stop at a luncheonette and order something of the pig. I thought it was strange that he could develop an interest in something that had never crossed our mezuzahed threshold. He asked me not to tell my mother about the pig. I didn't. Just as I didn't tell about the women he used to point to as we were sitting in the truck waiting for a red light to turn green. He'd share with me his appreciation of parts of the body—ankles, calves, hidden thighs, prominent behinds, and of course breasts. Sometimes he would even pass opinions about their facial features. (I spent about five years of the sixties on a series of paintings and sculpture called "Parts of the Body." More about that later.)

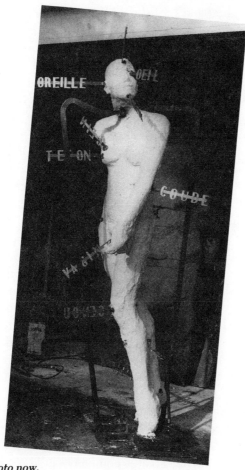

Photo now.

Pop paid for his transgression. He announced that he had to check into Montefiore Hospital for a few days to take some tests.

"What's wrong with my husband!" cried Mom.

Sore arm muscles.

"So? He works hard. So?"

His few days in the hospital turned into a month. The diagnosis was retribution in itself—trichinosis, a malady endemic to consumers of the pig.

Beyond Aesthetics

Being on the road, playing dance halls, auditoriums, and military bases sometimes till four a.m., then getting into a station wagon and traveling all through the dark of night to our next night's gig, put a crimp in the band's artistic ambition. We wanted to be recognized by critics and other musicians as a great and groovy band. But one-night stands, packing, unpacking, in and out of hotels, was incompatible with the composing, arranging, and rehearsing that was necessary. What we wanted was to fall somewhere between the lyric cool of Lester Young, the sonic regurgitations of Ike Quebec, the flatulent punctuation of Illinois "on-the-floor" Jacquet, and Eddie Lockjaw Davis. Was that asking too much?

It was asking too much. Three weeks in Old Orchard Beach, Maine, an ideal condition for adding to our repertoire, trying new ideas, getting seventeen men to play beautifully together, was also ideal for spending the summer the way everybody else spends the summer. Lavishly. Doing nothing.

During our stay there we were put up in a bungalow colony a few miles from the casino. We blew every night but Saturday, to a somewhat sparse house. On Saturday nights big bands with big reputations filled Cold Water Casino. Woody Herman and His Woodchoppers were playing the Saturday we arrived! Due next week was Lionel Hampton, who had played with Benny Goodman and was now a major independent contractor of a band that would heat up the same space we were working. And after Hamp, another Goodman defector, Gene Krupa, who was not only the most famous drummer in the world but the best-looking, whose hair when he played flew from his head like the wings of the Victory of Samothrace on the staircase of the Louvre, which I had not yet seen. And not only that, he was awaiting trial for possession of three joints of marijuana! What greater company could we have asked for? We had arrived! This was the Big Time.

We were really quite proud to be appearing the same week in the same place as the likes of Herman, Hampton, Krupa. Johnny Morris was certainly impressed, but he also felt relegated to the status of house band.

"Why Saturday night? Hampton could draw on Tuesday afternoon!"

"Lionel Hampton doesn't play on Tuesday afternoons in Old Orchard Beach, Maine," said the owners, Malcolm and Martin Beal, identical twins.

"We could use that Saturday night exposure." Johnny turned to me and whispered in my ear, "Did I say that or did I just think it?"

The Beal boys assured Johnny, "Look, it's nothing personal, it's just an artistic thing."

Johnny picked up quickly, pressing an idea he usually put down. "Artistic! Right! Bebop's the coming thing, and that's our band."

"Mr. Morris, we've been listening to your band. We like what we hear. And we think the way we have things worked out is just fine. It's the Lionel Hamptons of this world that pay your salary. That's policy."

All too true. The place was so packed and the crowd so aroused by Hampton's music and the dancers stomped so hard that Cold Water Casino almost collapsed into the waves lapping beneath. Johnny finally had to admit, "I was blowing in a blind alley."

Aside from those big-band Saturday nights, there was nothing whatever for us to do in Old Orchard Beach except ride the loop-the-loop and mount the lacquered back of the carousel horse. As for creative leisure, not only were we not composing or arranging anything new, we had given up feeling guilty about our pre-tour artistic ambitions. Nights were short. Playing music went quickly. The days were long. The way the band passed those days was to smoke pot and play poker.

Separate Tables

I could not play poker. Not that I didn't know the game. Only a few years earlier I used to accompany my parents on their card-playing nights just to sit with them and observe. Whether I was enjoying the privilege of being brought along by my parents, or whether it was the only live adult show available, I understood poker well enough for a seventeen-year-old Bronx boy; there wasn't too much to understand. At twenty, in Old Orchard Beach, Maine, playing poker felt like a step back in my evolution. As a young emergent snob I felt I was beyond a pastime that had amused my immigrant parents. Also, poker in Maine seemed to be one big bore.

Jack Freilicher was no poker player either. He was older than I and often exposed me to things that would broaden my view. He read a lot. Novels, politics, philosophy. He knew classical music. But he loved jazz. He and I had played lots of club dates in the dim social halls of Brooklyn, Queens, and the Bronx. In Manhattan we jammed with various groups that included players who later became known as Gerry Mulligan, Al Cohn, Zoot Sims, Allen Eager, and other members of the white avant-garde of bebop.

Brighton

Jack was from Brighton Beach in Brooklyn, a politically radicalized neighborhood of Jews. His cousin and close friend was Chester Kallman, the editor of the Brooklyn College literary magazine, whose epigrams and looks dazzled W. H. Auden. Eight years later I was living on St. Mark's Place with my friend Arnold, my stepson Joseph, my son Steven, my mother-in-law Berdie, and not my wife Augusta. Dr. Schwartz, the abortionist in the apartment above us, moved suddenly, probably against his will, to Ossining, New York. The two new tenants were a happily married couple, Chester Kallman and W. H. Auden.

Back at Brighton Beach, the 1945 advanced-thinking, fast-talking younger generation smoked pot and went to analysts, mostly Freudian. The more radical set preferred Reichian. Men had to eat cunt to amount, and women had to suck cock. This was the depths of their depravity! Pissing and shitting on people hadn't arrived. That was the lower depths. Sadism and masochism reared their heads only in the volumes of de Sade.

So I found Jack not a dull boy. He often made me question myself. Once at a gig in New York, during our break, he showed me an object from another world, the *Pocket Book of Modern Art*. He pointed to a reproduction of a painting vaguely featuring a bass fiddle. It had a lurking familiarity, and I associated it with the world of jazz.

Jack said, "That's cubism, man. It's by a French painter called
Georges Braque."

I wanted to say, "What's cubism?" But suddenly I knew what
cubism was. Cubism told a young man from the Bronx he didn't
know very much. Cubism didn't know about him or his nights
walking all over Greenwich Village with his big horn slung over his
shoulder looking for a joint where he could sit in and blow with a
lot of other desperados. Cubism certainly didn't smoke pot or get
high, cubism was history in which he played no part.

Where could I begin to catch up?

Jane Freilicher

Jack's wife arrived about four days after we arrived. She was nineteen, an artist, very funny and very smart. I caught that intelligent
thing about her right away. So did her high school; she was valedic-
torian of her graduating class, as were her two older brothers.

Jane did not seem sexy to me. She wore low-heeled shoes. For
me low-heeled shoes were something out of English movies. It
wasn't that only whores wore high-heeled shoes. My mother wore
high-heeled shoes. Jane was tall, a brunette, and had a thin nose
with a happy ending. She had an oval face. What you noticed about
her eyes was not so much the color blue, or their size, but who was
inside them. If someone asked me was I attracted to Jane I would
have said no. But I kept watching her paint. We went for long
walks, and we talked about literature and art. We'd get into our
bathing suits and go to the beach. There I couldn't help noticing
the power of her figure, her unique posture. She walked with the
confidence of a dancer, spine straight, head tilted back and up.

One day as the rest of the band was playing cards I was lying in
the sun trying at least for a tan. Jane was painting. It impressed me.
I became curious. How long had she been painting? Did she go to
art school? What were these paintings about?

Jack, who was also using the paint, said, "Why don't you try it,
man? I think you'll dig it."

Jane pushed some paper in front of me and handed me a brush.

"It's not music," said Jack. "But it's fun."

Every day after that, when the boys in the band would sit down
to an afternoon around a card table, Jane, Jack, and I nearby, on
one of those picnic-bench tables, laid out paint and paper, and with

33

one brush each spent a few hours painting. The weather was pleasant and the afternoons vanished. It's hard to think we suddenly discontinued gossiping, but the gossip was sprinkled with art, literature, and politics. I liked those spices. After a week or two I began thinking that art was an activity on a "higher level" than jazz. The blue romance that haloed jazz was still strong. Jazz reached into the past through songs with touching chord changes and simple words. I was still thrilled to walk into jazz spaces, where I could freely enjoy the faces, personalities, and speech patterns of young men and women, black and white. I had been caught up in this romance with jazz, blues, drugs, and night.

Now I began to have pleasure in the daylight, painting in the afternoons there in green Maine. In painting I could make nameable things, and I could do it alone. I liked putting a brush into a pile of color and spreading it onto a surface, making it come out looking like something, a foot or anything else. Music is abstract, it will always be abstract, and you'll always need other people to help you make it. Music was like sex. I wouldn't want it all the time. Painting was like living, a little lower-keyed than the life I lived, but something I wanted to hang on to.

Four or five days after Jane arrived, we were painting almost every day. Working with Jane, I learned how to mix certain colors. Blue and yellow make green, red and white make pink, and orange and white make Caucasian flesh tones, especially if you add a little raw sienna. I began to name colors I had only seen. Two weeks later I had already developed a repugnance for white-haired bristle brushes, not just because they were white and from the pig, but because they made furrows in the pigment. I hated furrows then and I hate furrows today! And in those same two weeks I already preferred thin paint to thick. Jane and I also looked at reproductions of Old Masters.

Nell Blaine

But it was the work of Nell Blaine that influenced the spirit of my first pieces. Nell was the only professional artist I knew. She showed her work at galleries and was reproduced in magazines and books devoted to abstract art. I saw my first modern paintings in the flesh on the walls of Nell's loft when Jack and Jane brought me there for the first time. For me, her loft itself, the actual having of it, was worth respecting. Three other accomplishments gave her work further authority. She lived and did her art in a manufacturing area on Twenty-first Street next to a Jewish graveyard. She was a southerner. And she was a lesbian.

Leaning against the wall in long racks, and on her easel, were large bright abstractions, bold simple hard-edge shapes contained in black outlines. My first efforts, bold simple hard-edge shapes outlined in black, somehow became transmogrified into faces and bodies and things, whatever I could manage at the time to make them somehow identifiable to the observer, Jack or Jane.

Some Changes

It took about two years down the bumpy road of my life to get from Maine to Main Street in the heart of Greenwich Village, where I enrolled in the Hans Hofmann School of Modern Art. Not that Hans called it the School of Modern Art. In retrospect, though, "understanding and doing" modern art was what he was selling. But first I had to go through some changes.

My daily activities, nocturnal music and drugs in Old Orchard Beach with the Johnny Morris Big Band and art in the afternoon with Jane and Jack Freilicher, continued. But the locale now was the Big Apple. I had traded the Johnny Morris band for other bands plus nightly jam sessions at Nola Studio. As for drugs, no change. Except more. As for art in the afternoon in Old Orchard Beach, it now took place in Nell Blaine's studio on Twenty-first Street.

At Nell's we drew, or as young artists say, "tried to draw," from a model. A ballsy older Nell, twenty-six and a graduate of Hofmann's school, told us what Art was all about, impressionist art and expressionist art and Giotto art. I still remember her attempts to show the relationship between the art of the past and the art of now, between new jazz and modern art. She introduced me to artists like Robert De Niro (the actor's father) and de Kooning, and critics like—well, there's nobody *like* Clement Greenberg, not that any of us liked him except Helen Frankenthaler, who had to love him to like him. Nell lent me art books and magazines. She suggested shows to see at galleries and museums: Matisse, Bonnard and—ah, but I'm jumping the gun.

First I had to disassimilate myself from an alchemy of my own devising.

A McAlpin Hotel gig with the Johnny Morris Big Band had come to an end. Jane Wrigley went off with her taped tits and her long legs and voice, to sing with, or to, Tommy Dorsey. I went to Local 802 to look for work. With the war over, the union floor was crowded with recently discharged GIs, good musicians anxious to reidentify themselves as saxophonists in name bands.

Occasionally I felt a remorseful twinge thinking of the competent musicians whose places I took while they were blowing reveille or getting their heads blown off. But when these veterans returned from the service, my sympathy drooped abruptly. The baritone sax was never essential to all reed sections, so baritone sax players were never too numerous. Suddenly it seemed that the entire United States Armed Services Orchestra was one big baritone sax section. Big bands were going out of style, and so were the dance halls, big clubs, big restaurants, vaudeville houses, and colleges that booked them. My opportunities for playing with big bands—or small—had depressingly diminished.

Newcomer

On Halloween Day, 1945, my son Steven Rivers was born. Wait a minute! He was born Steven Lester Rivers, and I was going to call him Lester, for guess who! After the first decade of this century, no parents faintly interested in starting a kid off on the right foot dared call him Lester.

I grew up in a family that named newborn children after dead grandparents. Augusta's father had died two years before. His name was Sydney ("Call me Jewboy") Burger. Well, I who had changed my name from Grossberg to Rivers was not about to lay the all-American Jewish "Sydney" on my firstborn, so I called him Steven, keeping Sydney's initial active. That took care of my Hebraic responsibility. And through the middle name Lester I could now broadcast my ineluctable passion for jazz, the pleas of family and friends notwithstanding. But finally, after weeks of hearing his middle name pronounced with escalating irony, forces stronger than my love for the President of the Republic of Jazz caused me to retreat, and "Lester" segued to the letter L.

On the day of his birth I was nowhere near the hospital. I managed a stoned and sentimental telephone call from Charlie's musician bar on Fifty-second Street and Sixth Avenue, three quarters of an hour by IRT from the mother and child. I was busy doing the proud father routine, buying drinks and shaking hands, becoming so absorbed in my act that I couldn't leave the limelight there at Charlie's for the offstage reality of a wife and a child in the Bronx Lebanon Hospital. In fact I never saw Steven Lester Rivers till six days later, when he arrived at our Crescent Avenue apartment as a bundle.

During the last month of her pregnancy, for reasons best known to herself, Augusta began redyeing her already dyed hair. It was frizzed yellow but still crowded with her natural dark hairs growing angrily back in. Of course I paid little attention to those details, continuing to satisfy myself sexually until just a few days before Steven L. was born. Not that I stopped because of the impending birth. I had a long weekend gig with Jack Freilicher on piano, and a bass player named Merv, and Dino the Greek on drums, on the bar in a bar up in Saratoga Springs, New York.

Meanwhile Augusta's hair began falling out in clumps. She was worried; she became frantic. To stop the fallout, she went to a hair specialist. At this point the child demanded out! Her days in the hospital were worrisome, not only because she was a twenty-year-old inexperienced child having a child and married to a child who seemed perfectly happy away from her, but because she saw herself going bald and looking so frightful that she imagined I would never come home, even for sex.

She had the baby, and with her mother's help began treating her hair, refusing to let anyone see her unless she wore some kind of Hedy Lamarr turban to keep things literally under wraps. And while I was playing and smoking each night away, far from home at this tender moment, she was content that I was not witnessing her cosmetic disaster. Better to be abandoned for a week while her hair grew back than to jeopardize the last slender strand of our romance.

The Bundle

I liked Steven's looks. No blotches, no abnormal features, nice big global forehead, five fingers on each hand, no split thumbs like my grandfather. Aesthetically he satisfied me. Genetically, I had to bide my time. I didn't see the beginning of my big nose in his, my sunken cheeks, my thin lips, my bushy brows. In 1945 I had not read August Strindberg's play *The Father*, which asks the eternal male question "Is this really my child?" No, I simply had a natural bent for paternal doubt, like every other man. Unlike Strindberg's obsessed father in the play, which opens on his child's twentieth birthday, I put my doubts to rest when at fifteen Steven looked like my twin.

My son Steven!

The Crescent Avenue three-room apartment soon became no more than a place for me to sleep from five in the morning till about noon. Then I would practice my horn or play with the kids, mainly watching with fascination as Joseph, age five, an electronic prodigy, worked electrical wonders out of the only outlet in our living room.

Monday, Wednesday, and Friday I'd go down to the union hall to look for a gig. There was some agitation in me to be identified as a musician, a modern musician, a funny guy hanging out telling inside jokes, speaking in hip code, seeming as black as I could seem, rather than being identified as an offspring of Russian immigrants who lived the grim reality of buying butter in the Bronx.

Downtown meant a different language, getting involved in collective mutual fantasy, honest casual hypocrisy; downtown was another polity. What gives on the Rialto! Playing till three or four in the morning with one customer in the place. Owners who chased you out with a gun when you asked to get paid. Booking agents in filthy offices with penciled black moustaches and crippled secretaries, who booked you into "toilets," as third-class night clubs were and are still called. That's what gave on the Rialto.

But you have to sleep, you have to return to the apartment, you have to play with your kids, that's family. I wanted little of it. Sorry. I was like a gangster coming home to his house, the opposite of excitement. What is every ad on TV about? Sitting around eating cereal, soaping up, discussing collars. Is that what life was about? Life insurance?

The Floor

Musicians Local 802 on Broadway met three times a week. There leaders or contractors would be hiring. All kinds of musical work could be had, classical, popular, jazz, swing, whatever you could get depending on what you could do. Every kind of gig for every kind of musician was at least possible, depending on your worth as a player, a reader, a reliable person. It was not easy for some of us to find work. A society bandleader like "pianist" Vincent Lopez, who could not play his way through his own theme song ("Nola"), insisted his sidemen play every note to perfection.

Musicians came for concert, club, or wedding work like longshoremen shaping up on the dock to haul bananas. The union met on the dance floor of the Roseland Ballroom. Monday was slender pickings, reviewing and recovering from our weekend gigs, if we had one. Wednesday was the busiest day. Contractors had to know by then who would work the weekend. Fridays, if we hadn't been assigned a gig on Monday or Wednesday, were frantic.

Sleeping Lion

At the union one Friday, Jack Freilicher and I literally bumped into Martin Flaxenhaar, alias Marty Flax (who cropped his name to hide the fact that he was German), with matching flaxen hair, a nice nose, wide blue eyes, and lips that in their natural position seemed ready to give you a wet kiss. He stuttered. I always admired him. He was a handsome, tall, golden Aryan who looked like an ideal candidate for Hitler's elite officer corps, and the least prejudiced person I knew, musically and ethnically. He walked and held his horn with style and wore a zoot suit; his head, which was adorned with the best duck's ass haircut on the union floor, tilted to the right. I tried to imitate him, never got it. He was a good saxist and always carried grass.

Marty said, as he struck a match to light a tiny pipe, "Th-th-this has got to be the b-b-best grass in the east!"

"Let's not get high here," said Jack.

"Wh-wh-where can we go to t-t-turn on?" said Marty.

"Let's go to the Museum of Modern Art."

"Where's that?" I ask.

"Oh, a few blocks from here. The garden is very peaceful."

We walked into MOMA past the gate, past the inner museum, across the surrealist corridor, without looking to the right or left; we headed straight for the open air, the trees, the breezy retreat of the sculpture garden, the horizontal Maillol, bronze backs of Matisse, cast iron of Roszak, marble of Moore, steel of Brancusi, and we immediately sucked in a great draught from the pipe Marty had deftly prepared in his pocket even as we filed past the guard.

Sock

When I go to a store looking for a pair of yellow socks I ignore everything else on display. I seek yellow socks. I buy yellow socks, probably with purple dots.

Certain homey artifacts remind me of the abstract art of some of my contemporaries. My dotted socks are early Larry Poons. I don't want to paint like him, but I feel perfectly comfortable wearing a pair of socks that shows my appreciation. Or shaping a dining room table as a toast to Kenneth Noland. Or placing a rug on my bathroom floor that seems hand-woven by the late great Josef Albers.

Where were we?

Oh yeah. We were in the garden of the Museum of Modern Art getting stoned among the statues, enjoying the flow of our thoughts. Finally, under the shade of a Gaston Lachaise bosom, I came to.

"Where are we? What is this place?"

Smoking marijuana could change my consciousness. I could look at my hand as if I was seeing it for the first time, and think I was thinking thoughts never thought before. At twenty you have a lot of energy. Smoking a little pot doesn't flatten you.

"Hey, let's look at this stuff. Let's walk around. Listen, Jack, do you remember that reproduction you showed me, the one with the bass fiddle?"

"The cubist painting by Georges Braque?"

"You think it's in this museum?"

In a special state of "wow," "gee whiz," and "how weird," we roamed the museum for half an hour and never found any Braques. But I saw Picasso's *demoiselles* and Dali's limp watches and Tchelitchew's elusive children and Rousseau's moonlit lion sniffing a reclining African female.

"That place was something else! I wasn't even high for the last half hour."

Dangerous as it was in those days to smoke pot in the streets, we took a poke on our way to the subway for our trip back to the Bronx.

Archeology

Next noon when I woke up on Crescent Avenue I got hold of little Joseph's paint set and started to make what I thought was art on those gray laundry shirtboards. After a few days of working on that size surface I felt a little boxed in. I couldn't get what I wanted.

What did I want? I wanted to paint something that was a bit more impressive. I grew up believing that size counts. And I did have going to waste an empty living room wall looming before me. Hardening under the sink was some enamel remaining from the paint job I had done a month before in that very living room. I bought some tubes of color and some brushes, mixed them with the enamel, and painted a mural.

If we were able to strip forty years of paint layers from the panel in that living room, we'd uncover my rendition of a tenor saxophone six feet long with a tiny bird flying from its golden bell. The sax signified, of course, Lester Young. From that horn and the painted music that came out of it emerged Charlie Parker, affectionately referred to as Bird, and depicted by me as such! It was so corny and so primitive it could hang peaceably today in Soho. I worked on it quite a while. Occasionally I would say to Augusta, "I'm going downstairs to buy a pack of cigarettes," and not return for three or four days.

The Street

I would spend whole nights on "The Street," Fifty-second Street between Sixth and Fifth avenues, where in one night you could hear Billie Holiday at the Onyx, Charlie Parker and Dizzy Gillespie at the Deuces, Coleman Hawkins at Kelly's Stable. I jammed nearby at Nola Studio, rehearsal rooms jazz musicians rented by the hour in one of the buildings that formed part of Tin Pan Alley.

In the privacy of a public toilet in that building Happy Bean first introduced me to heroin. Seated and sweating on a toilet seat, I watched him make a tiny brew by dissolving some heroin with water (from the toilet bowl!) and boiling it in a spoon over a lit book of matches. He tied me up, that is, he bound my arm with a belt, found a worthy vein, placed a hypodermic needle at the end of an eye dropper, and plunged it in. He waited for the blood to show up, then squeezed the rubber bulb at the end of the dropper, forcing the bloody concoction into my bloodstream. Twenty beauteous minutes later I was in the same cubicle over the same toilet bowl vomiting up everything in my stomach. The nausea was awful and remained awful for years. It took growing gray hairs for me to realize that my inability to stomach heroin, combined with my inability to sit still and just "be," saved me from a fate worse than etc., etc.

I feel like a woman describing in loving detail the unique sensation of losing her virginity, the how, the where, the with whom of it.

Homer Beniadakis

Happy was a trumpet player I knew from union meetings, jam sessions, and club dates. He was tall, had curly dark hair and a bold widow's peak descending halfway down a curved forehead. His nose was small, straight, and heroically angled. His deep purple lips were bow-shaped, and his full jaw had a no-relief blue stubble up to his ears. Put together, his looks hovered between cute and sinister. His horn playing lay somewhere between an excitable scurry of notes in bebop fashion and a soulful breathy tone with lots of reflective

L

A

R

R

Y

R

I

V

E

R

S

pauses all enmeshed in singable melodies. Without conscious aesthetic consideration, his playing on one level suggested a rejection of the brash success of the popular trumpet players Harry James, Ziggy Elman, Sy Oliver, and even the hero of many young jazz musicians, Roy Eldridge.

In conversation, Happy's silence ordained a particular discomfort. I had an ongoing hang-up about winning the approval of the strong silent dumbbells of music—not unlike my early need to be accepted by the few blond, blue-eyed, congenitally anti-Semitic teachers and classmates I knew from grade school through high school. Happy's put-down of anything he considered "square," which was pretty much everything, made discussion totally unnecessary. His dedicated lack of conviction made his silences seem comprehensible. The drug gaze raying from his eyes always aroused my sympathy; I felt I was present in a past full of tragedy. Perhaps it was the Sophocles in his Athenian soul.

Happy Bean was Greek.

I found out, I'm sure he didn't tell me, that Bean was not his real last name. Hardly any musicians I knew went under the names on their birth certificates. Consider. Whatever cultural or political circles ambitious people enter, they leave behind their families, and often their family names. Hitler, of course, was born Schicklgruber. His friend and enemy Stalin, which is Russian for "steel," was not born with the name we recognize but with the Georgian Dzhugashvili ("son of Douglas"). Lenin, who chose to go through life with the name of the river Lena in Siberia, near which he spent a lot of time thinking, was born with what he considered the unromantic Ulyanov. Leon Trotsky was a nice Jewish Bronstein. Juan Gris, the classical unchanging cubist, couldn't stand being branded a Spaniard in Paris with the name Gonzalès. Bernard Schwartz, a name you may not recognize, was born in the Bronx. Somehow, when he moved to California's seat of culture, he became Tony Curtis.

Larry Rivers = Irving Grossberg.

I swear to God, my name was given to me by a nightclub emcee on the first night of a summer job in Stockbridge, Massachusetts, the summer of my seventeenth year. I was heading a little band. One Eddie Gordon, at least that was the name he was using, at the end of the first floor show of the evening, after getting the audience to applaud the crooner and the flamenco dancers, asked the band to stand up. "Ladies and gentlemen, the music tonight has been

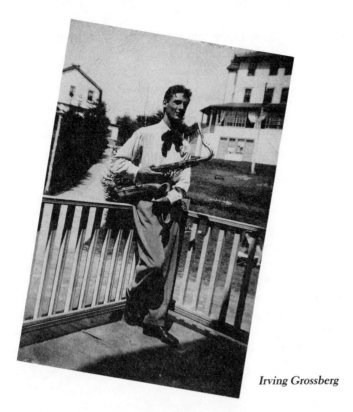

Irving Grossberg

supplied by Larry Rivers and His Mudcats." He thought the Rivers/
mud connection was very sharp. "Did you like their music? Let's
give them a big hand." Silence. Finally the audience responds po-
litely. "I knew you liked them. They worked hard. But remember,
young musicians eat a lot. Don't send your leftovers back with the
waitress, tell her to leave them on the table. When I gave these
guys this job, I promised 'em they'd clean up! So let's hear it once
again for Larry Rivers and His Mudcats!"

Let this version, the most authoritative version, of "How Larry
Rivers Got His Name" put to rest once and for all the apocryphal
tale known to at least two people: my sister Gerri (alias Gertie,
formerly Goldie) and my mother (Soora, Sara, Sonya, Shirley).
Their version tells of how I arbitrarily named myself after a black
appellate court judge, Francis Rivers, in order to give myself black
airs that might boost my jazz standing.

My sister still insists, "No! The story is that Larry's band got a
job and this required music stands with his name on it. He had a
little music stand at home, and 'Grossberg' had too many letters
and didn't fit on the stand, so one day when the family was driving

up Fordham Road, Larry saw the 'Vote for Judge Rivers' sign on the side of a bus, and we didn't know he was black, so Larry said, 'That name'll fit much better on a music stand.' "

Larry: "Yes, I see. Papa pulls up alongside the bus, I open the window, reach out, get a grip on a well-pasted poster, and—"

Gerri: "That isn't what I meant. You were giving yourself black airs."

Larry: "I thought you said we didn't know he was black."

Gerri: "What's the difference."

More Onomastics

Blacks of varied aspirations in the sixties disencumbered themselves of their Anglo-American slave names, the easier to untangle themselves from the web of the American Dream. LeRoi Jones reached to Africa for the significant name Baraka, which means "spiritual force." The pianist Orgonne Thornton became Sadik Hakim, Edmund Gregory, baritone sax, continued life as Sahib Shihab, and drummers Art Blakey and Kenny Clark as Abdulah ibn Buhaina and Liaquat Ali Salaam.

Variety

For a variety of reasons I spent so much time as an unknown on famous Fifty-second Street that I decided I might as well live there.

I moved out of Augusta's Bronx apartment into a furnished room two flights above the Three Deuces with a likable drummer I knew from Coney Island. This drummer heard extraterrestrial voices, saw flying saucers, spoke to the sky, and was appropriately named Napoleon. First name Andy. Lumpy, wall-eyed Andy was wonderful and easy to live with. He was the youngest of three jazz-playing brothers, one, Marty, a gregarious pianist who played with the great Louis Armstrong, no less; the other brother was a pianist too, suave, successful Teddy, then playing with Gene Krupa's trio. I fancied that with my new address and affiliations I was in a social and geographic position to find gigs playing alongside the musicians I most admired.

Is that the variety of reasons I moved from the Bronx?

No, I have a few more reasons.

Let us begin with the facial close-ups of Augusta, my pouting, unhappy, haranguing wife, vociferously accusing me every day of

Infidelity, Neglect, and Homosexuality.

Take Neglect first.

If Neglect means I didn't spend much time with her, I'm guilty. I spent three hours on the subway going from the North Bronx to the middle of Manhattan; I snooped around for work and took gigs that ended at four in the morning, not only to play, but to earn a few bucks in the small towns along the edge of the Hudson, like Secaucus, where they slaughtered pigs.

How did I know they slaughtered pigs in Secaucus?

I smelled them on the ferry crossing the river to the gig. And looking for marijuana and enjoying its effects also took time. An occasional brownout on a couch where I accidentally sat on a hypodermic needle full of heroin took time too.

What was I doing in such places?

I was coming to that! I had a lot of biz/socializing to do with my musician friends. Meeting with the boys, keeping my eye on the bouncing ball. I'm not saying it was *all* about finding a gig. I did enjoy myself with them, but they also knew of work, usually involving little pay and a lot of travel, that they'd turned down and were turning you on to.

From Augusta's point of view I just wasn't there.

As for the Infidelity accusation, let us take the Homosexuality first. Aside from a delicate gait with matching limp wrist, an imitation of what the average Joe would call a fairy but I called class, Augusta received a bizarre version of one of my more existentialist moments; at the time, all reasons were existentialist reasons, otherwise they weren't interesting. Some friend or suspicion had conjured up in Augusta's mind an image of me standing in front of a microphone in the middle of the crowded union floor and blasting three low notes on my baritone. The union floor was stunned quiet. Bending forward to the microphone, I presumably had announced, "I will suck the cock of anyone holding a union card."

Refute

I am going to dignify this absurd fabrication by admitting what I did not tell the Army Air Corps: I had had my homosexual moment, like any normal heterosexual boy of fourteen, on top of another boy. But what were Heshie and I talking about as we pumped innocently away? "A blonde walks into the room, she's got big luscious tits. Take your brassiere off. Slowly she does. Wow. What terrific nipples. I suck on one of them. Hesh, you suck on the other. Then we both take her bloomers off. . . ." And it is true that Arthur Newbold blew me at a party in front of fifty people, but Augusta knew I loved to entertain and couldn't resist a challenge.

One Way

The past comes to me in many different ways. Sometimes through a phone call.

"May I speak to Larry Rivers, the musician not the artist."

I was put on notice that the caller knew me in the days when I was only a musician. Did I have any need for a saxophone mouthpiece? My metal Otto Link mouthpiece sported a dent right at the top near the reed. I had recently been thinking that instead of keeping a scrungy piece of brass in my mouth for hours at a time, I should try an environmentally approved black Bakelite mouthpiece.

He introduced himself as Emile Neitraub, one of the few Jews in the music business using his real name. Maybe he kept it because it sounded like Amyl Nitrate. He was a saxophonist living in the Hamptons but was once a contractor for bands at Local 802. He said he knew me pretty well in the old days. He played in pit bands on Broadway and made $125 a week, but as a contractor hiring musicians and only paying them scale he ended up with $125 a night.

"Larry, forgive me for not giving you gigs. You played bebop. And you guys got high on the job. I respected you too much to ask you to play polkas and waltzes and the Star-Spangled Banner."

In the course of our ambling, he told me how I used to get high with Marty Flax and Jack Freilicher in the Museum of Modern Art and was inspired to make paintings on gray laundry shirtboards.

"You brought the paintings down to the union floor to show everybody."

Unsolicited art history. My first one-man show.

Emile arrived with a bag that had fifteen mouthpieces to choose from. I began trying them on my horn.

"I always wanted to play real jazz," he said. "But I guess I was too interested in the almighty buck. I was jealous of you guys."

I offered him some passion fruit nectar.

"I didn't smoke grass, I respect and enjoy drinking."

I put some vodka in his nectar.

"You were always a lot of fun, Larry! Always making far-out statements just to get a rise out of your bebop buddies. You once told the guys you were becoming an artist. And then you announced that you were a homosexual now."

"I what?!!"

"What what?"

"I said—what?"

"You said now you were a homosexual."

"But did I ever take out my—"

"Never!"

"Wait a minute! Did I ever take out my *baritone sax* and play three long low notes and say I'd suck the cock of any musician holding a union card?"

"Absolutely not. It was against union rules to play an instrument on the union floor."

Now for the Infidelity

In 1945, infidelity required the physical presence of a woman other than your wife, and some form of seduction. There was the Formal Date, which included dancing, dining, flowers, a movie, and possible success after a few such evenings. There was the quicker, old reliable Plying with Liquor, or Drugs, until her guilt about doing it was obliterated as totally as her ability to stand straight or talk coherently. Still, no 1945 seduction would have been possible to squeeze in in less than two hours—unless, of course, I asked Uncle Benny to order his friend Florence to fuck me on demand.

And then, if you found someone, where to find a proper place to finalize the act without a certain time expenditure? Well, a car if you had one, a hotel room if you could afford one. If not, you were an hour on the phone—who had a phone?—calling friends to borrow an apartment—who had an apartment?—for a half hour.

Even if I slept for a minimum of five hours, where in the twenty-four devoted to neglecting Augusta was I to fit in infidelity? Even if I was the fastest fuck in the east, which I was. And those five hours in bed included a half hour of sex with my wife, twenty-seven minutes of which were devoted to apologizing and explaining why I came in three minutes. It was Augusta's fault. She moved!

So how could I fit infidelity into my packed schedule? When were all these infidelities supposed to take place?

In further self-defense, the seduction period in the forties was longer than it is today; "giving in" was immoral, and unwise as well, in relation to pregnancy and opportunities for marriage. Mothers thought, and taught, that sex before marriage could mean no marriage. Men still existed who hoped to marry virgins!

But even if someone was open to sex, you still had to talk to her, it wasn't incumbent upon her to fuck. Nor did she feel guilty for not. It didn't get you anywhere, even if you had your hand under her dress, to imply that she was acting like a square fundamentalist from Missouri; and that rhetoric took another bite out of the twenty-four hours.

I slept home every night, or every morning, didn't I? Not out of policy, mind you, but because my bed was the only one I was welcome in. Jazz groupies in those days came across as weird but did not necessarily come across. The desirable, good-looking ones gravitated to well-known older players with a highly developed embouchure.

Except for this photo with two smoking guns cut out long ago in an early experiment with collage, my argument stands.

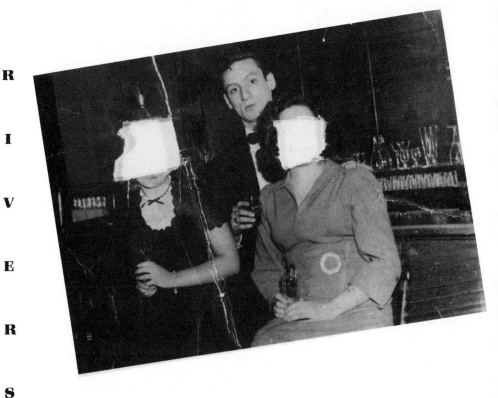

Actually, the last time I engaged in a no-seduction situation with any regularity was when I was sixteen and fucking the dark blue velvet armchair in my mother's living room.

My mother's living room? My father was alive. But everything that went into that living room was chosen by my mother, same for every other room in the house.

This armchair, bought at a bargain, somehow got to me. Perhaps I was attracted to its wide seat and its material, which went straight down to the floor and hid a pair of stumpy legs. In a way it was the least feminine chair in the room. But that soft chair, open and generously proportioned, was the most functional one for the purpose I had in mind. By pure coincidence or dumb luck, the distance inchwise from my knees bent on the floor to the pubic hairs at which my erect penis emerged was exactly where the bottom of the pillow rested on the body of the chair.

This armchair was also the youngest in the room. The rest of the furnishings, a faux French Provincial antique set of chairs and couch, were purchased a few years earlier, and on arrival covered in a fairly heavy-grade clear plastic to be unzipped and removed for special occasions. I remember none, except my wedding.

My dark blue beloved was always stripped, always available like that, naked and waiting. In order to keep from adding to the loaded family lore, I had to make sure my mother found no stiffened, wrinkled traces of ecstasy's scum. She plumped and turned the pillows every day.

Like what loaded family lore?

Like offering my five-year-old sister Goldie a dime to fuck her, or Papa showing his erection to eleven-year-old sister Joanie, or the more complicated one in the summer of '44 when Papa, unsuccessfully trying to stink-finger my first girlfriend, Peppy, in the living room, heard my sister and hid behind the piano, or when he asked my mother-in-law to satisfy him sexually, because, he swore, my mother, age fifty-two, was menstruating.

My solution to preserving the upholstered object of my affection for further use was to take a sock of mine, usually a dark one to go with the blue velvet, and place it over my cock just before I came.

What about preseminal flow?

Oh, my God, I forgot! No, I didn't know what preseminal flow was. My mother must have had some idea of what I was up to. That saint! She never confronted me!

To penetrate the crack between the cushion and the frame, first I would get down on my knees. There was always some foreplay. I'd lean forward and stroke the soft sturdy arm, pressing my face to the upright pillow and sliding my cheek across it, sometimes pursing my lips to give—or get?—a kiss. There was little street light in the living room, but the instinctual brain was glowing. I entered with a certain reverence, and began the usual undulations forward and backward, and reached ecstasy gazing up into the lace doily on the back pillow.

Illusion

Coming in a sock purposely rumpled to prevent seepage, I began to feel as if the original thrill was going if not gone. The sock was coming between me and my chair. I wanted to do it *au naturel*. Visions of sex unsheathed with one of the plastic-covered Provincials began to fly before me but were stopped in mid-flight by the painful image of skin moving against plastic. I quickly envisioned the Vaseline in my parents' bathroom, snuck down the hallway with an erection, and in the pitch black plucked the jar from the medicine chest, grabbing something to wipe up afterward and returning to La Provincial raring to go.

The darkness of my fantasy is suddenly interrupted by the living room light. My parents are standing in the doorway, my mother's hand on the switch.

"Irving, what are you doing?"

I'm on my knees with a diminishing erection, my boxer shorts down to my ankles, alongside a roll of toilet paper, and in my hand a jar of—Vicks? Vicks VapoRub?! I took it by mistake in the dark. Saved!

I began to rub my thighs. "Oh, Ma, my muscles are so sore! I played football today and I got kicked in the thigh blocking a punt. You know what a punt is, Ma? Pa, *you* know what a punt is."

"Go to bed, Irving."

I put myself and my fantasy to sleep. Being caught *in delicto* like that, even in my waking dream, frightened me into stopping sex with my blue velvet beauty. For about a year, a few times a week, I had used that blue chair for fancy masturbation. The relationship ended. From then on I resorted to pedestrian whacking off in bed. But my erotic inspirations were often based on the whole bizarre fantasy of my quasi-infidelity with the Provincial wingback, nude, kneeling with a half erection, crumpled shorts, Scott Tissue, Vicks. Sometimes, for the sake of variation, I would even picture the sudden blaze of light and my parents in the doorway as I reached orgasm.

Recent Chairs

The past comes to me in many different ways. In 1988–89 I did a series of works based on chairs and men and women in them in different positions. Mostly, chairs look like sitting people to me, ready to put someone on their lap.

Everything you experience is printed on a blank brain cell and stored in a file in a drawer in a cabinet of drawers. Looking for one file, you come across others as you agitate the system. In the time I have been working on this book, bombarding the page daily with vignettes of my past on every subject imaginable and unimaginable, the blue chair never surfaced. I can only think that its entry into the bio is a result of a brain rifling a chair file, which was cross-referenced with the sex file, and coming across the blue velvet chair. My recent paintings of chairs and dreams sprawled in them are connected with that childhood interlude.

Forward to '45

Fact or fancy, that living room pastoral took place when I was a boy of sixteen; now I was a twenty-one-year-old married man. I had a family of my own and a living room of my own and a bedroom, and I slept in it with my wife, each in the other's arms. That was part of the sleeping process. No matter how late the hour, how drained the body, how tired that most erotic of zones known as the mind, a twenty-one-year-old gets it up. And I did. Every night. And woke in the morning to accusations.

I left. Those are the reasons I exchanged a wife, a mother-in-law, and two children for Napoleon.

Economics

The GI Bill and my pension, along with my mother-in-law's small trust fund my and my occasional band salary, would provide meaningful support for the family I was leaving behind. Back when I worked steadily with big bands, I sometimes made more in a night than my father earned in a week threading pipe and draining toilets. For playing the music I loved, I made as much as $130 a week! And one time, doubling on clarinet with the Jerry Wald band, I made $180 playing the Loew's State vaudeville-movie palace. But when I left the Bronx to live on the right street and meet the right people, I was making nothing with no band, playing nowhere except at Nola Studio, where I had to pay to jam with other unemployed musicians.

Back on Fifty-second Street

While I was waiting for the phone to ring with an offer to go on the road with Benny Goodman, Count Basie, or the Duke—which was not too likely since I had no phone—my father appeared in the messy little room I shared with Napoleon. It was late in the afternoon and I was still in bed. He urged me to come back to the Bronx.

"Larry, come back to the Bronx."

I was glad he called me Larry in front of my roommate, who was absorbed at the window peering through a telescope at the heavens.

"Larry, you have a little boy. Why are you doing this?"

After a month with Napoleon I'd forgotten. I got up and began to put on my shoe. In it was a plastic bag of marijuana.

"What's that?" said my father.

"Marijuana I'm holding for a friend."

My father looked at me with pity and wonder. I remembered what Jack Freilicher's father had said to him when he discovered a few joints of grass under Jack's pillow: "Better dead than a dope."

My father, instead, offered to help me financially.

Back in the Bronx

I went back to the Crescent Avenue apartment where dwelt my child, my stepchild, my wife, and my mother-in-law, who was so gentle she seemed retarded, whose bladder control had so deteriorated that every time I told a joke, which was every other minute, she'd piss down the side of her leg. In that heady atmosphere of baby talc and baby and Berdie urine, I rested my weary bones. A week later I got a gig.

I was hired by the Herbie Fields band, probably with the help of Happy Bean. Herbie was a thirty-five-year-old tenor sax player, skinny and pock-marked, with cheeks that sank in even more than mine. He wore plaid jackets and respectable slacks; he wanted to be cool, sharp, but not black. He had no interest in the down-home look of hip jazz musicians. Sometimes he lectured. He advised young players not to think about chords. "Don't be afraid to get lost." Although he was quite capable of exceptional solos, he thought that what the music crowd liked and what would bring him commercial success was to stomp all over the stage. Carried away, horn in mouth, he'd go from one end of the band to the other, lifting his bony knees very high, bringing them down hard, bending his back almost to the ground. Sometimes he would even jump up in the air while blowing. He'd stop to work up to an octave, a high F above the high F on the horn, then he'd lift the instrument over his head, screech this one note with accelerating passion, quivering, looking as if all the blood had left his head and he was about to faint. At times he would execute a kind of concerto of notes, in the old honking tradition, slamming the sax against the inside of his thighs. In other words, he was serious about his commercial success. He was an older man, in his thirties, not too friendly, always preoccupied, hardly had a smile in him. But with the semiotic of the wink, the slap on the back, the upturned thumb, he could lead you to believe that everything was okay.

Addendum

As in the world of politics, rumors about Our Leaders were a pleasurable pastime. The rumor about society bandleader Vincent Lopez was that his notable green complexion was caused by years of having girls piss on his face. The rumor about Herbie Fields was that he had the biggest cock in the music business.

Miles

I wrote one song for the band. From the musical point of view it was considered innovative. It featured a wide distribution of sounds, from low notes on the baritone sax to some almost impossibly high notes on the alto. The harmonies were recognizably avant-garde.

I had gone to Juilliard to study musical composition at the same time as Miles Davis, who was living with Charlie Parker. If we arrived early for class we'd find an empty practice room with a piano. He'd play me some of the chord progressions he picked up from Charlie, as well as chords he himself was experimenting with. We were in one class together. In that class a female teacher would give us a test by playing single notes on the piano, and we students, with music paper in front of us, had to write what she had just played.

Miles and I would prepare for the exam by going outside to smoke some marijuana. We were convinced it improved our hearing, and we gulped down the smoke and the myth in big draughts. On the other hand, we didn't do badly on those tests. Put that in your pipe and poke it.

Miles was very thin and very quiet and—which seems amazing in the light of his subsequent public image—shy. It seemed I was the only white person at the school that he spoke to. I would invite him to some function or other; he always refused.

I saw Miles a few times over the next forty years. He always greeted me with a smile and a not so playful punch to the stomach. In 1990, after someone put the question to us, Miles and I agreed to collaborate on a project—a music box to be painted by both of us (he'd begun painting and was prolific but not terrific), and the sounds coming from inside the box to be a CD of a musical collaboration between us. I asked him, "What will we do for the music?"

"Oh, man, we'll get a rhythm section and blow."

This elaborate collaboration didn't make the six o'clock news. His death did, and did in our project.

About five years before his death I saw him at the opening of a show of his paintings. He used a cane and had grown a high forehead, and had a beautiful wide cape draped seriously on his shoulders. It was very majestic and moving. I told him he had gotten better-looking as he got older. He said he was good-looking back at Juilliard, I just didn't notice it, and he strode majestically away.

Headhunters

Much of the musical method of the song I wrote for the Herbie Fields band came out of those meetings with Miles in the practice room at Juilliard. My tune offered generous silences for solos and tasty tidbits to spur the soloist on. But what impressed—and amused—everybody more than the music was the name I gave the piece.

Back in those days, to discuss or request or demand the giving or getting of a blow job, you had to use the word "head," e.g., "She gave me head" or "I gave her head" or "Gee, I'd like some head." The tune's title was "Headhunters." Hidden safely behind anthropological images of Amazonian tribes hunting enemy skulls for religious and decorative purposes, as the initiated of the jazz world knew, were the real headhunters, hip guys constantly seeking to receive or administer blow jobs.

Of course, your ordinary square male would never think of this without a certain squeamishness about bad taste, and bad odor. Not you, you little pot-smoking hipster, you and the few like you who understood it was grand!

"Headhunters" was played every night, and the band's delighted, conspiratorial murmurs always followed Herbie's announcement of the number.

Roseland

The band had a week in Manhattan and two in New Jersey. In New York we played the Roseland Ballroom. Roseland in early '46 was the best-known popular dance hall in New York. The clientele ranged from young to middle-aged couples. The dances included the jitterbug, the Lindy, and the silly Big Apple, with steps like the shag, trucking, and pecking. And merengues and tangos, and the ecumenical rumba and the affable Peabody, and the immortal fox trot, and many more with names I never knew.

Our repertoire was a heavy book crammed with ballads and jump tunes and a smattering of contemporary ditties. Although Herbie took pride in this precious volume, reminding us that so-and-so who had some kind of name at the time had arranged this tune and so-and-so that tune, the book could not possibly fit the infinite needs of Roseland's various feet.

Big Breaks

So that evenings and matinees at the Roseland called for more than one band. So that breaks between sets were longer than usual.

During one of these longer than usual breaks Happy Bean and I found a toilet we could lock and proceeded to "take off" (slang for the entire ritual of getting high on heroin).

I was still green in the self-administering aspects of taking off. Happy was an expert, medically adept at tying up and needle plunging. He knew that I got loaded on a very tiny amount of heroin even when the heroin was cut generously with milk sugar. Happy also convinced himself that he was poorer than I—something about sending money back every week to his mother in the Bronx to pay

off an impatient loan shark.

So that when we "got on" (slang for "taking off") I paid for both doses. And given his voracious appetite both for heroin and for coming out on top of any deal, Happy divided the heroin, a lot for him, a drop for me, for my own good. He took off first. Then, after tying me up, he administered my shot.

There was a knock on the door. Our Leader came in to take a

leak just as I was vomiting into the sink.

"What's the matter, Rivers?"

"Chicken cacciatore. I had some at Mama Leone's."

"Uh-huh. Oh, I see." He looks into the sink. "Chicken caccia-

tore?"

"And it used to be such a good restaurant. Have you eaten there lately, Herb?"

"No." He unzipped and moved toward the urinal. Everyone

had to shift position in the tiny space.

The situation embarrassed me. I was splashing my face and cleaning the stuffed sink. He was struggling to free his organ from

his pants, trying to act cool in a minuscule toilet with two stoned members of his orchestra observing him. When he finally had it out and dangling before the open-sided urinal, I saw that the rumor about the size of his prick—cock, dick, penis, joint, johnson, organ —was not exaggerated.

"Don't let that snake bite you, man," I said, failing to break the ice.

He did not find the remark funny. The subject was becoming a big problem for him, and finally a tragic one. Despondent over a woman he loved, a black singer from Washington, D.C., who left him for a normally endowed man, Herbie Fields committed suicide just a few years later, the rumor ran.

I went home after the Roseland toilet scene, uncertain and fearful of Herbie's reaction to finding me in that obviously oblivious state. Chicken cacciatore! Not only didn't he approve of drugs, he didn't want to be reminded of their existence. Herbie Fields was of the real world, which viewed drugs as repulsive. Was this a way to proceed with my life?

Still, at those moments when I was high and playing, I felt uncontrollably drawn to some sorrow in myself that I never understood, especially while playing ballads. I felt as if I were crying.

The Watch

A few better days later, after visiting his mother on Adams Place in the Bronx, pretty close to where I lived on Crescent Avenue, Happy knocks on my apartment door. I open it. He doesn't move.

"What do you want?"

"Heh-heh." He walks in as if I said, "Come in." He forces a smile.

I ask him what he thought of our scene the other night with Herb in the toilet.

"Nothing's gonna happen with Herbie."

Happy makes clear what he wants to happen. He's looking to score for heroin and get high.

My doubts rolled over and played dead. I thought, Well we're not playing tonight, Augusta and her mother and the kids are visiting Berdie's sister. They were gone when I woke up. I felt sorry for myself. Nothing made me happy, what was the difference if I got high?

I didn't know then you could be unhappy and live.

We telephoned the local connection. Nobody answered.

Neither Happy nor I wanted to go downtown. We'd have to locate a dealer we didn't know, then hand him our money—sixty percent of the time we'd never see him again. If he did come back, three hours and eight cups of Bickford's coffee later, he's holding no junk, no scag, no horse, no smack, no schmeck, no shit, no H; all he brings back is a version of the classic tale of being robbed. Or if he has something it's odorless talc in a couple of gelatin capsules (this was a decade before the glassine envelope trend).

Happy and I decided to save a night by telephoning my good friend Murray, who lived in my old neighborhood around Allerton Avenue near my mother. I didn't think he'd have any horse, but it was possible that he knew someone in the neighborhood who might share or sell some. Murray never "got on" heroin, but he knew some local musicians and their friends who were beginning to "get on." He had a cousin, Solly, a jazz fan who, like me, "chippied"— dabbled in heroin. Murray, out of old-time affection for me and respect for Danny as a trumpet player who worked with name bands, enjoyed being the connection.

In a telephone call Murray triumphantly announced to Solly that he had actually spoken with the notorious Happy Bean. Cousin Solly agreed to donate two caps he had been hoarding for a weekend debauch.

Happy had become big in the small firmament of Bronx bebop, blowing that new horn style of cascading notes long enough to impress the young and aspiring. Happy's social style was just as awesome. His long silences punctuated by short blasts of disdain for everyone withered youthful opposition. His snap judgments were accepted as considered thoughts. And if someone dared disagree, Happy would comment, "It don't swing," in the tone of a judge passing sentence; he would follow through with a lowering of his eyelids, indicating that some questions weren't worth answering. The terse truths he played on his horn left no doubt about his authority.

Thrilled, Murray called back to tell us he found some H, but in accordance with his position as holder of the goods, he requested that we come to his apartment. Forty minutes later on a blustery afternoon, moving in great strides over the cement and tar, we arrived. Murray was playing Lester Young records in his bedroom. He was still living with his parents.

We had barely crossed the threshold when Happy signaled his anxiety; he was there for one reason. Murray, trying hard to project a solid jazz image, forgot himself for a moment and set down a sample of his mother's baked goods. Happy rolled his eyes.

"Cake!?" he said, amazed at so square a suggestion. "I don't dig cake!"

Inferring the way the social amenities had to go, Murray reached into his pocket and dropped the two capsules in Happy's small white palm. Happy smiled for the first time, moved immediately to the dining room table, pulled out his paraphernalia, and inquired whether everything was cool.

The Hit

Murray nodded. His parents worked and wouldn't be home for a few hours. Happy spilled the contents of both capsules into the bent, burnt little spoon he kept wrapped with his needle and dropper, his personal set of "works."

I didn't think I'd have much effect on this aspect of the operation. I left the division to Happy. Besides, I was filled with my usual dread about shooting up. If I did, how much? Would he give me more than I could safely assimilate? Miscalculation of the quantity and ignorance of the quality could be fatal.

Happy had no problem. He tied himself up with a tie Murray offered for the job, and in thirty seconds he was "booting" the liquid content in the eyedropper. (Booting: the sensuous process of squeezing the rubber end of the dropper just enough to send the mixed blood and heroin into the vein, then releasing the rubber so the mixture flows from the vein back into the dropper, giving the user an extra "boot." Some practitioners would keep up this ebb and flow in and out of the bloodstream until their heads sank down onto their arms in an ecstasy of warmth and oblivion.)

Happy took the dope that Murray's cousin had broken the law to find and without a word shot it up in its entirety as we stood watching and wondering. With six dollars' worth of glaze in his eyes, he didn't have the grace to answer Murray's request that maybe we could all "like, blow a little together?" Instead, Happy pushes his shoulders up and forward in modified Cagney fashion, and running his hands over his nose and mouth, a gesture recognizable as the junkie massage, he looks at me through pinpoint pupils.

"I've got to cut," he says. He picks up his horn and walks, real slow, to the door. His hand on the knob, he turns and frowns, speaking with the throatiness brought on by the opiate. "Come on, man!"

"Wait a minute, we've got to give him some money."

"Forget it, that wasn't heroin." Turns to Murray. "You got taken, man. We're not giving any bread for aspirin. Where's the bathroom?"

Tragically Murray says, "Through the bedroom."

While Happy was gone, there was a quick transaction between Murray and me. I paid him the three dollars per capsule, each of which could have turned on the two of us. Happy came out of the bedroom and headed straight for the door. In profound sobriety I walked with him, hoping my farewell expression to Murray would convey my regret at providing him with one of the gloomier half hours of his career.

The Right Time

We were two flights down the stairs when Murray called my name from his doorway; he asked me please to come back up, just for a minute. Happy said he'd wait for me in the street.

Murray was flushed, worried and bewildered. His father's watch was missing. Maybe Happy took the antique gold pocket Hamilton off his father's dresser by mistake when he was in the bedroom?

"I know what happened to your father's watch," I said, and ran down the stairs. There was Happy, calm, sitting on the stoop.

I reported the missing watch.

"So why are you telling *me*, man? Come on, *let's go!* I don't care."

I asked him for the watch.

Marbled with disbelief at my lack of faith, he started to walk away.

"The watch, Happy."

"I don't have it. Are you serious? I don't do things like that."

I realized that he was desperate, that the only solution to his mounting addiction and to my reputation was money. I offered to buy the watch from him. We struck a deal for ten dollars. He took the watch out of his jacket pocket, dangled it over my hand, dropped it, and gave me a Happy smile.

I ran up the stairs, made a quick apology, returned the watch, and ran down the stairs.

I could only justify this miserable episode by admitting to myself that I was, and always have been, a hopeless sucker for talent. But it wasn't long after that moment outside Murray's house that I began to wonder about my own talent. One night after the first set at the Meadowbrook in New Jersey, Herbie Fields took me to the bar, bought me a drink, and introduced me to a gentleman quietly sipping a coke. It was the baritone player Manny Album, the fastest fingers on the union floor. Would I mind if Manny sat in? A gong went off. I was right. The next night Manny Album was sitting in my chair in the sax section of the Herbie Fields band.

Another nail in my music box.

L

A

R

R

Y

Miami

In July of '46 I took my son Steven, nine months old, my wife Augusta, her mother Berdie, and little Joe on a train to Miami. It was off-season, and we found two rooms in the Hotel Floral on Collins Avenue about two hundred feet from the water.

R

In New York opportunities for playing with bands and making money were becoming scarce. It was beginning to take a lot of imagination to identify myself as a musician. I was spending more time searching for a situation to blow than blowing.

I

Going to Miami was geography as the hope of reducing my anxiety about my heroin use in New York. Living in Miami with my family was geography as the hope of making life happier and more meaningful. My father was equally hopeful. He loaned me money for the trip.

V

Miami in July was very warm and very bright. The Floral was full of slow-moving, fast-talking New York elders. Our rooms were situated in a structure that at one grand point in its history was a

E

hotel. Now, many years later, minus bellhops, front desk, all the romance of dining rooms and a bar and a lobby full of energetic traffic, it was a quiet, functional rooming house with a marble porch, maybe cement by then, painted in pastel colors hiding, or

R

rather not hiding, obvious disintegration. But there was still thick carpeting right out to the street.

Bare feet is my most memorable image of our stay. Bare feet

S

and Steven entangled in his bedding screaming for us to free him

as he struggled to keep from choking to death. Also, taking him to the children's clinic for a vaccination. As soon as needle touched skin a child ahead of us screamed in terror, setting off a chain reaction of howls. Steven, at nine months, calmly watched the hypodermic needle enter his little arm. I wonder whether his cool attitude was genetic.

We took him to the beach every day in a long, comfortably padded box that previously held four dozen eggs. We had lunch on the beach and came back late in the afternoon. We'd all have dinner well before the sun went down. Usually, if not always, Berdie made her version of spaghetti, a cross between canned Franco-American and Bronx buttered primitive.

Berdie's sainthood was confirmed by her total inability to cook. My idea of a qualified saint was a person of slightly substandard mentality with no conventional talent whose daily behavior was concerned only with satisfying everyone else's needs. Berdie couldn't sew, couldn't drive a car, found it difficult to dial a phone, could hardly tell you what day of the week it was, but would boil you an egg at 4:00 a.m., give you every cent of her income every month of the year, and except for Augusta's intervention would, I believe, have accommodated me a few years later the one time I asked her to let me fuck her, because according to Freud, according to Rivers, every boy wanted to make it with his mother; the next best thing was a mother-in-law.

After the pasty pasta Augusta and I would walk barefoot to our romantic bedroom across the hall. I would roll one or two joints and get Augusta to smoke with me. Once we were high everything took on profound significance, the box of soap flakes was of beautiful fuchsias and blues. And we would laugh at how square was the world with its conservative, closed attitude about sex. Augusta and I thought we were open for all kinds of sexual innovations, which at the time meant a blow job. I can now hear my New York friends chorus, "Big deal!"

And we would play with our baby. Then, leaving Steven with Berdie, we'd stroll out on the street along the Miami strand. Twenty-one years old, a few bucks in my pocket, happy.

Horn Over Miami

By the time I got to Miami I'd accepted the fact that I was not a professional musician. I played my horn whenever I could but rarely made money at it. I began to fortify myself with the idea that I was an artist. What did I think artists were? Artists were geniuses working unrecognized most of their lives, scuffling in obscurity for funds, until in the end if they were strong enough they would reap the reward of being the star of a room in the National Museum.

I may not have been hired, but I never went anywhere in Miami without my horn. Even later, in New York, when I became a full-time painter, I carried that horn from one joint to another many nights a week looking for a chance to sit in. At the very beginning, when I first started to sell my paintings and enjoy the symptoms of faint recognition, I went to Paris. I stayed at the Hotel Montana around the corner from the Deux Magots in Saint-Germain. Looking out the window, I blew my horn to all of Paris. Putting a crimp in this romantic image of serenading the City of Light was the horn I was playing: the baritone saxophone—a big, heavy, cumbersome instrument that your average Parisian homme in the rue found as lyrical as a runaway boiler. It was even less romantic to lug around at airports. Was I embodying the myth of Aeneas carrying his father from Troy to Rome? I don't think so. I've continued to carry a horn right up to the present. In 1967–68 I carried a straight soprano sax to East Africa and West Africa while making a documentary for NBC. I played in Mombasa, Kenya, at an all-night dance hall, in huts out in the bush, and in a Volkswagen autobus while photographing and annoying animals.

In 1979 I had a retrospective in Hanover, Germany, at the Kestner-Gesellschaft. I checked into my hotel early, not to prepare for my statement at the gala opening of the show, but to practice my horn, by now a tenor sax; the museum had found a blues band rhythm section for me to play with. My artwork wasn't enough. I had to spice it with my horn.

In 1985 I was in Stockholm for an exhibition at the Wetterling gallery. Red Mitchell, who often played at Bradley's in New York, and who rates somewhere among the top two jazz bassists in the world, lives in Stockholm. The habit of lugging my horn gave me a memorable two hours at the hundred-year-old Stockholm Opera Cafe. As the playing went on, the crowd became enthusiastic and the drunks came up on the bandstand to kiss me. In May 1990 I accompanied my horn (and twenty paintings) to Paris for an exhibit at the Beaubourg gallery. Again a jazz group—headed by Nico Bunink, a pianist I played with in New York—came to celebrate with me in Pigalle at the former home of Georges Bizet! In the heavily draped red interior, a pianist was playing Chopin as we entered. Soon we were off to being the center of attention, sweating a lot and enjoying the mysterious pleasures of playing jazz.

In my youth, playing my horn in strange cities, like Miami, accentuated my being alone. No one knew me, few people cared. And it was that very feeling that kept me playing. This mysterious attraction identified me to myself as a loner looking to express what as yet hadn't been defined. But I knew that being in the presence of art, making art, even making love, couldn't get at the feelings I felt when I played music.

There was no good reason for me not to carry that instrument on my back even on my strolls under the Miami moon with Augusta. We'd pass bars, nightclubs, and odd union hall dances or private parties where we heard jazz being played. Good or bad, it was jazz, meaning I could sit down with them and enjoy myself. We'd go in and have drinks. I tried ingratiating myself by dropping the right names—musical heroes and hip inside tunes—making it easy for them to say yes when I asked could I sit in. At the time, and maybe they still feel it, musicians felt obligated to share their good luck in having a job, and if the job was loose enough for it, to give a visiting or unemployed musician a chance to enjoy himself and keep in shape by inviting him to blow.

So, not long after arriving in Miami to see if living and loving in a family context could quell the unquiet heart, I was looking for thrills in the same old places with the same old accompaniments, jazz, pot, and sex. The difference between my behavior in New York and in the Southland was that wherever I went I took my little lamb, Augusta, with me. I would play with total strangers for whom I felt instant warmth and camaraderie. When I took a break, I would dance close up with Augusta to the band's music.

Augusta had a lower lip, always full of bright red lipstick, that drooped. The droop, which could seem like a snarl, gave her a kind of Dead End Kid attractiveness that said, "You looking for a fight, buddy?" My response was always the same. "I love you." It turned me on. Love is the translation of physical sensations into language.

Do I mean to say that love is a hard-on?

Well, no. I'll tell you, however, a hard-on is a compelling symbol. The sensations coursing through that organ are also the feelings filtering down your spine and through your body. All thoughts about the one who has given you and continues giving you said hard-on grow in the jungle heat of your senses, inspiring the language of romance.

The room in the Hotel Floral where Augusta, Steven, and I slept had an empty eight-foot-square space in the center. I decided to build a playpen for Steven, and to make it eight feet square. This would give him a generous and controlled area to crawl and walk and play with all kinds of things, and would lower our anxieties about what mischief and danger he might get into. Buying the wood at the local lumberyard and borrowing the tools from the Floral handyman, I built the pen. It took a few days, no drawings and very little planning. My only other carpentry experience, aside from a high school shop course where I suffered the making of Columbus's *Pinta*, sails and all, was a wooden box with a glass top that I built at age twelve. At the bottom of this three-dimensional rectangle I made a swivel arrangement allowing me to place inside it a frog and a snake I'd caught, and with great glee I would watch the snake make a meal of the frog.

The small bathroom in our hotel room was four feet from the edge of the playpen. For reasons inexplicable to me, then and even now, I would play a "fun" game with nine-month-old Steven Lester. While shaving, face loaded with cream, I'd begin a low *grrrowl* that gradually became louder and more violent. I'd turn a distorted face toward him, arms extended like wings and fingers curled like claws, and menacingly move to the edge of the playpen, where he'd be standing to watch me shave. At the point when he began crying I would change my frightening mien, bend toward him uttering gentle, reassuring sounds, and pat him affectionately until he'd stop. Slowly his confidence in me would return, and I'd go back to shaving. A few minutes later I'd begin the whole awful cycle again.

Magazines and newspapers and TV talk shows about child abuse always bring up the unbudgeable truth that abusing parents were subject to abuse at the hands of their own parents. I have no memory of abuse, as I understand the word, except what I think many children in the 1920s and 1930s had to deal with from immigrant parents. It wasn't always pleasant or the material on which to build unshakable confidence, but I can't remember anything resembling this terrible idea of "fun" I had playing with Steven.

And forgive me, Steven, I kept it up for most of our stay in Florida, for about six months, believe it or not. But only when I shaved. And only when you were in the pen watching me shave. And only when we were alone. I did not trust the others to appreciate my pedo-sadistic humor, not even my sainted mother-in-law.

Discourse

Meanwhile, the closeness I felt for Augusta enabled me to talk about my problem, premature ejaculation, as it is called in the sex manuals. Instant orgasm. Mine. I didn't have to read much or go to consciousness-raising seminars or adult education courses to know that women, after a while, become interested in experiencing an orgasm. In order to bring this about, since it was generally believed that a woman took longer to feel fully aroused, the man had to hold back his easily achieved orgasm and be sensitive and spend lots of time on foreplay, i.e., clitoral fingering or tonguing with no end in sight, breast nibbling, belly button kissing, etc., all the while straining antennae to feel how hot and close to orgasm she might be. That was foreplay.

How do you know it's doing its job? Your fingers are cramped, your tongue is tired. You don't know. Even if suddenly you hear moaning or feel the pelvic region moving with a certain viciousness or catch the quick breathing, the scream, the spasm, the whimper —was that it?

Well, all men know we can never know. There is no visible spillage, no instant shrinkage—no smoking gun. With her moans subsiding from a feral pitch to even breathing, with the pelvic region still, if she hasn't had her orgasm, she is at least trying to give you the idea that she has. She is signaling you to proceed. And you proceed with guiltless self-satisfaction, safe in the knowledge that you were as considerate as the sex manuals exhorted you to be. The ideal, of course, is for both of you to arrive at orgasm at the exact same time, two drowning in one groan of pleasure.

Intercourse

One night, returning to the hotel from the Flamingo Flame, a bar where I'd been sitting in with a small group, Augusta and I proceeded to our room. On the staircase we were already undressing. We had smoked some pot on the beach, as usual, but that night we also soaked the paper from a Benzedrine inhaler in Coca-Cola and drank it. By the time we were in bed and ready for It, we were also on our way to an all-nighter. As usual, I took the lead, with the usual result. Somehow knowing all that stuff about mutual satisfaction had little effect on the time it took, or didn't take, for me to come. I don't think I ever came without trying very hard not to. I tried splitting my mind from my body by running through chord changes: "Indiana," F, D7, G7, C7, F, B-flat, etc. From there to multiplying in the thirteen table. Thence to reciting the entire cast of *Forty-second Street*: Dick Powell, Ruby Keeler, Ginger Rogers, Warner Baxter, Una Merkel . . . But my will is always caught up and washed away in the surge of my urge.

No matter my explosive thrill, I always felt I was a flop in the Partner Satisfaction Department. Tonight was no exception. Except that tonight the Benzedrine wouldn't let us fall asleep and forget it. We talked through the night in stoned tones. It must have been a reasonable discussion; one by one, the neighbors—older married couples who shared our air shaft—complimented us on our honesty about matters they themselves could never broach in their day but wished they had. . . .

A Wrap

After six months of family adventure mixed with sun, sea, and sand in Miami, I forgot why I was there. The anxiety about my heroin use in New York took a back seat to a number of other anxieties. I was beginning to feel that down in Miami my life was standing still. Who am I if I am not doing anything?—a question I still ask myself.

I wanted to be an artist, and I had to do it alone. This was a trip that did not include a partner, a lover, a woman and her sainted mother and children. I had to present myself in a characterless context, or a context I could make up as I went along. But four relatives with the Bronx emanating from their faces, clothes, and speech only spelled failure—not to mention the rows of Franco-American cans in the cupboard and the Heinz and Hormel on the table, and a wife who washed her hands ten times before serving and made her family wash their hands ten times before eating. Augusta's germ phobia was getting worse. I had to take so many baths before sex that I was developing a chapped body. She was getting tough to be around—literally. She began yelling at her mother for hovering over the stove or for allowing the kids to get away with a single washing before dinner. And the fact that she did this when I wasn't there made me see her in an unattractive light. I had to begin somewhere else.

I didn't want to live in a family apartment. My life was not going to be about living, it was going to be about art. I wanted a studio and paintings in that studio, and brushes, canvas, and paint to produce those paintings. I had to fulfill my desire to study art seriously, even if I might have fun doing it. I wanted to be an artist with all the trappings of the day. I wanted to replace the image of a musician—zoot suit, duck's ass haircut, hip talk—with dungarees, rope belts, zany shirts and sweaters, outfits and language that would be thought original and full of invention. I wanted to experience the actual act of painting. Smearing. I always found painting walls or boards with a wide brush physically pleasurable. I even wanted to learn to draw. I wanted to come by some serious avant-garde ideas, then put the results on a wall in a gallery on Fifty-seventh Street and read all about it in critical articles in magazines and newspapers.

Once More with Passion

Once back from Miami on Crescent Avenue with my four depen-dents, and not playing much horn, I began spending time down-town drawing at Nell Blaine's studio on Twenty-first Street. The subway ride back from Nell's up to the Bronx and my family was becoming a painful waste of time as my interest in that scene diminished. I was young and, as my uncle Morris said, had "a lot of time in the bank." I didn't want to squander it on the D train.

I would usually wait until late at night to return to Crescent Avenue after hanging out as long as there was Something Happening: probably smoking pot, listening to jazz, a little drinking, and long, uninformed talks about art and seduction; not much was Happening Sexually. Many nights we'd go to Times Square to see a foreign movie, foreign meaning French, with the great Jouvet, Arletty, and Jean-Louis Barrault. *Les Enfants du Paradis* was one of the most artistic experiences of my life, especially that scene at the film's end, Barrault anxiously searching for the woman he loves in a crowded carnival street. The screenplay was by the poet Jacques Prévert. The love story inspired me to run out on Forty-second Street after the credits and look for the greatest love of my life. Having been told by friends and strangers that I resembled Barrault, I began to see myself as a thin, sensitive, odd-looking young man, disillusioned but still hoping to unite love and a life of art, for at least two hours after seeing the film.

My downtown friends and I would walk up to Times Square to see these films, and the buildings along the way were a show in themselves. The Flatiron Building, the Chrysler, the Georgian warehouses—every brick took on a new significance; we became sensible to seeing, we tried to cap each other in architectural observation. This was the first idea I had of new possibilities.

Augusta sensed that she was pretty far down on my People and Things to Think About list, which put her in a state of continual panic, confirming every negative view she intermittently held about herself. Her confrontations and accusations avalanched, leaving us little time for the fun of generalization. Augusta knew nothing about what interested me: jazz, art, old movies, fame (mainly in art, or anything else that might come along). She didn't have the social graces I began observing in women when I was downtown—not that we went anywhere to test them out. She was jealous and awkward. If a woman in the street, alone or with a date, looked at me for more than a moment as we strolled past the Paradise Theater on the Grand Concourse in the North Bronx, Augusta was capable of shouting at the innocent offender, "Hey! Like what you see? Turn your face!" I hovered between flattery and fear.

Sex with Augusta and guilt about leaving the children kept me on the D train up to the Bronx night after night. I liked my erotic sessions with Augusta—short as they were. I thought that part would improve, though I was convinced that the problem was more hers than mine. After all, I had the orgasm; she didn't!

But my sexual curiosity about different kinds of women was growing, and the world that would produce them for my omnivorous satisfaction lay waiting, I imagined, in a life of art and bohemianism. I went there.

I also found a way to leave those children to the wolves. I would continue to give what support I could by sending money. I would visit them, so that I wasn't completely neglecting them. And I'd be too busy to worry about them.

I never officially left. I never stood at the door, sax in one hand, bag in the other, delivering a farewell address. I never removed my clothes from the closet, my underwear and socks from the drawers. Nor did I peel the mural from the wall I painted. Sunday at 4:00 a.m. sharp, I would pay a visit wearing an outfit I hadn't changed in a week, and take a bath. The only space for me to sleep was in the bed with Augusta.

After a few months of the time between my homecomings lengthening, Augusta found a beau, one Aesop Gable, a handsome six-foot golf instructor. After Aesop's arrival on the scene, whenever I slipped under the covers in the dark, Augusta languorously pleaded with me not to try anything funny. She wanted to be faithful to Aesop. I made no immediate attempts to seduce her. I did try something funny. I stuck my middle finger up my ass and passed it under her nose. She jumped out of bed.

"Larry, you're impossible! I'm going to sleep on the floor."

"I'm sorry, let's just go to sleep."

So we tried to go to sleep. She turned on her side so that her more erotic parts, breast, belly button, mons veneris, and pubic hair, were the thickness of her body away from me. I would be hard put to try "anything funny" without having to climb over her. Well, I didn't need those parts in my hand to get aroused. I had this glass erection, my own, and it was difficult to fall asleep. Somehow tumescence and drowsiness are rarely experienced simultaneously. I waited till I heard her breathing evenly. In an extremely gentle and slow manner I put my cock at the opening in the natural turn of the thighs just below her ass. Taking my time and moving only on her exhale, I pressed my cock farther and farther into her vagina. After about twenty minutes I was all the way in. What I found surprising was how wet she was. I thought this occurred only after

73

foreplay and vigorous fucking. Maybe she had just been laid by Aesop and hadn't dried out yet. My rhythm method worked. I fucked my wife while she was asleep. A few times she woke up a minute or so after I entered, and with great anger and strength pulled my cock out of her, and with a critical groan got up and went to sleep with Steven in his folding cot about five feet from our bed. Did he hear us? Does it matter now?

Brilliant Idea

After the third angry removal of my cock, having spent a half hour of thrilling but difficult work, I was cured. I gave up necrophilia.

The next Saturday night I was downtown, stoned and drunk at a party deep in bohemia, probably Twenty-first Street, when I got the brilliant idea of fucking my mother-in-law. Fortunately phone calls are aural experiences; a visual one would have produced a fat gray-haired but large-breasted saint in a soiled housedress. I blubbered out my desires on the phone. Berdie, age fifty-six, said, "Oh, Larry, you're so funny. We miss you. Everybody's waiting to see you. Are you coming up?"

"Yeah, later."

I figured I'd stay at the party till it was certain that Augusta was off on her Saturday night date with Aesop, then sneak uptown to the arms of my wife's mother. I exhorted Berdie to be silent. "It goes without saying, Berdie, mum's the word."

"What do you mean, Larry?"

"Well, it might cause trouble."

"What kind of trouble, Larry?"

"Look, just don't tell Augusta."

An hour and a half later, I stepped off the D train at Fordham Road, walked around the corner to Crescent Avenue, poked my key in the lock, opened the door, and lurched toward Berdie, who was lying on the couch in the living room, her bed. I fell flat on top of her and said, "I love you."

The air was filled with shoes. Augusta stomped out of the closet and began pummeling me with a large black galosh. For five minutes I withstood her physical and verbal onslaught. I don't know what I said. But if something like this happened now, with the hindsight of a life in art, travel, reading, and psychoanalysis, I would say what I probably said that night. "I was only kidding. Let's go to bed." Which we did.

GI Bill

The GI Bill of Rights was a World War II military award, governmental gratitude putting its money where its lip was. By offering veterans the advantage and ease of getting paid to learn, the GI Bill, like the WPA educational programs of the thirties, sent thousands of servicemen into the territory of the humanities, unintentionally creating a mass audience for artists and their efforts, and even more unintentionally producing more artists per hundred thousand civilians than ever before to seduce this mass of new lookers. It offered the possibilities of education to lower-class kids in whose hovels going to college was only possible if their parents worked their lives away for them or if they themselves worked all day long and studied all night.

New School

The pedagogical star system was at its height in postwar Manhattan. Stella Adler was teaching a big sector of the acting community, including Maureen Stapleton and Marlon Brando. The New School was a renegade satellite of Columbia University. There you could study politics with Hannah Arendt or Earl Browder, head of the U.S. Communist Party. In that great hall of unacademic academe soulful William Troy thrilled masses of students with his course on Proust, Mann, and Joyce. His first lecture on Joyce began, "He wanted to be a singer, you know." The dashing Professor Meyer Schapiro, whose eyelids were of such purple hue he looked as though he wore makeup, taught the history of art. W. H. Auden, teaching Shakespeare at the same lectern, disappeared behind it in a faint one hungover morning after a big night at the San Remo, an ecumenical MacDougal Street bar where poets and thugs, artists of all stripes, sexes of all sorts, exchanged witticisms and addresses.

The popularity of the New School was based on such intellectual stars of America and world-renowned political exiles from Europe. It also had a well-merited reputation as a place where bohemian students looking for love could find classmates to accommodate them.

It was a delight to study with people respected for the uselessness of their ideas. You could be poor and think your life was worthwhile—the dance of the mind, the leaps of the intellect. If you made art that did not sell immediately, or ever, you could still be involved in a meaningful, inspiring activity that was a reward in itself, and you could show it to the people you dreamed of thrilling with your efforts; your friends were your audience. They were sitting on your shoulder watching you work. That was the opera of the time. You were not working to please swimsuit heiress Mrs. Jason Weisberger walking her groomed French poodle down Fifth Avenue and climbing up five floors in her mink coat to a spattered loft. Who cared that Joyce wanted to be a singer? Everyone in the lecture hall. Did Troy and Schapiro and Auden deal with making a living? Here were men and women teaching us nothing but the life of the mind, implying that the pursuit of a career and commercial success was *selling out*, losing one's soul. In painting, writing, music, and dance, nothing could be more shameful.

New School II

In the year 1947, on Eighth Street between Sixth Avenue and MacDougal on the downtown side, the main valve in the heart of Greenwich Village, one flight up in an unpainted rectangular room, windows looking right down on the busy street, thirty students of art from twenty to forty years old, male and female, myself included thanks to the GI Bill, were working, some standing at easels, others seated with boards in front of them, scrubbing away on their drawing paper, erasing, adding, leaving a trail of charcoal smudges down to their skin and clothes. We were hoping some interesting relationship between the nude model we were looking at and what ended up in our drawing might win praise from our teacher, the modern master Hans Hofmann.

Every Tuesday and Friday, morning and afternoon, starting at the first easel from the door, Hofmann began his assessment of our work. It ranged from compliments to deprecation, comparing the unlabored cleanliness of Matisse's line and the smudge of the student, or sometimes showing how an Old Master and a student handled the same problem. We stopped drawing and congregated around Hofmann, who moved from easel to easel saying things like,

Hofmann's class in Provincetown, 1945

"Simple solids are no longer relevant," which I took to be a reference to the figure. "Solids and spaces are of equal importance. Forces of action and reaction . . . expansion and contraction where all is risk."

Nick Carone, a former student, now a renowned art teacher himself, recalls that what with the unfamiliar content and the density of his accent, "we couldn't understand what the fuck he was talking about. But you felt your life was at stake with every word he uttered. The atmosphere worked on you; it was serious, you were serious, and therefore you were an artist." Wolf Kahn and Nell Blaine and Leland Bell and Paul Resika and Paul Georges and Jane Freilicher and Lee Krasner all studied there.

Sam Hunter was also there studying to be an artist. I feel personally responsible for launching him on his career as a top ten art historian, critic, and Princeton prof. It happened during one friendly moment in class as we waited for the arrival of the master. Hunter asked me to look at a drawing. Sauntering over to his easel in the last threads of my zoot suit attire, a pair of pegged pants held up by a stout frayed piece of rope, I looked at the drawing, not bad.

"What do you think, Larry?"

"Sam, you'll never make it as a painter."

"Why not?" said Sam with the ironic curiosity that characterized his critical style from that day forward.

"Because you wear a fuckin' bow tie when you paint."

Twenty by Forty-five

The class's work was mostly abstract, though based on certain observations of the nude model. For instance, if the model was seated, Hofmann expected our drawing to represent the air between the head and the lap, and totally to ignore what totally absorbed us: the naked sexual organs. The real subject matter at Hofmann's school, under his urging, was not the model but the use of the model, standing, lying, or seated, to create the feeling of space in the work. Foot in the door, Hofmann then led you to his theory of "push and pull."

In that quiet twenty- by forty-five-foot room I pretended, like everyone else, that the real issue was aesthetics. In the few years of my sexual curiosity, no nude female ever sat in front of me with her legs open in silence, allowing me to examine her body. Nothing in my experience resembled the scene here at Hofmann's. Take breasts. Your mother's were the first. That was not observation, that was functional. When I was twelve my ten-year-old sister had an eleven-year-old friend who already had little mounds of fat on her chest. We played in the dark under the dining room table. I would stalk her and catch her and squeeze them. It was not observation, it was dark. Later on, my teenage sisters ran screaming for cover when I walked in on them. And breasts you personally have freed from a brassiere, given where this act takes place in the sexual drama, cannot easily be examined for color and shape.

Our white-haired modern art master looked like Santa Claus, ha ha ha, ho ho ho, and all. Hofmann had a heavy round body that rhythmically accompanied his jolliness. He was always laughing, even when he crossed his arms over his belly to criticize a student's work. His German accent, thickening yearly, made him sound like Herman "Lederhosen" Bing, Hollywood's version of a Teutonic headwaiter, explicating cubism.

Hofmann's half-decipherable critiques were diatribes against all art that was not inherently abstract. Said with a smile. He reminded us every Tuesday and Friday that "push and pull," whatever that unresolved mystery is, was inherent in all great painting of the past. His ideas were transformations of the thoughts of Einstein and Whitehead. The painting was the universe and therefore a field of relative forces, and that he called push and pull. He showed us, as well, how the new abstraction derived from old art. All art, he reasoned, has planes and volume, and where there's planes and volume, there's push and pull.

Emergency Operator

I recently made a transatlantic call to a member of the class of '47, Paul Georges, now living in Normandy after being refused a variance to build a studio in the Hamptons.

"Paul!"

"What's up? Did I get the variance?"

"No. But you have the opportunity to appear in my autobiography. I'm up to the Hans Hofmann part of my life."

"What can I do?"

"Tell me: all the time we were at Hofmann's, we heard a lot of talk on the theory of push and pull from him and the students. And even though our old pal John Ashbery doesn't like to discuss what things are about, what was push and pull about?"

"That's a good question, Larry. I thought about push and pull for ten years after I left Hofmann. I was obsessed by push and pull. By 1957 I decided I finally understood it."

"I'm taping this, Paul."

"Push and pull is the tension between a painting's foreground and background as they move away from and toward each other.

79

L

A

R

R

Y

You know Bruegel's *Return from the Hunt*? That's where push and pull can be seen at its clearest, because the faraway figures and landscapes of the background are dramatic and they compete with those larger figures and horses of the foreground."

"Aha! Then push and pull is the pulsation of our eyes making quick jumps from one ground to the other."

"The son didn't have a clue!"

"What do you mean?"

"In Bruegel the Younger, the foreground remains the foreground and the background stays in the background. There's no movement, no tension, it's just flabby and still. You know, space was deeper in those days.

"You mean Renaissance space?"

"Today's space is shorter. In the modern world *and* in modern painting!"

"You mean push and pull is easier because there's less of a haul?"

"Think about it, Larry. A little square below a big square is different from a big square below a little one. And if it's yellow—"

At that point his voice started to fade, either because of emotion or failure in the line. Paul's words swirled in an art historical squall over the Atlantic.

R

"Mondrian . . . wh . . . fu . . . pu . . . pu . . . ."

"Yes! What about Mondrian!"

"In the . . . pa . . . he . . . ca . . . boogie-woogie . . ."

I

"Which boogie-woogie? The piano or the painting?"

Suddenly the line cleared.

"Mondrian's *Boogie-Woogie*. It's all push and pull!"

"What do you mean! I never saw a foreground or a background in Mondrian."

V

"The . . . uh . . . Mo . . . right out of the planes of Cézanne . . ."

"Cézanne? Which paintings of Cézanne's?"

E

Again we lost contact. I gave up, and hung up.

Theory

R

In Hofmann's theory size counts. So does repetition. A painted three-foot square in a four-foot-square painting affects us differently than that three-foot square in a nine-foot painting. Painting

S

is about the placement of volumes, not about God touching the hand of Adam on Michelangelo's ceiling, nor about the fruits of perversity in Caravaggio's *Bacchus*, nor the complexity of Courbet's world in *The Painter's Studio*. Right up to Matisse and Picasso and beyond, Hofmann emphasized, colors and lines, sometimes depicting figures and objects and sometimes abstract, move forward and backward.

The name Hans (which I heard as "Hands") Hofmann hardly ever passed my lips unaccompanied by some mention of "Foots Feldman," an abstract art competitor of my imagining.

Hans was not Jewish. Still, it was Hitler's policies toward modern and especially abstract art that extended Hofmann's stay on our shores. He was teaching at the University of California at Berkeley when the Nazis took over in the early thirties. By remaining here, he chose not to be a victim of artistic racism. Starving for abstract art in America during the Depression beat being incarcerated for it by Nazis convinced that there was something Jewish in the state of modernism.

He had a reputation as a teacher long before he arrived in America. He was born in Bavaria in 1880. At the age of twenty-four he went to Paris to paint. Paris in 1904 was the epicenter of the fauve and cubist movements. I wasn't surprised to learn that he worked in those genres with Matisse and Delaunay, who became early influences. In late 1913, still working hard and living hard in Paris, Hofmann contracted tuberculosis. While he was in recovery on the island of Corsica, the First World War broke out. As a German, he couldn't go back to Paris. He went back to Munich, managing to avoid a military career by virtue of his romantic affliction. Without one painting to show for his ten years in Paris, Hofmann altered the direction of his career as a practicing modern painter. Projecting another side of himself, he founded the Munich School of Art and in a few years made it famous. The hours devoted daily to the school kept him from any painting. He only did some drawings, a lot of long necks and small heads. Some of them were very good and some not so good.

Mercedes

Mercedes Matter is a painter who shows at the Sidney Janis Gallery and who is director of the Studio School in New York, one of the best art schools in the country. I visited her in her house in Long Island outside East Hampton. Her collection, which she would never characterize as a collection, includes some very wonderful pieces by Giacometti, Guston, Arthur B. Carles (her father), and our own Hans Hofmann.

MM: I studied with Hofmann in 1933 after he taught at Berkeley. We became good friends right away. He would teach even out in the street. Walking up Central Park West, you could see up to One Hundred Tenth Street this enormous diagonal and the buildings on the park, and he said, "See that building on Ninety-seventh Street? It feels closer than this one on Sixty-seventh, and this piece of sky above seems even nearer." I soon saw everything around me in that way. It was the opening of a door.

LR: Is that push and pull?

MM: He didn't talk about push and pull then. That summer he taught at Gloucester, Massachusetts. We took a house together there with two of my friends.

LR: Did they show up?

MM: The four of us had a house in a beautiful part of Gloucester just outside of town. There was a wonderful little cove with a fantastic huge rock that went right out into the ocean and had flowers growing on it. We were sitting on that rock one day and he said—he was so depressed—"All these years of school aren't worth one painting to me. I'm just not painting." I rented an empty building with lots and lots of windows. Twenty-five dollars —for the summer. I said, "Hans, go right to town this minute, buy paint and canvas, and start tomorrow morning." He started the next morning from the still life I put out. He went all the way back to the beginning, very impressionistic and pointillist.

LR: It was representational? You could tell what Hofmann was looking at when he painted it?

MM: If I hadn't done anything else in Gloucester that summer I did get him to paint again.

LR: Did Hans like you?

MM: We were very close.

LR: You continued to know him?

MM: Like part of the family.

LR: Speaking of family, what happened to his wife?

MM: Oh, Miz! She stayed in Germany for the whole war. But I'm not going to tell you about that. It's gossipy.

LR: What's gossipy?

MM: Larry, you won't use it? Will you?

LR: I promise it won't appear in this book.

MM: When she came from Germany Hans had a house in Provincetown and a big separate studio; he insisted on sleeping in the studio. He wanted to get away from his past.

LR: Did they slowly get together?

MM: Oh, and how! Once he did go back with her he was totally devoted.

LR: When the GI Bill came along, his classes were flooded with veterans. Did he feel he should have been painting?

MM: Well, the best of his teaching was when he drew on a student's drawing board. The worst was theoretical. Ideas like push and pull, volume, picture plane, deep space, shallow space, frontality of space, all that horrible rhetoric he learned as a student in the Munich academy. For God's sake, everything I hated about what he taught was not really his at all!

LR: In my student days, he acted as if push and pull lay at the basis of all masterpieces.

MM: What he meant by push and pull was plasticity. And plasticity was best defined by Mondrian himself at a talk he gave at Cooper Union. "Plasticity is an image of energy."

LR: That's as vague as saying truth is beauty.

MM: But when Hans drew on your drawing, that miserable little pygmy on your paper would get bigger and bigger until it was a colossus.

LR: What contemporary painters did he like?

MM: A certain French painter, Jean Hélion.

LR: Married Peggy Guggenheim's daughter. Strange he should like Hélion, who was abstract before the war, but after he was released from a German prison camp he came to feel that making abstract paintings was immoral. (Marrying a rich girl whose mother owned a museum wasn't immoral? [There goes Larry Rivers knocking a whole art form again.] [But I like Hélion's work!])

MM: The last time I was in touch with Hans I had spent two years as director of the Studio School. I wrote to him. "Do you remember that day on the rock when I saved you from teaching? Please help now, I'm really drowning, I can't take it." I didn't send the letter for months, and then he died.

LR: The last time I saw him was on Ninth Street. I walked with him for a block and a half. He said, "I see that you are doing well, Rivers. I saw your show. That's very nice, nikka. I'm very happy for you."

Up Against It

The film writer Pat All-Woman Cooper, who wrote poetry in those days, always said I had ten minutes of fame at the school when I "went up against Hofmann." For a year I had listened to him repeat from a hundred different angles that what gave a painting its character was the size of the forms, their volume, color, and the lines, in relation to the size of the canvas. In class I thought I understood his theory, and what I understood I agreed with. Back in my spattered furnished room on Twenty-first Street, where I was now living with my friend Eddie Aster, I pondered it further, and concluded that one could enjoy a detail or fragment of a reproduction without knowing the dimensions it sat in.

The next time Hofmann was standing in front of my work making his inevitable point, I sprang my prepared sass. "What about a detail like da Vinci's screaming face, huh, man, I mean Hans? It's terrific by itself without seeing the whole work."

"Ah yes, Rivers," said Hans, "das point iss interesting, nikka"— which was how we heard his rhetorical "nicht wahr?" "It iss good to ask qvestions, the artist should always ask qvestions, nikka. Vat ve have mit das detail iss das power of da Vinci's deep pseechological significance."

Hofmann was telling me, and everyone standing around waiting for the next *mots* to drop, that all rules and ideas, everything, are suspended in the presence of genius. What happened to line, form, and color? What happened to frontality? What happened to abstract art principles?

He was less interested in being right than in encouraging his students to paint without the benefit of theory; he let me think I had made a point. Most of the class thought so too. Wolf Kahn, Hofmann's monitor, came over with brushes sticking out of every pocket and one behind his ear. "Hey, Larry. That was pretty good."

Paul Resika, who I didn't know knew my name, said—well, he didn't say anything, he just nodded with the ancient approval of a seventeen-year-old.

Tess Zackenfeld, a new student, asked, "What made you think of that, Larry?" She was industrious, talented, and attractive—at least she attracted me.

"I'll tell you over a cup of coffee. Can we meet later?"

"Okay. Sure."

"That was an intelligent thing you said," Sam Hunter remarked.

"Thank you"—as I snapped his new bow tie.

Jane Freilicher, taking all this fuss as a sycophantic conspiracy, when I casually asked for her opinion of what went on between the master and me, said, "Big deal."

I am put in mind of an earlier refutation that earned me momentary notoriety. In high school science one of the going proofs that the earth was spherical was that it cast a round shadow. I stood up in class and argued that a flat, unspherical coin would also cast a round shadow if it was spinning. My teacher ran out into the hallway to call the other teachers and tell them that *her* student Irving Grossberg had just refuted one of the proofs of the earth's rotundity. That afternoon I played an especially hot game of ring-olevio in celebration; returning home, I realized word of my scientific breakthrough, brought by my classmate Hymie Horowitz's mother, had preceded me. And there before me at dinner I received the award, a beautiful brimming bowl borscht, with sizable dollop sour cream atop big boiled fuzzy potato.

My sister Goldie said, "Big deal."

I waited for Tess to put her drawing and drawing board away. She bent down to pack her stuff. The only time I am able to examine the outlines, the ins and outs, of a woman's body is when she has her back to me. Tess was tall and solid and in men's tight trousers something to be reckoned with. I looked at her and found myself swallowing. At Bickford's cafeteria nearby, where a bell sounded as you pulled the check stub from the dispenser at the door, we sat down with coffee and talked. We talked about what went on in the class between Hofmann and me, my brilliant idea about enjoying details of artworks out of context, Hofmann's remark about the suspension of critical disbelief in the presence of genius—a remark that still doesn't make sense to me, but I was showing off. We talked a little more personally as young artists. How much longer should we continue to be students? I strutted out my other talent and told her I played sax. She told me her husband had a great jazz record collection. "His name is Alvin Zackenfeld. Everyone calls him Al."

"Oh, you're married."

"Are you?"

"Sort of."

More questions. She asked if I had a studio. And what was I working on at the moment? Where did l come from?

She was my age and was also born in the Bronx. We both went to the zoo a lot as kids. If I made her laugh, she had a way of tossing her blond hair forward over one eye, reminding me of Veronica Lake. It was spontaneous but also something she figured out was sexy. I began the first step in satisfying my already clear desire to end up in bed with her. Would she like to come to my studio and see my work?

"I have to go home now, but tonight is Al's night out with the boys, and I have nothing to do." She hoped she wouldn't be too tired to come back downtown from the Bronx, where she lived with her husband way up on Mosholu Parkway. I knew what she meant. That was the same subway ride I had to take back to the Fordham Road stop in the Bronx to visit Augusta, Berdie, and the children. It was tiring, and for me it was becoming a big waste of time. Tess had to go three or four stops past Fordham.

She said she'd call me.

I went home and kept my door open to hear the hallway phone. It rang. Tess could be at my place at 8:30. I immediately asked my roommate, Eddie, if he could get lost between 8:30 and about 11:00 or maybe 12:00 that evening. He loved to stay at home in our little room, but like all of us, he got sentimental and helpful in relation to sexual possibilities.

I didn't have much work to show her: some earlier charcoal drawings I did at school and a few attempts on canvas with oil. I began to arrange the works I did have to their best advantage. Even now, in 1992, with piles of articles about me, collectors who own my work for a pretty penny, museums that hang my work on their walls, when I expect a visit to my studio, I create an exhibition that doesn't look like one. If something in the room is obscuring a work of mine, I put that work on the floor in front of the something.

Tess came. The viewing didn't take too long considering the amount of work I had. I offered her a glass of wine in a cup. The conversation drifted to life with Alvin, when she married, and the trouble she had with her mother, who lived near her. After the second cup of wine I moved to kiss her. She said she was hungry. But that was after the long French kiss and embrace. I didn't want to rush anything. We went to the Gran Ticino, a cheap Italian restaurant in the Village. Poor as I was, I insisted on paying. Our first evening together, and I hoped there would be more, ended with her owing me something. I walked her to the West Fourth Street subway stop. She went back to the Bronx.

Miz Hofmann

Even without Tess I had begun wondering about how much longer
to continue studying with Hofmann. But I was young and uncertain, and it was reassuring to hear Hans talk to me as if I were
already a working artist. Hans would put you in the same sentence
with Matisse, Michelangelo, and other past masters; he made you
feel as if you and they shared the same problems, satisfactions,
dilemmas, and wore the same purple mantle of artistic grace. I had
just come from life with Mom and Pop, whose big job was (1)
getting me to behave, (2) getting me to support myself, and (3)
telling me, not meaning any harm, "You're nothing."

When I was invited with other students to Hans's house, I stood
in awe before an original Kandinsky that Kandinsky had given him
in Munich when Hofmann was beginning his career.

"In Munich," he said, "artists gave away their paintings."

These were older, serious, rather well-known people who made
you feel—listening to them reminisce about Braque and Arp, sitting on kitchen chairs painted delectably in primary colors, eating
baguettes and pâté with mustard and buttered radishes—that you
were partaking of modernism itself.

Hofmann's wife, Miz (pronounced "Mies"), was a short, trim
woman of fifty-five when I met her. She kept her hair blond and
short and rolled under into a pageboy; she seemed attractive for
someone that age, an age that made her looks irrelevant to someone
my age. She enjoyed entertaining us. In the studio-parlor-kitchen

of their loft, she treated us students as guests. She was a gracious
hostess. Despite that, after first hearing Mrs. Hofmann's given
name, I could not see her as the Old World smoothie she obviously
was, so distracted was I. I had heard her name a dozen times a day
as a child when family and neighbors described pimples, moles, big
noses, hanging lips, missing teeth, double chins, triple chins, no
chins, and other forms of facial disaster. It came as a shocking fact
that someone was walking around being called "Mies," which
means "ugly" in Yiddish.

My teacher had introduced his wife to me as "Shitface."

My first reaction was to enjoy a private joke. My second reaction to this connection with my earlier Yiddish-speaking years, a
talent I was embarrassed to share after I left home, was to flash a
beam down to the hayseed in my soul. The innocent narrowness of
shtetl life did not become any broader or more sophisticated in the
move from Eastern Europe to the Bronx, where I was born and
lived through childhood. I was sixteen before I took a trip to Manhattan, playing hooky, the only time I ever did, to see the Benny
Goodman band at the Paramount Theater.

Growing

At about fourteen years old, up in the North Bronx, I was shocked
one morning to find the face I was beginning to stare at for hours
full of pimples and blackheads. A few days before, my dog Queenie,
who slept with me every night under the covers, had taken a big
diarrhetic shit. It covered me from the top of my head to my toes.
At first I thought these sudden eruptions of red and green and black
all over my face were caused by Queenie's upset stomach. It was
acne, not Queenie.

I was also very short for my age. When the teacher lined us up
by height in grade school, I was always second- or third-smallest in
my class. I liked a boy called Greenhut because he was even smaller
than I. (I also admired his name.) For the "problem" of my height
I could only wait and hope I'd grow. Adler elevated shoes as yet
hadn't emerged as a solution.

My nose was beginning to lengthen and turn down at a disturbing pace. My friends not only noticed this, they began warning me
that I was going to end up "looking Jewish." Vaguely aware of what
difficulties this would entail, I entered a beautiful and unrelieved
state of nervousness.

Along with these new misfortunes of life came an even more disturbing eruption. The nipple of my breast, not the one sliced open at birth that had a scar, but the left one, began to rise as if someone had deposited some Fleischmann's yeast there underneath the skin. The doctors we went to see about it told me not to worry. Okay, that was wintertime, and it nestled beneath my garments unbeknownst to anyone.

Ah, but summer came and the shirt came off. We were installed in a little out-of-the-way *koch alein* ("Cook yourself"), a rundown hotel that had gone out of business many years before. Now its rooms were rented by the season, and what was originally the hotel kitchen was transformed into tiny units that enabled the mothers to feed their families seated at different tables nearby in a common dining room. The Catskills were there long before their present ethnic association. There were birds, bees, trees, grass, etc. You know, the Country. For my father, with his endearing trait of no anguish about where he was, ladder-and-rung-wise, in society, this was a perfectly adequate way of getting us out of the heat of the city, etc. My mother acted as if it was some sort of comedown. I still can't figure out who or what could have given her the idea that she deserved a grander fate.

The place was full of girls my age. The pimples didn't disappear. My nose neither stopped growing nor changed its hooky course.

Fourteen years old

90

Worst of all, the swelling didn't go down. I couldn't make out what was happening there. I thought I was going to grow a real tit. This was hard to hide from my mother; so was my shame about it. But for the nose, pimples, and emerging tit that summer, I invented a simple arrangement. With one hand I hid my rising left breast, and with the other, my pimple-ridden all-nose face. My eyes, peeking through the opening between the fingers, attempted to convey some kind of serious thinking.

The kind of aid and comfort my mother administered was to draw attention *in public* to my affliction: "He's exaggerating his problem by covering up! You're drawing attention to it! You're doing a very unnatural thing." Her advice and attempts to influence me were conveyed with expressions and gestures ranging from an exasperated sizzle to rage that actually produced a colorless foam around her mouth. Did I magnify the real importance of my physical changes? Today I have nothing like a girl's tit rising anywhere in my chest. I am pimple-free. My face has broadened, which altered the ratio between the nose and its surroundings. What I thought was an endless appendage has become an average Mediterranean shnoz. With a respectable male height of five eleven and a half, an inch of which admittedly belongs to my ever worn boots, I can't excuse my aggression as an outgrowth of a Napoleonic complex. I'm not short, but I was.

My mom once came to P.S. 32 when I was in the third grade. I was serving the second day of a three-day sentence, facing a corner of my classroom on top of a high wooden stool. My teacher was a girl in her early twenties, blond and blue-eyed and of English descent. To Mom anyone who spoke without an accent was American, i.e., an anti-Semite. Still, she boldly ordered and then begged the teacher to release me. The teacher: "I told him not to leave his seat, Mrs. Grossberg." My mother: "After all, he only walked around the room so he could borrow a pencil. How could he do his work without a pencil? Two days, it's enough." No one was more Mom when I needed protection. In the classroom she wrestled with the language, ran through some seriously distraught expressions, tugged at her dress, etc. Nothing worked. At the end of it I still had my sentence to finish. On top of that, I was in debt to my mother for her energy expenditure, embarrassment, and failure. The kind of scene she played in the classroom was her thing. Basic Mother. Protecting her young. Clear and simple. A pair of tits, some sharp teeth, no confusion about what's bad or good for you.

Later this Basic Mother role could hardly minister to the complexities that arose. By the time I turned thirteen, we were at odds from the moment my head rose from the pillow in the morning to the moment I laid it back at night. The difficult thing was that for us it was the first time around. This was the first time she was a mother and the first time I was a child. I suppose I confused her, adding to the confusing dose of child psychology she got at a lecture given at the Board of Health. "Mothers, lifting your children from a crib to stop them from crying is one sure way of ruining them. Don't give in! It is BAD for them." She took this reductive Spartanism into every nook and cranny of our childhood. When aggressive looks and threatening pronouncements lost their persuasive power, she applied the slap and the pinch known by my sisters and me as the "knip." Several times, almost deranged, she used her nails and her teeth. The Board of Health meant *that?* Nothing was allowed to pass. A remark by me to my sisters at the table about someone whose looks I found funny got: "How do you think *you* look?"

One afternoon she cornered me in the bathroom after school. I was almost thirteen. It was on one of those feverish days right after we moved into the ground-floor apartment of a two-family house on Fish Avenue in the Bronx. It was much more expensive than our previous place; economically it was a bad time to make such a move, and she changed her mind every hour about whether she had done the right thing, whether she really liked the six rooms, whether they had enough light. She cried every day, she had a headache every day; she stalked through the house with a wet kitchen towel compress wrapped around her head. Our furniture was too old. My father wasn't troubled enough. "Look at him, Mr. Happy, with the long walks investigating the neighborhood. And your sister Goldie is eleven years old, she should know what to do, she should be putting dishes on the shelves, silver in the drawer, she should do something."

Mom had found a hot sex comic book that morning under my pillow in the first bedroom I had to myself since the day I was born. It was getting serious there in the bathroom. She threatened me, called me names, and began to slap and pinch me. I shouted, "This is the last time I'm taking all this shit from you!"

No one threatens Mother Courage and gets away with it.

It was worth the possibility of a sock on the jaw from her son to show me (a) she possesses no fear, (b) she possesses concrete proof of how disgusting I am. She pulled out all the stops: tears, rage, despair, and the customary plea to God that He open the earth to swallow her up. I didn't hit her. I could have, I was angry enough, but all I did was grab her by the arms, spin her around and plunk her down hard in the spot where she originally cornered me, and walk out of the bathroom slamming the door. Five minutes later she came out, still sobbing. I sat at the end of the dining room table. She sat at the other end. She didn't speak. We both knew that the confrontation in the bathroom was the last time she would attack me physically. Finally she spoke.

"Go to the drugstore and buy me some Anacin."

I was glad to do something for her.

Mother

It wasn't always frantic. Really. I even thought I loved my mother and she me. One forgets injustices. I often shimmied up her as if she were a telephone pole and kissed her. I kissed her every day when I came home from school, and even when I left the house for a few hours. For laughs I humped like a dog against her thigh. She, who passed negative judgment on almost everything I did, did not mind this. It made her smile. Sometimes after her Saturday or Sunday afternoon nap, if I wasn't playing ball she would invite me into her bed and read to me from the Yiddish daily, *Der Tag*, little parables and advice to the immigrant lovelorn. These back-and-forths between the adviser and the anguished advised were short clear pictures of the shtetl code of conduct translated to New York soil. "Rifka S., my advice to you is tell him either he makes up his mind between you and your daughter, or you're looking for a new boarder." I enjoyed listening to Mom's Yiddish. It thrilled me to understand most of it. These were our best moments. Even though I sprung a few embarrassing hard-ons lying beside her, I still accepted her invitations to lie down and be read to. It kept us friendly for hours.

Around that time I took a job in a tiny store on the Boston Post Road across the street from where we lived. I delivered bags of fruits and vegetables after school for three cents a bag. I'm sure it was to impress and please my mother. Some guys got five cents a bag. Why? How different an accomplishment can delivering a bag of vegetables be? The same disagreeable envy is still with me today. Delivering those heavy packages up all those flights of stairs has metamorphosed into trying hard to make paintings and sculptures.

Like my mother, the world of artists, museum directors, critics, and collectors has become something to impress and please. But no matter who likes my work, shows my work, who pays for it, I always feel the irritation of that old three-to-five relationship.

At the end of the week I gave my mother the money I made. She patted me on the head. "Good boy." During the next week she lovingly doled it back. In contrast to our usual frenzy, my mother and I found ourselves acting out the idyllic convention of a son appreciating his mother. It gave us a chance to come up for a good suck of air.

Picnic

Another point at which we came up for air was the spring picnic, an elaborate 6:00 a.m. to 6:00 p.m. affair including everybody in the family, aunts, uncles, cousins, and everything in their kitchens. Earth Spirit would rise at six and begin to cook a large, luscious pot roast. I performed my part by getting all the bakery stuff: rye bread, pumpernickel, seeded rolls, "pletzels," horns, and bagels. The fare ran pretty full. It was a little like those Northwest Indians trying to see which tribe could give away the most of its valuables to its close rivals and thereby win the day. There were always more than a dozen good-sized chunks of gefilte fish, a whole bowl of chopped liver mixed with hard-boiled eggs, radishes and horseradish for the fish, chicken fat for the liver, pickles for the sandwiches, and sauerkraut. As if this weren't enough, my mother boiled a big chicken, which naturally produced chicken soup and a mound of noodles to go with it. Then there were the other tidbits, like Greek salad. My mother always took pride in knowing that that was what it was called. It was composed of shredded lettuce and diced tomatoes and nothing else except salt. By about ten or ten-thirty we were ready. All we needed to get going were the Hochbergs—my mother's brothers and their families.

My first memory of these outings dates from about 1933. By the thirties my father's side of the family had been successfully discredited by my mother's side. Joe, my father's brother, was too argumentative, and our family suspected that he "used his hands" on his wife, Ida, who was too short, too skinny, and too ugly. (A man who struck his wife, even if the family thought she deserved to be dropped into a sewer with a mouthful of rags, was referred to with a scowl as a "lowlife." Everyone was ashamed of it. It was only supposed to be for the Irish. But the men on *both* sides of the family felt justified. Don't forget, the trick was to stay married. A little punch was the safety valve; denouncing it helped eliminate some of their guilt. I felt helpless and nauseous the one time I saw my father hit my mother.) Joe and Ida's children, Lillie and May, were out of the question.

Mary, my father's mother, was too silly. She sang at the drop of a hat and thought she had a voice. She worked hard, but selling housedresses door to door wasn't the family's idea of chic. Benny, my father's youngest brother, went to yeshiva his whole life, making him too old-fashioned for the Hochbergs. He was very sweet, but his sweetness was interpreted as weakness, for which they further dismissed him. He was very protective of me, stood beside me in all adversity, and arranged my first sexual experience, with Florence. Rootie, his sister, got upset if you looked too long in her direction, and her marriage at fifteen to a gangster hung a little heavy over any meeting.

So it was my mother's brothers, their wives, and their children I saw on occasions like the picnic. Since there was no phone in our house until well into World War II (and then only because my sister Goldie-Gertie-Gerri was becoming marriage material), we just waited until we heard the car horns blow.

The first Hochberg to be ready was my mother's brother Dave. Cranky, belligerently loyal Uncle Dave rolled up in his spiffy blue La Salle. He'd already forgotten the bootstraps by which he had lifted himself manufacturing "new" hats from old ones. He had a fairly good market in the South but enhanced his income through insurance claims resulting from fires of "Jewish lightning" (the insurance scam of burning down one's own business). Dressed for the occasion in beach pajamas was Dora, his second wife. The first, also Dora, he found a little too interested in sex, without him. Years later, after Dave died, the second Dora was also accused of excessive interest. With them were his two daughters from the first Dora, Goldie, the older one, and Fannie, six months older than I. Before Fannie turned fourteen and began seeing my cousin Abe Kores on a steady basis, I always thought that when we "grew up" we would get married. Today Goldie is Gertie. Fannie is Faye, and Abe, her husband, is Al.

Then there was Paul, Dora the Second's tall, dark, and handsome son from a previous conjugal encounter. When Paul and I walked into a gathering of near and distant relatives, the female sighs were audible. He had a straight nose, a joy and relief for Jews to behold. His black, moist hair was slicked back, and at sixteen, six feet tall, he sported a 1920s matinee idol moustache à la John Gilbert, Ronald Colman, Warner Baxter, Clark Gable, George Raft (in *Bolero*), and the ever popular Warren William. I was much shorter than Paul, my Jewish nose dangled from the center of a pale green face already full of angry acne, and all five foot three of me stood beside him feigning joy at his good fortune while waiting for a pause in his compliments to tell a joke or run over to a piano, if there was one, and give a chord-crammed demonstration of jazz that I can safely say interested very few members of my family and made even the near ones distant.

Paul's compliments did not fall on deaf ears. My father, usually a gentle contrast to hard-hitting Mom, couldn't resist suggesting, "Maybe in a few years, sonny, you know, maybe you can get yourself a nose job. When you earn enough money to pay for it."

I had to pay to change a nose that came down the genetic pike? He seemed to overlook the recognizable relationship between his nose and the one he gave me.

Paul's comment on looks and art was that all artists were ugly, that's why they went into art, look at violinists! Years later, in 1954, Paul came to study art with me when I was teaching for the Adult Education Department in Great Neck, Long Island. He came to study with his cousin who was forced into the arts by virtue of his nose.

When I was at Juilliard my thoughts on the subject went into a song. This much I remember:

> You have a nose that puts Pinocchio to shame;
> Though he fibbed to lengthen it, his lying was in vain
> But ah don't fret, cause I love it so. . . .
> Please don't come too near me or I'll scream and shout.
> You might put your nose in my ear, sneeze and blow my brains out.
> But then again, dear, what is in a nose?
> It isn't what it looks like but what the nostril grows.

Gogol, you are not alone!

Mother's brother Moishe, now Uncle Morris, was sometimes absent. His excuse for pulling a no-show at the picnics—that his four sons were older than most of their cousins—didn't convince anybody. We knew he was bored being anywhere with his wife. Poor Brontza! Over a period of years her shapely calves, originally responsible for keeping Moishe interested, disappeared beneath elephantiasis of the ankles. All her dresses seemed to be dark brown and go all the way down. She waddled when she walked. She looked like some lumpy fire hydrant. I liked her; her looks didn't matter to me. Since she could only understand Yiddish, I enjoyed practicing my limited repertoire with her whenever we found it necessary to communicate. She lived a blank day. At her most unattractive she was dumped by Morris and had to squeeze out a life from the monetary and social benevolence of her sons.

When Morris did come to the outings he was generally silent. Now, of course, I realize he had a number of heavy themes to ponder, but silence always made me nervous. I always gave, and still give, silence an interpretation of sternness and disapproval. When he opened up he usually spoke on a more abstract and intelligent level than anyone else. He was considered cool, the philosopher of the family. He often took a whole minute to respond to a question. My mother summed him up. "Look, it goes to show you, brains are not an insurance policy for happiness." At fourteen, a teenager with problems, I went to work for him in his business removing the leather bands in old hats soon to become new ones. Morris's laconic tendencies reduced the flow of advice about what I should do with my life, how to behave with my mother.

Uncle Herman, who came to the picnics with Tante Anna and their kids, was the family's greatest commercial and amatory success. He manufactured and sold an enormous quantity of lace dresses, which he contracted my father to haul, which enabled my father to begin S.B.S. Trucking. Herman insisted on speaking English and got rid of most of his accent. He married Anna Silverstein,

*Uncle Herman,
a good Republican*

L
A
R
R
Y
R
I
V
E
R
S

highly regarded for having come to America before she was nine and not looking Jewish and having no accent. Between his mouth and nose sprouted a dark square patch of hair. It was a conversation piece. Why did he want to imitate Hitler? He refused to remove it. The rift that making money brought about between himself and the rest of the family was accentuated by his refusal to vote for Roosevelt in 1932. Then he took the more traitorous step of joining the Republican Party. His "making it," especially during the bleak economic reality of the early thirties, must have given him a good-sized head.

Uncle Herman moved to Yonkers, bought a large brick home in a quiet green street. Lots of Friday nights I'd sleep over so I could play with his son, Irving, for the weekends—a luxury of bare feet and red rugs. The idea of a staircase inside your living space was a thrill. The attic! The sound of good china. Pretty maids who all seemed to have red hair. And Tante Anna had a marvelous pair of tits hard to hide under her loose and silky garments.

At the high point of Uncle Herman's zoom he commissioned a copy of a Rembrandt, perhaps the self-portrait. He made a huge party for its unveiling. No one in the family knew Rembrandt from a hole in the wall, but they all got the point. Hail Herman. He had become a celebrity to his family.

They all borrowed money from him "just to live." When he saw signs of the borrowers spending money, he asked, from his parked car, why he wasn't being paid back first. One of his rewards for his help was to be labeled "crude." But a wave of the family flag kept them together. Considering the potential in his experience, he still paid more than the minimal attention to the amenities of family and remained what my mother could call "a good brother." Whatever may have been unforgotten was also unspoken at these picnics.

By 11:00 or 11:30 we'd be on the road. All nineteen or more of us. There was less traffic then, but the roads were one-laners and not always paved. There were about three places to go. Uncle Dave had discovered Grasslands and usually suggested we go there.

Grasslands is the name of a town north of Tarrytown on the Saw Mill River Parkway. But the specific spot where we picnicked was just an ordinary field of uncut yellow hay. The one tree whose shade we needed was a good trudge from the highway where the cars had to be parked. The walk from the highway resembled a safari. I could never find a stone in the entire field. Its main draw-

Family portrait, Glen Island

back was that there was no water either for drinking or swimming, and what bothered my cousins and me even more was that there was no place to buy soda or ice cream.

Choosing Grasslands was a convention to make Dave think he really had an eye for nature; it was not an ideal place to picnic. Everything had to be dished out on the ground. For a good part of the afternoon you were either on your knees or on your ass trying to find a comfortable position for your legs. The hay was too high for any running games and after a while became irritating to my bare legs. Sometime in the afternoon I managed to get my father to throw a rubber ball back and forth. I was convinced his peculiar overhand arc was the way they threw a ball in Europe. Did they throw balls in Europe?

After a season or two of going to Grasslands the exploratory instincts of myself and my cousins were satisfied in twenty minutes. We usually made our way back to a tablecloth on the ground, spending most of the time nibbling and listening to our parents gossip and watching them play poker. It was pleasant, the sun, the sky, the breeze, being with the loved ones.

But the place we usually went to when cranky Uncle Dave could be talked out of Grasslands was the place I really relished. Glen Island, off the Long Island Sound near City Island, New York, was a state-run setup. There was a tremendous parking lot. It was hardly any distance from there to where we laid out the goodies on a long wooden picnic table. These tables—there was a football field of them—were situated in a shaded area. It seemed as though the bottom of a small forest had been cleared. The tables were four to six feet apart, pointing in all directions as they adjusted to the trunks of the tall trees sticking up all over the place. During the course of an afternoon, most tables would receive a short visit from the sun. Beyond the shade toward the sea, there was a huge area soft and green as a lawn. You could see below the gentle slope to the ocean and the bathers and the beach, and of course the soda and ice cream stand. My cousins and I, plus hundreds of other kids, would use this soft field for all sorts of games.

Quite early in my life on this earth it was apparent that I was a skinny boy. It was also obvious that I was a faster runner and better dodger than almost any boy I knew. From the day I realized the gift I had been given, I had the impulse not only to express it in various forms but to have it noticed. Ringolevio was one game well designed to give me satisfaction on both scores. There were two sides with three or four or five boys each. The side that was "it" had to chase and tag the members of the other team. Once you were tagged, you were put in a marked-off pen, usually on one of the boundary lines. Aside from the fun of running around and arguing decisions, the obvious thrill of the game was to free the captured (tagged) members of your side from the pen. If you could touch the ground of the pen with your feet before you were tagged, they were free to run out, and naturally the whole chase started all over again. If everyone except you was captured, you could become a hero. A run straight at the boys guarding the pen, a feint, a change of direction, either a flop roll or a beautiful slide, and your team scattered out free, though you were now a prisoner. To play ringolevio was too much to ask of my cousin Irving, whom I loved but who was fat. My cousin Fannie, well, she was a girl. Paul and the others considered ringolevio a little rough, the kind of game kids who hung around the street, which they were not, were more likely to play.

In 1972 Emmett Grogan, the flower-child revolutionary, wrote a book called *Ringolevio*, about his life from New York in the forties to Haight-Ashbury in the extraordinary San Francisco of the late sixties and early seventies. Emmett got ringolevio down.

There was one aspect of Ringolevio which attracted players and made the game a permanent part of the cultural tradition of the streets of New York. Sooner or later during the course of a contest, each participant had to look into himself and face his physical and mental limits. You just inevitably learned who you really were whether you liked it or not.

I did the cover. I took a three-dimensional map of the United States I bought in a toy store and created an uneven, disrupted, colorful surface—a 1972 visual State of the Union address. Originally I used this idea for a poster to inspire the public to vote for the down but never out George McGovern. There were more posters than votes.

Early Collecting

In our Bronx apartment the only art on the walls was a print that crossed baroque with burlesque, Fragonard and Minsky. It was a Woolworth reproduction of a Spanish maiden with a flower between her teeth; her exposed nipples, like cocoa-brown eyes, followed me all over the room. There was a dark piece of cloth two feet by six feet that my parents called a tapestry, depicting joyous peasants around a rude table partaking of the fruits of their agriculture. The peasants and the señorita went with us from one new apartment to another. One of the features of the Depression was a tendency to change apartments frequently in order to take advantage of the three-month concession (i.e., free rent) offered as a lure by landlords with more apartments than tenants. The only other artworks my parents acquired were two Van Gogh prints, *Young Man in a Black Hat* and *Sunflowers*—the one that was bought by the Japanese for $49,000,000? Yes. The *New York Post*, formerly the *Bronx Home News*, in order to induce people to part with the two cents their newspaper cost, tempted them with free Van Gogh prints for coupons cut from the paper. In the thirties Vincent was considered pretty much of a screwball who cut off his ear and gave it to a prostitute; his overly vigorous brushwork suggested a similar imbalance. Giving a free print of Van Gogh at the time was not giving too much.

My painting Memory *(1989):* Young Man in a Blue Velvet Chair *with* Young Man in a Black Hat

Ours was a small collection that in all likelihood, except for the Christs on Italian walls, was more extensive than any in the neighborhood. Is my art in any way a reflection and response to this early pictorial information?

I managed to acquire a certain taste in music listening to the radio, going to the movies, stopping in the local candy store to hear the jukebox. I never went to an art museum. I never had anything presented to me as art, except maybe what there was in the Museum of Natural History. I don't think my parents had heard of Michelangelo. Certainly he wasn't a household word.

I remember Ralph Robinson, fifth-grade Géricault, the boy who sat in front of me at P.S. 78 and drew horses, running horses in the bargain. I considered him a genius. Why did I associate genius with the ability to recreate a horse on paper? Ralph did something that seemed difficult. My only attempt at art was drawing some maps for my geography class, which I enjoyed doing. I thought they were pretty good. I also thought maps were easier than horses. Maps lack perspective, chiaroscuro, volume, frontality, and push and pull.

Through my attraction to music, I observed and mingled with different kinds of people; I engaged in activities that took my brain out of the diasporic pale. And I experienced joys and disappointments that had nothing to do with an Aunt Dora appreciating the biannual suit my parents bought me for the High Holy Days. The Air Corps lifted me one step up the ladder that led to the world beyond the hills of the Bronx. But after a year of one-nighters all over the eastern states and living and studying in cosmopolitan Greenwich Village under the husband of a woman whose name I heard as Shitface, I realized I was still pretty low on the ladder.

I was still a hick, a cookie stamped out of parents whose highest aspiration for me was that I be a mechanical dentist. From their point of view it was something they could answer proudly when a neighbor asked, "So what does your son do?" "My son's a mechanical dentist," they could say to the neighbor, a sewing machine operator on Seventh Avenue and Thirty-eighth Street, a lifelong member in good standing of the ILGWU. I tried to imagine what a mechanical dentist was, perhaps one of those robots you sometimes saw in store windows imitating human gestures by means of an ingenious arrangement of gears and batteries. I was to become a dentist who would open an office, come to work every morning, stick an insulated electric cord up my ass and plug it into the wall, then with wooden motions begin working on a patient moaning in a chair like the one I saw in W. C. Fields' *The Barber Shop*.

I had taken a few saxophone lessons and had some ambitions of my own, along the lines of being an ace player in the Benny Goodman band and the blackest white saxophonist in the land—a fantasy that did not include shelves and shelves of dentures, rows and rows of gums, gums with teeth, gums without teeth, stacks and stacks of bridges. The color of these pink organs still remains fondly fixed in my mind. It would seem that I would have banished from my work any reminder of the colors associated with these mandibular objects. *Au contraire!* My work is full of gum and inner-body-part tones.

I know my parents were being practical, suggesting a way for me to make a living. It was the Depression, and their suggestions came out of a mentality that saw no end to the hard times; they were trying to ensure that I could feed, clothe, and house myself, of course without depending on them.

In choosing the mechanical dentistry field they passed a pretty clear opinion of me. A student of denture manufacturing didn't have to be too smart, didn't have to study too many hours, maybe didn't even have to study, and could probably get it all in a six-week training course, which wouldn't cost much. You didn't need to have money to start making money. You didn't have to take a chance investing in tools, office space, rent, workers. You could be earning a fortune in six weeks sculpting fake ivory, with the perk of receiving false teeth at half price.

"Son," my mother assured me, "one thing about people, they're gonna be always losing their teeth. Slow times, depressions, they'll always need a new set of teeth. Look at your father. Oh, by the way, how are your teeth?"

Why didn't they suggest I become a mailman with all those civil service benefits? Mail, in slow times, depressions, through snow and sleet, must be delivered. Because mechanical dentistry sounded more like a profession to immigrant Jews.

Toilet in the Hall

The room I shared with Eddie Aster on Twenty-first Street, across the street from Nell Blaine's studio, was in a rooming house called the Penzone; it was big enough for one big bed, mine, and a cot Eddie slept on. We lived on the top floor. It cost four dollars a week, two bucks each. Thirty cents a night. Nell Blaine told us the Penzone had a long, interesting history. If you peeled enough layers of wallpaper off the wall you'd find designs going back to the Civil War. There were about four rooms to a floor, and the occupants shared the toilet in the hall. Our room looked out on Twenty-first Street; during the day it had a decent amount of light.

I met Eddie through Jack and Jane Freilicher at Nell's studio. Eddie played drums. So did Nell. By the time I poked my head into Twenty-first Street, Eddie was part of an ongoing scene. Nell, who made no effort to closet her lesbian feeling, was married to Bob Bass. I never heard anyone refer to her as Mrs. Bass. I thought being a lesbian and married was so fantastic it became a lighted gateway into the art, the jazz, the parties, the banter that went on in her studio. If anything could be the relieving opposite of "square," Nell's life of avant-garde sex, abstract art, and a loft was it! In social terms, all you needed was enthusiasm for whatever came along—enthusiasm and energy and openness of the kind that accepted the validity of contemporary painting. Such an attitude could convert middle-class ideas of immorality into heavenly passion. You didn't have to bother with the I-love-you's.

Eddie found some way, as we all do, of overcoming the God-given unbearable hand-me-downs in life, the ancestral genetic print. In his case shortness, the blue cast of his skin, kinky hair, and a face full of tiny holes. He was born into a family of Dutch jewelers from Amsterdam, Jewish and hardworking. He lived in Brighton Beach and probably flirted with the four unavoidables of that time and tide: socialism, jazz, cunt lapping, and psychoanalysis. He married young, a girl who carried the heavy last name of Einstein. That lasted a year. If there was nothing tragic about Eddie, all this would not be worth mentioning. He was an early ditty-bopper, on the outside a St. Vitus lip-licking dancer with a lizard tongue who seeded a bed of coals on the inside. He carried his drumsticks wherever he went and played on every surface he was near enough to get at, accompanying his rhythmic licks with excerpts from jazz choruses we are all supposed to recognize. He woke in the morning with five o'clock shadow, shaved, and by five o'clock in the evening had ten o'clock shadow. A hand caressing his face came back smaller and smoother. His nose was a short hard beak. After he became a heavy heroin user he developed the slow blink that gave him the look of the last dodo bird. He liked every artistic figure he was supposed to like, respected every highly re-

Jane Freilicher, Eddie Aster, Nell Blaine (right)

106

garded jazz solo. No wonder I loved Eddie. We agreed on everything and thought that Nola Studio's nightly jam sessions were the great thrill of any given day. At those sessions you could hear the new jazz before it went public, get a glimpse of the up-and-coming Brew Moore, Stan Kosow, Al Cohn, and other personalizers of the Lester Young academy.

Bed in the Toilet

There was a new arrival in town. He was handsome, tall, fresh from the West, with a brilliant head of red hair, red eyelashes, and green eyes. He walked into Nola one night. It was Gerry Mulligan. When he entered, to find a seat and a place to put his big horn, it was with a very confident stride. There seemed no doubt on his part that he was the best saxophonist in the room. He blew his baritone choruses, waited a polite amount of time, and left with a look on his face—as I read it—that corroborated the notion that he was still the best saxophonist in the room. When he walked in to play he thought he was the best. When he walked out everyone thought so. It was hard not to like him. His playing was likable and so was he. He had the freshest-scrubbed rosy face I had ever seen. As a musician he wasn't as taken by Lester Young as the every-nighters at Nola, which in that scene gave him the stamp of originality.

Gerry and I were never any closer than our mutual interest in heroin—the great leveler. After playing at Nola, we arranged to meet the following evening at his place, go buy some heroin together, and get high. When I arrived he told me he had no money. Guess why. Something happened. I offered to pay for both of us, thus weaseling out of going with him; for the few bucks I put up, my chances of being apprehended by the fuzz were considerably reduced.

He told me to sit there and wait. He was out of the room before he finished the sentence "I'll be back in a . . ." I sat down. Five minutes later I began to feel uncomfortable, claustrophobic. In relation to my darker downtown abode, Gerry's room was very bright. I sat on his bed. I saw that the floor was tiled white from wall to wall. I looked straight ahead. The walls were tiled. The ceiling was painted white enamel. Gerry was living in a large bathroom, minus toilet bowl, sink, and bathtub. These had been removed to make room for his bed, night table, and one-drawer dresser. The one homey note was a soft rug in the center of the floor. I lay back on the bed and felt I was in a glistening tomb. I became anxious for Gerry to return. Considering how long it might have taken, his run was short. When he got back we instantly introduced the substance into our bodies. We had an affectionate dialogue with tune-ins and tune-outs till he said he was due to blow somewhere. Out in the West Sixty-eighth Street night we parted.

I next saw him forty years later, sauntering still tall and slim through the doors of O-So-Ho, a restaurant in Soho where I was blowing with the East Thirteenth Street Band. Karel Appel, celebrating his sixtieth-something birthday, had hired us to liven up the night. At the end of a punchy blues tune of ours I walked over to Gerry to say hello and go wherever our hello led us. He had that same pixie expression around his mouth and eyes, and the red hair, always a knockout, was now knocking me out white. We gave each other a cursory facial review to assess the damage of time, and then I invited him to blow with us. One of the jazz rarities of our era is to have the big baritone sax as part of a small band. David Levy, our baritone player, dean of the Parsons School and now director of the Corcoran in Washington, relinquished his horn, and Gerry, hardly batting a long eyelash, played with us for over an hour. Nothing in our book fazed him. He gobbled it all up and "blew his ass." He played so great that evening he made us sound great.

Nell's Gatherings

My furnished room was not conducive to practicing what Hans Hofmann preached. But I didn't feel deprived with my small table in my small room and only my bed on which to throw the equipment necessary to produce my first timid, maybe not so timid, works. I wasted no time putting together the bare necessities: an artist's pad, hand-sharpened pencils, an eraser, five brushes; for color, gouache, water-based paint with a lot of body. It came in little jars.

At school all was charcoal paper and charcoal. Considering what you had to overcome with this dull duo, just finishing something at Hofmann's was an accomplishment. Let me put it this way: If you didn't fall asleep at the easel, you were at the beginning of a promising career. I didn't know then how valuable it could be to work with charcoal's limitation of color (I now know a smudge is color). At Hans's school I was a student. In my room on Twenty-first Street, in a spattered smock, I was the artist.

I usually came back to my room in the afternoon. Eddie was always there waiting. I'd find some excuse to go to Nell's studio across the street. My visits became more frequent. Nell made me feel comfortable. I admired her. I must have asked hundreds of questions, all of them giving her the role of a practicing expert. Through her I met many artists, writers, filmmakers, young men and women in publishing and advertising, an occasional heiress, and the odd English nobleman.

At Nell's gatherings there was a brimming presence of male homosexuals. The few ideas I had about homosexuality were quickly adjusted to my new experiences. I began spinning in an ever expanding reality. Most of the gay guests, if not as well read as they tried to sound, showed a great interest in literature. Literary heroes' names were dropped constantly.

"My dear, I've been reading Dostoyevsky's *Raw Youth*. It's marvelous. I found the spirit of the book to be—"

"Spirit, my ass," someone interrupts. "He filched it all from Dickens, who has everything Dostoyevsky has, plus being—"

"What, a social historian? How about the honorable Honoré? You're not telling me that Dickens had more balls than Balzac."

"Ronald Firbank held more balls than Balzac."

"Where?"

"In a ballroom, honey. Where do you hold balls?"

"I don't hold balls in a ballroom. I hold them in a bedroom."

"I hold them in a men's room," someone chirps up from the end of the couch.

"Anyone know a nice quiet spot where I can finish part twelve of *Swann's Way?*"

"Sure. Try the San Remo bar."

There was pressure to exhibit a talent for the well-turned phrase. Being in touch with silly bits of information was very useful as well.

"Did you know there was a case in Michigan where a mother ran off with two objects? The Renoir hanging over her fireplace and her equally well-hung nineteen-year-old son."

The end of the couch pops up again. "That's adding incest to injury, Mary."

Men often referred to one another by women's names. Even things and places were given female proper names. Out at the beach in the Hamptons, if our new friend Waldemar went for a swim, either Frank O'Hara or Jimmy Schuyler flat on the wicker would sit up: "Oh, look! There goes Wilma, off to Ophelia Ocean for her afternoon dip."

And then there was the "-ola" suffix, used to an excess that didn't necessarily lead to the palace of wisdom, but I picked up on it like everyone else I knew, gay and straight. I heard the first example of it in a conversation with Chester Kallman and Wystan Auden at their housewarming when they moved one flight above me at 77 St. Mark's Place. ("Carriages at 1:00 a.m.," said the invitation.) Chester invited a tall, muscular sailor who showed up in uniform, a boy from Iowa, who after three cups of Chester and Wystan's concoction of English tea, white wine, and hundred-proof vodka slipped into a pair of black silk stockings and sheer lace panties and demurely worked a kosher salami into his asshole, singing "Anchors Aweigh."

Wystan told Chester in a loud stage whisper to "get that hidee-ola out immediately." Wystan may have been a snob, but he was not a prude. What he was was a gracious host. His rage was provoked by the frivolous misuse of the kosher salami brought by Mr. and Mrs. Noah Greenberg of the Pro Musica Antiqua ensemble.

Queer

For the first time in my life I began to feel sexually attractive. There was so much talk about beautiful asses and burgeoning baskets and the ins and outs of sucking cock—nary a word of the abominable cunnilingus—that after a few hours of such high-toned banter it became apparent I was some sort of dish.

With women, until then, I was not aware that they might be feeling something sexual about me. For women, I thought I was a boyfriend possibility, or that I was an interesting guy, or simply that I was the proof that a man found them attractive. In my estimation sex with women was achieved only by my urging them to do it.

Sex with men wasn't exactly my bag, but if they got my cock hard they could have it. I felt what I imagine women feel: that if they're young and mildly attractive, most men would be happy to sleep with them. If a homosexual of my world had the opportunity to get me in bed, he would take it. Is this an ordinary heterosexual conceit? Megalomaniacal omnipotence? But that's where I was.

What was the code word for "homosexual" in those days? In my immediate group of friends it was "queer." What was it out there beyond my circle? "Fag"? No, that was much later. "Pansy"?

"Fairy"? "Sissy"? Those terms were insulting. What else was out
there that was not insulting? You could tell where people stood on
the subject of homosexuality by the word they used. There was
"queen" (more neutral), and there was the aggressive objectivity of
"cocksucker." I didn't mind being called a cunt lapper. I thought it
gave me stature. I thought the word "cocksucker" gave homosexuals the same pleasure. Both terms marked us as standing outside
the pale of society. That was then. Forty years ago.

Zoo

I grew up in the Bronx Zoo, born across the street from the main
entrance. Starting at about five or six years old, I went to the zoo
alone almost every day the way other boys and girls might go to
their neighborhood playground. I walked about a quarter of a mile
from the entrance to my favorite beasts, on the way enjoying the
camels, wild ducks, and zebra herd as a kind of hors d'oeuvre, but
I didn't really stop until I reached the Cat House, where a serious
sculptured portrait of a lion guarded the entrance. The building

*Doorway to my
birthplace, across
from the Bronx Zoo*

was late-nineteenth-century government-sponsored architecture trying to look as Greek as possible.

In the winter the cats were inside the Cat House pacing nervously before the audience. I took great pleasure in examining their coloration, their spots, stripes, muscles, toes (like the chair in my living room), their specific faces, even their whiskers, moustaches, and beards. The only feeling nearly as intense was the fear of what they could do if there was no wire grating between us. A cat in the Cat House was not an enlarged house cat. In the wild I couldn't spend five seconds observing them.

Each cat had a particular lore. The lion was naturally king of the cats. The male was not only the cat king, he was grandest of all the beasts. He had the biggest rib cage, he stood the tallest, and with his specially coiffed furry hairdo, he couldn't be beat. His face in repose was strangely serene, to me not frightening. One could see the relationship between the king and other evolutionary strays like the bear and the dog in his rudimentary snout.

The tiger, on the other hand, was the quickest destroyer and eater of anything he found fit to do in; he seemed capable of killing just for the pleasure of using his extraordinary equipment. He had a mean face when he smiled. Leopards were smaller but still quite frightful; the first moment you would be aware of their presence would be when they were one yard in front of you, already leaping. Or you would never even see them drop silently from a tree to the back of your neck. The black panther was a thrill down my spine as he caught my brown eyes with his green ones, pacing nonstop and rubbing his fur against the grating.

After I passed in front of all the cages, I'd head for the elevated platform lined with benches and plants some thirty feet away. I'd sit where I could view almost all the cages and wait until I heard a roar, then quickly run over to the cage of the roaring cat. The lion's roar filled the building with the most beautiful tones as it reverberated and rolled in the stone and concrete space. It never stopped. The lion's roar would inspire a leopard's growl, which in turn got the tiger off his belly to join in. And so on, until every cat was in on the act. It was beautiful. It was why I came to the zoo.

My next stop was the Monkey House. Above the entrance was an extraordinary frieze of five or six primates contemplating the bust of Homer. I was an ordinary kid. I liked the chimps and the howlers. And I enjoyed the gentle demeanor of the gorillas, despite all those Hollywood denizens running around in gorilla suits trying to scare everybody.

Then to the Reptile House, where I looked at a lot of sleeping coils. The crocodiles excited me, but they never seemed to wake up; occasionally they would raise a thick lid and eye me with something between disgust and boredom.

I gave the yelping sea lions five or ten minutes. They had a really interesting physical setup, a kind of free-form pool lined with lumpy cement dwellings that they could either withdraw into or climb onto, and roll beatifically into the liquid below. Later some bright administrator figured out an extra source of income for the zoo by charging kids a fee to throw fish to the seals.

There was another attraction at the zoo. Cigarettes. I'd follow a man who was smoking and wait till he threw down his cigarette, and if he didn't stamp it out I'd pick it up and have myself a few puffs of what was left of it. There were many failures. I would sometimes tail a man for a few hundred yards only to have him flick his cigarette over a fence I couldn't climb. The cigarette was a perfect end to a few hours of adventure. In the winter I used to come home in the dark.

There was a final and much less enjoyable feature to those late afternoons: one Manny Schwab, eleven years old, very tall for his age, black hair, black eyes, heavy lips, and a mesmeric talk that put my six-year-old mind in his control. In a bushy undergrowth that he would pretend we were exploring, Manny would spring his dick and push my head down on it and shout, "Suck it!" I don't remember whether he came or not, but he was always harsh and brooked no guff, and threatened to tell my parents that I smoked cigarettes. Leaving out some important details, I reported him to my father as someone who mistreated me. In the street the following day my father grabbed Manny and with one slap brought an end to my sexual slavery.

Patronage

At seventeen, spring, fall, and winter, I walked about a mile to school every day. I crossed the Boston Post Road, past the vegetable store where I carried packages for three cents apiece, to Holland Avenue, which led without a twist or turn to the Evander Childs High School yard. This was a popular route. On it every so often I would meet Eugene Agin, a sixteen-year-old whose face never broke for a smile. At first he was reluctant to talk, but after I made a few remarks on some subject, no matter which, he would let loose a flow of ideas on politics, literature, the human condition, and why he was a Communist. In the great American tradition, he was rooting for the party of his dad, who was a Communist. He was living with Dad and Mom at a cooperative housing project called the Coops, best described as Russian Tudor. It was the first such housing where each family could own their apartment. It was built and financed by the International Ladies Garment Workers Union, the ILGWU. It was a two-block-square affair, and as you would expect, it was inhabited mainly by members of the union who were nonreligious Jews, Communists and Socialists, with perhaps one percent of the tenants divided evenly between Negroes and Italians. Canada "Lifeboat" Lee, a wonderful actor, had a wife and a son named Carl who lived there. Carl briefly dated my sister. I knew Carl well; he starred in *The Connection* by Jack Gelber. In all our intercourse over the years, I never found out whether he had intercourse with my sister.

I had two attractions to the Coops. One had to do with Eugene Agin, who made me feel like a wastrel because he was always carrying, cover out, Marx's *Das Kapital*. And reading it. As politically inexperienced as I was, I knew the neighborhood bible when I saw it. When we were graduating from high school, the yearbook's undercover observer penned these words about Eugene:

> All night he thinks about the human race,
> he's Karl Marx without a hair upon his
> face.

I thought that was the finest tribute in verse ever paid to one of my peers. I'm not sure whether he ever became the statesman implied by the yearbook doggerel, but what was said about me—

> He laughs and jests the whole day through
> as if there's nothing else to do

—is as true today as when it was written.

Attraction number two: By this time I was in a small band that played for dances when we had a chance. The Young Communist

My first band

League from the Coops hired us to play for their dances. Hence Jewish Communists were my first patrons.

My second patrons were the taxpayers who paid for the art I made at the Hofmann school, though no citizen received any of that art.

My third patrons were my first patrons with literate and artistic interests. Ted and Gloria Branfman had little money, but it was more than I had; they frequently bought paintings by their unknown friends. At twenty-two Ted was already a Freudian analyst intern, which automatically gave him authoritative insights into every friend's sex life, love life, and social situation. They had migrated from Ted's parental bedroom in Brighton Beach to a snappy red-brick apartment house on Twenty-second Street, around the corner from the hovel where Eddie and I lived, laughed, cried, and pissed in the sink when we were too stoned to go to the bathroom down the hall. Ted and Gloria, with encouragement from Nell Blaine, wanted to buy one of my paintings. I was still going to Hofmann's school. My first exhibition was to be a viewing of one painting in their apartment with no one but them.

As I was splashing my face in preparation for my exhibition, I heard festive noises coming from a room down the hall occupied by Mr. O'Hatteran, a paunchy middle-aged fireman who lived with a small woman named Nora. There was a knock on my door. I opened and Nora was standing there, serious and slightly drunk.

"I'd like you to come to my room."

Did I say small?

Ordinarily she did not appeal to me, but as she swayed in my doorway I began to wonder whether it was time to change my opinion. We walked down the hall together silently. Halfway to her room I put my arm around her waist. She felt soft. In the room a lot of men and women of all ages were drinking beer and whiskey.

Mr. O'Hatteran was there too, all dressed up like a painted corpse. He in fact was in a coffin. This was a wake. Not Finnegan's. O'Hatteran's.

How was a Jewish boy from the Bronx who felt nervous in the presence of a crucifix to behave in a roomful of Irishmen toasting a dead man? Nora wanted me to commiserate with her about her loss and her bleak future; all I could think of was James Joyce, who I knew was a great cultural figure—there wasn't an issue of *Partisan Review* that did not substantiate this—and I vowed to read him at the next opportunity. As Nora offered me one drink then another, I wondered whether she knew what I was thinking when she stood in my doorway and when I walked with her, to what I thought would be my first sexual experience with an older woman.

Between the stiff drinks and the thrill of the moment, complicated by the fact that my sexual feeling for Nora hadn't totally subsided, I needed a change of scene. I found myself walking down the stairs, still hearing the laughter of the mourners. In the street the air hit my forehead; I realized I had a headache.

Indian

On the corner of Seventh Avenue, a woman in her late thirties was behaving strangely. She stopped a man passing by and said something to him. The man looked at her and quickened his pace. She followed behind him until another man drew close in the opposite direction. She turned and followed the second man and began the same kind of urgent dialogue. He too ignored her. She had a good deal of makeup on her face, funny old-fashioned rouged cheeks. She was drunk, and upon closer examination I decided she was mentally disturbed. This combination—drunk, desperate, and slightly out of touch with reality—kept afloat the sensual feelings launched by Nora in my doorway.

"Mister, can you help me? I have to pee very badly. Can you take me to a bar or restaurant? I'm afraid they'll throw me out if I'm alone. Please?"

I brought her back to the Penzone. She preceded me up the stairs. Her figure did not meet my standards of amplitude, but it wagged invitingly side to side in the rayon dress she wore. She turned and said she was an Indian, as if to explain something about herself that perhaps I was missing.

The toilet on my floor was occupied by a happy singing pisser, one of the last guests of the deceased. I led her to my room and pointed to the sink.

"I'm an Indian," she said again, and ran over to the tiny sink, sat on it, pulled off her underpants, lifted her dress, flaring it delicately around the sink, and took a blissful piss, undistracted by my erection, which rose proudly from its humble beginnings at the foot of the stairs. Somewhere among the rayon folds I found her vagina. She objected and tried to push me away. But I held her exactly where she was and kept my cock inside her. The tussle itself could have triggered my orgasm, but she projected, by positional accommodation, that what was happening would continue to its logical conclusion.

An unexpected knock aborted the logical conclusion.

"Larry! Larry, are you there?"

Almost, I thought.

"It's Ted and Gloria. Are you all right? We've been waiting two hours!"

I withdrew from the Indian on the sink. She reached down for her underpants. I decided that Four Characters in Search of a Conversation was unfaceable.

"Can you come back in about ten minutes?"

I heard their steps as they moved down the staircase. They came back and bought a small work on paper, nine by twelve inches, in bright gouache stripes inspired by my bed, that is, the mattress on the floor of my room in the Penzone.

My first sale

Habits

Life with Eddie Aster. Except for sleep we are beginning to reduce the number of things we do together. His ambition for a conventional career of drumming dwindles. It's hard to know if he's decided he has no talent or if his galloping interest in horse has paved flat any ambition. My memory of the spring of '48 in our small chamber is of Eddie's radio murmuring twenty-four hours a day, a belt wrapped around his biceps, and a hypodermic doing its job.

Penny, his teenage girlfriend, was shorter than Eddie's five feet four and a half inches. They met at a Jazz at the Philharmonic concert. A serious liaison ensued; she adopted his habit. Penny and Eddie, the Bonnie and Clyde of Twenty-first Street, soon started stealing.

At first their life together had the attractive literary quality, for me, of being on the thin edge of nothingness, passion, and danger. But this wasn't happening in a book, it was happening in my room.

I felt sorry for Eddie, but when I joined him for a "taste" I ended up sorry for myself. We talked in moans, sometimes all night, passing out and waking each other up at different times. I was always nauseous and remorseful, thinking that I would soon begin to look as ugly and sound as pathetic as Eddie; I'd ruin my health, steal to keep myself in drugs, and wind up in the Tombs with a green face, kicking a habit cold turkey on a cement floor.

L
A
R
R
Y

Countering the attack of Monday morning blues, I went down to Hofmann's class early and spent a longer day there than usual. By Wednesday I was finally feeling better and lighter. There was actual physical pleasure in drawing. Life had a purpose. I was studying to be an artist, maybe even a great artist, and I had no anxiety concerning the amount of time it would take. On bright mornings I imagined I had some special talent that would speed up the process. Other days I felt just being a plain old-fashioned hardworking artist was a rose in my tattered lapel.

Not that I was ready to burn all my bridges from music to art. Although my ambition to become an artist put me in touch with new people, I still found it easy to be with my old lowlife friends, so long as I saw them apart from my serious friends—my new friends who had highly developed middle-class attitudes about breaking the law and didn't think you were accomplishing much by taking dope.

Ink

By Friday I was in class at Hofmann's, the dreary scenario gone from my mind. I was drawing, absorbed in my work. Then Eddie walks in. He doesn't enter the class proper, he stands at the edge of the class near the storage units. He has been indicted by a New York grand jury and is awaiting trial on two serious charges: statutory rape and car theft—oh, and possession of drugs. Everyone in the room sees him and knows he's there for me. I walk over to him. I feel as uncomfortable as I always felt when my mother or father showed up at school, my father in his overalls with a long pipe wrench in his back pocket, or my mother with one wart on the bridge of her nose and another on the flare of her nostril.

Eddie looks very much as if he knows no visitors are allowed. Why is he here? To look at my work? Probably to look at the models he knows pose nude for us.

He tells me he has some heroin.

"Man, what are you doing holding?" I ask.

"It's good shit, Larry."

"Oh, man! How many times have I told you good shit gets me sick!"

"It's not *that* good."

Five days have gone by since the last time I had some. Maybe I'll have a better reaction today. "Okay, let's try it."

R
I
V
E
R
S

We go into the toilet out in the hall. There's no lock on the door, but there is one in the cubicle with the bowl. Two minutes later we're trying to find something in which to cook up the heroin. Eddie managed to bring the injection part of the paraphernalia, an eyedropper jammed into the back of a hypodermic needle, but he forgot the small spoon.

Sometimes the cap of a soda bottle would work instead of a spoon. I go back into the classroom. Nothing there to use. I go to the office and take a cap lying out on the desk next to an open ink bottle. I come back to the toilet and give the cap a thorough rinsing; it looks clean enough. Eddie taps the heroin from its plastic capsule into the cap, draws water from the flushed toilet bowl into the eyedropper, and squirts it into the heroin powder. I bring a few matches under the concoction. Eddie stoically suffers the heat, and in a few seconds the water boils. We drop a tiny ball of cotton scraped from the tongue of my shoe into the cap. Eddie places the needle in the cotton and starts to draw the mixture from the cap. It isn't until the entire mixture fills the dropper that we realize ink, loosened by the heat from somewhere in the cap, tinctures the solution—now water, heroin, and blue-black Waterman's.

We look at each other. Are we really going through with this?

"Has ink got poison in it?"

"There isn't *that* much ink in this."

"Listen, Eddie, if you think it's okay, it's okay. You go first."

This isn't as villainous as it sounds. Eddie always goes first. He pushes half the contents of the dropper back into the cap, ties himself up, and does the deed. A minute later, he's still on his feet, and I am convinced everything is perfectly all right. Supremely tranquilized, he administers my shot.

We exit the cubicle. I make my way into the office and put the cap back on the desk sooty side down.

Five minutes later, the rush of the drug subsiding slightly, my thought process returns. "Maybe the poison in the ink takes a few hours to kill you. Oh, man! What have I done?"

I not only recovered from the ink shot, but there was no manifestation of my usual nausea and pallor.

Rome wasn't built in a week, nor was leaving Eddie and drugs and Twenty-first going to take a quick pack, a ten-minute speech by me about values, and a split. While my criticism mounted, life continued.

Tess Zackenfeld and I saw each other five days a week at school. Her interest in hanging out after school into the evening grew. Hanging out meant going to museum and gallery openings, drinking wine and smoking pot at Nell's, seeing movies, attending parties, and beginning to fit into the outlines of a couple.

One night I gave a long wine bash in my Penzone attic, to which my fifteen-year-old sister Joan was invited. I had just read about the poet Byron's affair with his half-sister, and I thoroughly approved. It was hardly more shocking than what I had read in *Psychopathia Sexualis* or what Wilhelm Reich was urging on a suppressed and unhealthy public. I thought an affair with my sister would give me an admirable position outside respectable society, leading to the logical conclusion that I could be as great as Byron. And because my sister, unlike Byron's, was under age, I could be even greater than Byron. Don't get me wrong, we are not talking a long romance with Sis—just one little night of love.

I got drunk and demonstrative with every woman in the tiny room. My sister started to leave. I caught her at the door, dragged her to the bed, and fell on top of her, kissing her and declaring my love. I began sobbing, and in a few moments began sexual undulations—dry humping, as it is known in the Bronx, which I clearly hadn't left too long ago. I stayed on top of my sister until some guests finally peeled me off and splashed water in my face. I looked down and saw that it was not Joan; it was Tess, lying there with her clothes ruffled. But Tess, five long years older than my sister, was not too ruffled.

Love in the Afternoon

A day or two later Tess invited me to see her paintings in her apartment on Mosholu Parkway, where she lived with her husband. I was nervous as it became obvious that this visit was going to be more than seeing her paintings. I'd never had sex with a married woman still living with her husband.

Tess's body was an improvement on what I already thought was beautiful and sexy in clothes. She was blond from head to toe and had the most perfect breasts I'd ever seen. She was as sexually unexperimental as I was—nothing much more than the basic blow job. I was in love.

Still, I was very uncomfortable with her deception. When would she start lying to me? Of course I didn't give my own betrayal of Augusta a moment's thought. Tess, sensing my discomfort about our sneaky sex, took me one afternoon to a deep doorway where we stood in the shadows and watched her husband leave a rooming house with a dark woman who looked like a small, curvaceous Puerto Rican.

That June Tess wanted to go to Provincetown to study with Hofmann, whose school moved up to the cape for the summer. She asked Alvin whether he approved of her going up there. Al— even I began calling him that—not only approved of Tess's continuing art education with Herr Hofmann, he also approved of her plan to save money by sharing a place with me, "a homosexual student of Hofmann's."

We found a cheap studio a stone's throw from the beach, one flight up, with a widow's walk where in days of old the wife could see the husband pulling into port before he could see her.

The Dream

When I decided to search for the Holy Grail in Provincetown, indecision set in. Could this be like my trip to Miami, an idea for some kind of salvation, a geographic shift into the unfamiliar? No matter how depthless was my tie to Eddie, Twenty-first Street had the virtue of familiarity. The feeling that I had to leave for my own good was well mixed with a dolorous wave of sympathy for a pal sinking before life had even begun. My wife and kids and mother-in-law up in the Bronx had the virtue of familiarity plus family, but being there with them for more than a few hours failed to quiet my anxieties. Provincetown, in my best projections, was going to be a no-jazz, no-drugs life with Tess, its meaning never put into words.

Provincetown looming, little green me went through my tiny bag of accomplishments. There was the saxophone career virtually abandoned. There was the art student whose teacher in less than a year gave up on me, either because I was so early set in my ways or because Hofmann perceived in me and my work an inability to understand and use any of his teachings. The Branfmans, who bought that painting for a few free meals, made me feel like a professional, but the elation soon dwindled; I suspected that the sale was motivated more by friendship and affection than by aesthetics. Then I whipped out the list of my sexual accomplishments:

123

(1) the blow jobs I gave at age six in the Bronx Zoo; (2) at eight, dancing with my penis in Ida Shisselman's eight-year-old hairless crack in a Catskill meadow; (3) my mother's blue velvet chair at sixteen; (4) a retarded friend of my uncle's; (5) erotic sessions with my alluring wife lasting as long as ten seconds; (6) and now the newness and fascination of Tess (though the time hardly lengthened).

On the Provincetown bus these wearisome ruminations tumbled one into another like the landscapes whisking by. It was night. The lights went out. I fell asleep and had a dream.

> Hans Hofmann is playing my saxophone under a skylight; he is standing in front of an easel with a sheet of music on it. Every so often he stops playing and talks very fervently to an imagined audience, pointing to the sheet on the stand. He begins playing again, and I notice that the light coming from the skylight has a dingy bulb quality. I come forward out of the dark part of the room and put my cock in the bell of the saxophone and begin dancing with him and the horn; only now we are outside in a field. I notice my mother moving toward me. I quickly zip up my pants. When my mother comes closer I see she is Tess. She asks me sternly, "What is your sperm doing on that horn?"

P-town

Provincetown was a corny seascape made in Rockport, Massachusetts, up the mainland coast, painted by all kinds of artists. I mean, gulls flapped and landed on pilings, docked boats always had a twin wiggling in the water below. Along Commercial Street the air was full of fish and salt. On the dunes stretching outside town, you tilted your head to catch the odorless breeze. Decor in all the bars and restaurants was a variation on a theme of sea things: fishermen's nets, some stretching for yards from one part of the space to another, trapped dead fish and crabs and clams and starfish nailed to the walls. Spray-painted purple or green with lots of dancing dots, this decor suggested contemporary homosexual frivolity—not very serious, not very good, but perfect for a saloon hangout in Provincetown. From talking to some of the community decorators I gathered I was supposed to give these efforts more than passing recognition. After all, they were getting close to what modern artists were up to. They created the decor in the bars and restaurants, and

in the bars and streets they themselves were decor, young, energetic, and publicly happy. And no matter what outfit they wore,
their asses were hugged tight.

Our P-town home, one room and an alcove, was bigger than
my place in the Penzone. It was a construction made of one-by-
four knotty pine floorboards, walls, and ceiling. It smelled like a
pine forest. You walked and your footsteps echoed. We arranged
the few bits of furnished furniture so that the place could serve as
a studio for some serious artwork.

Over the first few days we clarified P-town's social life. We knew
plenty of people, mostly connected to the Hofmann art school, and
there were plenty of bars to go to, beaches to lie on, and future
parties to meet new people. Romping and bathing in the nude was
a popular activity among the young, i.e., my friends. And I soon

Painter friends on the cape

found a job as a saxophone player in a bar called the Sea Dragon
on Commercial Street. Buddy Worth on drums, on piano a thirty-
year-old Portuguese lady who taught music appreciation in the
local high school, and me. This left little time for Tess and me to
be at home together.

Lots of jazz musicians I knew passed through P-town and visited me on the job for a bit of blowing. There was Johnny Andrews

of the breathtaking good looks. And any tenor player who had the Lester Young bag down to the soft-shoe shuffle Johnny had it down to was immediately given star status. Tess showered on him an unusual amount of attention, for her—his looks, his playing. The mere mention of his name made women wet. And when I had to play at the Sea Dragon, and when Mr. Andrews did not show up to sit in, and when Tess did not appear to pick me up by the last set, I suspected that it could only be because he was busy fucking her.

The job at the Sea Dragon was quiet, and when it wasn't quiet there was a crowd that came to drink beer, dance, and make a lot of noise. Not, mind you, to hear all the wonderful musical ideas we weren't able to execute. The trio produced some weird sounds. But as I mentioned before, playing saxophone, no matter the quality, high or low, exercised the embouchure and kept the lip muscles in shape. And that had value for a saxophonist. Our drummer and new friend Buddy Worth, a stoned Li'l Abner, tall, no hips, wide chest, one thin polio leg, had a very delicious-looking girlfriend name of Anne Tabachnick.

Now, I don't know what the rest of the country was doing at the time, but in P-town it seemed that trying to get laid was the number one preoccupation. Number two on the list was getting happy, either with alcohol or pot. Number three was making art at Hofmann's and at home, and looking forward to the weekly crit show of student painting. All of us were hoping to be nominated Best Student of 1948.

Bob De Niro, Sr.

The recipient of Hofmann's Best Student Award in 1939 was nineteen-year-old Bob De Niro. He was up in Provincetown painting in the dunes with Virginia Admiral. There they were friends of Tennessee Williams and Robert Duncan, the best one-eyed beat poet outside of Robert Creeley. Virginia was a bright and peppy independent WASP De Niro had just married. She produced good paintings and a movie star. Among the many who sought her favors were Manny Farber and Clement Greenberg, causing the first of many one-rounders between these two. Every Friday night Bob and Virginia had a rent party. You danced, you drank, and you brought money.

Bob was skinny, six feet, and blondish. When he walked he hunched his shoulders. When he stood still he hunched his shoul-

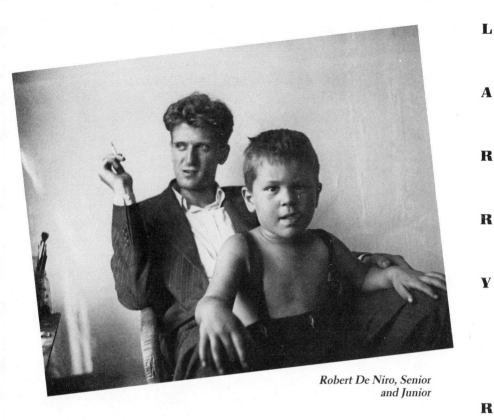

*Robert De Niro, Senior
and Junior*

ders. When he spoke about his own art and art in general I couldn't hear anything in his remarks that invited me to add to what he was saying. He had the air of someone with a long and complicated history: he was a kinetic dandy, he was Baudelaire in New York. His obsessive attraction to French culture, its literature, art, music high and low, even its cuisine, put him and his work ahead of the rest of us, certainly me.

"Bob was a great dancer," says Jane Freilicher. "He would whirl around and around until his movements had no relation to the music or anything. Squeamish women sort of pressed against the wall trying to hide from him."

Bob was also unabashed in his assumptions about the role bourgeois society must play in the Artist's life. This was not mere theory, this was telephone calls two and three in the morning to lawyers, doctors, Madison Avenue people, art dealers, collectors (Joe Hirshhorn told me Bob used to call him)—anyone he had some acquaintance with—asking for cash (he'd take a check) so that he could continue working on his art uninterrupted by the time it took to make a living. These were more demands than requests. I wasn't successful enough to warrant a call. But Bill de Kooning, at the first stages of becoming a revered figure, received urgent calls and was happy to help out. De Kooning for his generosity got some good charcoal drawings from Bob.

As a young artist I was impressed by Bob's work. Painting Greta Garbo elevated him in my affection and respect. I always looked longer at his paintings than at the work of other unrecognized artists. Bob used Greta Garbo as subject matter not only because of the lines and color that would make her recognizable, but because he was crazy about her—as an actress, as a beauty, as the kind of creature she was. In 1962, when Andy Warhol did Marilyn Monroe, he chose her for a media profile that reached across the American scene. She was a natural choice for Andy, allowing him to be comfortable about his color exaggerations for the features of the face. Like Greta, Marilyn was a superstar, but choosing her had nothing to do with Andy's personal feelings about her. Andy, I'm sure, if asked, would have answered that he sincerely admired Marilyn. But he was not physically in love with her, as Bob was with Greta.

Cape Rhetoric

The difference between the Hofmann school on the cape and the one in New York was how much more visible were my fellow student bodies. Even Hans sported a pair of hairy legs. The summer school had more students who looked Mom and Dad's age, men and women perhaps accomplished in areas other than art who had the summer off to pursue dreams they failed to pursue in their youths. From our point of view these were Sunday painters—not to be taken seriously. Little did we know then of Douanier Rousseau, the French customs inspector who began his great career by painting only on Sundays.

In P-town Hofmann's school was one large square room with a high ceiling and a skylight in a tall gable. There the light of day swept out the gloom inherent in most art classes. I don't remember going to class as regularly as I did in New York. And I don't remember the exact moment, but sometime that summer a desire to draw like the Old Masters swept over me—by which I do not mean to exclude such near-contemporary stars as Matisse, Degas and Courbet, Ingres, and possibly Picasso.

I had a pencil and pad with me at all times. On buses, on the job, at home, anywhere and everywhere, I drew. I began to look over my own shoulder as I laid the groundwork for a personal history that might equal the obsessions of artists of the past.

To try to draw well was natural for an ambitious student. Every artist of the past who has come down to us through history had an ability to draw. Painting was drawing, drawing with a brush, with color. Sculpture? Sculpture was a hundred drawings that kept changing position. So how could I think of myself as an artist coming down in a later history unless I too could draw? If I repeatedly made drawings, as did the artists of the past, it followed that I was an artist. It's hard to imagine the lack of confidence this humble beginner had and what kind of crutch I needed to support the little there was of it. I needed the support of history. What is true for a beginner is not necessarily untrue for an Old Master. My draughtsmanship is not as terrific as some have said, but I don't argue. To this day, from time to time, I still wipe crumbs of humble pie from the side of my mouth.

Up in P-town my idea of taking on history was to draw people, to ask people, perhaps children, sometimes perfect strangers, would they mind posing for a while? The while took quite a while, and since I was not a quick sketch artist, being barely able to draw, hardly any of my subjects were enthusiastic about their portraits.

Four years later, after hundreds of attempts at a decent drawing, I was offered a job at Bloomingdale's at a specialty counter demonstrating ballpoint pens with three colors. Each sale entitled the buyer to a quick sketch by me, an artist who despised the notion of a quick sketch. People stepped their faces up to the counter, on which was a sign identifying me as "Jack Harris, Quick Sketch Caricaturist." No one at that elegant store knew from Larry Rivers, but just in case . . .

Ladies carrying bags full of I don't know what with faces coming only as high as the counter would buy a pen and seriously wait for their portraits, some combing their hair and looking into their compacts before setting the angle, which I would ask them to change so they'd feel in capable hands. One pleasantly absurd moment was when Rudy Vallee stepped up to the counter. I asked for and he sang sotto voce the first line of the song synonymous with his name, "My Time Is Your Time." It didn't do much for the drawing; even with his handsome gray Homburg I couldn't achieve anything distinctive. I have never done a pen drawing since.

A

"The only job I remember Larry ever having was one Christmas when I was thirteen and Steven was eight, a job selling colored pens in Bloomingdale's. You pressed a button and different colors came out. These pens were really neat, and my brother and I, I'm sure, got about a hundred of them. Larry made ninety dollars a week. To us kids, Larry had attained success. 'Cause basically we had heard rumors he was a bum, ha ha ha ha, because he was an artist. What's an artist but a bum? Then the job was over, and he slipped back into being a bum and returned to painting. I felt threatened, I mean our survival, a parent not having a job. You know, a kid can't go out and make a living. And yet we were proud of Larry. Though the art scene hadn't exploded as yet, it was exciting to grow up in a cocktail party, meet wonderful people, go to a nightclub sometimes when Larry was playing. We felt kind of bad that he had given up his name even temporarily just to pick up some extra Christmas money for his kids."

R

R

Y

Talking Art

The weekly crit show at Hofmann's summer school was attended by hordes of people other than the students whose work was going to be criticized. A bunch of paintings turned to the wall would be stacked at two sides in front. The cleared space between was the so-called exposition area. Two monitors, the now respectable land-scapist and Hofmann school authority, Wolf Kahn, and a well-built recently arrived Pole—Bronislaw Something-or-Othervich—would line up about six paintings, face-out, few larger than twenty-four by forty inches—small by today's standards, but normal and ade-quate for most artists' ideas in the late forties.

Hofmann and sixty or seventy people were jammed into the hot room; as the time drew near to start the proceedings, perhaps at 1:00 p.m., there was an extra rush of thrill seekers, some standing in the large window frames. The atmosphere was reverential. Hans worked modern art and the artist into a theatrical performance. Howard Kanovitz, artist and friend of mine for thirty years, was studying with Kuniyoshi in Woodstock that summer; he drove eight hours to catch Hofmann's act. It was so crowded, he says, that he could only find a spot for himself on the landing of an outside staircase and look in through a window. He couldn't see anything

R

I

V

E

R

S

of Hofmann, but he could hear him and was able to catch the
corner of a few of the paintings being discussed. He didn't feel too
sorry for himself when he looked down the staircase and saw people
who did not even have a window to peek through, but they, like
him, stayed put, knowing they were in the presence of Something
Important. It was what you did in Provincetown those summers.

Hofmann taught until the middle fifties, when he finally
stopped teaching and began applying his theories to his own work,
which he did over his dead body. He was sixty-seven when he had
his first show, only three years before I came on the scene. He
didn't receive full recognition until he was seventy. Wanting more
years of painting under his belt, when Hofmann heard anyone
sneeze he raced out of the room. He had waited long enough for
success and didn't want to die on account of a runny nose. In
P-town he worked with an exaggerated energy, behaving—it struck
me in my judgmental youth—like an old codger in an old Hollywood musical, "trucking" with an index finger raised and shaking
his ass. This vitality produced splattered, dripped, poured, thickly
stroked canvases that predated abstract expressionism.

Waiting for Whiting

The poverty level of daily existence drove some of us, especially
our drummer at the Sea Dragon, Buddy Wirtschafter, alias Buddy
Worth, to visit the P-town wharves where fishermen gave away
bushels of whiting, a tasteless little fish that seemed to number in
the thousands as you looked over the daily catch·aboard the fishing
boats.

Buddy was born on the Atlantic City boardwalk, of parents who
ran a small boardinghouse whose large silverware supply he kept
using up to his death. On the cape Buddy lived on a sailboat. No
need to spend money he didn't have for gas. The wind was free. He
got a genuine boot out of not having to pay rent. He went to get
free fish off the fishing boats every day and knew exactly which
wharves had the shortest queues and when. Buddy's day was the
clearest example of one of bohemia's important codes: No one willingly works. To submit to a job represented failure, a loss of face.
He was not ashamed to scrounge food, showing up not too frequently but at the right time for a plate of spaghetti or a sandwich
or a hard-boiled egg. He knew how and where to dig for clams and
mussels. He had learned for very practical reasons how to cook

cheap meals. When we lived in Paris at the same time in 1950, in the same hotel with cooking facilities, he'd show up every day with a price report. He'd change his shopping habits for a reduction in the price of an egg.

In the winter he'd hitchhike to Mexico, "a great country for goofing." The food was cheap and there were no heating bills. And always with a pretty teenager, usually from Scandinavia. With no need to work, since the Mexican government wouldn't allow it, you could live nicely on fifty dollars a month, supposedly, leaving you time to paint or write or "do your thing."

It took twenty-five years for his worn-out clothes, worn out of necessity, to make it in high fashion. He lived in faded denims, ripped at the knee; shuffled in sandals and no socks; hated underwear; and grew a beard, further reducing expenditures: no razors and no shaving cream.

In P-town poverty was no stigma. Most artists were used to it, coming from working-class backgrounds in the thirties. Anyway, you don't need as much money in your youth: no doctor bills, you have your health, and distracting activities like dancing, seduction, and self-destruction cut down on appetite.

There were cocktail parties. Some Tess and I gave, most we went to. The urgent matter of those cocktail parties, the sirocco breeze coming off the Atlantic, was to get drunk enough to leave with someone you didn't arrive with. Brown whiskey was the designated alcohol; potato chips, cheese, and peanuts the food. Hors d'oeuvres were something you experienced at the homes of the rich.

Tess and I gave one dinner party. The painter Fay Gold came with Milton Klonsky, who came with Delmore Schwartz, who came with two uncovered loaves of day-old challah and Anne Tabachnick, who said Delmore was crazy in private long before he went public. Elaine de Kooning came without Bill, looking like a Ring Lardner escapee, rouged cheeks, red lips, short skirt contrary to the long new look, talking a mile a minute about everything from drawing to capital punishment with her customary verve and intelligence. She came with Pearl Fine, proving her fidelity to Mr. de Kooning, as well as to Tom Hess and Harold Rosenberg. Jane Freilicher, up for the week, walked in with her husband, Jack. They brought some Basie records and bruised tomatoes from her tiny garden. John Grillo, the first grid painter in the abstract pantheon of New York, now a Mardi Gras figure painter, came alone, hoping he would not leave that way. Grillo was a great cook, and so sweet you wouldn't mind if he slept with your girlfriends between the times you slept with them. He made a delicious dinner for us, something between chicken, pork, lobster, and pâté, which he later announced was three dozen fishnet specials—whiting!

No one we knew was seriously married. At these shindigs you felt part of a happily beleaguered community. In '48 art was still looked upon by mother and father, aunt and uncle, the grocer— the Common Man—as a way of escaping the reasonableness of working for a living. What stuck in the Common Craw was the passion of art, its thrills and leaps of the imagination. How far could all this be from what artists' lives were about? The only professional arena where it was not social or economic suicide to be shameless about being homosexual, or fond of drugs, was in the arts.

Visit

In August Alvin came up to P-town to see how his wife was doing, perhaps to see *what* she was doing as well. The sleeping arrangement in our studio, one double bed and a pullout couch, could reasonably represent to Al a clear situation: Tess is his wife, she has their bed, I'm her gay friend, I have my bed. Before Al's paranoia could take wing about what was really "going down," Tess decided to calm him by hinting that here in P-town, a major queer watering hole, Larry's homosexuality had escalated to hog wild!

I put on what I thought was a queer act—how much of an act could it be?—offering Al a blow job. Had he accepted, out of love for Tess I would have given him one. But Al, the kind of discreet fellow I would have liked to have as a friend, pretended not to hear. The painter Anne Tabachnick says:

> Larry didn't have gay episodes to have sex but to improve himself! He thought by hanging out in gay company he would learn to be classier. That was the only time I saw his insecurity. He was insecure about his manners, he confided to me. He really wanted to learn how to dress and talk! I got him ready for the evening, got his wardrobe together, practiced eating with him. No, it wasn't the homosexuality, it was the upward mobility.

Like a certain evening. At one of Nell's parties some guy, a friend of hers, said he wanted to give me a blow job, right there in front of everybody. I lay down on the couch and pulled off my pants and underwear. Quietly on his knees he began. Shortly afterward the party disintegrated into a lights-out, lights-on affair; when the lights were out, there were lots of bodies on the floor groping and kissing, dresses being drawn up, flies unzipped. Then the lights would go on, and everybody got up and began dancing. In a few minutes the lights would go out again. It was innocent, in a way. There was a team of budding psychoanalysts present, actively interested. Anne Tabachnick was right there.

One party night, Larry took the dare of being blown. I got very drunk and very high and took my clothes off and danced naked around the room. But I didn't want anyone to touch me. I felt everyone had contempt for me because I started and didn't finish. A psychoanalyst wanted to touch me. I didn't want to be touched. He had a leering face. His wife didn't want to join in, but she would have enjoyed watching him with me. Larry asked why I took off my clothes. Maybe I was demonstrating that I didn't know what I wanted. He said, "That's okay, kid, let's go over in the corner and have a quiet little fuck." But we didn't. Few of us did. We were all pretty brazen and really pretty innocent.

Modern Romance

During the first month of our stay in P-town, Tess and I behaved pretty much like two people in *Romance* magazine. We "found" each other. After a few hours at Hofmann's we'd go to the beach together, often in the company of other artists and new friends, and just as often we'd go by ourselves, sometimes in early evening, with the sun sinking orange into the gray-blue. I often wonder if Tess, now living in Bombay with her guru, remembers those days with the same affection I feel right now. I was sexually attracted to her, even if I had my ordinary knee-jerk reaction to other women, which was to practice and improve my sexual act.

There was one night when Tess suspected, correctly, that I had arranged to meet another woman. Tess was not home when I finally returned from my evening out. I went looking for her on Commercial Street. I found her walking with Bronislaw, the Hofmann monitor, in what looked suspiciously like hand in hand. When I got closer, I was relieved to see they were not holding hands. Commercial Street has narrow sidewalks, and they were just walking close. They gave vague answers as to where they were coming from. My response to her inquiries was equally vague. Fifteen minutes later, at our place, she told me she had slept with the muscle man. "How was it?" I asked.

She made me feel that it was vulgar to ask that question. An involuntarily lowering of her lids suggested there was nothing to complain about. I had an erection through the entire catch-up, as well as a flipping heartbeat. I began to hear myself breathing. I felt weak. I drank a whiskey, and another. And our romance took a giant step forward.

Possession

The first night of Alvin's visit that August, it was natural for him to have sex with his wife after a month away from her. I was on the other side of the screen and could hardly avoid hearing everything. The sounds created pictures in my mind—which worked to relieve me of the apprehension of our being found out. That night I was not a happy bohemian.

For the next few days we all smoked pot, played records, talked about art, and went to the beach. Whatever Al might have been uneasy about between Tess and me never surfaced; either our cover story was successful, or he realized he couldn't know the truth. When it was time for Tess and me to go back to New York, to that other life of hers with Alvin Zackenfeld and mine with Eddie Aster, there was no talk of her changing her arrangement with her husband. She would never leave Al, nor ever tell him, nor ever, if possible, have him find out about us.

Madison Street, 1948

I decided to leave art school and find a new abode, live by myself, and paint, but I stayed enrolled at Hofmann's to collect my GI Bill money. I was anxious to begin the serious chapter of an artist's life. I moved to Madison Street, one block south of East Broadway, on the Lower East Side.

On Madison Street I began thinking for the first time about how I got to be me and the role played in this everyday drama of mine by my parents, early toilet training, and sexual sublimation. Our group's young Freudians soon to become psychoanalysts, and my friends who were patients, discussed what went on behind closed doors. All this rich material gave me lots of ideas about how to think of myself.

My mother and father, but mostly my mother, were in my mind almost all the time. By now she thought I was nuts. I'd left a wife and child, I blew a saxophone with no sign of getting serious about a steady living, I smoked pot (which I remember offering her, convinced of its instant consciousness-raising potential). I wore all-black outfits with a black cap that placed me somewhere between a Russian ruffian and one of Conrad's men from the sea. And now I was in a house with no heat, alone, painting pictures!

My father continued on an intermittent basis to be in touch with me. Unable to hide her distaste, my mother cut communication. He once came by to bring me some of her home-cooked delights and asked me to call her. I told him to go back to that cunt and tell her she's a lousy cook and I have no intention of calling her.

Goldie, my sister, would also deliver food from my mother. Goldie says:

Where Larry lived was full of prostitutes, bohemians—you know, artists, dancers, writers. The floor of the apartment was so out of kilter that if you placed a ball down on it, it would roll from one end of the apartment all the way over to the other. And the only heat in the place came from his small kitchen stove. My mother never hated Larry, but she always felt that he didn't like her—especially later when he lived with Berdie and showed such kindness to her. His habits started to become too obnoxious for her. My father had no opinions about behavior. He was very good that way. Also, my mother wouldn't let him open his mouth. But she always let him help Larry: fix the heating in Larry's house, help him move, he even swept his floor when it was too dirty! She couldn't live by Larry's rules, but she never stopped my father or anyone in the family from being good to him.

The only social interaction around our house was with my mother's brothers and their children. She never had outside friends; she was afraid of people, and public opinion meant a lot to her. She really thought Larry was a little nuts. As a matter of fact, the rest of the family did too. I was the only one who kind of defended him. And when he got famous, they didn't know what to think.

My mother's whole building was Eastern European Jews, all garment center union members, raging Communists who made my parents feel as if they were just Jewish nationalists. Every Sunday morning from the windows of forty different apartments you'd hear the radio blaring, "Arise, ye soldiers of starvation." After dinner, all the Communists would congregate on the avenue. It was like walking through Red Square.

Larry was always coming home in this long overcoat with his strange haircut, saying a lot of things no one understood, telling weird jokes without a punchline, and using a lot of "hey man, you dig, man, go, man . . ." Mama was beginning to learn how to read and write English in the Communist Party night school when Larry comes around talking black talk. They thought soon he'd be bringing black people home with him. Which of course he did. So it wasn't only the language but also their position that he was subverting. Here's their son, the firstborn, wearing ridiculous outfits, talking incomprehensible talk, playing incomprehensible music, and generally wending his way down the road to disgrace.

The source of Larry's taste became obvious when he brought his friends up to visit. With their vague idea of what it was to be high-class, they would wear these moth-eaten chesterfield coats. They all wore costumes. You'd see a guy in a doctor's uniform, you knew he wasn't a doctor. He even had the stethoscope around his neck.

Artist at Home

I began to paint canvases, about thirty inches by forty inches, of women sitting in lumpy chairs as if painted by a blind Bonnard. The style was short little strokes, the setting crossed Bonnard's rooms, tables, and food with Madison Street space and the objects I threw on my table, for realistic renditions of course filtered through the French master. I tacked Bonnard prints on the wall next to where I painted and introduced whole passages from them into my paintings.

My place on Madison Street was more than four times the size of my Twenty-first Street room; it had a single bed, a table, two chairs, no refrigerator. Except to heat Campbell's split pea soup, I never cooked anything on my small stove, not even coffee.

After only a few hours of beginner's struggle I would usually stop painting and go for walks nearby or go uptown to Greenwich Village or Chelsea to meet some of my painting pals, or to lug my baritone sax to the nightly jam sessions at Nola Studio. Or I'd chuck it all and go to sleep, refusing to give my depression the satisfaction of affecting me.

One night, an especially cold one, the burners on the stove turned up, I fell asleep and dreamed I saw my father's face in a dark floral landscape spotlit under the surface of the sea. Octopuslike tentacles hung limply from his ears. The scene turned into an enormous tank full of luminous tropical fish. In the dream I was in a bed alongside the tank. Whenever I raised my head to check what was in front of me, my father would open his eyes wide. I thought, I'm not sure why, that he was going to die. And he was angry with me and I was afraid of him. I woke up with a rapid heartbeat. I got dressed and went for a long walk, wondering why I had such a dream.

Maybe I was afraid of my father my whole childhood and was ashamed to admit until then that he was powerful and lost his temper easily. He hit me three times in my life. Once, when I was nine, I was making a commotion in the back seat of our Buick riding into the city from the Catskills because Maxie, a teenage cousin of mine, had suddenly died. Without warning my father swung his fist from the front seat and hit me under the eye. I saw real stars. Later my cheek and temple turned black.

When I was sixteen my friends and I pushed the same Buick off the lot beside our building. With the keys I took from my father's pants we drove off. He must have woken and looked out the window. The car was gone; guessing why, he waited till I came home, about midnight. He asked for the keys and came after me. He was

L A R R Y

Papa a Little Later, *1964*

R I V E R S

especially infuriated since he often let me drive with him sitting next to me. I had been taking boxing lessons since I was twelve and could ward off quite a few of his blows, but not all of them.

The last frightening time he expressed his superior strength was in our living room. I was sixteen, and I was hacking out what I thought were jazz sounds on our upright piano. He asked me to stop a few times. I didn't take him too seriously. He rarely asked me to stop anything, or do anything. His idea was to achieve peace and quiet with my mother, his friends and neighbors, and his children with as little fuss as possible; he would agree to polish our furniture on Saturday rather than argue with my mother about whether a man who worked all week should be obliged to polish furniture on one of his two days off. I was looking at some chord changes on the piano in front of me when suddenly I saw a wall where the music was. With no warning he had come in and punched me in the jaw. I punched him back and made his lip bleed. We sparred for a moment and then put down our dukes, both ashamed of the incident.

Color

In one of the moments of thaw between my mother and me, we went to the Bonnard exhibition at the Museum of Modern Art. My mother had never been to a museum. I'm not sure she ever identified something specifically as an artwork, but she had strong opinions about color and style in clothes and apartment accessories. There was no way to know that any opinions I had were superior to hers.

Take green. Every Easter Sunday the streets would be filled with young people and old proudly wearing their spring outfits. She always said, as if she had never said it before, "The Irish have no taste." And as far as she was concerned, Easter was an Irish holiday. Nobody could tell her different. She didn't know that Jesus Christ was a Jew. A lot of people didn't know that. I myself didn't know it until I enlisted. The subject of Jesus certainly never came up in Hebrew school.

On an early January evening of 1943 in Sioux Falls, South Dakota, when I was studying radar and Morse Code communication as a private in the Army Air Corps, there was a general call for GIs of all denominations to come to a large quonset hut chapel for a program of orientation and prayer. It turned out to be prayer first and orientation second, led by a lieutenant. His main point was that anti-Semitism had no place in the Air Corps. It was hard not to turn my head to gauge the response of the congregation. There was no need to turn my head when the lieutenant, to sounds of disbelief and discomfort, went on to explain that in fact Jesus was a Jew, not only a Jew but a rabbi, who died for his belief that he lived more strictly than others according to the ancient Jewish tradition.

This came as news to me! If Jesus wasn't a Christian, who was? However, I did not immediately fire off this theological update to Mom, who would have assumed I had fallen under some Gaelic spell.

Painting with Mom

Green (and sometimes purple), reasoned Mom, belonged to the Irish. No matter how fine their Easter outfits, the Irish preference for green ruined whatever they wore. For good measure she threw in their hats, with those creepy little light green veils.

Since the beginning of my interest in painting I have been unable to use any green unless it is blunted with small amounts of yellow or raw umber or white. In 1948, in my painting infancy, my use of color swung between two aesthetic poles. I either used a color to represent some object I was looking at, or I used color to brighten and enliven something or to dull it. Color was a means to connect an idea from one part of the canvas to another, to make something handsome or simple, based on instinctual likes or dislikes. No one is right in the use of color, as no one is wrong. In looking back at Mom's remarks about the tragic use of green by the Irish, I'm almost certain that her odd opinions had more to do with ethnic slights she experienced from the Irish than with an instinctual dislike of the color. I see some connection between my mother's antipathy to Easter Parade green and my own difficulty in using it. My mother's criticism was transformed into an instinctual aesthetic.

In 1942 Philip Wylie wrote a popular how-to-think-about-Mom manual called *Generation of Vipers*. Its middlebrow popularity brought into New York semi-intellectual circles the word "Momism." The Mom role in human history has had a great many faces. Wylie's book presented a Mom full of shit and exposed the insidious nature of her cover-up. It's hard to imagine that a yokel like me, descended from a tradition of deifying Mother, could tell my father,

141

"Mom's a cunt," without some kind of social backing I felt had greater authority than what existed at home. I thought Wylie was mean and modern, just what I wanted to be.

Life with Mother

When my mother was pregnant with my youngest sister, I was six years old. Instead of the usual swelling distributed in a gentle line from the breasts to the vee between the legs, which makes pregnant women look as if they are leaning backward, she had a huge pro-tuberant bulge. I thought about my mother's body for the first time,

and I began to examine my mother's looks.

There were those two warts on her face, one where her left eyebrow met the bridge of her nose, the other at the rear of the right flare of the nostril. The warts were grayish, three eighths of

an inch in diameter. At home, like any other feature of the house-hold, the warts didn't matter. However, during open school week when my mother was invited along with me to the principal's office, her warts, her hips, her bowlegs, and everything else European about her put me—my drab clothes, shortness, accent—into an excruciating context. Her face was raw umber, orange and white, her eyes were brown and too small. Three soft bumps made her

nose look comical. All of which never stopped my father from com-menting over the years, "She was always good-looking, and you know she gets better as the years go by."

She rouged her cheeks, a substitute for the winter snow Rus-

sian girls applied to their faces. When she transferred the red dust from a small compact to her skin, she narrowed her eyes in the mirror, ran her tongue over her lips, then alluringly puckered them

in grand satisfaction. To the end of her nose she applied a light pink powder with a mangy puff, brushing off the shelf of her bosom that caught the falling dust. To put a noticeable amount of red on her mouth she had to create a larger pair of lips than she had. I'm

still not sure my ability to draw is inherited. My stubborn insistence is more genetic than my skill. Mom could never draw a satisfactory pair of lips. She couldn't do much better than a red smudge.

Her hair was dark brown and had a naturally moist look. Con-

vinced that it made her younger-looking, she kept it short and close to her skull. She ran a brush through it every day. A single wave traveled a few inches in all directions down to a pageboy hairdo. I

often wanted to ask her to let her hair grow longer, curious about what it would look like. I finally did.

"What's the matter? You don't like it this way?"

"I like it this way, Ma."

Anacin

Mom always had a headache and a reason for it. Before my birth, what bothered her was naturally limited to my father. Some of the annoyances:

1. He didn't know anything, but she couldn't convince him since:

2. He talked too much. Except when she needed his support on some issue, so that most of the time:

3. He never opened his mouth. Except at the table, where:

4. He had the appetite of an animal, which she was convinced had nothing to do with hard work.

5. He kicked when he slept, pulled the covers off her, snored, kept her up half the night, and:

6. He had the gall to take a Saturday afternoon nap, probably because:

7. He did not care about his children. In fact:

8. He was nicer to strangers than he was to his family, and:

9. He was always trying to lay her friends, especially after entertaining with his violin at get-togethers, because:

10. He was a big show-off.

Romance in Her Heart

That her husband was a lower order of being was established three months after their marriage by the following rebuff.

"With romance in my heart," she recounted to me, "I brought him breakfast in bed on his day off. He told me, 'Get out, can't you see I'm sleeping!' " Which to the day he died justified the development of her various talents: frenzy, voice pitch, tears, despair, and conviction based on her superior intelligence.

After I passed through Milk and Toddling, for which I wasn't grateful enough, she made a list of what bothered her about me.

1. I was too skinny.

2. My skin was green (I was called Grina, "the green one," from the time I was six years old until I left home). But if I ate her food

I could improve my unattractive condition. Instead:

3. I didn't eat. Why? Because:

4. I joked during mealtimes, which was the reason that:

5. I never finished her rice-and-tomato soup. Which I needed to sustain me because:

6. I ran around too much.

7. And I played handball, punchball, mushball, football, stoopball, basketball, boxball, baseball, softball, stickball, and other dirty, dangerous games. So that when grade school finished at three my mother was never certain I'd come home because:

8. I lingered late in the schoolyard playing all the above games, plus ringolevio, Johnny Jump the Horse, and Kick the Can, because:

9. I had four hundred friends, each one a worse influence on me than the next. A lot of these boys wore knickers at the age of nine. After two and a half years of begging, at eleven and a half, almost twelve, I was finally allowed one quiet pair, "only for special occasions." In the P.S. 78 schoolyard back then, the elastic grip of a boy's knickers was worn below the knee kind of loose, which was the in, hip thing. My mother succumbed to my demands for knickers, okay, but forced me to wear the elastic grip above the knee, where it was hidden from view by flaring the pants almost down to the calf. They looked like the Bobby Jones plus fours in the golfer series on the covers of Horton's Ice Cream Cups. "What's wrong with that?" asked Mama. "Millionaires play golf." I didn't want to dress like millionaires, I wanted to dress like my friends. Hence:

10. I didn't know how to dress.

Back to Bonnard

As my mother and I went through the first room of the Bonnard exhibition at the Museum of Modern Art, she let me know which of his paintings were bad, not so bad, and passable. In 1948 Bonnard's reputation was not as solidly established as it is today. Bonnard vied with Matisse for first place as the French master; Picasso was also in the running, blinding us with his razzle-dazzle, opening new categories every day. In '48 I knew very little about all this. I thought Picasso more "modern" than Matisse or Bonnard, if only because his paintings of faces were superficially ugly, or because where normally you found one head there would be two, or a face composed of a front view and profile. I hadn't as yet understood the

Mama a Little Later, *1964*

idea of the avant-garde, nor how wildly admired it was.

My mother stopped at Bonnard's *Sunday Afternoon,* circa 1934.

"This is already something! You should paint like this!"

But right next to it was *Still Life and Figure,* drenched in colors no one could resist.

"That's a lousy painting."

"Ma, that is considered one of his great paintings."

"Yeh? Well, where is her head?"

From the hip, right next to the umbilical cord: "Ma, you don't know anything about modern art. In today's painting it's not necessary to put everything in."

"Look, I'm just an ordinary person. I cook, I clean, I don't know anything. It's enough, let's leave."

She was the perfect candidate for Stalin's rumored method of deciding whether art was good or bad. He'd call in a peasant woman and show her a painting. If she liked it, it was socialist realism. If she said, "That's a lousy painting," the artist was relegated to the boondocks.

Beyond their use in bringing me to orgasm, women, and especially Tess, now began to play a more complicated role in my life. On a bench in Dante Alighieri Square, horns honking, forty people a second walking by what is now Lincoln Center, Tess, in a purple gauzy bandanna and a skirt that came over knees I kept staring at, again swore never to leave her husband. Whatever her vows, we did continue to meet. Her long rides back to the Bronx from wherever our evenings ended seemed to get longer, like my trips back to my wife and kids in the Bronx eight months earlier. Tess phoned Al many times to say that it was too late to take the subway home and she was going to stay overnight with one of her painter friends, Nell or Anne or Jane, and that she'd come home in the morning or after finishing at the Hofmann school. Not too much later she and Al found a three-room apartment near Madison Square Park in Manhattan. No more rides, no more overnight stays.

Tess began to play hostess; in spite of her art and her talent for reminding us all of the absurd and other delightful digressions, she was an efficient and uncomplaining household engineer. I don't remember if in her twenties she went so far as to make dinners, but social life slowly shifted from Nell's studio; the somewhat well-known writers, the less well-known painters, and the well-off psychoanalysts-to-be appeared at Tess and Alvin Zackenfeld's apartment. Tess and Al, in turn, were invited to the lofts and apartments of friends. When he was working nights, as a part-time stagehand, Tess would go to these gatherings alone or with me. With their move to Manhattan, Tess had no excuse for not being home.

Tess's development as an artist and the amount of time she spent with our spirited gang began to bother her husband. I'm sure it started well before she told me about it. But Tess still came to my Mad Street place in the afternoon. We'd look at my attempts at Bonnard imitation and talk until the place got too dark, and too often, too cold. Sleeping with Tess was boiling down to: (1) the blood-coursing passion that can mount with familiarity (even sober I was becoming less embarrassed by my nudity); (2) her figure—as beautiful as sculpture from the Greeks to the exquisite Houdons—which felt better each time we were in bed; and (3) the never-ending anxiety about the control I didn't have over the time between insertion and removal. But her tender moans relieved me of my anxiety that Tess would look elsewhere for satisfaction.

One anxious but thrilling Friday afternoon in my place after Tess
came from school, we were at the point of being carried away when
there was pounding on the door. It was Augusta. My wife Augusta   **A**
—plus a guy.

"Open the door, you lousy bastard." That was Augusta.

"Yeah! And now! Right now!" That was the guy.   **R**

The door, latched by a small chain, suddenly opened about two
inches. The chain held, and we caught a slice of Augusta, who
managed to see what she was looking for. The male voice accompaniment was provided by Aesop Gabel, Augusta's lover, a six-foot- **R**
four golf instructor who had recently begun managing a few boxers.

Augusta: "You're fucking her, you bastard. Open the door, I
just want to talk!"

I was sure she wanted to talk. I didn't open the door.   **Y**

"I'll come up to see you on Sunday afternoon. We can talk
then." Never losing sight of sex's bouncing ball, I chose Sunday
afternoon to allay Tess's suspicion that I might sleep with Augusta
if I came up Saturday night. Tess, living with her husband, had no
choice but to continue fucking him. I had no such responsibility to
Augusta; we were separated. If I fucked my wife it was because I
wanted to.   **R**

Let me not step into the same naive river twice: I thought then
that Tess, because of all she felt for me, was only doing her duty
when she made love to her husband. I know now that married folks
having affairs can perform sexual duties with their spouses and have **I**
a pretty good time during the sacrificial act. Was I an extramarital
taste for Tess, one that I took more seriously than she? Even had I
suspected she was enjoying sex with Al, I would have approved, as   **V**
it helped keep our secret a secret.

Augusta and I have been divorced now for thirty years. She
remarried, and is redivorced. I feel close to her. I like Augusta's
spunk, her softness, and her brightness, which produces some   **E**
clear-headed off-center writing. Recently Augusta told me that
until the Mad Street fiasco, she always believed we would somehow
"get back together." After that Friday afternoon she didn't think so. **R**

Listen to Augusta.

I loved Larry in a very different way from any young fellow
I had ever known. He was odd-crazy, fascinating. At   **S**

twenty, he could have been considered almost homely but beautiful, sinister but sweet-faced; high cheekbones in a thin face, sensuous mouth; loud but almost girlish laugh; thin, tight, inquisitive, wondering eyes, evil but charming glance wandering over his face. Even then he looked as though he was destined to be infamous and famous. At times, there would be a pensive, faraway look on his face. He had a lean beautiful body, agile as a ballet dancer, fast as a young horse, wild and brilliant. Mr. Sensuality, Mr. Personality, Mr. Masculine, Mr. Nonmasculine, Mr. Crazy-man, Mr. Wonderful.

Before Larry I had only been attracted to masculine, dark, not very bright Italian boys, the local home-types who had their own particular beauty. I was now exposed and indoctrinated to something completely different that would change something in me and stay with me forever. After knowing Larry, I would find beauty and desire in thin, feminine-looking, aesthetic-looking men, totally devoid of any macho Latin "toughness" that I may have been a slave to in my earlier years. I would get stimulated, seeing him play the piano, hunched over, bopping away with some melody he had written. Give me his ballet-style pirouette through the room and I was "had." What I didn't know, never thought about, was that he had also captivated my mother, who had never seen anyone like him.

When, several years later on, I could no longer have Larry, I would meet and be attracted to Aesop Gabel, who was as strange-appearing as Larry. Another weird young guy: even higher cheekbones, long lean body, but hardly any brain (at that time). There's the difference between the two of them. I can only excuse my action by my agonizing and dreadful loneliness. Still, I couldn't shake off my feelings for Larry. Whenever Larry came up to visit he acted attracted to me. How angry I must have been with him. I would be with Aesop one night making love, and if Larry happened to show up the next day I'd have sex with him too, but he had to pay me for it—so little (in those cheap old days) that I get infuriated with myself at the thought. Was it only three dollars that got him his moments of love from me? How could we? I guess we were all a tad crazy in those days.

At seventeen, when I had Joseph, I could never have been a mother. At twenty-two, I could have been. Larry destroyed everything the moment he walked out of the Crescent Avenue apartment. With him went my marriage and my motherhood, cruelly removed from my life. I remember the pain and disbelief when he left, since he had always told me how beautiful I was. That in itself, of course, could never bind a man like Larry to me; he knew what he wanted from life much too strongly for that—his freedom, his drugs, his women, his men, his music, his taste for everything wild and different, his intense desire for immortality whichever way it would come; I was minuscule, I had entered into his life for a very short period.

I would call him incessantly, wherever I knew he would be, track him down to the holes downtown he was lying in with his junkie pals (with my big pregnant belly), because it took a hell of a long time for me to let myself know he wouldn't be coming back to me. I functioned to a degree—I worked every day, as soon as Steven was old enough for me to return to my job. But I was beginning to feel the psychosomatic pains and fears and feelings that would plague me for years afterward. I couldn't stop washing my hands, and I was getting worse. I had feelings that I was dying. Panic attacks in the street would send me flying into any doctor's office I came upon. I was sure I would fall onto the tracks of a subway station and be killed. I would awaken in the middle of the night, telling my mother I couldn't stand the needles in my head, thinking I was dying. The ambulance at four a.m. began to know me too well. I begged my mother to put me away. But she loved me so much that it blinded her to what was happening.

Every so often, my mother and I, with Joe and Steven in nearby St. James Park, would see this skinny, lightning-like figure coming toward us. His visits were always brief, and he'd be off again to his very private drug-jazz-art life in the streets of Manhattan. It was bad enough meeting someone smart like Larry and feeling that I could never keep up with him. He was the sky and I was a small star somewhere, that's about how big his personality burst out to you as soon as you saw him. I wonder if he ever knew how he came through to me.

There was nothing in the color and subject matter of my 1948 Madison Street paintings that pointed to my daily miseries and dissatisfactions. These works were of bright, upbeat rooms and primitively drawn figures looking neither happy nor unhappy. The mood was neutral. Mine wasn't. It was all blues. Then, as now, I had no interest in showing my private preoccupations to the viewer. Painting, for me, was not about that. It's enough to be bothered by these feelings a good part of the day, I don't have to carry them into my painting. Rousing myself to paint in these blue moods gave me heart to disentangle myself from them and pursue something less fraught in the aesthetics of art. When painting, I was lively. I was painting. A visit by an artist or musician acquaintance also livened me up a bit, and so did evenings with a sexual conclusion. Tess was withdrawing. If my manic seductions flunked I'd end up home alone, depressed, cold and drunk. Shaving in front of a mirror, I always saw the unattractive things in my father's face exaggerated in mine. That still-unfixed nose and those sad, dilated eyes.

Then there was my neurotic behavior. Drug taking, promiscuity, great bouts of insecurity. . . . "Neurotic" was the newfangled term my friends and I used to characterize my behavior. The psychoanalytic connection kept it from being an ordinary put-down. I heard the word so often I looked it up in *Webster's*. Neurotic: "showing undue adherence to unrealistic ideas."

Listen to this adherence to an unrealistic idea.

One early evening, going to a movie on 42nd Street, I picked Tess up at her apartment and greeted her with an enthusiastic report of how I'd made love that very afternoon with a seventeen-year-old girlfriend of my sister Joan's.

"And Tess, she was Persian! She had long black hair and big black-and-white eyes, she looked like a Picasso! I thought Persians were dark people, didn't you? She had the whitest, smoothest skin, and her lips seemed to shine the whole two hours we were together. She had a chunky shape that made bulges in her black dress, and she looked like the Renoir female in that painting you like, I think it's called *The Box at the Theater*."

"Uh-huh."

"We had to get under the covers with our clothes on! You know how cold it gets on Madison Street! Remember that afternoon we ran into the street to get warm? Ha ha!"

All this I recounted as if for Tess's applause. There was no applause, and no "How was it?" I went to the movie alone.

Soon after, Tess decided to stop talking about psychoanalysis and became a patient.

A Joke for Passover

I was invited to the yearly Passover first-night dinner. It all started well. My mother served a holy and delicious meal. Between each course she handed me a healthy portion of shit, about my way of life, what I looked like, what I wore, etc. To lighten the atmosphere I told a joke.

Two Jews, Abie and Moe, are walking down Fifth Avenue. Outside St. Thomas church there is a sign reading, CONVERSIONS $400, BECOME A CONVERT. Abe says, "I can't do that." Moe is broke and has some big expenses to take care of. He walks quickly up the steps and enters the church. Abe says he'll wait outside. A couple of hours later Moe comes out of the church and walks down the steps. Abie says, "Nu, Moe? Did they give you the four hundred dollars?" Moe looks at Abie and says, "That's all you people ever think of!"

Everyone laughed except my mother, who said, "What's so funny . . . Irving. Yes, you're still Irving around here. Where did you hear that joke? Downtown by your intellectual friends?"

Thomas Wolfe says you can't go home again.

I say you can. But keep it under an hour and a half.

That was it. I took the train downtown.

Romance in the Dark

Somewhere in this rapidly declining period Tess threw what we at first called a party and later something else. My mood changed to excitement as I walked from the subway station to the party. I knew Al was at the theater that night. We could dance and drink and be sloppy without his silent discomfort. I rang her bell. I didn't hear any music. Slowly the door was opened by a guy without a shirt on. I'd never seen him before.

I walked in. It was dark. The light in the kitchen beyond the living room was so bright it was difficult to see what was going on. From the kitchen Nell waved her arm frantically. "Come in here, Larry! In here!"

As I moved toward Nell, I thought I made out some moving figures, some standing still and embracing, one or two people slumped on a couch. And in the corner on the double bed I discerned a big lump of bedclothes. In the kitchen Nell nervously asked me what I'd like to drink.

"Hey, what's happening, Nell?"

My eyes adjusting to the dark, I see Eddie Aster with a drink in his hand, wearing nothing but his five o'clock shadow. I take my drink and walk into the living room. Nell asks me to stay and talk with her in the kitchen. The lump in the bed is now moving. I get closer. A friend of Nell's comes over in her bra and no panties, takes the drink out of my hand, and downs it in one swallow. I see now that the lump on the bed is Tess on her back, fucking this guy I don't know. The lump is now in the pit of my stomach. The nausea becomes worse as I pass Tess and the guy on my way to the kitchen. Nell says I better sit down. I sit, quiet, and think I must try to leave. Tess appears in her panties in the streak of light from the kitchen. She beckons silently. When I reach her, she takes off my jacket—I was still fully dressed—embraces me, leads me to the bed where she has just been fucking, pulls me down, and tells me she loves me, that I shouldn't be upset by what I saw. With my eyes closed I kiss her long and lovingly. She looks more beautiful than she ever did. She tells me to take off my clothes. I don't know what to do. I feel as though I have no center and will do anything she wants. I am no longer nauseous. The low light, the various smells of sex, the entire trauma gave me an erection and is giving me one right now, even as I write.

Well, sort of an erection.

The Shoals of Peyronie

I have had erections in all sorts of situations my whole life, most of them for easily understood reasons. But why I always had one when I found my loved one doing it with another or just telling me she'd done it with another has remained a mystery. During those years of figuring out the human beast with the help of psychosexual analysis, one much-voiced theory was that Pop was making it with Mom, who was having the first of her multiple orgasms, and as soon as he came and withdrew, I had to be ready.

I don't remember wanting to make it with Mom, but as Freud points out, its verbotenness doesn't allow the urge to rise to a conscious level. Trying to figure out how a later loved one replaces Mom in the throes of multiple orgasm is replacing my hard-on with a headache.

The much-hushed explanation, offered mainly by the animated John Myers, my dealer from 1951 to 1962, is that your hard-on proves you are basically homosexual and sexually excited by visualizing what's going on between your women and this supposedly gorgeous guy.

From Freud to Myers the upshot is that when an erection arises from these sexual betrayals, you are watching a porno movie you are not starring in.

The Syndrome

Being aroused by my loved one's carnal adventures with another man is part of a personal syndrome. *Why* this happens to me is still a mystery, but *what* happens to me is not. I get an erection. To my surprise, I recognize an added, bizarre twist to the syndrome, given how long ago Tess's carnal adventure took place.

About four years ago, at age sixty-three, I developed another kind of syndrome, called Peyronie's Syndrome, named for the French doctor who isolated the condition, which distorts the penis when it is in its erect stage. There are a number of theories about its cause. One is that some kind of internal bleeding, either spontaneous or from exuberant sexual performance, causes clotting in the penis. As the tissue heals, it forms a scab that does not have the resiliency normally found in the penis. The scab hinders the expansion of the penis the way a piece of tape would if placed anywhere on a frankfurter-shaped uninflated balloon; with the infusion of air the balloon will expand, except in the spot where the piece of tape is. This retardation of expansion creates twists and turns that deform the penis in ways that would be comical were the consequences not so funny. It takes about a year for the syndrome to reach its final stage of distortion. Some men end up with a member that, engorged, looks like a J-shaped sausage with the hook curved up or down or sideways at the end, or like something with which to open a bottle of wine. Since Peyronie's Syndrome is rare and has an embarrassing aspect, I have seen very few erect examples, in the flesh or in photos; in fact, only one, my own. (How did I get the erection? It was given to me by a friend.) Allen Ginsberg, sexually active his whole life, tells me he's had Peyronie's since the fifties.

Another theory about P.S. is that it is caused by taking Tenormin, a beta-blocker, over a long period of time. For over a decade I have had a condition called arrhythmia, for which I have taken Tenormin. Arrhythmia describes the abnormal aspects of the heartbeat rate. A rapid heartbeat is called tachycardia, an uneven one is called fibrillation (popularly known as palpitation). There are atrial (or upper heart valve) fibrillations and ventricle (or lower heart valve) fibrillations. Atrial fibs are frightening but usually not life-threatening; ventricle fibs are more serious and under certain conditions cause death. Bradycardia, a slower-than-normal beat, produces dizziness and sometimes fainting. Bradycardia responds very well to pacemakers, which are buried in the chest and bring the heartbeat up to a normal rate. That is not my particular arrhythmic problem. I have atrial fibrillation: a sudden, seemingly out-of-nowhere increase in the heartbeat rate, with a pronounced irregularity. The normal pulse rate of an average adult is anywhere from 60 to 90 per minute. My first episode of atrial fibrillation came on in August 1977, after a night of drinking and jumping for the first time on a trampoline at a Long Island art extravaganza hurled at the summer night by Christophe de Menil. My pulse rose to a rate of such speed and irregularity that it could only be determined correctly when I was attached to a piece of equipment in Southampton Hospital. It was a hearty 160 per minute. My heart seemed loosened from its moorings, bouncing and bumping against the inner wall of my chest.

Next morning in Intensive Care the healer making rounds told me, "Mr. Rivers, it's nothing that serious; tachycardiac fibrillation is more common than you think. It used to be called Saturday Night Syndrome, brought on by all-night dancing, carousing, and strenuous sexual activity."

"And trampolining?"

"Any kind of strenuous sex, Mr. Rivers. Is there anything I can get you to make you more comfortable?"

"Yes. A mirror."

Saturday Night Syndrome? Well, I had spent part of the night drinking and dancing and trampolining, but a very small part; I didn't stay up late, and there was no strenuous sex. The party at Christophe's new $8,000,000 shack was a grand affair, two hundred guests. Once inside I noticed with a great deal of agitation that not one work of mine was part of Christophe's art collection. Not that she considers herself a collector; she just likes a lot of things and

154

buys them. In 1970 her parents, Jean and Dominique de Menil, responding to a fast-changing world, commissioned me to do a work that would cover, as they put it, "the black experience." They offered $250,000 for a work comprised of painting-constructions I called *Some American History*. Three hours of guests asking me, "Where's your painting, Larry? How come she has nothing of yours?" stimulated me enough to produce a chestful of Saturday Night Syndromes.

There are operations for dealing with some arrhythmic problems, and other procedures, like electric shock. But the usual way is to give patients chemicals. Pills. Over a period of ten years I took Tenormin for my atrial fibrillations. Taking chemicals for one set of symptoms can produce a whole other syndrome, often very surprising. One of the side effects of Tenormin—listed third in the Tenormin literature, in capital letters—is Peyronie's Syndrome. No doctor ever mentioned this, few of them had heard of it. If they had, they knew little about it. It's no use feeling miffed at my attending physicians: even with the knowledge of Tenormin's side effects I would have chosen to help the organ that is more important than the one wherein lies the hope of eternal happiness—my penis. Dead men don't get erect.

I mentioned getting an erection while watching Tess and the guy that night and getting "sort of an erection" while writing of it here because to omit the modifier "sort of" would be to omit an important detail and could ruin my reputation as an informer on myself.

And how do I manage sex with my affliction? Well, when I was fifteen I asked my mother how a man we knew with a very big stomach could make love to his wife. Her answer is fifty years old and useful: "They find a way."

Pulse Rate

Until recently these episodes of my wild beating heart would wake me in the middle of the night. At first the doctor's recommendation was to take pills only when I had these "attacks" of atrial fibrillation. On waking with my chest thumping, I fiendishly took pulse and pills and a tranquilizing warm bath, sat up in a soft chair, read a book, and checked my pulse every few minutes. Anywhere from four to six hours had to pass before normal heartbeat returned. The intervals between episodes were as long as six to eight weeks. As time went on they occurred much more frequently, until in the second year I was put on a daily program of pills to get rid of the symptoms and shorten the period of fibrillation. Like heroin or cocaine, antiarrhythmic drugs gradually lose their effectiveness unless you increase the dosage; but upping the dosage finally becomes more threatening to your life than the condition for which you are ingesting the drugs. After years of my trying this and that, a stalwart M.D., unable to ignore my daily brushes with death, took the long withheld step of suggesting the controversial drug Tambicore, a very powerful heartbeat inhibitor given mostly for life-threatening ventricle difficulties. A month later, Tambicore sent me to the hospital. Two months and many deaths later, it was taken off the market.

Meanwhile, I had a dinner date with the ex-wife I never divorced, Clarice, and one of our daughters, Emma. Clarice and I were intensely married for six years, from 1962 to 1968. Then we separated. In my own sweet way, from the song of the same name, I continued to love Clarice, but from other spaces that contained other lips and limbs. I wasn't always rich and admired. I had an uncomfortably long period from the late sixties to the mid-seventies of continued glitter but little gold. Even so, when Clarice and I split I left her in a ten-room apartment on upper Central Park West that I was allowed to rent in exchange for one pencil drawing. I supported her with enough money for food and clothes and the cost of sending our two daughters to Walden, a private school on Eighty-eighth Street. There was a brief period of blaming each other for the breakup, but we are short on remembering slights and long on swinging through the network of our social existence, dinners, parties, musicales, theater, discussions about our daughters' welfare, etc. and so on. In fact, when Prince Rainier von Hessen moved into 315 Central Park West as an affectionate mate for Clarice and the girls, he and I became friends and he joined our civilized network, to the point of sitting down with me and submitting a proposal for the role he should take in the finances of the household. He and I also made two short films, starring Clarice, that still give me pleasure to look at.

At 6:45 on the evening of that dinner date, Clarice and Emma came to the loft they had once lived in to pick me up. They picked me up off the couch, where I was sweating and groaning in justified fear. Clarice, who had been a nurse years before in her native Wales, took one feel of my fibrillating pulse and said, "Let's eat at a

For C's 35th, *1974*

hospital." I stayed in Intensive Care for three days, and six more in a private room at University Hospital.

A week earlier, on my way to the opening of my 1988 exhibition at the Marlborough Gallery, I was in the midst of yet another atrial episode. I felt so awful I couldn't decide whether to go to a hospital or my opening. I decided, "Fuck death. I'm breathing." A mob awaited me at the gallery, old and new faces, collectors, dealers, a museum person, art magazine people, old groupies seeking autographs, artists whose shows I had recently attended. This unauthorized autobiography's embryo went up for auction that day, triggering the arrival of such publishing luminaries as Aaron Asher, publisher, and Ann Getty, owner, and Barney Rosset, founder, of Grove Press; Jeannette and Richard Seaver of Arcade Publishing; and Crown vice-prexy Carol Southern. Back on Fourteenth Street my studio was festooned to decorate a dinner for a hundred guests, music by the Climax Band, with me on sax. So there it was, as it has come to be in the last twenty years, another evening where I

L

A

R

R

Y

am artist, entertainer, father, husband, ex-husband, boss, friend, enemy, and doorman.

At the Marlborough, an anxious Pierre Le Vai, my dealer, asked me, but knew, what was wrong. Denton Cox was there, Andy Warhol's physician, facing silent accusations of incompetence after the recent death of the pop star (he was later exonerated). I told him I felt awful. He said it was nice of me to show faith in him, took me to the john, pulled out a stethoscope, and told me what I already knew. I was surrounded in the gallery office by doctors of mine attending the opening, who took my galloping pulse and gave me Tenormin to squelch my fibrillations and my anxiety about perishing in the next five minutes.

About an hour after I arrived, my show sold out. The high prices my work fetched, the highest at any gallery exhibition of mine, would have marked a fabulous moment for my demise; carried out of the gallery by my bearers on a litter of money.

First Ending

R

I

V

E

R

S

Clarice and Emma support me as I enter the emergency room. I am laid out, stripped and covered with a sheet, rolled into a makeshift room, and attached to a battery of equipment. With me under a bank of bright lights are men and women moving quickly. Clarice and Emma, biting their lips, are silent and serious in the shadows cast by the lights. They are still in their coats, three feet away. It all adds up to the most life-threatening scene I've ever played. A technician is calling out my blood pressure every few seconds. Off an operating table, we want our blood pressure to go down. Here, mine is descending at a rate I think doesn't bode well. The youthful medicos assisting my doctor, who is miraculously in the hospital, begin a folksy banter, hoping to calm down me and my adrenaline.

"Mr. Rivers, everything's going to be A-okay."

"Why is my pressure dropping?"

"Let us worry about that." They've already found out I'm an artist. "Just think of your next beautiful painting."

I am injected with a good dose of Lidocaine. In five seconds I feel very high and very talkative. My eyes flutter.

"Try to keep awake, Mr. Rivers. It's very helpful."

"Fellas, is this the last curtain call?"

"Mr. Rivers, we don't accept that kind of talk here. Everything's going to be A-okay."

I feel like fainting but decide if I pass out I'll die. The Lidocaine is now telling my doctor he's handsome, has a beautiful head of hair, but "you shouldn't call and shout at me to pay my bill." Another doctor, contacted by my internist from his car phone, pokes his head in and blocks me from heading for the last roundup. It's becoming very difficult for me to stay conscious.

My blood pressure, reaching 60, is still descending.

In the midst of this deathbed drama I suddenly have to piss. A female assistant brings a plastic bottle, pulls back the sheet, and unravels my shriveled penis, stretching it to fit into the neck of the bottle. I don't think my daughter, as a grown-up, has ever seen my organ. Not only am I dying, but she has to see it under these conditions, and in its smallest, most withdrawn state. I stop fighting my desire to pass out, though it may lead to my death. I decide to die. I close my eyes. My whole life does not pass before them. All I can see is my obituary in the *New York Times*. Will it begin at the bottom of the front page, "Genius of the Vulgar Dies at 63," continued inside with one of the *Times*'s awful photos of me and the usual reference to the name my parents gave me, Yitzroch Loiza Grossberg? There won't be much sympathy, of course: I am dying at a pretty ripe old age, and I have lived my life to the hilt, had success, money, fame, accomplishment, and an abundance of sensual satisfaction, and I am leaving this life loved by friends, cherished by a grateful family, and adored by some pretty sexy women; I should die happy. But if I'm happy . . . After choosing death over struggling to stay awake, and feeling I've arrived at some saintly height because of it, my eyes open.

L

A

R

R

Y

R

I

V

E

R

S

Back to '48

Up to the time Tess moved out of the apartment she shared with
Al and moved in with me on Madison Street, she continued to tell
me with the same light of determination coming from her green
eyes that she'd never leave him. I don't remember it as a surprise.
Considering our romantic meandering, I didn't take this change of
address as a step on her part to bring herself closer to me, although
that's what happened. I thought her leaving was the first step in
getting on with the business of her own life, taking herself more
seriously as a working artist. What I do remember is using the hot
plate to make my delicious lamb chop and veal chop sandwiches
smeared with mustard on Wonder Bread. She was terrific in the egg
dish department. She taught me how to use eggshells as a spoon to
scoop up the bits of shell that fell in the yolk.

　　The difference between my place and the comfortable apartment she lived in with Al prodded us to go out every night. I had
no furniture, no lamps, and some stolen utensils; the walls were
tall, but we didn't appreciate that much at the time. The place
looked even emptier than it was, like an apartment being shown by
a rental agent. But this empty look has remained in my mind as a
natural space for painting to take place. While the work I produced
there was a reverie on Bonnard and not very important, the habits
I began to develop were. I felt a compulsion to paint or draw something every day.

She didn't stay long. Nor did I. Tess moved uptown to share an apartment with a girlfriend. I moved to 122 Second Avenue, off St. Mark's Place, to a loft divided into three parts.

Nola Again

During this period I felt some neurotic pull to the jam sessions at Nola Studio. I held a pretty low number in the pecking order and had to wait until greater unknown jazz luminaries wiped themselves out with long solos of endless choruses before I could blow. I wasn't an equal among equals. By my third chorus I imagined no one was listening. My baritone sax playing in those days stressed energetic rhythmical patterns with lots of low burps that didn't take into consideration the melodic line, something like Ornette Coleman's playing a few years later. If the song called for a G-major chord for four bars, I'd play anything that had a loose connection to the chord. The luminaries, like Jerry Horowitz, part-time taxi driver, were much more oriented to a melodic line and natural rhythm patterns.

Nola was a gathering of six to eight musicians each putting up a little bread to pay for a rehearsal room with dark chairs and an upright piano. The only conversation we had was about what tune was next. The two or three hours of playing could go anywhere from "gee whiz" and "wow" to "ho-hum." Tess would go with me at first; soon I went to the sessions myself.

Dancing Feet

Okay, so she stopped going. We had a few other things we could do together at night. One of them wasn't staying home and having long discussions about art. Another wasn't trying to figure out why we were together.

Sometimes around midnight we'd impulsively take a subway up to Forty-second Street, mostly to see some Hollywood film, the silliness of which gave us a feeling of superiority. I didn't find the Forty-second Street regulars as silly as the films. These unfortunate humans in greasy garments darting along the sidewalk, halting abruptly to argue, sometimes in tears, also made me feel superior, but sad too.

Eating a hot dog in Times Square at one in the morning at one of Grant's twin bars was like being in an enormous cacophonous operatic chorus, one half watching the other half eat, flanked by oversized tubs of ketchup and mustard. We avoided eye contact with the mess around us by acting as if Grant's was our after-theater boîte and the two hundred frantic food chompers mixed with beggars and pickpockets two blocks from the Metropolitan Opera were a comfortable background for our Forty-second Street slumming.

We thought we were broke. We were broke. But on Forty-second Street we understood the theory of relativity. Downtown we had a roof over our heads. For the Forty-second Streeters, the night was their roof. Every so often, I'd see a flower in this peculiar garden I'd like to have uprooted and transplanted to my bed. Some of them were prostitutes; that was a guess, because soliciting then, unlike today, was undecipherable. For the next thirty years I kept promising myself I'd go up to Forty-second Street in the daytime and have an entire afternoon of physical thrills with one of these wretched beauties. But there was always something else I had to do that postponed the trip. I agree with Oscar Wilde: What we really regret in life are those things we did not do.

122

The ground floor of 122 Second Avenue between St. Mark's Place and Seventh Street, across from the still-existing B & H All Dairy Restaurant, contained a foundation shop, an endangered species in those days, specializing in corsets and brassieres. It was owned by Joe Eppy (Epstein) and enthusiastically run by his wife Rose.

My mother, who sported big tits and a sizable stomach, wore a corset. On the many evenings when my parents were invited to celebrations, like those given by the Drushkapolia Death Benefit Society, my mother struggled into her corset and walked around collecting her earrings and necklace, putting on rouge and lipstick, before slipping a dress over this laced harness. A condom dulls erotic sensation, even if you have so much sensation you can afford a dulling. A corset is like a condom on your eyes.

Rose Eppy, Joe Eppy's peppy wife, wore a corset. It must have been good business tactics—being at one with the customers—because she had a svelte little shape and didn't need one. Women went in and out of the store all day long. I never ceased looking into the window.

Five stories above, just below the roof on a stone rectangle, was chiseled "Milgrims Dept. Store"—a kind of early Lower East Side

Macy's without an elevator. Just below that engraving were four giant windows starting two feet from the floor and going up to the fourteen-foot ceiling. A black wrought-iron railing like a balustrade kept you confident as you leaned out the open window doors to observe the full flow of life and traffic below. From here, in the fall of '48, I looked down at Harry Truman riding in an open limo, fedora, Margaret, Bess, and all, waving to the multitude on one of his many presidential campaign trips.

The studio behind these windows was the largest and lightest of the three on the fifth floor. Harry Holtzman, an artist, held the lease. He brought Piet Mondrian to the United States and offered him the use of that space. Piet walked up the five flights to look Harry's place over, decided he was not up to the climb. Harry found him a studio a little more down to earth, uptown. If 122 had had an elevator, Mondrian's *Broadway Boogie-Woogie* would have been called *Second Avenue Boogie-Woogie*.

There was another studio in the rear, fairly grand for those days, again with many windows, not as high as in the front, but allowing ample light and a view of Brettschneider's Funeral Home. I rented a space between these two studios, about fifteen by twenty feet, for twenty-five dollars a month: no window, thin walls, a chair, a table, a dresser with a mirror, and a nice long bed to lay my wasted body down.

I continued painting in a Bonnard framework. One work I remember was called *Woman with Dog*, a figure again in a chair

taking the frontal position in relation to the observer. I didn't feel comfortable with profiles or three-quarter views and never painted figures unless they faced the camera, so to speak. It took many years for me to try a seated figure in any other position. I liked shoulders to run parallel to the bottom of the canvas. Each canvas I work on has a hidden grid, lines running across, up and down, consistent with gravity. Putting the oval of a face at an angle to this grid, or the shoulders, or even the seat or back of a chair, puts holes into that grid, creating space. Without realizing it at the time, I found shallow space more to my liking. Don't get me wrong, I love the Renaissance, deep space and all. And although I compete with the art of the past, deep space is too tough an opponent.

Over the next years in the studios at 122, different artists, writers, and dancers rotated in a game of musical chairs. The rear studio overlooking Brettschneider's Funeral Home was inhabited by an heiress to the Brunswick bowling ball fortune. Chubby, gregarious—life is just a breeze—and angry, the nonwhispering Louise Gutman was a modern dancer, mildly adorable, a twenty-four-year-old Jewish girl from Cincinnati, Ohio, an older-sister type who could sit on your bed late at night in a slip that sometimes rode up, lecturing you about your bad habits, as if sex with whomever she was talking to was out of the question. She had lots of energy and was a perfect tenant; she paid her rent on time, cleaned up whatever mess she made in our common kitchen, played music at a socially acceptable audio level, and got you tea if you weren't well. But she disagreed with every idea you had, and put you in your place if you put just a forefinger on any part of her body including benign spots like the upper back. Landing a hand on her tit got you the windup for a slap. If it remained, she slapped. It took me six months of living with her with a weak wall between us to admit I wanted to put my arms around her, kiss her, and if it didn't scare her to death, penetrate her and pin her down, until she stopped complaining and acted affectionate. When Louise had had it and vacated to more suitable quarters around the corner on St. Mark's Place, I rented her studio on the other side of my wall.

A month or two after Mondrian rejected Harry Holtzman's front studio space, Harry subleased it to Martin James. Martin was from the U.K. and spoke with an exaggerated Oxford accent that led you to suspect he was born a Cockney. Except for his evanescing blond hair, he looked and sounded like Basil Rathbone playing Sherlock Holmes with a tennis racket instead of a magnifying glass.

He was a professor of art history at Brooklyn College. At 122 Second Avenue, he was engaged in researching the field of female sexuality. I had heard, from my unreliable stunted grapevine, that Professor James was a respected figure out there at Brooklyn College. In the studio next to mine he walked around nude and, from what I was unable to escape noticing, held a natural advantage.

His other chosen field was the unrelenting search for art trivia. His pet obsession was egg tempera. He felt that the turning point in the history of art occurred—he claimed to know the exact date! —when the first yolk was introduced into pigment. He felt that the discovery moved art out of the primitive realm associated with fresco painting. He made a list of every tube of paint in my studio and often asked, "Do you intend to use egg tempera?"

It was hard to make a living as an art historian specializing in the subject of egg tempera. He reserved his obsession for symposiums spontaneously formed by the artists who worked at 122 Second Avenue and their artist visitors, such as Lester Johnson, Wolf Kahn, his brother Peter, Paul Resika, Al Kresch, Nell Blaine, Anthony West's son Tony, and Margaret Stark, a Westchester housewife who commuted with her white dog.

Martin James's temperamania helped us one day in a very practical way. There were city building codes in the forties and fifties that made it illegal to live in lofts registered as businesses. On a surprise drop-in by building inspectors we had to prove we weren't living there. We could have a bed for afternoon naps and for models to pose on, even a hot plate for coffee. But a full stove and refrigerator were telltale evidence that we were committing the crime of dwelling. Professor James came up with the perfect artistic *raison d'être* for these appliances. The stove was for boiling and stirring egg tempera! And the refrigerator served to keep it from going bad when I wasn't using it.

I liked Martin James. He was friendly, silly, and occasionally brilliant. He was one of my first fans. If you were interested in some topic, so was he, and you invariably went away with information very few people knew or had any interest in knowing. If you knocked on his studio door, he opened quickly, nude, and smiled.

Nell and Al

Nell Blaine, my Twenty-first Street painting pal, was not only a pal, she was trying hard to help me get started in the slow climb to

*Hyde Solomon,
Nell Blaine,
and Al Kresch*

artistic recognition. She was an important member, almost the boss, of an artists' cooperative called the Jane Street Gallery. One blinding bright day, Al Kresch, sent by Nell, came to my studio at 122, acting as emissary and talent scout for the Jane Street cooperative. Al was also a close friend, meaning we smoked "tea" together, drank wine, and walked through the city delivering short emotional paragraphs about corners of buildings, shapes against the sky, and certain artworks.

Pat and Will

Accompanying classically featured Al was a young woman from Westchester County, not long out of high school, who wrote poetry. Patricia Hoey was the first person I knew who identified herself as a poet on introduction. I thought of her as advantaged: she was Irish in a sea of Jews. Skimpy according to my galloping Rubenesque lust, she presented a fashionable figure in a long gray flared skirt, brown low-heeled shoes, and high woolen socks, all of which, after twenty years of associating that style with schoolmarms and hikers, I was growing to respect. But nothing I ever respected gave me a hard-on. Which was a problem then and continues to be one to this day.

Pat (who also wore clothes of the type men usually find sexy) could match and double anything you had to say, backing it all with impeccable literary references, sociological insights, and for good luck, ideas about the art of painting.

If I was sloshing around in the low end of my romantic sludge, the bright froth of her optimism flushed me out of it. Even at this youthful stage Pat enjoyed an aura, the biggest glow coming from the information that certain literary figures associated with *Partisan Review*, like Delmore Schwartz, Philip Rahv, and William Barrett, began inviting her to some of their quiet stand-up social occasions over in the West Village. Barrett, the youngest trained philosopher in the business, was the most assiduously interested in our Pat. I believe they saw each other one on one.

A thirty-two-year-old man's exhibition of platonic interest in our twenty-year-old Pat I saw as sexual. It was almost as appalling as my father trying to seduce my teenage girlfriend Peppy! Today, with a forty-year exhibition of interest in very young women, I am the person I accused Will Barrett of being, with a vengeance. Forgive me, Will, wherever you are.

Barrett and Pat had literature as a common interest to help their budding romance. They had something else in common. Which Will approached from this angle, as reported by Pat.

Pat Hoey

"Why weren't we born Jews, Pat? Don't you feel deprived?"

"You wouldn't be Will Barrett if you were born Jewish."

"In New York being Will Barrett isn't enough."

My negative feelings about Will Barrett were never aired. Dating between Pat and Will stopped. He went on to write an important book on existentialism in America, which I read, partially because I knew him, but mostly because if the subject of existentialism came up I would know something other than the name and that Jean-Paul Sartre was its spokesman and that it was popular in France.

I've met Will a few times; he's tall, well known, a keeper of the information about how far he went with Pat. I generously swept that out of the conversation. I don't hold grudges that no one knows I hold.

Ah, Youth!

I have been looking for, and finding, women in their early twenties my whole life. The faces have changed, the places have changed; their age has not changed. Is this my way of confronting the inevitable? If I can attract a woman that age at my age, is time a defanged monster?

There is always some contemporary at a party nowadays who corners me to level with me.

"Larry, let me level with you. You know that your interest in young women is to seem young yourself; everyone knows you're not! You just haven't gotten past the notion that youthful flesh has a privileged bounce. You are a lifelong hedonist, hunting for a thrill a week, congenitally incapable of a serious relationship."

My first sexual experiences were with women in their early twenties, and their look and sound and feel have been programmed into my erotic mechanism.

"I can't help it. What did you say your name was?"

"Ned Barlow."

His sincerity inspires me. "Look, Ned, I'm like a computer that refuses to take new information, a kind of fully packed soft disk."

At an Andy Warhol party in the early seventies, an electric violinist gave a concert with tiny blinking lights moving around the frames of his dark glasses. There I met a young woman with a big red flower clinging Hawaiian-style to her temple. After dancing and rolling on the floor with her, I asked her age.

"I'm twenty-four. . . . How old are you?"

Something in the way she moved made me hesitate. Forty-eight would sound better than the fifty-one I was. Something in the way my mother lied about *her* age forced me to be honest. "I'm fifty-one."

"Oh," said the girl with the mouth red as her rose. "What a drag!"

On another level, listening to the aspirations and difficulties and previous romantic experiences of these young women, and offering my sympathy and advice and maybe a little money, put me in the incestuous Daddy seat. I told you, dear voyeur, that I was convinced at a very early age that young women only did it to please men—another notion that has become part of my erotic mechanism. I am not aroused by women who feel sexually aroused by me. Sorry to say, it's their shape in clothing that gets me hot.

"Oh, you artists," says Ned. "You never stop looking."

"Right, Ned, but not because I am an artist, but because what I see before me plays on the retina and is transmitted to the medulla oblongata, where messages are sent calling for blood to flow to the appropriate zone. So I keep looking. I never lie back and close my eyes."

Ned goes to get a drink for his wife and rushes back to continue leveling with me.

"What about a blow job, Larry?"

"Thanks, Ned, not now."

"No, Larry, I mean if a young woman is using you as a sex object."

"If I'm being used as a sex object, it's usually without my knowledge."

"What about arousing a woman? Does that give you pleasure?"

"If we've never gone to bed before, I try to arouse her. It's my way to get her consent."

"Consent? . . . For what?"

"Entrance, Ned."

Exit Ned.

Talent Scout

Expecting Al Kresch, the Jane Street Gallery's roving scout, I purposely arranged a small but unarranged-looking exhibition of my latest things on a wall directly under a skylight. On this very bright day I realized for the first time that I didn't like my art seen by strong daylight. I usually painted on the opposite wall, which had an even but duller light.

About a decade later Philip Guston, painting abstractions then, told me one quiet night at the Cedar Tavern that one of his great joys was to take a work of his outside into the bright sunlight somewhere in a field, set it down, and look at it for hours.

"My works are like nature itself. I want them to be enjoyed as you enjoy a field of flowers on a bright afternoon."

Not me. I felt then at 122, and now even more, that my work looks better at the level of ordinary house lighting. The fusing of my colors, where and how they join, the faces I paint, the bodies, whatever, contain a logic that under a strong beam of light can give you that pimples-and-all quality. And this feeling about light on things follows me into the bedroom, where I prefer light that lends itself to blurring the edges, like the forms in my work. *Kunst* is the German word for art as well as for tricks. Art was for a long time thought of as tricks ("Less art and more matter, Polonius"). You don't see a magic show performed in sunlight.

There certainly is pleasure connected to seeing clearly what and how you're doing under a dazzling beam in the bedroom or the studio. But my instinctual response to blow job or work in progress is to lower the rheostat. What I prefer to shine a bright light on is a book I'm reading, where I can experience life, at last.

Tour

Al comes in with Pat. Silently they go from work to work, some on paper, some on canvas. After about three minutes Pat stops, looks at me, and says in her very enthusiastic and lovely low voice, "Larry, these are wonderful compositions."

"Listen, cuntface, I don't paint to make compositions," would have said Jackson Pollock as he pissed in your fireplace. I had often fantasized saying this to someone, because I agreed with the mad master that painting had more to do than hang on a wall like a candid photo of placements. What appear on canvas or paper are your interests and desires: color, subject, line, space, someone's looks, relationship to old masters, new masters, how great, how silly. It took a lot of graying to accept the idea that where you put the fruits of your interests and desires could be called composition. I don't believe in composition. I don't mean this in the way people say they don't believe in God. There is salvation, but not in losing oneself in composition. Again, I have desires, and seeking to satisfy them gives birth to composition. Sex produces babies. But you don't have sex to have babies. Even if you want one. And the church can stand on its head.

Those were the years, late forties, early fifties, when my friends and I read books about the concrete in art, dada, the Bauhaus, and futurism, and came away from these books with such fashionable revolutionary stances as my ideas on composition. Everyone had notions to peddle, and young artists in New York bought them. Marinetti's manifestos were like Mussolini's edicts. In fact, Marinetti designed the Fascist blackshirt. Duchamp thought that breaking a glass and filling the crack with lead would produce not only new art but a new order. The smell of Trotsky's "big garbage can of history" is still with us today.

I didn't share any of these ideas with Pat or Al. I didn't have enough of them to go around. I was glad to hear Pat repeat, "Larry, I really mean it, these are wonderful compositions."

Lest she swing her book bag at my head, all I said to Pat was, "Thank you very much."

I was more concerned about Al's opinion. He was an exhibiting artist, and about to decide whether to offer my name to the Jane Street Gallery cooperative members as a possibility for an exhibition. I don't remember whether Al was as much a believer in composition as Pat, but her compliment helped reaffirm his good feelings about the works.

The Jane Street Gallery was run by artists who chipped in eight to ten dollars a month to pay for rent, the printing of invitations, and mailing costs. Sometimes they even took an ad. Each member had to tend the gallery one day a week. The average membership was ten. They kept it pared down. No one else could join unless someone got kicked out. Each person's show was about three weeks.

Cooperatives

The Jane Street Gallery was the first of the coop galleries, at least in my experience. There was another cooperative artists group at the Hansa Gallery, a name that implied descent from the Hanseatic League, hardworking and honest men and women producing art of high quality. You smoked a pipe, wore corduroy, and were serious about what you were doing.

At one time or another, I knew most of the Hansa members. Jane Wilson, a beauty born on a farm in Iowa, painted and paints large, sometimes bright, and sometimes dark landscapes from memory. Her husband, an internationally known fact dealer (see his prophetic book *The Party's Over*), was John Gruen. He was a composer, now is a dance and art critic, and is adorable for someone his age.

Richard Stankiewicz, also from the Midwest somewhere, founded the junkyard-and-rust school of sculpture. He lived with my co-student of Hofmann days Jean Follet. Everyone showed up at Hofmann's with clothes that dirt wouldn't be noticed on. Jean wore a white powdered face, a long clean skirt, and chunky high-heeled shoes.

Wolf Kahn, brilliant, perennially boyish, never quite lost his German accent, painted and paints small structured landscapes with attractive bright colors and sells them all. In 1949 Wolf and I sat and drew on a tree-lined street in the Bronx after visiting Augusta and the kids. He was married for some time to an elegant, conservatively dressed black woman who wore a loose bun and spoke gently. She earned Wolf a special place in my affections. You have met him as the monitor and translator of Hofmann's English.

Miles Forst's work eludes my memory, but his escorting Billie Holiday for a few years doesn't. He later married Barbara Bottom of Norfolk, Virginia. This information is being passed on to you by virtue of my delight in Barbara's name.

Allan Kaprow was Mr. Happenings. Happenings were the precursor of performance art, installation art, and *arte povera*—abstract art as theater. He talked about his work with a warm, winning smile. He influenced Oldenburg's and Rauschenberg's theater pieces. Within a few years it was hard to distinguish his work from that of his many imitators, until finally everything that happened was a Happening.

George Segal and I went to NYU together, where I did a color dot portrait of him and his standing hair. He raised chickens and worked hard on his sculpture in New Jersey. He is the Hansa's most successful member, but still a believer in the brotherhood of artists. He is almost as sweet as he sounds when he speaks.

Fay Lansner was Fay Gold before she married editor in chief Kermit Lansner, then of *Newsweek*. The mixture of the recognizable and the abstract in her work has made us members of the same family.

The Hansa's director, Dick Bellamy, sat and slept in the store for years and did a lot for all his artists. It hardly ever made him look happy—which got him the role of the preacher in *Pull My Daisy* (1960). In that film I acted alongside him (and Allen Ginsberg and Jack Kerouac and Gregory Corso, and Dave Amram and Alice Neal and Denise Parker, wife of Ray Parker—who else?—and Jack Youngerman's then wife, Delphine Seyrig of *Last Year at Marienbad*). I never understood this goofy little masterpiece as it was being filmed, but it was pleasurable playing the part of a stoned train conductor carrying a kerosene lamp in the company of such beat luminaries. *Pull My Daisy* was made by Al Leslie and Robert Frank, who have been arguing for thirty years over the rights.

Clockwise from Larry: Jack Kerouac, David Amram,
Allen Ginsberg, and Gregory Corso between takes of Pull My Daisy

Ivan Karp, the other director of the Hansa, began as a writer; as an assistant to Leo Castelli he was forced to praise works other than his own in order to eat and drink. After he left the Castelli Gallery and opened his own, the O.K. Harris Gallery, the praise continued and made him rich.

The artists in the Jane Street coop included Al Kresch, whom you just met at my loft but know little about so far, and Luisa

Matthiasdottir, the only Icelandic artist, or for that matter person, I ever knew. Iceland is a cold country, and the air that lay between Luisa and myself at any meeting never warmed up. She was always considered a major talent by all of us, but hardly ever by those tastemakers whose interest gives your work at auctions the outrageous prices that every artist knows are important but is uncomfortable facing. Her husband, Leland Bell, was never given a show at the gallery even though he was a paying member. He never got enough votes. He was a strong influence on Luisa aesthetically and philosophically. By 1990 he and his wife were highly appreciated in the uncommercial corners, mainly by Hilton Kramer and friends in *New Criterion* magazine. Lee considered André Derain the greatest modern artist and continually said so. Over thirty or forty years he never wavered from this position, even when he found out Derain hated Jews. Anti-Semitism and aesthetics are difficult to square, e.g., Ezra Pound. Lee and I had one love in common that formed a thin but lasting bond. He was a musician, a drummer, and like me, he never stopped loving Lester Young. He lived miraculously with leukemia, always loved Lester, and continued to admire Derain until his death in 1990. A Rock of Gibraltar.

There were two middle-aged women in the gallery, Ida Fisher and Frances Eckstein, lesbians who wouldn't be caught dead in black leather. The bolder, Ida, painted bold abstractions, studied with Hofmann, and before that studied in Peking under a Chinese master. Sensitive, frail Frances was the dark horse of the gallery; she limited herself to painting flowers, usually in vases. They were so good, so intense, so beautiful, that they challenged the idea I swallowed whole hog, that painting in our time must answer the question, What is modern art? Frances's paintings were answering loftier questions. Ida and Frances's friendship was innocent, possibly sexless, and lasted forty years. A word to the wise!

Hyde Solomon was the gallery's founding member along with Jack Levitan, prizefighter turned artist. For a lighthearted, sweet guy Hyde painted dark abstractions. As he became more intellectual and older and darker, his paintings brightened up. He lived long periods in artists' colonies like Yaddo and MacDowell. He also made a living selling his paintings. His highest point of public recognition came when Princeton University offered him a professorship that he held until Alzheimer's carried him away in 1983.

Several of the original members were kicked out of the gallery when Nell and the rest of us were cordially invited to join. Howard

Mitchum was among them, a deaf mute, a vigorous and interesting **L**
expressionist painter who could be heard a block away after he
learned to speak. After leaving the gallery he became a writer.

More Nell

Nell Blaine came to New York from Richmond, Virginia, in 1942.
The war didn't get in the way of her ambitions to be an artist. She **R**
too studied with Hofmann. She bit the bohemian bullet. She was
always broke. In the streets she kept a sharp eye out for deposit
bottles, which gave her money for food. Through Jack Freilicher,
myself, and Leland Bell she became interested in jazz, which nat- **R**
urally led her to play the drums. She rushed from revelation to
revelation, a tireless spokesperson for all her enthusiasms. Anyone
within mouth range was given an earful of what was the latest in
jazz and art. When Dizzy Gillespie came on the scene, Nell pro- **Y**
nounced Dixieland dead.

In her art Nell at first was influenced by Arp. Gradually that
influence fused with Léger and Hélion. As early as 1943 the already
great Clement Greenberg came to her studio and claimed that her
eight-foot-square *Great White Creature* was one of the first big abstractions. In our circle this passed for the beginning of a raving
success. From the 1947 showing of her paintings in the window of **R**
a Chinese gallery on Fifty-seventh Street, she went on to be in the
Metropolitan Museum of Art, the Museum of Modern Art, the
Virginia Museum of Fine Arts, and collections all over the country.
In 1959, vacationing in Greece, she contracted polio and lived for **I**
months in an iron lung. It is impossible to tell from her optimistic
and colorful paint jabs and what they finally describe that she has
been confined to a wheelchair ever since. She is a good painter, a **V**
terrific colorist, and an archivist who can produce, on the table,
before your eyes, just what you are looking for. She is that rare old
thing, a wonderful person.

More Al

Al Kresch, a member in good standing, had a pointy nose, a pointy **R**
chin, pointy fingers, and a point in the middle of his hairline, a
widow's peak. Adding up these points produced the face of artistic
sensitivity, which, combined with his very dark eyes, sweetness,
and sincerity, laid flat half of downtown New York's female popu- **S**

lation, sotto voce. Al did a series of figure paintings with heads entirely in unadulterated cadmium red deep. Al's strong red heads had no rhyme or reason, nor did my sudden decision to imitate them. With nothing I could point to as original or even fresh in my work at the time, Al invited me to be number three in a two-man show of his and Bob De Niro's work. Al worked quietly for years in the tradition of good painting. He still works quietly, so quietly I haven't heard from him in years.

The Jane Street Gallery

In the spring of '49 the Jane Streeters decided that being downtown on Jane Street had its limitations. We moved uptown. Collectors, private and public dealers, and gallery directors hung out uptown, those we thought counted in making our recognition and success dreams come true. They could shop and look over the goods in their own neighborhood. Critics, thinking we had uptown backing even if they didn't think much of what they saw in the gallery, would be prone to review us.

In my case, never was such a blind shot so immediately rewarded. We opened the uptown gallery late in '49 with my first show. Two individuals who played a pretty important role in my not so slow climb to recognition saw the exhibition and liked it, for different reasons. One was Clem Greenberg. Writing for the *Nation*, he snapped out an extraordinary review—not for its brilliant critical reasoning or for pointing to a new wave, but because I as a beginner read Clem saying that though a beginner, I was already better than Bonnard.

Judging superficially, one is liable to say that everything Larry Rivers displayed in his first show (at the Jane Street Gallery) is taken from Bonnard. There is the same niggling, broken touch, the same conception of the illusion of three-dimensional space, the same color often, a similar approach to composition, similar subjects. The similarity is real and conscious, but it accounts really for little in the superb end-effect of Rivers' painting, which has a plenitude and sensuousness all its own. Rivers is a better designer than colorist—or rather, more obviously a designer than a colorist; for his color does everything he asks it to within the relatively narrow range he sets for it; and part of

176

the artist's originality comes from the way in which he ac-
commodates earth tones, ochers, umbers, etc., to the
brushstroke and flat design of full-color impressionism.
Eventually Rivers may acquire a lusciousness of color and
surface more traditionally appropriate to the vein he paints
in, but I for one would rather see this amazing beginner
remain with his present approach and exploit further a native force that is already quite apparent in his art. That
force, so unlike anything in late impressionism, he owes
entirely to himself, and it has already made him a better
composer of pictures than was Bonnard himself in many
instances.

The other important eyes to see my first show were those of
John Myers (John Bernard Myers, he was quick to tell you), partner
and director of the Tibor de Nagy Gallery, which was in the same
building as our cooperative gallery. It took him two years after his
quick peek at my work, and me, to ask me, at Louis' Tavern downtown on Sheridan Square, if I'd be interested in a show at his
gallery.

Up, Down, and Even

I discussed my early surprise success with Rudy Burckhardt, whom
I met when we both lived on Twenty-first Street, and continued
hit-and-miss to know from that time on. He is a photographer,
artist, and maker of funny films, including *Mounting Tension* and
A Day in the Life of a Cleaning Woman.

> RB: We didn't expect to have shows uptown. You went up
> early. I used to have a theory about you, that your life was
> very difficult. You had a big success at twenty-five, which
> means the rest of your life you have to make comebacks.
> So you had to make about six comebacks. In a way it's
> better to advance slowly.

> LR: If you can.

> RB: Elaine de Kooning once said, "In America an artist has
> to advance by stealth." Not by a big sudden hit. Critics give
> you a very good review the first time, then they think they
> own you, and then the next time you don't do what they
> expect you to do—

Rudy Burckhardt

LR: They love you at the beginning and then—

RB: You know more about this than I do. You were a young big success. Everybody else was much slower.

LR: John LaTouche was an early success in the forties because of *Ballad for Americans*.

RB: He wrote some Broadway shows.

LR: Was he supposed to have sold out because it was Broadway?

RB: No, because of *Ballad for Americans*.

LR: Commercialism was all right, but patriotism wasn't?

RB: Walter Auerbach was very simple about the whole subject. "No career! Don't try to be successful! Don't ever be jealous, don't be possessive." He was a saint wandering around in the Village. He had nothing to do, nowhere to go, nothing was pressing. It was a wonderful quality, to live without ambition. He was very angry at people like you who had a career. He was morally disapproving.

LR: It was easy if you didn't want recognition and money.

RB: You couldn't get it, so you might as well pretend you didn't want it.

LR: When I started out I didn't think of success. I was content just to get a little experience. I thought I knew nothing and had everything to learn.

RB: Actually we had plenty to learn from you. Hofmann once hired a bus to take us students to Philadelphia to see a Matisse show. One student said Matisse had no content. You said, "What do you want, the painting to reach out and shake hands with you?"

LR: What else did you learn from me?

RB: You did a lot of people a favor by showing up stoned. I decided not to try heroin when I saw you looking so green. I put you in one movie, in a coffin. In the story you took thirty kinds of drugs. We hadn't heard of most of them. I got a list from the *New York Times*. We used your paintings after Bonnard for the movie. They were in the Jane Street Gallery uptown, your first show.

John Ashbery, Jane Freilicher, Larry Rivers,
Sigmund Freud, and Ann Aikman in Rudy Burckhardt's Mounting Tension

Criticism

Clement Greenberg was connected to *Partisan Review*. Before he wrote art criticism I think Clem wrote poetry. He also painted.

Respect for the intellectual was with me from the time I crawled out of the crib. *Partisan Review* was a neon sign over the gateway to the fields of measured thought and thrilling argument. I knew little, in the year 1949, of the practical value art reviews had relative to ambition and career. Greenberg's review of my first show, aside from the pleasure I got from the attention swelling an already swollen head, didn't help me figure out what my work was about or what direction it should move in. I certainly didn't believe I was better than Bonnard. Did he mean overall or in some specific way like colorization?

I never sat down and wrote him a thank-you note, because I thought it would seem like sucking up. Seem? What's wrong with a simple note telling the writer you enjoyed his article, which you did, and offering one or two passing reflections. That seems natural. The artist exhibits his wares, the critic reviews them, then you send your note. You perform, someone in the audience claps, and you bow. Not me. Coming out for a curtain call would be sucking up. I still don't send thank-you notes.

In exaggerating your independence and the support you already have, the critic ends up feeling he needs you. He has a lot to say about art, but it flows from the choice of artist he writes about.

It becomes a matter of who is more famous. People read about an artist if the critic is well known. And people will read a critic because the artist is well known.

I first met Clem Greenberg through my Delmore Schwartz connection, Milton Klonsky, who brought me to a Sunday cocktail party Delmore was giving. I think Milton's stature for me, aside from being—I'm sorry—an unpublished and not too productive poet, was that he was a friend of this literary figure. By now, 1992, I've read a good deal about Delmore in informative articles and in Saul Bellow's fictional version supposedly based on their long on-again, off-again palship. Delmore Schwartz was not only a writer who had been writing and publishing for a number of years, he was an editor of *Partisan Review*.

For a literary lion, Delmore, stretched out in a wide, soft chair at his party, looked more like a primate on the branch of a tree. He wore a white shirt, a dark blue suit, and a wet chin he kept bringing his sleeve across to dry. It took a while to get used to his speech. He had an unusual lisp and a very special timbre that ranged higher than the normal male voice and trailed off into a cross between Brooklynese and a chuckle: the delight he seemed to take in the content of his sentences. He waved his arms when he spoke, punctuating his points. The color and texture of his skin were noticeably attractive. He was tall and had Mongolian eyes and a scar in the middle of his forehead. What are Mongolian eyes? Ovals put into the face below the brow at a slant. Well, maybe they were more Tartar than Mongolian.

Schwartz was a very common last name for Jews. I'm not sure whether Black (Schwartz) was more popular than White (Weiss). I don't even know how colors became the last names of individuals. But the name Delmore I had never heard until then, and except for him until now. If you want to get rid of the Jewish tag a last name gives you, "Delmore" couldn't be a better choice to confuse a bigot. "Delmore" could have been some relative's name, possibly some hero the family wished to immortalize. Historical investigation points suspiciously to an apartment house on Ocean Parkway, a high-rise with high rent called the Belmore. All this ethnic stuff was never a topic for discussion below Fourteenth Street, though Jews and the Jewish Question were occasionally, if diffidently, broached.

There was much more interest in the New York art-lit scene. Manny Farber, same age as Delmore, an art critic for the *Nation* and a painter himself, wrote an unflattering review of one of my early exhibitions in 1951. The review was animated largely by Manny's certainty that I was headed for commercial success in the art world; he even had the feeling as he wrote that he was already defeated, that the steamroller of my success was going to flatten his critical opinion of me. Delmore must have read the piece; he spent a good deal of time talking to me, putting Manny Farber in a context meant to ease any bad feelings I might be having about the article. "Listen, Larry, he's jealous, he's a hermit, no one ever gives him a show, no one even knows he's a painter."

Sometime during the party, Delmore told me that Manny Farber had received a clout or two or three from Clem Greenberg at an opening when Manny failed to show proper deference to Clem's self-evaluation. Greenberg had a reputation for punching anyone who gave him the slightest excuse. He felt that words on a page contemplated in the quiet of your home were the proper setting for art criticism. Any face-to-face discussion was okay if you accepted most of what came through his naturally curled sexy lips and acknowledged with some sign, verbal or bodily, that he was the most important contemporary art critic of our day. Unfortunately he was.

Manny didn't quite agree with Clem that Jackson Pollock was the greatest painter since Botticelli. Manny himself was pretty outspoken, and if pushed, insulting, choosing to ignore the pecking order of the MCA (the Major Critics Association), which was purported to meet every month in the editorial office of *Partisan Review*. I can't remember the repercussions of this rather one-sided fist fest. Delmore told me Manny went down for the count. I finally met Manny Farber. I liked him. Most people punched by Clem Greenberg I liked. Manny was slim, with uncombed hair. He had a serious look full of the clouds and storms of life's disappointments, and when it broke for a moment the smile winging its way through the features of his face brought on pleasant feelings.

Delmore introduced me to Clem. "Meet Larry Rivers."

Greenberg's first words, before "Hello," were, "What was your name before you changed it?"

Meekly: "Grossberg."

"Sounds like you're ashamed of being Jewish," he said, reminding me of my parents, who were hurt when I legally changed my name. I always feared I'd run into someone in my new world who would call me on this. I never dreamed it would be someone whose

Studio Interior, c. 1948
Oil on paper, 17½ x 23½"
Collection of Gloria and Dan Stern, New York

Interior, Woman at a Table, c. 1948
Oil on canvas, 39 x 49"
Collection of Pat Cooper, New York

Washington Crossing the Delaware, 1953
Oil on canvas, 83⅝ x 111⅝″
Museum of Modern Art, New York, anonymous gift

OPPOSITE

The Next to Last Confederate Soldier, 1959
Oil on canvas, 60 x 46″
Marie-Hélène and Guy Weill Family Collection, Scarsdale, New York

Joseph, 1954
Oil on canvas, 52½ x 45½″
Private collection

OPPOSITE

O'Hara, 1954
Oil on canvas, 97 x 53″
Collection of the artist

Double Portrait of Berdie, 1955
Oil on canvas, 70¾ x 82½"
Whitney Museum of American Art, New York, anonymous gift

The Family, 1954–55
Oil on canvas, 82 x 72″
Private collection

Parts of the Face: French Vocabulary Lesson, 1961
Oil on canvas, 29½ x 29½″
Tate Gallery, London

French Money II, 1961
Oil on canvas, 36 x 60″
Collection unknown

opinion about my work would be so important and whose feelings about an odious weakness of character would probably influence that opinion.

Fight Night of the Stars

One of the artists connected to the Tibor de Nagy gallery after 1951 was Helen Frankenthaler. Her work, from the first time I saw it, was abstract. Tall, with a good figure, a red mouth without lipstick, power in her background, her father a New York State judge, she herself was good-looking and cool, and her art conveys that, at least to me.

There must have been peaceful moments, but the stormy side of the affair between Helen and Clem showed itself one people-packed evening at a show for Paul Feeley, Helen's painting professor when she was at Bennington College. At the opening of the show, with the help of the very drunk John Myers, Clem got word

Helen Frankenthaler, LR, Tom and Audrey Hess

that Helen, younger than he by a couple of decades, had fallen in love with Howard Sackler, a young poet-playwright. Clem's legendary ire exploded. He punched John Myers, the cheerful messenger of the tidings; then he made his way across the room to where Helen was talking to the new boyfriend, and before she could answer his spittle-strewn questions he slapped her. Then he took Howard on, which landed Clem on the deck of the gallery.

As I was the one who helped him off the floor, we remained fairly friendly, and once he even gave me some critical advice. Dustin Rice, a Columbia professor of art history, once called me "the Elvis Presley of art" (not bad!) in a *Village Voice* article. Clem's advice: "Sock him in the jaw, Larry." Generally, after the fight at the Feeley show, he lost his enthusiasm for fisticuffs in public places, but he continued verbally to confront those who showed improper respect.

In 1960 I was asked by Tom Hess, who ran *Art News*, to review a Monet exhibition at the Museum of Modern Art. Here is part of the review, in which, from Mr. Greenberg's point of view, I showed the proper disrespect to inspire confrontation.

About ten or eleven years ago there was an old masters show in Philadelphia. I think it was the exhibition of the Berlin Museum paintings, and I was there. Somewhere in one of the galleries I ran into Clement Greenberg, a New York critic, whose preferences in modern painting are already part of our morbid history. I was mad about the Titians I saw, and in the wake of this enthusiasm asked him what he thought of them. His answer: "You know, Larry, he [Titian] never learned how to put a head on a pair of shoulders." Facing the task (as I am) of saying something about a much loved master produces more spleen than insight and in some individuals so much spleen that there is oodles and oodles for the master-loving public, and still plenty enough to heap on the poor old dead master himself. "What about Monet, Larry?" I think it will be hard to match Clem's arrogance and inaccuracy but I'll take a whack at it.

Monet's Legs

Standing in the Museum of Modern Art listening to MOMA curator William Seitz's rambling enthusiasm, full of "fabulous" details about his Monet show, transformed me into the Clem Greenberg I

ran into in 1952 in the Philadelphia Museum. Clem tried to shorten
Titian's legs. I wrote to cut Monet's legs off completely.

I've been to the Monet show at the Museum of Modern Art
about six times now. I keep going back, sometimes with
someone else, mostly alone, hoping to penetrate those
pinks, purples, deep purples, alizarin crimsons, blues,
green-blues, the no-reds of nature (Kandinsky loved them,
read the catalogue), those trees, Turner fogs, roads, huge
rocks, water and more water, and I hear no voices. I keep
thinking time has been unkind to hard-working and con-
stantly-in-his-boat Monet. . . . But along with time and the
minds of men grinding his work into countryside clichés,
this show limits his virtuosity and his range of interests and
brings together a lot of works that look very corny to me.
The selection reduces Monet by its emphasis and its ideology. . . . What we are given is a controlled and severe arrangement by subject and place that makes Monet very
modern and very weather-bent. A painter with no prior idea
of the outcome, only sure he wants to paint something—
all very "New York School." Many paintings would be better titled, "5 o'clock, wind from the south, barometer 29.9
and falling, fair tomorrow with a high near . . ."

On a brisk fall evening, a few days before publication of this
review, I went to the Martha Jackson Gallery for the Karel Appel
opening. Earlier in the day Tom Hess had called me to say that
Clem had seen a prepublication copy of the review and wanted the
lines about him withdrawn. Tom wanted me to know he didn't
flinch one bit in the face of Clem's threat to sue both me and the
magazine. Guess whose curly lips I saw coming through the entrance to the gallery! Clem and I didn't come near each other for
fifteen or twenty minutes, and it was very crowded. I moved my
feelings of discomfort to the back of my head. All of a sudden I was
looking into Clem's face.

Out loud above the din he said, "What an asshole thing to do,
Rivers. You and Tom are full of shit."

"You're full of shit too, only you don't know it."

Okay, everyone is full of shit, some of us know it! Making me a
little less full of shit?

Clem flung a few more insults, then moved closer and said, "I
should really punch you one, Rivers," as if this crowded opening

made it cumbersome to throw his customary roundhouse.

I'd had my last bout as a teenager, with boxing gloves. But I moved even closer and said, "Would it be better if we went outside?" I began to remove my coat. Before Clem had a chance to respond, Martha Jackson came over to thank him for coming.

Clem was known to be smart, his criticism clear, his points of view so persuasive that museum directors, gallery keepers, even artists themselves were impressed—which had a very strong influence on the tastes of our time. I was too busy with art, sex, drugs, and pre–rock and roll to have an opinion. I read some of his criticism, like his influential 1948 piece on art and kitsch. He was the first to bring Pollock to public attention. He gave an important lecture on the subject of minor and major painting. Jane Freilicher came back from the lecture with this synopsis: Major painting, according to Greenberg, was not only an adventure in line, form, and color but continued the evolution of modern art. Minor painting was the endeavor to produce art that could be of high quality but was based on older forms and therefore lacked the inference of the unknown.

Another opinion of Clem's I remember well was that easel painting was finished—Pollock painted on the floor, didn't he? And didn't other greats and near-greats, Bill de Kooning, Franz Kline, Joan Mitchell, Mike Goldberg, Nell Blaine, Larry Rivers, tack large canvases to the wall, ten feet and beyond? All this convinced Clem that we were in the Era of Large Painting, which the easel could no longer accommodate. Greenberg's idea about the demise of easel painting seemed original, growing out of his experience with new painting in New York.

Because I'm currently doing a series of paintings called "Art and the Artist," I've been looking at books containing the works and writings of Matisse. I just came across this statement of his, made in 1929: "I believe that easel painting will cease to exist because of changing mores. Murals will replace it." The cotton gin was invented in seven different places at the same time. It's possible that Greenberg, without having read Matisse's statement, could have come to the same conclusion eighteen years later.

Clement Greenberg's mesmerization of the tastemakers reached its zenith when Jackson Pollock won prize after prize in the Fifty-seventh Street sweepstakes. He later went on to say that Pollock, and all of abstract expressionism, deteriorated after he wrote about them, even Kline and de Kooning. Franz affably went on painting bigger and better and never confronted Clem, which would have been difficult, since Clem rarely went into the Cedar Tavern, the G-spot of the art scene. Clem considered it "sordid and filled with doomed artists." Bill managed to leave the Cedar long enough to pick a fight with Clem.

Bumping into his many strong opinions in different important magazines, I was curious to see if he had any opinions about me. I think I exist, but if my dog barks when I come home I know I do. An artist has to feel that the value of his work is not just his imagination. I was among the many people impressed by Greenberg's powers, and I behaved accordingly. I held the door open for him, helped him on with his coat. When his shoelaces came undone, I tied them. When we ran out of drink, I ran out to the liquor store. When he told me I should be ashamed to have changed my name, I hung my head. But when he told me I was full of shit and he'd like to knock my teeth down my throat, I began to think, "Hey, what am I getting out of this? He's not that important! I guess I'm going to have to make it on my own. How many times can I count on him to say I'm better than Bonnard?"

Helen and Howard and Murray

What happened to Helen Frankenthaler and Howard Sackler?

Here's one thing that happened.

Murray Schisgal is a writer of comic masterpieces of all lengths and forms, like the film *Tootsie* and the plays *Luv, The Typist and the Tiger,* and *The Petomane,* a hilarious tragedy about a virtuoso farter down on his luck. Murray, who knew Howard in those days, tells us:

MY LAST CASE

It was sometime late in the 1950s when my friend Howard Sackler asked me to represent him in a legal dispute he was having with his former girlfriend, Helen Frankenthaler. It seems that Ms. Frankenthaler had left a chaise longue in Howard's apartment and wanted it back. Howard refused, claiming it was an irrevocable gift. Ms. Frankenthaler hired a lawyer and Howard hired me. He made it clear that I wasn't getting a fee but that he would consider my services as essential affirmation of our deep affection for each other.

L

A

R

R

Y

I had quit the practice of law to write. I lived on Riving-
ton Street, in a fifth-floor railroad apartment. My rent was
thirty dollars a month. I did not have a phone. I arranged
with the owner of a candy store downstairs to pass on any
calls for me by shouting in the alleyway under my window.
That would start me running down the five flights of stairs
to answer the phone before the caller hung up.

Ms. Frankenthaler's lawyer phoned. Did I realize that
the chaise longue belonged originally to Judge Frankenthaler, his client's father? That it was the very chaise longue
that Judge Frankenthaler rested on during the afternoon
recess? How could my client deprive a daughter of such a
priceless remembrance of her beloved father? I called Howard saying that perhaps he should return the chaise.

"It's mine, Murray. She gave it to me. I'm not budging
on this. I'd sooner give her my arm."

One sunny afternoon, reaching the candy store phone
breathlessly, I heard Ms. Frankenthaler's lawyer say something to the effect that we were scum, that to wash his
hands of us he was offering two thousand for the chaise
longue. And he hung up.

R

I

V

E

I was overjoyed, bursting with pride. Two thousand
buckeroos! It was the best settlement I had made in my
entire legal career! Whoopee! I called Howard immediately.
"Howard, buddy, I have terrific news to tell you! They're
giving you two thousand for that fucking ugly chair! Isn't
that great? Isn't that terrific? We did it, buddy, we did it!"

A pause.

Howard, grimly: "Murray, the answer is no. I'm offended that they would even think of buying me off. I re-
sent that. Deeply. And I'll tell you something else. You're
fired. I cannot tolerate treachery."

I don't know who eventually got Judge Frankenthaler's
chaise. *I swear I don't.*

R

S

This put an end to poor Murray Schisgal's legal career, forcing
him to eke out a living writing hits. Howard Sackler went on to
success as well, not surprisingly, with a play about boxing called
The Great White Hope. For readers of Proust and believers in "Life
is stranger than fiction," Mr. Schisgal, defending attorney for Howard Sackler in the Case of the Coveted Couch, todays lives on
Central Park West in the apartment below Clement Greenberg.

What happened to Greenberg versus Rivers?

Well, there was one more round, covered by Grace Glueck in an article in the February 13, 1966, Sunday *Times Magazine*, entitled "Larry Rivers Paints Himself into the Canvas." Dream coverage: in-depth reporting, photographs and interviews, several pages of appreciation of my work, à la:

> Rivers has made it big in an avant-garde milieu where "success," in the popular sense of the word, still means you must be doing something wrong. His recent 15-year retrospective at New York's Jewish Museum drew 35,000 art-gazers in its month-and-a-half run—fellow artists, rabbinical students, parents, children, hipsters, squares, the poet Stephen Spender and the maestro Lenny Bernstein. Big business collects his work and commissions him to paint its profile; private patrons collect not only Rivers' art, but Rivers himself at their parties. His sell-out appearances on the lecture-symposium circuit include (besides Cambridge University) London's Royal College of Art, Brown, the University of Southern California and ladies' think-and-chatter clubs in places like Great Neck. And his larger paintings sell for anywhere from $5,000 to $10,000 at Marlborough-Gerson, the wheelingest, dealingest art firm in the business ("I mean they don't exactly take beginners," Rivers says). . . .
>
> He was one of the few non-abstract painters to be accepted as a peer by the crowd that frequented the famous Cedar Bar. His hero, Willem de Kooning, said once that looking at Rivers' painting was "like pressing your face in wet grass," a statement from which Rivers still draws nourishment.
>
> It is, of course, far too early to judge his place—if any —in art history. Like most of his fellows, he is both damned and praised. He has powerful detractors—as he did even in the heyday of abstract expressionism. ("Jackson Pollock once tried to run down one of my sculptures that was standing in a friend's driveway in East Hampton," he remembers, with a certain bitter glee.)
>
> But others find much to praise in his work. "An extraordinary entertainer," a Los Angeles critic summed up when

Rivers' museum show appeared last fall at the Pasadena Art Museum. This newspaper's critic, John Canaday, has called him "one of the most high-spirited and inventive stylists at work in this country right now." Many of his artist contemporaries look on him as a "big" talent—a superb draftsman and a particularly subtle colorist. More than that, he has shown them that contemporary modes may be reconciled with more traditional painting ideas.

Then there was this: "Greenberg, in 1949 the first to cry up Rivers in print, today says coolly, 'His work began to deteriorate soon after I wrote that *Nation* article. You can say now that I think he stinks.' "

I last saw Clem in 1977 in Mickey Ruskin's restaurant the Locale, opened after the closing of his illustrious Max's Kansas City. Julian Schnabel was his cook. I was speaking to Schnabel, a close friend of my assistant at the time, Rainer Gross. Julian was in his kitchen whites, a pleasant young man whose work I hadn't seen, and when I said goodbye to him I walked toward the bar. The place was empty. It was early in the evening. A man sitting with a woman turned his face to look at me. Clement Greenberg.

He didn't seem much older; he was rather handsome, better-looking than I had ever noticed. My temperature shot up, my heart beat faster. I stiffened and slowed my pace. He was smoking, had a drink on the table. Once our eyes met I stopped walking and kept looking at him until he turned back to his companion. Our last brush.

Today I'm not sure why I wrote those provocative sentences about Clement Greenberg in a review about Claude Monet. I accepted a chance to use *Art News* as a bully pulpit. A word in an art magazine is worth a thousand pictures. I had stepped into the ring once before with Tolstoy when I translated *War and Peace* into *Washington Crossing the Delaware*. But Tolstoy was dead. Tolstoy couldn't undermine my career! Greenberg was a tough partisan in politics, women, and sports. He liked one painter at a time. Pollock in the forties, Morris Louis in the fifties, Noland in the sixties, me for ten minutes. He hated art scenes. "They eat up artists," he told John Gruen in a 1969 interview.

It wasn't that he lacked some simple democratic generosity we all grow up with, a built-in tolerance for differences that would extend to art. Culture is full of stubborn opinions. His seemed more

Clem

informed than most, bolstering his sense of always being right. Philip Pavia, who "sort of ran the Artists Club," said, "Clem put a railroad track in the middle of every gallery—'This guy's good and this guy's bad, the right side is good and the left side is bad.' He was always making good and bad on everything."

Perhaps I never forgave Clem for criticizing my change of name to one that didn't carry the identity his name stuck him with, which stung me all the more because somewhere not too down deep I agreed that changing my name was shameful.

Or maybe it was the curl of his lip.

Or maybe our scrapes are part of a long tradition of artists and critics not getting on too well.

Let's give the critic the last word. John Gruen, who can get anyone to say anything, got this from Clem: "As far as art is concerned, I just prefer good art to bad art—if I can tell the difference."

The Difference

Greenberg, by preferring good art to bad—if he could tell the difference—joined a large number of individuals carrying the same unresolved question. At the university, museum, and art school lectures I have given, during the question period, it rarely happens that people do not ask, "How are you, Mr. Rivers," meaning they themselves, "able to tell the difference between good and bad art?"

Like most artists, if they don't take their remarks as ready to go down in history, I haven't figured out an answer. I have some ideas, but it is not my area of expertise. My work is the best answer. There are too many other questions of greater interest that I haven't found the answer to. One that has elated and depressed me my whole life is about career and the making of art, or more bluntly, "making it" and making art.

Leon Trotsky, exiled in Siberia as a young man and in Mexico as an old one, before he ended up with an axe in his skull, was seated on his porch talking to some visiting admirers when his dog snouted his way through the screen door. As Trotsky was answering questions about his revolutionary philosophy, his leadership of the Soviet army, his signing of the Brest-Litovsk truce to get the Germans off the Bolshevik back, etc., his dog ambled up to him wagging its tail, exquisitely happy to be licking its master's beard. Trotsky stopped his commentary, pointed to the dog, and with a wide grin told the waiting assembly of budding revolutionaries, "Behold, man's best friend."

What did it avail Trotsky to go so far in politics and philosophy, and to deal with such brutal vicissitudes of life and death as the shelling of his own sailors at Kronstadt, only to end up sounding like my uncle Yonkel Bloom?

What did it avail Clem Greenberg to spend a lifetime looking at new art, thinking and writing about new art, curating art shows, visiting artists' studios, talking to the latest hotshot artists, only to end up with the ancient conclusion that he prefers good art to bad art . . . if he can tell the difference!

Lexington Public

A little before my show at the Jane Street Gallery in 1949, Tess and
I had moved out of our barren cubicle on Madison Street up to the
Second Avenue loft. I kept painting every day, still accompanied
by my Bonnard reproductions pinned to the studio wall. But in my
quiet moments I was preoccupied with Tess's obvious desire to find
some other male to make her happy—a preoccupation that made
Tess, and subsequently other women in my life, even more beautiful and desirable. But she complained that a clearer look at our
situation together would reveal that it was more about my asking
her to find her own place and that it was I who was trying to find
not another female but about a dozen. There was no reason anyone
could see, including myself, why she should be with me. And
"being with me" was becoming hard to define. She slept with other
men, spent more time with her female friends, went to parties
without me, and told me there was more to life than art.

"What, go ahead, tell me what!"

In fact, after finding a new job, Tess did begin to search for a
place of her own.

Number two preoccupation was my off-again, on-again use of
drugs and the fear of becoming an addict. I didn't know what to do
about Tess. I thought of something to do about drugs. I had heard
about "Lexington" from some of my confused musical friends with
some drug experience. It was both a prison and a mental health

center for convicted drug addicts, located in Lexington, Kentucky. Maybe I would go there voluntarily for specialized psychological counseling.

As yet I hadn't identified myself as an addict. I hardly ever took heroin for more than two days in a row. My nausea shortly after the shot was so sharp and debilitating I had to lie flat on the bed for hours. It was easy to let a lot of time pass between episodes. The uncomfortable cycle of pleasure, guilt, and shame didn't seem worth it. And aside from Charlie Parker, an addict and a genius, none of my heroes in the history of art was addicted to drugs. Unless you considered alcohol a drug.

I defined a heroin addict very narrowly as someone who had a condition of serious discomfort if there was no steady ingestion of heroin. By this definition I was only a weekend joy popper who had no right to so grandiose a title as Junkie.

Ulysses

I return on weekends to the Bronx, chuck the kids under the chin, drop off a few bucks, don't know where I got them, and try to fuck Augusta, who is now with Aesop and will have none of it.

I no longer feel light about how things are going. Berdie reports that unhappy Augusta yells at her and pulls her hair. Funds are running low on Crescent Avenue; we allow some bookies to use our phone to take bets. One morning I'm in the bedroom writing poetry and playing with four-year-old Steven when there comes a loud knocking on the fire escape window. Five cops enter. We are all put under arrest, myself, the bookies, Berdie, and the kids. The one cop in civvies identifies himself as Sergeant Bernard Bopp.

Bernard Bopp!

B. Bopp the cop asks me what's on the papers in front of me.

"Poetry," say I.

"Yeah, I'll bet."

I am put in jail for the night. In the morning the boss of the bookies bails me out. Three weeks later, after delays and postponements, the charges of bookmaking against me are dropped.

I find little comfort in my family or my friends. Even sex is beginning to take a back seat to my preoccupations with my state of mind. Everyone convinces me to go to a psychiatrist. I scare up the money and see a German refugee, Edith Nachmanson, perhaps forty years old. Each feature of her face seems to come from a different member of my family; I spend half of my fifty-minute hour examining her face instead of my problems. She's intelligent, kind, even motherly, but nothing helps with my conviction that I am hopelessly neurotic. And being neurotic in 1949 is synonymous with being a full-fledged failure.

The only way out is to become a great artist—Baudelaire beseeching the Muse to give him the secrets of his art so he may rise above those who have little regard for him!

So—onward to Lexington.

I took the train trip at midnight to arrive in broad daylight. I didn't want to reach this southern hillbilly town in the evening. I imagined getting lost walking in the dark, and when I ask a stranger on the street for directions, I am recognized as a New Yorker by my accent, a Jew by my nose, and an addict by my sallow skin. Ozark beards, shotguns, overalls, and tall tattered hats; drawls and jokes about "furriners." No arrival in the dark for me. I wanted a bright and early one.

I descended the steps of the train at 7:45 a.m. and took a taxi to the local courthouse. Volunteering to enter the hospital required a hearing before a local judge who had the authority, under the state's "blue grass laws," to place me in the prison-hospital with "the key," prisoners' jargon for the right to leave whenever you want. All that was required for this free therapy was a confession of drug addiction and a willingness to break with your past bad behavior.

Slam

Inside the joint I share a room (two cots, a four-drawer dresser, and a small window) with a short doctor from Cincinnati, about thirty-five years old. Minutes after I take up residency he admits to having had an addiction back there in Ohio, where the pain of his daily existence, like the pain of a broken leg, could be relieved by a shot of morphine. Before too long he forgot why he started, but he couldn't stop. He ordered far more morphine than was necessary for his patients. He was apprehended.

Before I went to Lexington I imagined most of the prisoners would be either jazz musicians or jazz hangers-on, all with that special kind of hip jargon I enjoyed. In reality an astonishing number of prisoners were doctors and just plain Joes.

As part of my rehabilitation I was given a job in the kitchen peeling potatoes. It was another life, like being in the Air Corps, and for a few days I had no regrets.

From the beginning there was talk almost without end about drugs, all kinds of drugs, the infinite variety of highs and how the speakers outsmarted the police. And how they were caught. And how much pain they endured having to kick cold turkey. The one thing I'd never heard of until I got to Lexington was the gospel rippling through the entire prison, that nutmeg was capable of getting you high. Plain old nutmeg, the ordinary spice sprinkled on custard pies and Christmas eggnog?

A friend who considers himself a great authority on mind-altering drugs did an eighteen-month stint in 1949 as undercover reporter for the *Lester Young Newsletter*. He asserts that the right dosage, half a large match box, could indeed get you stoned.

What were dozens of cases of nutmeg doing in a rehab prison in the Ozarks?

"There was a lot of baking going on," he says.

I never bothered to test the nutmeg theory, just as in high school I never tested the rumor that two aspirins in Pepsi Cola could produce euphoria and—if you were able to get a girl to drink it—a sexual experience. To me, stealing nutmeg and passing it out to fellow prisoners only meant trying to be a bad boy in a bad place. And did you ever taste nutmeg by the spoonful? Not that it tastes half as bad as peyote, the substance taken for religious purposes by some American Indian tribes, which I had the nerve to try about five years later. After soaking the peyote buttons in water for an hour I swallowed a solution that produced the sensation of drifting over the earth, but it was like drinking liquid shit. I held my nose and gulped it down, as I did cod liver oil in childhood. Cod liver oil was backed by the science of motherhood; like spinach, it tasted bad and had to be good for you. The results of peyote were objectively visible out west among the Zuñi. But nutmeg and Pepsi with aspirin, from any point of view except gossip and hope, for me lacked credentials.

The prison had a research center probably out of sight of "bleeding heart liberals" or "lock 'em up and throw away the key" conservatives. While a rather civilized detoxification program gave addicts four weeks to clean up, there were other programs hard to name. For example, there were experiments with synthetic opiates and amphetamines, pride of the Nazi medical high command, commonly known as speed; and there was a rudimentary attempt at a heroin cure using methadone, otherwise known as Dolophine,

Hermann Goering's pet high. That program was called "Ten-Eight-Twenty." I don't know what it means and don't care; I hate people who use their past experience with drugs to become lifetime experts on the subject.

There was also research into drugs not necessarily of the mind-altering type, called medicine. Inmates would volunteer to be guinea pigs testing untried cures to ease the life of man. And for this worthy involvement, they were rewarded with several weeks' worth of morphine. A center to rehabilitate drug addicts dispensing drugs over the counter down at the lab! They were in the avant-garde of legalization!

Stitt

Potatoes peeled, pots washed, floors scrubbed, I still had enough curiosity to mosey down to the auditorium, a small theater where the prison band was rehearsing. I hung out until they were finished and asked the piano player how I could get to play. Everyone pointed to a man who was walking toward me, Bruce Munson, a hospital official in charge of the band.

"Ask him."

"How can I get to play with the band?"

"What do you play?"

"Baritone."

"Can you read?"

"Yeah."

"Well, come down tomorrow about eight. We can always use a baritone."

The eighteen-piece band was mainly about bebop and mainly black, with spiritual traces of Count Basie, Lester Young, and Roy Eldridge in some of the solos. Practically everybody in the band wrote charts. A youthful, thin, head-shaven black alto player was obviously the band's star. He soloed first and he soloed long, and he sounded like the already legendary Charlie Parker. Lots of alto players picked up qualities from the Bird, sometimes directly quoting him or attempting the speed and flow of his supreme logic. But this alto man played with Parker's authority and variety. It didn't take too much time to conclude I was looking at and listening to another legend. Sonny Stitt, of "Ooh Bop She-bam" fame, one of the great bebop hits, which he recorded with Dizzy Gillespie in 1946. Like Parker, Sonny played alto and had the same pleasant

L
A
R
R
Y

R
I
V
E
R
S

197

piercing tone, plus many of the general assumptions of bebop. Lots of double time, use of the flatted fifth, tender arialike melodies mixed with the sadness of slow blues. Parker recorded before Sonny did, with the underground but well-appreciated Jay McShann band of Kansas City. There, still under the influence of Lester Young, Parker took some tentative steps later identified as bebop. Because of that he was credited with inventing the entire musical phenomenon of bebop. Questioned about his following Parker into bebop, Sonny in interview after interview in no uncertain terms insisted he came to bebop all on his own. He suffered for years from the scourge of being considered an imitator. He finally gave up the alto and blew tenor sax.

It is more natural now for me to admire and experience soothing sensations when listening to Sonny Stitt. His music touches on previous jazz, much the way I feel my paintings touch on old art. Parker was more clearly separated from the jazz of the past, so much so that Louis Armstrong dismissed his playing as "fast noise and no feeling."

Back there in Lexington, Stitt was not very friendly to me, or for that matter to anyone in the band. He registered, when I blew, neither disapproval nor approval. Outclassed by his great talent, I experienced again that old self-sorrow about not being born black.

There were other stars of the new jazz at Lexington, not all of them there on a voluntary basis: Dexter Gordon, great tenor player with Billy Eckstine way back, who would portray Lester Young in the 1986 French movie 'Round Midnight, and Tadd Dameron, amazing pianist and composer. And there were famous ofays formerly of such renowned bands as Stan Kenton's and Woody Herman's. And the gaunt Joe Albany, a great pianist of the Charlie Parker band, who in a speeding cab to 110th Street, between sets at the Three Deuces on 52nd Street, could score, get back in the cab, pull out a spoon, fill it with water from an eyedropper, add the heroin, light two matches under the spoon, cook up, tie up, and shoot up at fifty miles an hour down Fifth Avenue at 1:00 a.m., and arrive in time to play the next set.

Help

The psychological counseling that originally drew me to Lexington was not scheduled frequently enough for me to feel I was being helped. The psychiatrists were young, with crew cuts and midwestern twangs, not a middle-aged German refugee among them. And what was more offputting, certain subjects were off limits. How do you talk about crime to a federal physician? How do you discuss the following degrading episode?

Early in 1949 at a jazz club I met a girl who asked me if I could buy her some heroin. I had about as much connection with connections as a plumber, but I figured I'd supplement the little heroin I was carrying by adding some meaningless powder to it and make some extra money, maybe her too. Alas, I had nothing with which to increase my cache.

Urinating in the club's toilet, I spotted a container of Bon Ami cleaning powder. Without hesitation I used it for the mix. Most pushers use milk sugar or crushed aspirins to keep their trade alive for future business. I think my attitude toward women then, which I'm not too proud of now, allowed me to pull such a stunt. I assumed this woman was more interested in being thought interested in heroin than in the pleasure derived from the drug. What was even more mindless was that in order to prove that this transaction was on the up-and-up I shared the mixture with her. We shot up in the men's room.

I recovered from the possibly lye-laced Bon Ami shot. In Lexington, in the doctor's office, it was impossible, and illegal, to admit my fear that she might have perished. I didn't trust analysts I couldn't tell a story like that to. They were keeping me from expressing myself!

That I voluntarily chose to go to Lexington Federal Prison Hospital gave me no privileges except one: I could leave on three days' notice. Apart from the music and my intermittent curiosity about American drug lore in the prison population, I didn't get anything out of my experience. Ten days after I arrived I threw in the prison towel, and in three more I was out.

Told to get on the next train and not to find the town interesting ("It might prove too interesting for your health"), I went from the hospital straight to the train station.

Lexington Epilogue

On my trip back to New York I arrived in time to drop in at the Open Door or Club Bohemia or the Nineteenth Hole for a drink, for a listen, for a possible encounter with a woman. I found myself in the club of the Bon Ami fiasco with the young lady who was shopping for heroin. Guilt struck like a twelve-inch brush dripping peanut butter.

Turning toward the bar, I saw the very woman. I walked over. Slowly and with emotion, in a stage whisper, I said, "Oh! You don't know how glad I am to see you!"

She moved closer. Returning my stage whisper, she says, "Listen, motherfucker, I've been looking for you for weeks."

Uh-oh.

"I haven't had shit that good since the last time you and I got high."

Puppets

In my absence Tess had flown the coop to a cold-water flat in the West Village. Our get-togethers had longer spaces between them, and soon we gave up the little left of the feelings between us. Considering all I was doing as this affair suffered its death throes, I concluded either that love was not as crucial as I had read and believed or that perhaps there was someone just around the corner waiting for me.

Back downtown, entertaining a profound self-pity about my art and my ineffective trip to Lexington, I was busy at the same time meeting new friends, mostly literary and homosexual. John Myers, not yet an art dealer, was uptown and broke. Subways had just gone up to a dime. His poverty didn't keep him away from cocktail parties. At a party given by versatile writer Randall Carter, John met Tibor de Nagy. Already attracted to famous artists and intellectuals, John willingly broadened his attractions to include titled aristocrats rich or poor.

Tibor was an impoverished Hungarian count out of *Grand Hotel*. Managing to stay alive during Hungary's occupation by the Nazis, then the Communists, he made his way in 1948 to the USA. In NYC all that was left of the fortune in the pocket of his Savile Row hand-tailored suit were two pieces of bread on the lookout for content. Out of his chance meeting with John Myers a partnership was formed. Tibor agreed to put up his last piece of bread for what he hoped would turn into meat and potatoes: the Tibor de Nagy Marionette Company.

John was a talented marionettist who performed in nightclubs, most often on Fifty-seventh Street in Spivvy's Room. These performances made him feel part of the underground avant-garde. Major

Count Tibor

surrealists—Ernst, Leonor Fini, Eluard, and other practitioners of
the New, including Léger—spent some of the war years here,
though by 1949 most had gone back to Europe.

In Buffalo, before coming to New York City, John was an editor
of the surrealist magazine *Upstate* and the leader of the New Art
and Cultural Club at the Albright-Knox Art Gallery. As a dedicated
reader of such literary and intellectual magazines as *Dial*, *Criterion*, *Horizon*, and *Scrutiny*, he understood the role played by Parisian nightclubs in bringing the public new ideas in theater, music,
and the visual arts. The dada movement itself had come into being
at the Voltaire, a nightclub in Zurich that presented theatrical
pieces by Tristan Tzara; what you looked at was designed by Oskar
Kokoschka. (Tzara was still organizing Happenings in his apartment when I was in Paris in 1950.)

In a secondhand station wagon John and Tibor brought their
marionette shows to schools, country clubs, churches, and even
hotels. Cecil Beaton, an international success who allowed himself
to be adored by John, got them a booking at the Sherry-Netherland,
and through aristocratic channels Tibor could tap, Prince Obolen-
sky got them a few one-night stands at the Plaza Hotel. In 1950,
with the Howdy Doody show breaking new ground in puppetry and

in money-making, John and Tibor worked hard hoping for similar rewards.

But an outbreak of polio frightened parents, who kept children from mingling with other children. The epidemic put a serious crimp in the marionette biz. As their bookings dropped, Tibor and John agreed with artists and friends who suggested they open a gallery for the new art of young artists. I was one of the young artists.

Money was promised for this venture by, among others, two poverty-stricken downtown artists, Willem de Kooning and Franz Kline. The first person actually to come across was Peggy Osborne, a lovely and lonely uptown Wasp who wore Hedy Lamarr turbans day and night. In company she tilted her head so far back, probably to pick up the slack in her jaws, that you got a good view of the inside of her nostrils. She was a chic, thin lady who after her well-handled divorce had more than enough to chip in and inspire other angels to help form the inchoate Tibor de Nagy Gallery. One of these was Babs Simpson, sometimes known as Barbara, editor in chief of Vogue magazine. At cocktails in the middle fifties, Babs in her forties was a five-foot-two-inch woman always in a black dress topped by a powdered white face with bright statuesque teeth and a nose wrenched from a drugstore Indian; her hair tight to her scalp always made me think of Balanchine's ballerinas. Jeanne Reynal, rumored to be a big bread source, also came through, as she came through for many of the surrealists during the war. She was a Sunday sculptor with earrings the size of the Ritz and floor-sweeping Mexican skirts to match. She had a silent Negro boyfriend who smoked a pipe and looked like a history professor, and whom she finally married.

Such were the humble yet noble beginnings of the careers of Tibor de Nagy, John Myers—and Larry Rivers. And Fairfield Porter, Jane Freilicher, Al Leslie, Nell Blaine, Neil Welliver, Grace Hartigan, et al.

John

John Myers was homosexual as James Baldwin was black. It was instant, almost unconscious recognition. Gore Vidal writes that there are no homosexuals, only homosexual acts. Well, a man who I am able to predict will only engage in homosexual acts is what I mean by a homosexual. Except that homophobia exists, what's so bothersome about identifying someone as homosexual? A white European in a big black fur hat, long curly sideburns, and a beard could be an actor in *Fiddler on the Roof*; he could also be a Jew.

John Myers' special identity is hard to lay out on paper. The forties and fifties social and sexual style of New York gay lives is now part of history. Flashes of that style still bring on a pleasant rush. No one but a gay Rip Van Winkle, coming out of his twenty-year sleep as if it were the morning after, could clearly demonstrate the gestures, language, and ironies.

John Bernard Myers—as I said, he insisted on the Bernard: there were too many plain old John Myerses in New York—was a man with a rubber face, a little over six feet tall, and had a paunch he sometimes successfully held in. He had frog-belly-white nicely shaped legs and silken dirty blond hair that he constantly pushed off his face. His eyes were green and changed size with every idea that crossed behind them. He read endlessly. John never made a point that wasn't backed by some intellectual highbrow or cunning surrealist, or by Corbusier, whose brilliant one-liners appeared in every art or architecture magazine you picked up in the forties and fifties.

John Myers broadened my cultural and culinary horizons at many a soiree or dinner. Not that he or I ever thought that my cultural development was the purpose of those events. John wanted to be near me whenever he could and would entice me with opportunities to meet fairly well-known cultural figures: W. H. Auden, Stephen Spender, John LaTouche, Lotte Lenya, the artistic wing of the Ford family, and Tennessee Williams. Broadening of cultural horizons included Tennessee drunk and almost nude answering my questions about making the *Streetcar* film while grabbing at the flies of three or four handsome young hoods invited off the streets by his lover, Frank Merlo.

What I singled out in the passion of John's many discussions was the upward turn of his large mouth and his limber lips, and that was what I was later to be moved by when he talked me into practicing fellatio in my presence—on me. Since I was technically unsure of myself in performing fellatio, John graciously allowed me to use his organ for practice. My cunnilingus style at the time was probably okay. While labia and hair weren't my visual idea of heaven, the act was always inspiring. With John Myers, fellatio was okay, but I always felt I was doing him a bigger favor than I was doing myself.

John's interest in me went beyond the physical, if there is such a place. He was genuinely interested in my growth as an artist. He devoted a lot of time to talking with me about art, my art, and literature, especially the theater; he even gave me the opportunity to do my first set, for *Try! Try!*, a Frank O'Hara play that John produced with his director boyfriend Herbert Machiz. Under John's prodding and beseeching, Jimmy Merrill, the poet son of Charles Merrill of Merrill Lynch, put up the down payment on my house in Southampton, Long Island. I am still living in that house, which cost $10,500. Jimmy's $2,500 allowed me to procure a mortgage that cost $54.11 a month—for an eight-room house a short walk to Main Street and the beach.

At one point, when I had moved out of the Bronx with my tribe of children and mother-in-law and needed temporary housing, John put us up. His East Ninth Street establishment included one-man symposium Waldemar Hansen, John's loyal pal from his days in Buffalo, plus lots of other old pals in need of one-night put-ups. It was a three-room ground-floor flat with a small backyard where my boys played when they weren't ruining the rest of the place. Joe Rivers, my stepson, on John Myers' Ninth Street apartment:

> There were mysteries solved when John put Larry and the rest of us up. Before I moved downtown, the Village to me was a place where Indians lived.
>
> Ninth Street had a reputation as a lesbian block, not that I knew what a lesbian was. I thought it was a tough woman who could kick my ass and was physically stronger than a man and did not like males, for no particular reason. I wasn't aware of the sexual aspect. I was terrified of them. At eleven years people could easily kick your ass, men or women—and if they didn't like men at all who knows when they might take it into their head to make an example of me and pull me into their clubrooms back of a store on Ninth Street. How many kids get to grow up knowing that world, not to mention the world of art, Kline, de Kooning, O'Hara, even a madman like Pollock.
>
> Many people around Larry at the time drank so much that Larry, by not drinking, appeared to me to be stable—though he did shoot dope, but I didn't know it. I was very glad to live with Larry, an artist who gave us a lot of contact —riding on Larry's shoulders, things that directly influ-

enced how I deal with my children now. Since he was so active sexually, every time a new woman, a girlfriend, would come over, we would immediately set up a situation where we could see something happening, or the woman naked, and that could be done by climbing a tree, or drilling holes in the floor, or sneaking into the bedroom, or opening the window shade about two or three inches, just enough to peek in.

Steven hated Myers intensely, not only because of the homosexual connection. John once hit him and yelled at him. Steven never forgave him, although he probably fully deserved it—if we had lived in any other family, we probably would have been sent to reform school. Also, Myers was always reminding Larry to send us kids to bed at night so John could have Larry to himself.

John always had a lot of parties on Ninth Street. To get a little spending money, we kids would go through the coats of the guests and take money; once we got a small fortune, three dollars in change. All kinds of stars showed up, Gore Vidal, Tennessee Williams, Lotte Lenya.

W. H. Auden and Chester Kallman came over once. Chester invited the thugs from the Holiday Inn on St. Mark's Place to John's; these neighborhood hoods at knife-point began robbing everyone at the party; one stuck his knife in a gay guy's ass and asked him how he liked it.

Dealing

Not many moons after John Myers and I began to include sex in our art-and-dealer association, I excluded it. I rejected him. He was too dramatic, weeping outside my studio door when I refused to let him in. In a letter he wrote that he felt like "Rilke's Portuguese nun who sat at the gate, looking up and down the road for the rest of her life after she had been abandoned by her cavalier. . . . But the worst thing of all about being rejected is the grotesquerie, it sits on one's back like a hump, a horrid tumor, which cannot be shaken or cut off or wished away. It *is*. And there is no making it *not* what it is." It took some time for the "hump" and "horrid tumor" to wither away. I was fond of John, it was always fun to be around him, he was a lovable pain in the ass. I had to find a way to make him understand. I can't remember exactly how I managed this. Perhaps a few sexual backslides allowed him to feel he wasn't a repulsive object. Anyway, I succeeded.

In time he was back on the phone with tidbits of malice about everybody but *everybody* we knew, and even people we didn't know, inviting me to "cultural and culinary events," sending me letters about our latest commercial and aesthetic opportunities. More than a flowery romantic, John was a compulsive seller of talent. There was no telephone call or letter or lunch that didn't serve to promote his artists or the gallery's current exhibition or the next one. If all that highbrow PR was basically about money, it didn't change his unshakable loftiness.

John's first difficulty grew out of his enthusiasm for Helen Frankenthaler's work. Her boyfriend, Clem Greenberg, didn't think she was "ready." But John lined up a publicity barrage and a one-woman show that gave her all she needed to take herself seriously as an artist. The idea of being "ready" for an exhibition sounds like the artist is about to enter battle and the works are missiles. I see an artist's first show as an onstage spot-lit introduction. For Helen there was no retreating.

Whatever had happened to me in art up to that point rested on my own work and talent—I hope. But John Myers' role is important and must be recognized. He recognized it so well that he cursed me in 1962 when I signed a contract to show exclusively with Marlborough. Five thousand sunny miles away he phoned me from Venice and vowed, "I'm going to destroy you." This is not the unique compliment it seems. In 1968, when John and Tibor's partnership ended, Tibor asked the whereabouts of certain artworks the gallery had acquired. John's answer was a low growl: "I'm going to destroy you." Grace Hartigan, quitting the new John Myers Gallery for the Martha Jackson Gallery, received an even greater compliment. "I'm going to destroy you *and* your marriage."

Marlborough and Me

In 1962, when I bound myself exclusively to Marlborough, John Myers instituted a million-dollar suit in addition to vowing to destroy me. Marlborough and I had hopes of accomplishing a mutual onward-and-upward in the New York art world. The matchmaker was my accountant, Bernard "Heart-to-Heart" Reis, later destroyed by his questionable role in the Rothko scandal.

I did not know then that the Marlborough, with Frank Lloyd

as director, couldn't help me grow to be a healthier and bigger artistic celebrity. The talent of the Marlborough dealership hardly included nurturing. I was expected to be on my own two feet as an artist, famous and accomplished, and Marlborough, equally famous, was to reap the nourishment. In 1962 I was on my own two feet, sort of famous, sort of accomplished, but I still could have used nurturing—the kind John Myers gave me during the ten years he was my brilliant and adoring but not too adorable dealer at the Tibor de Nagy Gallery, which I shamelessly abandoned for the Marlborough glitter that did not turn into the gold I envisioned. John Myers' nurturing consisted not only in foraging for funds to keep me alive and painting, but in all those other ingredients necessary to produce art.

Nurturing Myers Style

On the phone.
"Are you painting, honey?"
"Yes, John."
"What kind of mad avant-garde storm are you up to today?"
"One look will eliminate a thousand words."
"In that case I'll come down and look as soon as I close the gallery. By the by, this doctor from Pennsylvania, Dr. Moss, is finally buying your luscious Augusta painting. He wouldn't pay more than seventy-five dollars, but I got him to agree that after a year he'll donate it to the Allentown Museum—"
"If they'll take it."
"Face it, honey, this painting is an important example of the school of Everyday Surrealism—"
"*What* school?"
"—of which you are the brightest proponent."
Starting in 1951, when I first showed at the de Nagy gallery, John Myers, sitting alone in the gallery at a plain desk with a phone, surrounded by little more than paintings, rained letters on me for over a decade. Here are a few.

Urgent: Send a small page of writing on how you felt about THE BURIAL being taken by The Museum Purchase Fund and what you think of that whole setup for buying new art. Do this immediately. They have a deadline. ART DIGEST— 116 E. 59th St. O.K.? It will be printed in the next issue. They must have it by Monday.

He wrote the address in the letter to save me time looking it up, to avoid delay, to make sure I met the deadline! Like a mother writing to a child whose best interests she has at heart, or like a father at a Little League game, he was always applauding from the sidelines.

> You have no idea how VINDICATED I feel to have your *Washington Crossing the Delaware* taken into the Museum of Modern Art. Now if they will only start studying all my artists, oy! my cup would be overflowing. . . .
> Larry, I can't *wait* to see your new paintings! I am in need of just such a LIFT—to be fired with enthusiasm for next season's shows! It's so much easier when one is in love with the work. They sound fabulous, a gorgeous new phase of elegance and maturity.

In another letter John pointed to something about me in the fifties that kind of continues to this day.

> I think that this last period of yours when, like Bill de Kooning, you paint a stroke and then stare at it, might be alright to do for a while—but I cannot see it as intimately related to the physical you whose whole basic ferment is the need

for action and completion. . . . I think you have a peculiar
idea that if a picture doesn't take a long time and isn't fussed
over a lot that it will lack richness and depth. But that is
absurd, as a reading of the lives of a great many old masters
as well as modern painters will reveal.

I still have the feeling that if a painting or sculpture or even a
drawing takes a short time it is suspect, it can't be great. But why
do things have to be great? What's wrong with pleasant, colorful,
rhythmical, mildly fascinating? No, it must be great! Why? I've been
reading a biography of the peculiar Ludwig Wittgenstein subtitled
The Duty of Genius. The author, Ray Monk, deals with Wittgenstein's Vienna in the twenties, where life for some writers, artists,
musicians, etc., was worth living only if you lived the life of a
genius. For all my instant ironies and jokes on and off the canvas,
am I hiding a seriousness I equate with genius? Unfortunately,
genius is only recognized by *others*, so I can never answer that
question.

John's letters were always full of news and gossip about the art
world.

Matta has broken with Tchelitcheff! Matta complains that
Tch. has stolen his palette (colors). Max Ernst has quar-
reled with Breton since Max believes that Breton has carried "automatism" to the point of absurdity. Anyway he is
jealous because Breton has taken up someone named
Gorky. Matta has introduced the theory of the cubed crystal. Giacometti sculpting again—with figures 1 and ½
inches high!

After seeing a synagogue show at the Kootz gallery, he wrote me
that it looked "exactly like a smart Lord and Taylor window. . . . I
simply can't take candelabra by Lassaw, or a Motherwell rug, too
seriously."

But John could also wax philosophical. Once, writing about the
role of the dealer, he invoked what Kant called "disinterested joy."
"I long to exercise judgment as dispassionately as I am able, and
then to convince the world that it really agrees with me," he went
on, adding that he could think of no greater happiness than to have
been Vollard or Kahnweiler, two great art dealers: "Even though
they had to be involved with commerce their love of painting was
so intense that they transcended their own *worst* motives."

And of course there was plenty of correspondence about my
painting and my career, always full of encouragement: "I want you

to feel secure that the gallery will continue to buy your work and fulfill our new contractual agreement with you." With other galleries here and abroad beginning to breathe pleasantly down my neck with all kinds of offers for shows, and with my work selling better than that of any other artist in the de Nagy gallery, and for higher prices, Tibor and John guaranteed me $25,000 a year as an advance against sales. Painting was beginning to sound like a career!

Louis' Tavern

Like I said, I met John Myers on a high stool in Louis' Tavern on
Sheridan Square in Greenwich Village. It was 1951. I was just back
from Paris after a half year of deliberating whether I should continue a life devoted to making art or write poetry. I was fortunate
to meet a fancy art connoisseur like Myers, even on a high stool in
a low bar. I was in bad need of someone to make a fuss about my
paintings. He told me how much he liked my 1949 exhibition at the
Jane Street Gallery. "It was divine! Full of energy and a natural
propensity for the perverse." He also seemed transfixed by my person. He never stopped talking, never stopped flirting. He offered
me a show on the spot.

"But you haven't seen my new work."

"It doesn't matter. I know they'll be fantastic."

Just as some women judge the size of a man's cock by looking
at his fingers, some homosexuals go by nose size to judge cock size.
I wonder if my nose gave John the desire to see more of me.

A week later John Myers was whacking my studio door. He had
Clem Greenberg with him. They stayed for half an hour or so,
seated in two chairs about eight feet from where I placed works on
the floor and leaned them against the wall. I suppose John brought
Clem along to corroborate his evaluation of my worth, as well as to

impress on me the pull he had with the most important critic of avant-garde art.

A week later, alone this time, John was in my studio choosing works for the future Larry Rivers exhibition at the Tibor de Nagy gallery. Everything he saw was of course "fantastic!" By then German expressionism and its broad stroking had begun to replace my fascination with the gentler strokes I borrowed from Bonnard. After his studio visit we repaired to Louis' Tavern.

Louis' was a loud bar packed to its rafters with young bohemian heterosexuals lightly sprinkled with homosexuals who walked over from the San Remo, their main hangout on MacDougal Street. Its popularity was based mainly on the excellent chances, after entering alone, of going home with somebody. There was so much traffic in and out of Louis' that it's hard to remember if the doors ever shut. There were booths and tables for four that usually contained six or more excited talkers ordering food and calling to friends across the room. It was three or four deep at the bar, and the last row couldn't catch the bartenders' attention without shouting. In warm weather the overflow extended outside and up the eight or nine stone steps of the building next door.

One night I saw Bob De Niro, Sr., sitting on those steps.

"What are you doing out here, Bob?"

"Oh, I've been insulted by the owner and I'm boycotting the place."

It made sense. How would anybody know he was boycotting it if he stayed at home?

Those steps led up to the dressing rooms of the new theater that had just opened, Circle in the Square. Its members dropped in after their show: Ted Mann, the producer; Jose Quintero, the director; some new faces onstage, Geraldine Page, Jason Robards, and recent arrival Steve McQueen; and coming down after his Birdland gig, a new singer, Harry Belafonte.

Mixed into Louis' crowd were some unfortunate types, male and female, a notch up from the bums on the Bowery. What they wore made the sloppy togs of us bohemians seem like evening wear. Except for one woman with a body like a wet question mark, none of these tramps was sexually attractive. They had some vague exposure to the arts, and they shuffled through the bar sensing correctly that bohemian clients would respond to their requests for a handout.

Stanley Gould was a part-time sandal maker and drug dealer who took a long slow dive into the fifties, sixties, and seventies, in the eighties came up with a case of AIDS acquired from a needle, and died. At Louis' Stan would ask me for a quarter, the price of a cheap whiskey, promising to repay me the next night. The next night, drunk or stoned or both, he'd ask for another quarter. After four nights of extending him a twenty-five-cent loan, I'd say, "Listen, Stan, you promised to pay me back!"

Insulted, with a look of self-pity and a voice of vengeance, he'd say, "Okay, man, I'll never borrow another quarter from you as long as I live!"

He always forgot his threat and forgave me, condescending to negotiate with me again. He had a certain bizarre charm, a folksy philosophic way of delivering two-minute news clips of what "went down" last week, yesterday, and earlier today on the Main Streets of Greenwich Village: Eighth, MacDougal, West Fourth, and Sixth Avenue, in Bickford's, Riker's, and Stuart's cafeterias, where you could sit all night discussing truth, justice, drugs, sex, and art.

On the street level, Louis' was easily scanned through the windows for a personnel check. There was action until about two a.m. After that, if you were unhappy enough to drop by in search of sex among the last few souls draped unconscious over the bar, the place, according to John Ashbery, "looked like the bottom of a pocket."

Desire

Around the corner from Louis' Tavern, down Seventh Avenue at the Cherry Lane theater, Judith Malina and Julian Beck's Living Theater was presenting their first production outside the living room they had been using for a stage in their West End Avenue apartment. The play was Picasso's *Le Désir attrappé par le queue* ("Desire Caught by the Cock"—or "by the Tail," depending on the translator), a very brightly lit, up-tempo surrealist work featuring seminude young men and women speaking interesting surrealist nonsense. The great name of Picasso so impressed me I saw *Désir* two or three times a week. A more compelling reason was that two poet pals of mine, John Ashbery and Frank O'Hara, were playing two dogs, both called Bow Wow. After their last bowwow, the night for John and Frank began.

The Living Theater does Picasso.

Ashes

John Ashbery was a little more assiduous than Frank O'Hara—not much more—in dealing with his case of Young Man's Randiness. Miraculously, he found time in those same twenty-four hours to work, eat, sleep, write, and even play a part in the Picasso play.

My clearest picture is of a very thin twenty-two-year-old with clear skin delivering hilarious accounts of all sorts of things, noticeably searching for a very particular sequence of words or phrases that gave him a great deal of pleasure and his listeners even more. He had and still has a sense of recall that makes everyone else seem to have Alzheimer's. If his talk—where he went, what he did, with whom—was an indication of what preoccupied him most, I vote for sex, French cooking, and writing. At the time, he worked at the respectable Oxford University Press for peanuts and wrote poetry on the job. During the evening, in a bar or restaurant, he'd pull a poem out of his three-button J. Press jacket's inner pocket and hand it to us to read right then.

I

We see us as we truly behave:
From every corner comes a distinctive offering.
The train comes bearing joy;
The sparks it strikes illuminate the table.
Destiny guides the water-pilot, and it is destiny.
For long we hadn't heard so much news, such noise.
The day was warm and pleasant.
"We see you in your hair,
Air resting around the tips of mountains."

II

A fine rain anoints the canal machinery.
This is perhaps a day of general honesty
Without example in the world's history
Though the fumes are not of a singular authority
And indeed are dry as poverty.
Terrific units are on an old man
In the blue shadow of some paint cans
As laughing cadets say, "In the evening
Everything has a schedule, if you can find out what it is."

Not that Frank O'Hara walked around with empty inner pockets; nor Cincinnati's poet laureate, Kenneth Koch; nor, before he defected to the playwrights' union, Arnold Weinstein. Arnold once offered John some of Louis' lousy antipasto, consisting of three olives, two slices of salami, and a chunk of Velveeta cheese. John refused.

"What's the matter?" asked A.W. "Are you anti-pasto?"

"No," said John. "I'm pro-volone!"

One of John's specialties was leaving parties before anyone else, including parties he hosted; first a few bottles of wine, then a nap right at the table or on the nearest flat surface. On waking he found his J. Press jacket and split for Louis', or more likely the flamboyant Blue Parrot, a new bar that offered a delightful change from the sexy but potentially frightening atmosphere of the San Remo. Just to give everyone a sense of the world they came from, the Remo's waiters walked around with baseball bats, making sure no fag came on to them even if they did look like pink piles of shit.

John rarely spoke about poetry and said nothing about his own. Even today he acts slightly miffed if I ask about the source of some

Top: John Ashbery, Nell Blaine, Barbara Epstein, Seymour Krim.
Bottom: Barbara Cobell, LR, Leatrice Rose (back to camera), Nell

line. This attitude predates Susan Sontag's "Against Interpretation," which appeared in *Partisan Review* during John's tenure as its poetry editor.

John Ashbery is now breathing backward on sixty and is admired from Oxford University to the St. Mark's Poetry Project in the East Village. He appears in so many literary magazines and newspapers he can't keep up. Perhaps he frowns upon discussing source material because he himself doesn't know exactly where everything comes from, and strictly speaking, what difference does it make?

John spent eight years in France, from 1956 to 1964, and the few letters I received from him included few poems and lots of laughs.

> Dear Laresville,
> I've been meaning to answer your letter for a long time, honest I have, but right after I got it I made tracks South with the money that was in it. . . .
>
> I was slightly taken aback by your characterization of me as a modern-day Montparnasse Caligula, though subsequent events have proved you right . . . and anyway I am always tickled by your seemingly endless capacity for being shocked by my modest adventures, as well as your amused puzzledness by my refusal ever to "talk serious," which is really just lack of intelligence on my part. Gee this letter sounds so analytical that you'll probably find it out of character. . . .
>
> Jane [Freilicher] wrote that Emily Genauer [art critic for the Paris-based *Herald Tribune*] had asked you whether I would like her job. The answer is probably yes—but I can't very well write her since she hasn't yet announced publicly that she's leaving (I checked with the Paris office). With your customary savoir-faire maybe you could find out more and *SUBTLY* hint that I'd be very interested. . . .
>
> Love, J.A.

I saw him each time I went to Paris in those years. He did get the job on the Paris *Trib*. For my 1962 exhibition at the Galerie Rive Droit he wrote me a rave review, as well as this essay for the show's catalog.

Larry Rivers paints whatever comes within his reach. This is what Lautréamont was thinking of when he wrote about the sublime logic of making love to the first person who comes along. Rivers used to paint his mother-in-law, because she was around the house a great deal. He was not trying to confer any universal significance or its opposite on her. Today he paints portraits of cigarette packages with

L A R R Y

R I V E R S

the serious grace of Tiepolo. He is not trying to say that ordinary objects have their place in the scheme of things. He is certainly not trying to say either that nothing is more important than anything else. It is hard to say what he is doing. He is a machine like Mozart that has gone haywire and cannot stop producing symphonies, sonatas, everything beautifully clothed in colors but that is not quite it either. You see you cannot put yourself in a position toward his work that he himself has not just taken and is now walking away from into some pleasant shadow or pastel probability. He is breathing in some inevitable oxygen and expelling it in multicolored bubbles which may break but who cares. There are certainly beautiful accidents of paint in his work and you can enjoy these if you wish, only he cannot wait too long because he is going somewhere fast. What could be more beautiful and stirring than a colored picture of Napoléon on a French banknote; what could be sexier than the artist's own wife? Here, wait a minute, he is going to label all the parts of her body including the ones that interest you most, because he is really in quite a hurry and by the way did you know that you are coming with him? Oh yes you are. There is no more time to try to think what his work is like because the train is slowly pulling out of the station. *Premier service au départ.*

By 1962 John had exchanged his Ivy League jacket for a Parisian model with no inner pockets for the poems he used to pull out at a moment's notice. The necessity of friends' opinions about our work had diminished. By this time, we had both developed an audience outside our friends. In the early years of our artistic development we spent a lot of time showing our work to friends and seeing and hearing theirs. It was part of our reason for getting together. Who were we painting or writing for? Well, for our friends, and history. Who was looking over our shoulders as we worked, adjusting our aesthetics? The whole New York art world! But it didn't know it. So the time we spent showing our work to one another was reduced and formalized into exhibitions and publications. For a long time I didn't mind. I was busy with that unseen audience I had developed outside my friends. It gave me certain satisfactions, and definitely some self-confidence, notoriety, and money. But my friends' reactions always excited me and meant a lot, and still do.

Years ago friends who visited couldn't escape a studio tour. Nowadays I don't suggest they look at what I'm working on. Neither do they. We no longer talk about sex—nobody's "into" it; no one asks for another drink—no one drinks; no more talk about acquiring property—it's more about deacquiring, putting it in your will. Health is of some interest, blood pressure, fractures that won't heal, how to distinguish a memory lapse from the onset of Alzheimer's, and the ever popular discussion of how old so-and-so is getting to look. These conversations take place in a mirrorless room. Then food appears on the table, which sends the conversation careening toward diet as the low-salt, fat-free fare is wolfed down by guests glad not to be hosts.

So far nobody all evening has volunteered to take a peek at the art in the studio, or read a poem, or listen to a sonata. Well, they're artists, they've been thinking about art all day long, and this is the time for a much needed break, so we rationalize. After a few jokes, a tumble down memory lane, there is a mad dash for the door, a trading of kisses and handshakes and *buona seras*.

Where are the animated aesthetic discussions of yesteryear? Are we less interested in art? Have we no more problems to solve? I used to think that part of being an artist was to show an interest in the art of others. Looking around me today, I see that for most of the artists I know this is not true. It's something that's never spoken about. Who wants to share this truth of the recognized artist's complete lack of interest in anyone's work but his own? Too busy? One-upsmanship? At this point no live artist is doing anything that will have the slightest influence on my work, nor will mine influence them, at least not my contemporaries. Could I go to a psychiatrist at this age and stage to change my character? It's too late.

An Active Life

I'll try once more to set down the 1950s exuberance of the Everyminute Theater of Gay Life starring my close friends. The stage changed every night. A studio, an apartment; a cocktail party, a gallery opening. A walk through a museum. The cast was never the same. What remained the same were the gestures, the arms, fingers, lips, eyebrows, eyes, tossing heads. And the content of the short verbal bursts and abundant name and phrase dropping to signal how much Mallarmé and Valéry and Reverdy you'd read, in the original.

Nineteen fifty-one, circa early spring. The stage is now an automobile speeding south to Philadelphia. The cast: Jane Freilicher, John Ashbery, Frank O'Hara, Larry Rivers. We are on our way to a bunch of Old Masters paintings from Berlin. Muriel Oxenberg, now Murphy, has loaned me a Studebaker for the day. In my mind, delicate Muriel is always surrounded by herring: I never got over her being the heiress to the Vita King fortune. Muriel's brother Howard dreamed up a plan to make his own fortune by cornering the mustard market, intending to do in Gulden's, Dijon, even Grey Poupon, the Rolls-Royce of mustards. It didn't work.

Why do I know so many heirs and heiresses to the fortunes of mercantile adventurers?

Like who?

Like Jane Watrous of Parker Pens; Saint Louise of the Bowling Balls; Phyllis Lambert, Seagram's whiskey; Elaine Lorillard, Kent cigarettes; François and Christophe de Menil, Schlumberger (pronounced "Shlum-ber-*zhay*") oil drilling equipment; Jean Stein of MCA (now Matsushita); Niki and Elizabeth de St. Phalle, Crédit Lyonnais; Jimmy Johnson of Johnson and Johnson; and Michel de Grèce of the throne of Greece. I don't know how to fit in Prince Rainier von Hessen, who isn't heir to anything but deserves a variance to be included in this compilation on the basis of his being the nephew of Queen Elizabeth of England.

On the road to the Berlin Old Masters show our exuberance about the bright light streaming into the car, about being out of the Big Apple for a day, about the amazement we felt was in store for us, led us to write a long collaborative poem. Each of us in turn would contribute one line. Frank, who sat next to me, started the poem. If you liked what you heard you added something that related, or you countered with a ninety-degree turn toward something totally beside the point. We each contributed anything we wanted. I was second. Jane, a serious contender for producing the best lines, was third. And John, with his special gleeful yelp after each of his offerings, brought up the rear. It was difficult to tell from the result that John and Frank were the poetry pros in the car, the whole piece was so goofy and good. Someone who hadn't traveled with us would be hard put to know whose lines were whose or how good it was. The poem has disappeared, but each of the creators remembers the genesis of this lost masterpiece.

More Ashbery exuberance from the fifties:

Dear Rivs:
I have been meaning to startle you with a letter for some time now but the "oppressor's wrong, the proud man's contumely, the pangs of dispriz'd love, the law's delay, the insolence of office, and the spurns that patient merit of the unworthy takes" have been keeping me busy. Except for these my life has been unevenful. . . .

Rumor hath it that you are sore annoyed with me for not going and having breakfast with you that day when you were indisposed. But, my dear fellow, surely you remember that before I made the fatal phone call to Jane you had unequivocally stated that you would be unable to have it with me! It was only then that I received the inspiration to call her. Of course, I should have stayed with you and smoothed the pillow of your illness, but it seems to me that I offered to and you uttered a demurrer. And I was so hungry! Please, please, in these days of factions let there be no feelings of rancor 'twixt you and me. . . .

This letter, in a style I have not indulged in since the age of sixteen, may be a product of the dexedrine I have been taking to lose weight and of several gallons of black coffee, and some typhoid and smallpox shots I had this morning. For I am going to Mexico, did you know, with the mysterious Jane, the positive Grace, the reluctant Joe, and the redundant Walt. We shall leave May 28 and be gone for 3 weeks. I don't know how far the peso stretches these days, but will attempt to bring you back some trinket to make up for the slight you have suffered at my hands. Would an Aztec headache band make you feel any different? . . .

The dexedrine has made me much thinner—last night at Bill Weaver's coming home party everyone marveled at how slight I was. Perhaps people will be taking us for brothers once again. . . .

A Fan

I told you that when I was six the Bronx Zoo obsessed me, and I went almost every day. Of all God's beasts in that neo-Greek zoological park I was most drawn to the big cats, their rippling bodies pacing from one end of the cage to the other, their reverberating meows. If I arrived at feeding time I considered myself lucky to be able to watch them tear apart the giant chunk of meat thrown into

221

the cage. Next to each of these great cats was a plaque stating where they came from and could still be found. The most usual place was of course Africa. How envious I was of Africans lucky enough to inhabit the same regions as my mysterious cats!

When I began playing saxophone and got hung up on jazz and it became clear who the greatest jazz musicians were, again I was envious, and at the same time madly attracted to blacks.

The reasons for such adoration are not always appreciated by the adored, but I was not conscious then that my reasons could be regarded as an insult, and when life carried me into contact with yet another world, the world of homosexuals, which gave me such

laughs and thrills and boundless joy, I developed the same unreserved admiration—at least for the hundred or so homosexuals I knew.

Flash Forward

In 1975 Earl McGrath and his wife, Countess Camilla Pecci-Blunt, were throwing an elegant pasta party. The blood running in McGrath's veins is Cherokee Indian and Irish. He is a poet who sailed the seas on merchant ships with his close friend Richard Baker, who settled for being the head of Zen Buddhism in the United

States. Earl assisted Gian Carlo Menotti in setting up the Spoleto Festival. Many years and positions later, he became an executive at Atlantic Records, producing the Rolling Stones and finally man-

aging them. During his reign the Stones sold more records than they ever had before. After giving up the impossible life connected with them, he went on to peace and poverty. Having befriended artists for most of his life, he possessed a modern art collection of

consistently good quality. His collection gave him the feeling that he knew something about art and the nerve to open a gallery in L.A.

Earl drinks too much and smokes too much, and he's my best

friend. He's also an irrepressible fun lover and laughs hysterically at every joke he tells. He figured in several of my early videotaped improvisational scenes. In one memorable sequence Earl comes home early to find his girlfriend—played by my girlfriend at the

time, Donnie—entertaining a friend of his. After a long, fruitless interrogation about "what's been going on around here" he says, "Wait a minute!" Sniffing his friend's face, he ad-libs, "I smell pussy

on your breath!"

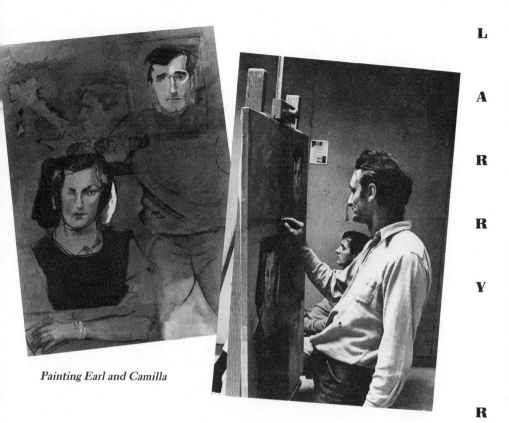

Painting Earl and Camilla

That blood in Earl's veins probably runs dark brown, as any painter will know who mixes the red of the Cherokee with the green of the Irish. His wife's blood runs a rich blue. Her title was given to the family by papal decree. Pope Leo XIII (pontificate 1878–1903) was a great-grand-uncle of our Countess Camilla. Leo XIII was known as the pope with big balls because of his remarkable encyclicals against the tide of extreme conservatism; he dreamed of a church that could relate to the problems of the present world. Another Leo (X, 1513–1521), son of Lorenzo de Medici, was also renowned for the size of his *coglioni* by virtue of his remark "God gave us the papacy, *let's have a ball with it*" (his italics).

Speaking of balls, sometime early in the history of the Catholic Church it became apparent to the Vatican Council of Cardinals that they had elected a woman as pope. She comes down in history as Pope Joan. Divesting her of her papal robes because she gave birth to a child in the streets of Rome, the church vowed never to be fooled again. There then came into use in the Vatican a chair built with a hole in its seat, through which the nominated pontiff's

nude genitals hung, to demonstrate for the select committee posi-
tioned on their knees that he was indeed a man.

Countess Camilla's father was Cecil Blunt, who made his living
on the phone. His mother married the Duc de Montmorency; you
meet Camilla's grandfather all the time in Proust. Her family owns
a theater in Rome that is considered one of the most beautiful in
the world. Her palazzo in Tuscany isn't bad either. Camilla grew
up in Paris and Rome, went to the best schools, knew the best
people, spent the war years safely in Santa Barbara, California; after
the war she returned to Rome. She assumed her first public persona
in 1958 as the international student coordinator for Gian-Carlo
Menotti's Spoleto Festival, where she met Earl McGrath. She is a
photographer of avant-garde figures known and unknown, and photographs dinner parties, even her own. True to her Blunt nomen-
clature, Camilla is renowned as the straightest-shooting friend and
hostess who ever whipped up a Spaghetti alla Matriciana.

Light of Foot

On exhibit in our country, among straight people, is a wide range
of attitudes about homosexuality. There are the physical bashers,
there are those embarrassed by it (you don't mention it without
some unflattering reference, and you *never* mention it to children),
and there are parents marching in big-city parades with signs saying
"I'm Proud of My Gay Son." There is the AMA, which only a few
years ago altered its position: no longer a disease, homosexuality

became a choice. There are politicians with sizable homosexual constituencies trying to pass equal housing laws, and there are legions of Grant Wood look-alikes who adored Liberace. It is a crime to loiter in a men's room or to give or get a blow job. Homosexuals, if found out, cannot hold a position in the CIA, the FBI, or any of the armed forces: they might be blackmailed into divulging our country's secrets, which most of the world can read about in any number of publications.

During the reign of LBJ, a close adviser of his was caught making a pest of himself in the men's room of a fancy Washington restaurant. Before the adviser could be brought up on charges, he was advised to get lost. LBJ, unable to save him politically, tried to keep him out of jail. As gossip had it, he spread a story that the adviser had been overworked and, feeling faint, went to the men's room to splash water on his face. Bending over the sink, he became nauseous and rushed into a cubicle to vomit, only to find a man seated on the bowl. Too late. He threw up right on the man's naked lap. He got down on his knees, trying desperately to brush the disgusting stuff into the bowl between the open legs of the occupant. Misinterpreting the adviser's attempt at neatness, the man began to scream, "Help! Police! What are you doing? Get away from me!" A police captain's retirement was being celebrated at a table near the john. Immediately five cops in plain clothes burst in on this tragic scene. A month or two before, to show the country how economy-minded he was, our president had had the White House lights dimmed way down every evening. This conjunction of low lights and a scandal involving a presidential adviser in a men's room gave columnists a rare opportunity for wit: "Aha! So that's why the lights in the White House were lowered!"—insinuating that this most macho president was not averse to a blow job from a close buddy! Which endeared LBJ to me, for all his Vietnam lies.

Then we have David Bowie, Michael Jackson, Mick Jagger, and scores of others who gain attention through theatrical homosexual clichés of dress, gesture, lingo, while maintaining their heterosexual steadfastness.

I guess nobody's reviews have been improved by pretending to be a sodomizer of pigs. I did, however, see a Cuban-Jewish conceptual artist kill chickens at a gallery performance, but he got bad reviews. He said the critics were anti-Semitic.

For some morally minded individuals, theatrical homosexuality is still about reaping commercial advantages; for plainer folks like us the advantages are more diffuse. Case in point. At Earl and Camilla's pasta fest Andy Warhol, whose apartment no one had ever seen the inside of, was once more a guest of the McGraths, balancing a plateful of spaghetti, walking around with a tape recorder in his pocket and a microphone in his hand, being his pleasant insightful self. Forgetting his advice on how to remain thin, which was to eat only what you don't like, Andy, slurping Camilla's prosciutto-tomato-mozarella combo, puts his mike in my face.

"Larry, what was your day like? Anything interesting happen?"

Never for a minute can I admit that I went through a day without something worth reporting. Mix this with my need to excite or please and you'll hear me telling Andy, "On my way over here I saw this good-looking young guy in a tight shirt with rolled-up sleeves. He was kind of posing against that wall at Central Park and Fifty-ninth. His hips were thrust forward; anyone passing by would have to notice the big lump of his crotch. I guess he was a hustler. Some man about fifty thought so too. Just as I was putting my watch away to ask the kid what time it was, this man walked up to him, had a two-second conversation, and they walked off together."

"Larry. Are you trying to tell me how attracted you are to young men? Come off it! You're not gay." Andy was accusing me of trying to make myself *interesting*!

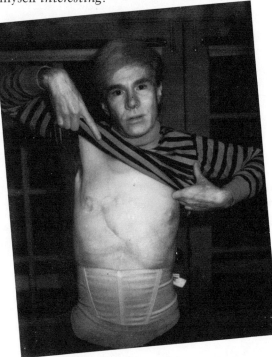

Andy's
wound

How?

By adding homosexuality to my other frowned-upon sexual activities!

Such as?

Attempting to screw my poor old mother-in-law.

And?

Sexual interest in the young.

And by adding pederasty to pedo- and gerontophilia, what was supposed to be gained?

Attention. Which leads to the palace of access.

Access to where?

The Whitney? MOMA? Studio 54? On the other hand, was I gay or not? Or queer? Or whatever it was called that week. The English use the expression "bent" (as in the play of the same name about homosexuals sent to concentration camps). There's also "light on his feet." Was I bent in one ball and straight in the other? Light on one foot, heavy on the other? The guy leaning on the Central Park wall did have nice muscles and an unusual protuberance, but I was just reporting this; maybe also trying to give Andy a warm feeling. "You know you're not gay, Larry," was only Andy expressing his territorial rights.

John Myers had an unbendable theorem that "bent" sex is better than straight because "men have more to play with." (I hope for his brain's sake that he was kidding.) Chester Himes, the detective story writer, did a lot of time in jail. He had anal sex with men, him always on top; in his autobiography he came to the conclusion that sex was better with women because of the rub and resistance of their pelvic bone. Sex via the rectum lacks the hard part above the vagina, and for Chester that put the thrill on a lower level. Homosexual sex, for me at around twenty-seven, was an adventure, for a while on a par with trying a new position with a woman.

I also tried petophilia with my dog Amy, but she howled and I stopped and we remained just good friends.

But for all this pseudo *psychopathia sexualis*, something happened that resembled a romantic fling in the realm that dares not speak its name.

227

L

A

R

R

Y

R

I

V

E

R

S

Sketch

Frank O'Hara and I met in 1950 at a party John Ashbery gave when Frank arrived in New York after graduating from Harvard. We shook hands and talked our heads off for two hours. Repairing to a quiet spot behind a window drape, we kissed. To know modern poets and poetry was number one on my list of "things to experience." Kenneth Koch, John Ashbery, and Jimmy Schuyler were the poets I admired most. And Frank was their favorite! And they said Frank and I would hit it off! I liked his Ivy League dirty white sneakers, he liked my hands full of paint. He was a charming madman, a whoosh of air sometimes warm and pleasant, sometimes so gusty you closed your eyes and brushed back the hair it disarranged. He was thin and about five seven. He walked on his toes, stretched his neck, and angled his head, all to add an inch or two to his height. I never walked the same after I met him. Through a moist pair of lips like Cupid's bow, he smoked and spoke with enthusiasm about the virtues of a thousand subjects. His days, no matter what he was up to, were divided almost equally between getting over what he drank the night before and drinking toward the same pleasant haze. When he was sober he was careful, objective, more a listener than a speaker. He always had something to add to anything I said. Anything. It was comforting being understood; until then I had the suspicion that I was a court primitive with privileges among the highly civilized.

Drunk, Frank could be an aggravating monster, sometimes to the point of my deciding, along with everyone else in the room,

never to speak to him again. At cocktails he was affectionate and bright, the Frank everyone loved. At ten, after a bottle or two of wine and a little food—he didn't eat much—his wit and information were unceasing. By midnight he was dancing and drinking, singing and drinking, and holding in thrall the group around him, beating everyone verbally to the draw. From then till one or two in the morning, he never stopped talking. After two a.m. there was nobody home. And there he began to find the world a pretty disgusting place, full of awful individuals—one night you, the next night another close buddy. He'd become more and more moralistic, implying that you were hypocritical, self-contradictory and evasive in facing any issue. Or if you made fun of someone in absentia, Frank came to his or her defense, protecting that night's martyr, like the nun he often called himself, from our unruly mob. By three we all sounded and looked smug to him, cocksure of our mates and our immortal youth. Most infuriating to him was our refusal to be charitable to our enemies—those who had become successful, or slightly successful. Through it all, no matter what the hour or his condition, there was no change in his conventional courtliness. He always reached the door first to hold it open for you. He might just have dropped a bomb on your head, but if you needed ice in your drink he'd run to the refrigerator and fetch it, then continue where he left off, gnawing at the little that was left of your ego.

The next morning he was on the phone; some control mechanism alerted him to the damage he'd caused the previous night. His recasting of insults as insights into your character became a performance you had to admire.

Visits

From the earliest moments of our friendship we were enthusiastic about each other's work. Frank O'Hara was a big influence on me, but I think I influenced him too; I was already a working artist in New York. This is not to exclude all sorts of sexual undercurrents. "What are you working on?" was interwoven with "What are you doing later on?" Between the end of his day at work and his evening plans, he often came by. First the ritual drink. He liked martinis (as some of you may remember) very dry, meaning lots of gin and a pass of the vermouth bottle over the glass. Then I would show him what I was working on.

Once I pulled out a painting, a horizontal rectangle with two life-sized nude females reclining on something that looked like sand and weeds, twisted in an expressionist embrace. "Why don't you call it *Les Amies?*" Frank said, making the connection with the Courbet painting at the Met of two women in bed. He thought turning down the volume on the name I'd given my painting, *Lesbians at Fire Island*, would help it to be judged as a painting. Nothing could have helped that painting to be judged as a painting.

Frank's remarks in my studio were usually complimentary. More than that, he substantiated the direction my work was taking: I was a natural colorist, and my work always made him think of this, that, or the other.

Painting has the advantage over writing, dance, theater, and music. Painting can be enjoyed or despised at a glance. So how long can you discuss any subject, especially behind three martinis? If any moment of our getting together began to resemble a seminar, we'd switch to social gossip, art gossip. Soon after, Frank would pull out a poem he'd written that day at lunch in his office. He wrote lots of poems over lunch, enough for Lawrence Ferlinghetti's City

Lights Books to publish a delightful volume called *Lunch Poems*.
Here is one of the more dramatic ones.

THE DAY LADY DIED

It is 12:20 in New York a Friday
three days after Bastille Day, yes
it is 1959 and I go get a shoeshine
because I will get off the 4:19 in Easthampton
at 7:15 and then go straight to dinner
and I don't know the people who will feed me

I walk up the muggy street beginning to sun
and have a hamburger and a malted and buy
an ugly NEW WORLD WRITING to see what the poets
in Ghana are doing these days
                              I go on to the bank
and Miss Stillwagon (first name Linda I once heard)
doesn't even look up my balance for once in her life
and in the GOLDEN GRIFFIN I get a little Verlaine
for Patsy with drawings by Bonnard although I do
think of Hesiod, trans. Richmond Lattimore or
Brendan Behan's new play or *Le Balcon* or *Les Nègres*
of Genet, but I don't, I stick with Verlaine
after practically going to sleep with quandariness

and for Mike I just stroll into the PARK LANE
Liquor Store and ask for a bottle of Strega and
then I go back where I came from to 6th Avenue
and the tobacconist in the Ziegfeld Theatre and
casually ask for a carton of Gauloises and a carton
of Picayunes, and a NEW YORK POST with her face on it

and I am sweating a lot by now and thinking of
leaning on the john door in the FIVE SPOT
while she whispered a song along the keyboard
to Mal Waldron and everyone and I stopped breathing

An affectionate grope at the door sent him optimistically on his toes off to dinner, to one, two, or three of the four hundred people who, like myself, considered him their best friend. He was a professional fan. By the early sixties he knew so much about what was going on in New York painting and sculpture and had written so much in little magazines that he went pretty quickly from a Christmas job selling postcards at the Museum of Modern Art to being one of its most outstanding curators. He had an informed brain to pick, and Alfred Barr, director of MOMA, wanted it so close that he wouldn't have to take his frail body downtown or anywhere else to find out what he thought he had to know.

Life and Letters

Frank's knowledge wasn't limited to the modern scene. Letters he wrote from the navy when he was seventeen contain opinions about every art of every age. It was no coincidence that at Harvard he became close to John Ashbery, a former quiz kid who at twelve toured the country on network radio as an eighteenth-century French painting expert.

From 1950 on, Frank and I wrote stacks of letters to each other. We wrote as if the committee that decides who goes down in history was looking over our shoulders at them. We kept every letter. When Frank died, his sister Maureen inherited the letters I wrote him. The ones to me from Frank I xeroxed and sent to Maureen in exchange for mine. I use these letters to show what was going on between us and around us.

I was living in Southampton and had just written Frank a letter that hurt his feelings; I had finally gotten around to telling him I was uncomfortable as the object of his affection. Pursuing the objects of *my* affection, females, was more usual, subsequently more comfortable. I felt his dependence on me was becoming a strain. I don't have my letter to present here, but I have his answer.

> Dear Larry Rivers,
> You are very sweet but very stupid. I'm not dependent on you. You are like a mouse blinking outside the maze not realizing he's out. On one point you are remarkably wrong and completely lacking in self-knowledge: you always feel that you never equal *anyone's* desire to see you, so that shit is hardly pertinent in this relationship. And exactly what means do you have of computing all these marvelously clear equivalences? Don't talk like someone in the Duchess de Langeois, we're not tied together while the ants gather. You can fondle or masturbate all you want and it won't break my heart. I'm not always going around kissing you, what right do you have to say these things when we hardly see each other? If you want to be pleasant, then we'll remain friends and allies, I don't have to go to bed with you to admire in you what I've always admired, don't get so fucking confused. If you feel the way you do in your letter

it's because of *you*, *I'm* not bothering you, and I'll certainly take steps to bother you even less in the future. Who asked you to "feel" anything? Don't be such a whiner. I "understand" you all right, even through your pomposity and affectionate anxieties; you are simply not being truthful when you attempt to reduce me in this way. If you were busier about other things than trying to imagine my feelings you might stop complicating one of the simplest and least troublesome little affairs you've ever had. Relax, and it will all have disappeared in a few weeks and then you'll be free and happy and all the things you've always had until you met me will come back to you with fat sissy yelps of joy.

Frank

Frank one night and, if I could manage it, a woman the next. I was so convinced of being heterosexual I could be homosexual. It will become clear, as you read, what pressure caused me to write him a letter to "end it all," which elicited the above response. I mostly felt happy seeing Frank. He was a good friend, he was kind to my family and took an interest in some of our problems, and he persistently remained an aesthetic ally. He wrote poems about me and my work, "Second Avenue," "On First Looking at Larry Rivers' *George Washington Crossing the Delaware*." In his articles on art he usually found some way to include my work. Eventually he wrote articles that featured only me and my work, without the slightest self-consciousness about giving a public forum to a close friend everyone knew was a close friend.

In 1957 Frank and I did a lithographic series together called "Stones," produced by Tanya Grosman's Universal Limited Art Editions. With his own hands, using a mirror to write backward, he

put his poetry on the litho stones in and around my images. There were also many literary collaborations between us, two of which were published, "How to Proceed in the Arts" and *Kenneth Koch: A Tragedy*.

Frank blandished me with social opportunities he knew I'd enjoy. Through him I met "Babi Yar" poet Yevtushenko. Swimming down Eighth Street one afternoon with Frank, I was introduced to good-looking, all-smiles Ned Rorem, the composer. (Good-looking? Ned was considered one of the beauties of New York and had the pick of all the lesser beauties!) I was also introduced to the ever-critical pipe-smoking lay analyst Paul Goodman, who told me I must be sick for refusing to go to bed with him.

"But Paul, you're married. You have a beautiful wife and child. What future would there be for me?"

And there was the evening Frank was invited to Virgil Thomson's Chelsea Hotel apartment and brought me along to meet the composer-critic-curmudgeon extraordinaire. A minute after we shook, Virgil told me he hoped I agreed with him about the impor-

Virgil T.

tance of the skylight in painting. In Paris in the twenties, Gertie—Stein, that is—took him to the studios of Matisse, Picasso, Bonnard, et al.; they all told him how important was the light of Paris, which could only be truly seen through the well-placed skylights of their ateliers.

"How's your skylight, Mr. Rivers?"

"I keep it covered."

Frank became a central switchboard. So many artists, writers, dancers, museum personnel, etc., were part of the swirl he lived in that I eventually got to know most of them. Some were interesting, others were a pain. I didn't have to like them to enjoy them.

Entrances and Exits

Sex with Frank—I'll spare you the details—was not very thrilling. "The man who lies flat on his stomach and allows anal entrance is definitely homosexual," says the Man in the Street. The Man in the Gutter, Larry Rivers, says, "Who giveth and who receiveth doesn't tell you too much." Gore Vidal, the Man on Mount Vesuvius, says, as I said, "There are only homosexual acts, not homosexuals."

Because Frank and John Myers found me sexually attractive, I concluded that I was some kind of physical catch. There were a few trios and foursomes that included men, but only sex with Frank, and earlier John, ever went past one night. If I jerked off with eyes closed, the image I conjured was always a woman. Eyes open, it was a woman in a photograph. Open or shut, it was never a man.

Except for one brief shining moment, I hardly ever made the first move toward a man, the lucky exception being a foggy, fat saxophonist who possessed a purple nose stacked on a pockmarked face. I wanted to shock him. On my knees with Fatty seated in a chair, I delivered a fifteen-minute blow job as the light went down to darkness in my Second Avenue studio. If you swallow sperm shot into your mouth, you earn the title Queen for a Day. As much as anything else, I wanted to show him that I was in another world now. Jazz and taking drugs to end up in comatose heaven was no longer my interest. Still, I can't unravel even today what that quarter of an hour was about.

Dear Frank,
You speak as if everything is my madness my stupidity my blindness etc. You are very nice. Also convincing. Almost. It is true as you have noted that I seem to want to end things—I don't know why.

I did know why, but what I wrote was more in tune with my cowardly character. I abhor the confrontation.

... I am also very worried about what is happening in my painting. Because I don't know if "Berdie Burger a Picture" is over I keep doing sculpture; although I enjoy it, it's become a way of escaping what is more important. A sentence: "Can two people who have prides as high as the Chinese wall who have dirtied the same sheets know happiness as friends?" It is rare. But we 'neath the philosopher's tree are always open for surprises and always full of hope. Maybe the silent slip-away approach employed by everyone we know including you and me in different lands and other seasons has features that are recommendable, but it is really silly for two old cheats and phonies like us to carry on so commonly. I really admire your mind, and many of your sentiments feel very breezy meaning lofty. If Courbet knew Byron would he throw away such joy and juice? No, Byron, I mean Rimbaud, destiny has assured us of our holding hands forever. Besides which at this moment in life I need money. And you promised that I would be dressed well for the races. Can you send five for the telephone and five more for a $65 debt covering gas elect phone doctors dentists lumber, just for good luck? If not I'm afraid we're through. Reread the money part, it is serious—forget about the rest. Would you like to visit the first week in August? I think that would be nice.

Larry Rivers

How was I supposed to say, in a few sentences, that the thrill was gone, that the closeness of our friendship and all he meant to me was not alleviating my discomfort at being involved with a man? How could I admit I was not very different from the Man in the Street? What brought the physical between us to a "civilized" conclusion were the women who slept with me, and their price, which was my (almost) undivided attention. What existed between Frank and me was never matched, and finally had to die. I gave Frank pleasure, I owed him nothing. Fidelity among men in my circle was a subject no one spent a minute thinking about. Because women gave me such sexual pleasure, I owed them something. I know that women enjoy sex as much as men, and according to Tiresias the Hermaphrodite, even more than men. But back in the fifties I was still carrying the baggage of my Bronx beginnings, repeating working-class catechisms.

"Sure you like sex with me, Larry. But what are your intentions?"

"To continue fucking you at the lowest price possible."

The lowest price I paid women was more than Frank asked of me.

Dear Larry,
I really feel relieved that we are going to see each other. When I have thought of you recently it's been with regret because we seemed an unusually lucky combination, and certain things are developing in our talents with more rapidity than we could have managed separately; but something did go wrong, not that it was a surprise and not that everything is irreparable. Perhaps this rest from seeing me will make us get on well—as a matter of fact we always do when we are together, and I would like to pose for that statue, since we began it we may as well have some seaside monument to our friendship if it does wane. Sometimes I feel as if we were both made of glass, but what the fuck, it's ridiculous for toughies like us to act like a pair of nuns counting each other's rosaries. People care very little about anything but the gratification of their own emotions. I am neither starved nor sated by you alone, and I'm sure it's the same with you, but we do interest each other in some way a larger portion of the time than anyone else does I guess. I know that I can be perfectly happy and interested without seeing you but for my part I don't feel like giving you up until we've finished KK [our collaboration, *Kenneth Koch: A Tragedy*] and it's in production. When you feel irritated with me you might think of the nice things about me such as my hatred for so many people and my prose and my leopard look, and I in turn will temper my temper by reflecting on your nervous stomach, your love of mankind and your sublime baritone. I'm not an infant in swaddling clothes after all and you're not the Blessed Virgin Mary.
                                                        Frank O'Hara

The menacing flare-ups threatening our friendship, sex or not, subsided. I invited Frank to my place in Southampton for weekends. Sometimes he came alone, sometimes with someone who wanted out of the city, someone I liked or wanted to get to know. Mostly our times were friendly and fun, lots of visits crisscrossing the Hamptons. There were occasions when I let him have my house for a few days.

When Frank visited me he had to contend with Joe and Steven trying out their energetic rituals, and Berdie floating gently through the rooms like a Chagall, tolerating everything, and the occasional visits of a wife still carrying a small torch.

Frank never dreamed of getting married, but he was an extraordinary family man. He was the oldest of three children, and he always felt it was natural to care for his brother and sister after their father died and their mother became incapacitated by sorrow and drink. Out of his meager paycheck and sporadic, scant royalties he always put aside a portion for the family, to help Phil and Maureen through school, to pick up his mother's medical tabs. Even as a wartime sailor, he wrote the most delightful letters to his parents, rife and juicy with critical comments about books he was reading, music he was hearing, wonderfully confidential, charmingly judgmental, and with a lack of condescension rare for a person of seventeen. It wasn't a big leap for him to become interested in my kids.

When Frank came back to the city we continued our letter writing; he was both Goncourt brothers, and I was Sainte-Beuve of the Bowery. Poets in general enjoy writing because they write so little, according to Virgil Thomson, who wondered, "What," after their half hour of pouring out their passion, "do they do with the rest of the day?" Well, Virgil, Frank talked a lot, saw a lot of people, drank a lot of whiskey, had a lot of romances, and did an amazing amount of writing, including stacks of letters to his myriad friends. He continued "honing his craft"—Frank, excuse this phrase I promised never to use! but the statute of limitations on all promises to friends runs out after twenty-five years. Frank's letters connected him to the great literary figures of the past. The trinity that Irish writers—the likes of Swift, Sheridan, G. B. Shaw, Joyce, O'Casey, and Beckett—were not ashamed of was Emotion, Invective, and Wit, right, Oscar?

If I made drawings to give myself the credentials of an artist of the past, Frank wrote letters to bolster his image as a writer, for himself as well as for those who received them. Let me not forget that it was also fun and natural for Frank, who felt compelled to put down on paper as much of his thoughts and experiences as he could cram into any one week. His letters are an amazing surge of single-space enthusiasm; like all his friends, I was flattered to receive them and careful to save them.

Dear Larry,
. . . I expected to see you before now, especially at Arnie's [Weinstein] cocktail Sat—it was quite WILD enough even for you, if you can picture such thrilling scenes as J. Button, Jimmy and me smoking grass in the john, while Joey

[Le Sueur, Frank's roommate] pounded the door shouting "Frank! let me in, I can smell what you're doing in there" or [trying to pull] Ann Truxell's skirt off while we rumbaed and she [fumbled trying] to unzip me or Ann's pearls falling all over the floor while she cried "Oh never mind, it happens at every party" or Jane [Freilicher] falling on top of me when she was saying good night or John Myers answering a severe critic of Adlai Stevenson's principles with "Well, Tom Hess is for him and all the artists are going to make posters, NOW COME ON!" or Kenneth going out at eleven to get another bottle of liquor. Well, you see what it was like. I had already gotten drunk at Ned Rorem's (where I had a nice ugly repartee with that professional pig Christopher Lazare). . . . How much I like your picture at the Whitney! . . . your Lavinia [from my *Titus Andronicus* work]. What a gift you have! And everyone else who amounts to anything here (the only people I speak to), says so too. I did think your painting, with Bill's (de K), Helen's [Frankenthaler] and oddly enough, Rosenquists'—and Oh yes natch, Jasper's, which I liked very much, were the best, if not the only, things in the show. The Newman I liked very much in his studio, but it was so badly lit that you couldn't tell the stripes from the non-existent frame, etc. The Rauschenberg was quite glaringly terrible. What hath Andy wrought? . . . I should confess that I'm not so hot on the Berdie two nudes [in the Whitney collection] (don't tell her), for reasons which I can tell you some time but which don't make much difference anyhow. . . .

Love, Frank

Joe Le Sueur, nephew of Lucille Le Sueur (otherwise known as Joan Crawford), lived with Frank to ease the rent crunch in their loft on Broadway and Tenth Street. Blond and tan, Joe was a gorgeous import from California. His family were teetotaling Salt Lake City Mormons living in L.A. His father told Joe off the record, "I was forced to give up booze by your mother and the church." Once a year, until he left his East Village walk-up to move to East Hampton, the Mormons sent envoys in black suits with matching Bibles to knock on Joe's door and urge him in soft voices to change his ways and come home and go to church.

My sons were close to Joe Le Sueur because they knew that Frank and Joe lived together, not that they quite knew what that meant. Joe complained about Frank's drinking, and Frank complained about Joe's flirting and everything else he did. Joe would

take Frank's abuse with a white smile. There was a dinner once when Frank cut him in two like live steam. Joe responded with joy and affection, "All that energy just for me!"

Paul Goodman advised Joe, as a friend, to admit to his Mormon parents that he was a homosexual. Joe wrote them a letter, but before mailing it he showed it to his analyst, who said, "Don't send it. They couldn't possibly handle it." But his father, on his death-bed, told Joe that he knew and that he admired him because he was devoting his life to joy.

As I said a chapter ago, I made the sets—with my own hands, without assistants—for Frank O'Hara's *Try! Try!*, produced in 1953 by John Myers and Herbert Machiz as a project for the Artists Theater. With its fancy ideology, the thrust of the Artists Theater was to distinguish itself from the aesthetics and interests of Broad-way. Frank's play ran for a week at the Theater de Lys, not long before another poetic play began a seven-year run there, Brecht's *Threepenny Opera*. Two decades later the street where the Theater de Lys stood became a "notorious" gay strip.

In 1951 I had begun doing sculpture and had learned how to make inner supports, called armatures, for each plaster or cement figure. A few years later I showed these sculptures, which wore the expressionless gloom of George Segal's work, at the Stable Gallery.

The Stable was a new gallery. One of the memorable works shown there was a Rauschenberg goat with a rubber tire around its middle. Anyway, the armatures I made for my figures consisted of iron pipes I cut, threaded, and joined, a technique I picked up helping my father in his plumbing business. Usually I wrapped the pipes in chicken wire to secure the plaster or cement. I always thought the pipe arrangements themselves were interesting as pieces of metal sculpture, and that gave me an idea for Frank's set. *Try! Try!* takes place in the apartment of some bohemians in Boston, Frank's hometown. I wanted it to have an arty look and thought an armature, now sculpture for me, would be perfect. My set was an empty stage except for a dilapidated wicker couch I found in a secondhand furniture shop, some floor pillows, and the six-foot-high former armature on which characters improvisationally hung coats, hats, socks, shirts, and pants. A giant pencil-and-charcoal drawing of some clumsy reclining nudes formed a wall behind the couch; later it was given to MOMA, where after a couple of decades it has yet to emerge from storage. *Try! Try!* was my first collaboration with Frank. There would be more. About a year later we collaborated on a piece of writing, "How To Proceed in the Arts," driven to it by articles on art, half of them incomprehensible, by name-dropping exhibitions, and of course by other artists and their statements about art receiving more attention than we could bear. Almost thirty-five years later I can still recognize which lines are mine and which are Frank's. I could point them out, but I am inhibited by the collaborator's code, which frowns upon naming lines and goes back to the *Iliad*. Here are some excerpts from our "detailed study of the creative act."

1. Empty yourself of everything.
2. Think of faraway things.
3. It is 12:00. Pick up the adult and throw it out of bed. Work should be done at your leisure, you know, only when there is nothing else to do. If anyone is in bed with you, they should be told to leave. You cannot work with someone there.
4. If you're the type of person who thinks in words— paint!
5. Think of a big color—who cares if people call you Rothko. Release your childhood. Release it—
6. Do you hear them say painting is action? We say painting is the timid appraisal of yourself by lions.
7. They say your walls should look no different than your work, but that is only a feeble prediction of your future. . . .
8. They say painting is action. We say, remember your enemies and nurse the smallest insult. Introduce yourself as Delacroix. When you leave, give them your wet crayons. Be ready to admit that jealousy moves you more than art. They say action is painting. Well, it isn't, and we all know abstract expressionism has moved to the suburbs.
9. If you are interested in schools, choose a school of painting that is interested in you. . . .
13. Youth wants to burn the museums. We are in them —now what? Better destroy the odors of the zoo. How can we paint the elephants and the hippopotamuses? How are we to fill the large empty canvas at the end of the large empty loft? You do have a loft, don't you, man? . . .
15. In attempting a black painting, know that truth is beauty, but shit is shit.
16. In attempting a figure painting, consider that no amount of distortion will make a painting seem more relaxed. Others must be convinced before we even recognize

ourselves. At the beginning, identity is a dream. At the end, it is a nightmare.

17. Don't be nervous. All we painters hate women; unless we hate men.

18. Hate animals and birds. Painting is through with them. . . .

Besides thinking about modern painting and painters, Frank enjoyed and raved about dance and music. He was a pianist long before he began writing poetry. He often made reference, as he was writing me, to a symphony or opera he heard on the radio.

> I was listening to a Chopin Nocturne when I woke up and suddenly felt so unalterably great just by the contact with it that I swear that I must have thought I was Homer at the edge of the sea, and suddenly thought of how words in one's head boom and crash like the sea and do, corny as it sounds, keep ebbing before one "gets" them. The most one can seize is merely a splinter of some magnificent edifice one had just apprehended like that famous submerged cathedral. Someone who didn't like me could say, "Sure all you have to do is show him Larry Rivers or the sea and out comes a poem."

As for dance, to Frank it meant the genius of Balanchine's New York City Ballet and specific dancers in the company he never stopped talking about. Merce Cunningham's group ran a close second. I was not the raver Frank was; nonetheless I considered ballet the most beautiful of the arts.

Frank and I showed up at dance concerts, sometimes two or three times a week, sometimes for just one number we couldn't resist seeing again. The boyfriend of Aaron Copland was a quasi-commercial success as an official of the ballet company. We managed to cultivate his friendship. (Use a sentence with the words "commercial," "official," and "cultivate." Give up? "Come, Moishel, catch a fishel, it's too cul ta vait.") We'd arrive after the crowd at City Center had cleared out of the lobby into the exotic theater, originally built by the Shriners as Mecca Temple. Our friend the cultivated official let us in free.

Opening night at the ballet attracted a mob filled with a mob of my friends and acquaintances. Coming down the steps of the grand staircase during an intermission, driven wild by Frank and me looking happy, John Myers shouted, palms cupping his mouth, "Here

L

come the divine Verlaine and Rimbaud with their lips full of blood and semen"—at least that's how Frank and I remembered it in one of our prints in the collaborative "Stones" litho series.

A

R

R

Y

R

One of the twelve "Stones"

I

     Here is part of a letter from Frank originally written as prose made to read like one of his odes.

    The ballet opening last night
      was sublime I did think of you

V

especially in Scotch Symphony, the slow movement
    of which was drenched
      in tears for this reviewer.
Seldom has the essence of movement been more clearly
    delineated

E

      than in Miss Tallchief's arabesque
        seven inches
          from the apron of the stage,
her breath hung in the conductor's baton

R

      her tibia grandiosely extended and
so on. Really

S

she was perfection and more
            itself
and in the fast concluding movement she seemed
to be conducting the orchestra
            too
so precise were her entries and stops in the various
    nifty positions.
        She has a way of coming
            to a halt
after some violent business
        which is so startlingly abrupt
            and immobile
                that the set
seems to be shivering by comparison.

L

A

R

R

Y

R

I

V

E

R

S

Gray Days

Meanwhile, back in 1952, I sustained a broken heart when Jane Freilicher, the woman I didn't know I was in love with until she left me, left me—for a man who seemed an improvement over me. I underwent months of cardiac rehabilitation casually showing up almost everywhere she showed up.

I liked Jane before I entertained any ideas of getting any closer than liking implies. We went to the Hofmann school at the same time. Nestled calmly against my physical attraction for her was my attraction to her generosity about people, which wove brilliantly with her humorous criticism of them. Jane was now about twenty-four years old, and divorced from Jack, whose Freilicher changed for good her Niederhoffer. She was only seventeen when they married, and they had been sliding apart for a few years. She was no longer just that bright neighborhood girl.

This was the same Jane Freilicher I still remembered on the beach in Maine in 1945. Her enthusiasm for practicing art with me then brought to an end my afternoons of poker and pot with members of the Johnny Morris band and began the activity and identity that involved me for the rest of my life. She had more integrity than anyone I have ever known, and still does.

I'm not sure when or after what series of events we got together. But as time passed, like Tess, Jane claimed before, during, and after going off with someone else that I didn't behave at all like a man passionately in love. I believed her version, but it didn't help the distress. I don't know why I chose this moment to act so hurt and bothered by a rejection. I'm sure I had been told to get lost before. Did her goodbye corroborate the low opinion I had of my body and its ability to give slow pleasure to others? Was it all my posturing about the depth of my involvement in art and my total self-concern? Was it because she was a woman with a mind plus a body?

No, son. She wanted to marry someone whose behavior she could predict. I didn't know it then, but she did me a favor. I didn't have to think about her art, which was already beginning to challenge me.

In the beginning she made paintings looking at what was in her studio. Later she painted looking out her window. It took years of sticking to her quiet guns to overcome the power of the avant-garde. The power of her own aesthetic created a place for her art outside the narrow judgment of the day. For me she personifies Ezra Pound's dictum "Art is character."

Cardiac rehabilitation included parties, gallery openings, evenings at the ballet, where she'd see me acting as if I hated her or

L

A

R

R

Y

R

I

V

E

R

S

Jane Freilicher and her Still Life with Calendulas

L
A
R
R
Y

R
I
V
E
R
S

loved her, depending on my latest drug or drink or session with Dr. Edith Nachmanson or discussion with Frank O'Hara and other psychological experts in the art of surviving the cold sentence "Get lost." Actually, when we did meet, she tried to calm me down—a kindness sharper than her disaffection.

I kept trying to sleep with other women, as if they would dilute my sense of loss. I went more often to the Bronx, spending time with Steve, Joe, and Berdie. Occasionally I saw Augusta there, my estranged wife, almost always getting ready to meet her boyfriend, Aesop. I became more serious about acquiring a teaching degree at NYU. I took a job selling tickets to special lectures at the New School, which I attended for free, tried sculpture, and scheduled as many jam sessions as I could.

On one of those nights of jazz and drugs and drinking stirred into my vat of self-pity, two musicians and I rolled onto a mattress on my studio floor with Jenny Schecter, an enthusiastic exponent of the no-holds, no-holes barred school of humiliation. Consciously neither of these two hale fellows had the remotest interest in a homosexual act; so six arms, three tongues, and three cocks had to scramble for two breasts, one vagina, and one rectum. Poor Jenny. Poor me! There were no parts of the body left for my use. I guess I could have kissed her on the lips, but I forgot. I got off the mattress, deferring to the pleasure of my guests, found a drawing pad and began to draw.

There are art teachers who still believe that quick unreworked sketching is a tool for learning to draw—not to be confused with the automatic drawing of the surrealists, plumbers of the unconscious, who were not concerned with coordinating the eye with the hand. That night's rare opportunity to record changes in the sexual positions of the two men and one woman was wasted on an artist like me in the tradition of Cézanne looking at Mont Ste.-Victoire: no matter how much time went by, when Cézanne returned, backpack and all, the mountain he was painting had not moved. For four in the morning, the mattress manipulations on my studio floor were nothing close to immobile. Trying to be a camera with pencil and paper was a childish conceit. What my drawing pad showed was a flurry of lines hardly connected to the innocent orgy before me. This sexual still life was the last quick "sketch" I ever tried to make.

The next morning I was back on Rejection Street searching in Distraction Alley, where I met Jean Garrigue.

248

Jean was a published, established, highly respected poet anthologized by Theodore Roethke in *New American Writing*. Although her poetry seemed dense, there were lofty overtones. She was a tender person about ten years older than I, maybe more. John Ashbery, my part-time adviser, had read her work and thought having an affair with her was worth a serious try. Jean and I began to see each other pretty steadily, expanding each other's horizons socially as well as sexually. Through Jean I met older literary mavericks of the left who showed no interest in us Off-Bohemia newcomers. They were writers with political axes to grind and hornrim glasses and meerschaum pipes and corduroy jackets with suede elbows, and memories of the Spanish Civil War. They spoke familiarly and with authority about things I had vaguely heard about that interested me—like the fact that Joseph Stalin was five foot three. Jean was a close friend of the poet Conrad Aiken and introduced me to his "Senlin," a dead ringer for "Prufrock" written a few years before Eliot's poem. And she knew Auden and Roethke, and a young writer named Hilton Kramer, who still writes respectfully of those people and that time. Central to that set was Jean Garrigue.

I was never able to figure out why she let me fuck her. It was always late at night after the San Remo or the Cedar Tavern or Louis' held no hope. I would wake her with a romantic pebble thrown against her window on Cornelia Street, and she'd toss me down the keys. And she had to get up in the morning and go to work.

Jean took me to Bucks County, Pennsylvania, to meet the novelist Josephine Herbst, her lover. Bucks County was a popular artists' and intellectuals' summer version of the Village. Until the sixties it gave the Hamptons some competition, but it lacked ocean, and fashion.

I spent my visit on Josephine's farm, inside the farmhouse with no plumbing, barely looking out the window. I hated landscapes. I did not and do not worship the sun. Toward the end of the stay I spent a few hours in the backyard, where I painted a picture of the old farmhouse and the garden and the girls. Josie's Caribbean blue eyes were full of understanding about Jean and me and Cornelia Street. Notwithstanding her understanding, I slept alone in the "spare" room. Josie had one of the more open minds of the day (and was in fact dogged for years by witch-hunters). She let me chop wood and fix the barn. Then they fed me, garden stuff. Both Josie and Jean were in the avant-garde of healthy eating back then, thirty-five years ago.

Did I like Jean because she was an established poet or because she was an intellectual lesbian who selected me for an encounter? Before I could find out, she got pregnant. We went to Rutherford, New Jersey, to the office of Dr. Williams, a small-town pediatrician who often helped people in the arts out of medical difficulty. That is, Dr. William Carlos Williams. He performed Jean's abortion, free of charge, simply because she was a friend and a fellow poet.

Jean didn't exactly fit my young man's image of a sexy woman. She didn't complain about her mother, she didn't have a roommate, she knew what she wanted to do and was doing it, and her father never wanted to fuck her. The subject of her former sweethearts did not come up. This was different. Most young women at my prodding not only told me of their former lovers but how their former lovers loved them. These images I conjured, about who and what who did, were the song and dance of my sex life. Who would have imagined that there could be passion without confession? She was a kind, smart woman, easy to talk to, and had a lot to say. I loved her medium-sized breasts on a ribbed chest. She had some

gray hairs and the faint beginnings of crow's feet; being aware of
our age difference didn't lessen my physical feelings for her, which
were intensified by the tight skirt and high heels she wore on occasion. She had a voice with certain breaks in it, kind of tragic, that
drew me to its sadness. Her eyes were lightly beaded at all times,
though she wasn't crying. Her tongue came out of her mouth very
often to moisten her lips. We were so different that we got along
nicely. Maybe she identified with the sadness in me. We never
spoke about it.

Before I could find out, we went our separate ways. She died in
1972. Many people felt the deep loss of a friend and a woman of
importance. I didn't know. I just liked her and the sex we had for a
restful while. Here are a few lines from her poem "A Demon Came
to Me."

> A demon came to me in love's disguise,
> One of the lower order of hell's guard,
> The devil's angel, as it once was coined,
> Cool as marble, with a heart like iron. . . .

Family

After I was apprised of Jane's preference for an Other, I moved
Berdie, Steven, and Joseph out of the Bronx to a five-room apartment at 77 St. Mark's Place (below lovable old Dr. Schwartz, the
abortionist, whose notoriety brought many a young woman from
Pennsylvania, New Jersey, and New York mistakenly knocking on
our door). It was bright, with high ceilings and a high rent. Arnold
Weinstein, studying on the GI Bill, shared the place with me and
the family. He spent long hours learning two useless languages and
working for the Phi Beta Kappa key he has never worn. He usually
did this seated on the floor with his back against the wall. Considering the audio level of our abode, he must have been wearing ear
plugs all day long. I appreciated his rent money and his presence;
since he had a fuse as short as mine, he could squelch some grave
flare-ups, and when necessary could make a phone call, which the
boys and Berdie hadn't learned to do. Arnold has been a subtenant
of mine intermittently over the last forty years, and now, even as we
write, is living in a fixed-up barn on my kibbutz in Southampton.

When I left Steven and Joe in the Bronx with Augusta and
Berdie in 1947 to become a serious artist, out on my own, I knew I
was increasing their chances of having a lot of bad days. Under the

Arnold poses for Jane.

siege of my own unhappiness, and not only because of Jane, I decided to have one less thing to feel bad about. Before moving I discussed the plan with Berdie: all of us living together—without Augusta. Berdie accepted, happy at fifty-nine years old to spend the time left for her a little more peacefully, a little more comfortably, and a little more amusingly. She agreed that it would be a terrific thing for the boys to have me around. At least part of the time. For Augusta this rejection was mitigated by the family-free use of the Crescent Avenue apartment for her and her lover—or that's what I thought. Augusta didn't say anything.

My father moved my Bronx contingent with his truck, his back, and his helper Big John. They brought a great load of stuff from the Crescent Avenue apartment. That building had an elevator, 77 St. Mark's didn't. There Arnold and I lent four more hands. My father's experience in trucking was limited to the ladies' garment industry. Tables, chairs, cabinets, dressers, beds, couch, and piano were another matter. The gigantic refrigerator was the last item out of the truck and went smoothly up the twelve steps of the brownstone and through the outside double door. Between that door and the hall was a single door. The fridge wouldn't go in, but after we worked on it for five minutes it also wouldn't go out. I remember my father's desolate "Oy, Oyving, have we got a wedge!," practically apologetic. Other tenants couldn't get in or out either. We removed some door trim and lugged the fridge up to the apartment door, where we did the same. After a full day's moving he had a Dr. Brown's Celery Tonic, went to the toilet, came out, walked past us out of the apartment, came back a minute later with an enormous red wrench, and began fixing the toilet.

That was my father.

He was my mother's cousin. Although they came from unpronounceable Russian towns only fourteen miles apart, he from Knehinia-Gebhernya, she from Drushkapolia, they never saw each other until they were formally introduced "over here" with a union in mind. He was a plumber. When the building industry failed in 1931, in-laws set him up in the trucking business in the garment center. For twenty-five years this reluctant trucker gave his back every day, but he wasn't tough or bright enough to extract from the business anything more than a meager existence. Five years after he moved us to St. Mark's Place he threw in the sponge and sold his trucking business for $5,000. He dusted off his wrenches and torch, and minus the worries of a small businessman, also minus a head of hair, he returned to his first love.

He played a bad fiddle. Starting on the other side of the Atlantic, near the fountain in Knehinia-Gebhernya, then on this side, at weddings and bar mitzvahs, he played polkas, mazurkas, horas, and kozatskis. His American repertoire consisted of "Bei Mir Bist Du Schoen," before the Andrews Sisters recorded it. He conventionalized what drinking he did into three categories: appetizers, bracers, and toasts. Only five foot seven and a half, he had a strong physique; off the beaches of Glen Island, where we picnicked, he could swim a good distance with my sister and me hanging on to his back.

Six days a week of plumbing grew terrific muscles. The coordination of these muscles was put to use early one Sunday morning when I was five or six years old. Finding a pack of Camels on the kitchen table, I went back to my bed in the dining room and began smoking. Suddenly a little flame danced on the mattress. I rushed to the dark kitchen, pushed a chair over to the sink, and filled a white pan large enough to boil two eggs. When I got back, spilling part of the extinguisher on the way, the flame was fiercer. I threw the few drops left in the pan into the fire and yelled to my father, "The bed is burning." In his underwear, letting out a loud "Oy!," he folded the burning mattress in half as if it were a newspaper, ran into the bathroom, flung it onto the tub, and turned on the tap.

I have no memory of his doing or saying anything afterward. He was capable of giving me a whack if I took the sugar cube or egg he looked forward to. For especially serious situations he displayed a remarkable restraint. At about nine years old, I offered my sister Goldie, seven, a dime if she'd let me put my cock in her. She giggled and refused. Next day the house became very quiet. My father asked me into the bathroom. The door closed. Those muscles suddenly looked awful. He placed me square on the bowl, trying to hold back his temper, his face ashen. He looked at me for a full minute without speaking. Then he pointed a finger. In a lower than normal tone he said, "Don't ever do that again." I didn't deny anything or move. He opened the door and let me out. In the face of firebuggery and attempted sister buggery his behavior for the time was in the avant-garde of permissiveness.

Two months before World War I my father, Shiah, arrived in New York Harbor with his mother, Miriam. Shiah soon became Sam. As the war went on, Sam went to England to enlist in the

British army's Jewish Legion and fight the Huns. Within a year Miriam was calling herself Mary. "Jesus Christ's mother!" incanted the family. During the 1930s she hawked towels and sheets and housedresses. Door to door through Westchester County in restricted towns like Scarsdale, Larchmont, Tarrytown, Mary went with her dark healthy hair. Her face in rare moments of repose was passable, which meant "not too Jewish-looking." Mary's nose was straight. (The nose, after all, isn't just a Jewish preoccupation. Gogol and Rostand took quite an interest.) Her lips, like mine, were a little too thin. Eyes, we know, are either bright or clear or dull. To look into hers was like looking into the eyes of a dog; they barked back if you wanted obedience. From my mother's point of view, Mary was a shrewish wife, a bad mother, and an inefficient housekeeper who sang and minced around in her fifties, showing no respect for herself.

One summer she took as job as a cook in a small hotel in the Catskills. Her red-haired daughter Ruth, called Rootie, firstborn this side of the Atlantic, twenty-one years old, had a gorgeous face and body and no patience with my preteen goofy flirtations. Lovely Rootie was a diabetic. She had to get up every morning to pee into a jar, bring it to a boil and judge the sugar content by the color, then give herself a shot of insulin. Mary felt that her lack of talent as a mother was responsible. So this scorching August in 1936 as Mary overfed the patrons of Rosen's Catskill Mountain Lodge in Kiamesha Lake, New York, she got a call from the city that Rootie was in the hospital. Mary wanted to leave the next day, but Mr. Rosen had no time to get a substitute cook. Wednesday she took the afternoon train to New York and the subway up to Fordham hospital in time to arrange Rootie's burial.

Mary herself died fifteen years later, in 1951. There was plainly no money, nor caring. A few months before, I had come back from Paris, where for almost a year I had been asking myself, "What is Art? What is Life? Twenty-five years old and what have I accomplished?" My admiration for the Old Masters was growing, as was my envy. It all took six giant steps forward when in the Louvre in the flesh I saw Courbet's gigantic *Burial at Ornans*. The painting was as serious about the act of painting as it was about the subject. By the time Mary died our relationship had dwindled to seeing each other at events like this one; as I got into one of the cars in the funeral cortege, I decided to keep an eye artwise on the proceedings. Mary sunk in her simple box sent pleasurable bubbles up my back. Here was an opportunity to relate to "serious" painting, like Courbet's, and to the drama of his life. Quel balls! From this grandiose decision came ten drawings and a six-by-nine-foot enamel flurry called *The Burial*, the first painting I did after my father moved us to St. Mark's Place, sold to Gloria Vanderbilt for $750.

My father's father was Moishe, which is Moses, a heavy name for a heavy cat. From an old photo I looked at recently it is obvious that what passed for wisdom was profound self-pity. In Europe he was a scholar of the scriptures; in the tradition of the yeshiva bucher he was supported, fed, clothed, cleaned up after, even after he married Miriam. When they got to New York and he sat down at his books ready to continue being supported by his wife, Miriam-Mary said, "This is America, Moishe. Here there are no yeshiva buchers. Go out and get a job." In Europe he was a scholar, here he sold brown paper bags. Still, you could find him every Saturday hanging out at the Arthur Avenue synagogue, where because of his knowledge and fabulous piety he was given the distinction of calling congregation members up to the podium, featuring four or five scrubby "elders" in prayer shawls gathered round a load of enormous dog-eared books reading incomprehensible Hebrew incomprehensibly. Moishe would leap into action and lead them to the Big Book, pointing out the passage to be read. But first that portion had to be kissed by touching the page with the shawl, then bringing the shawl to the lips. The more passionate members put their lips directly to the page, giving it something between a kiss and a good suck. This proved the depth of their feelings and made holy nonsense of the germ theory. Grandpa Moses died in 1931 and was buried after lying in our living room for twenty-four hours across three blocks of ice; he chose the hottest day in August for his

demise. A bulb fuzzed away all night about his body to keep us from bumping into him. He died as he had wished to live, with people making themselves uncomfortable for him.

On the same boat as my father and his mother and father came his brother, Yussel, six years younger. Shloyma, another brother, a hunchback, was left in the sunny Ukraine to bring luck to Mary's mother, a woman called Entza Shtuff. Lucky Shloyma died. Entza then sailed to New York. Entza became my greatest protector. The only thing she asked from her God was that she live until I was thirteen and "ceremonialized into the race." My sister and I played lots of unpleasant tricks on this bony, saggy-skinned woman, whose eyes were so deep-set in her yellow face that she seemed already dead. As she lay sinking in the vast ward of the Jewish old folks' home, she promised to spend eternity bargaining for me. The Yiddish word for "grave" being *keyver* (pronounced "*kay*-vuh"), I pictured her kneeling in a cave halfway up a billiard-green hill begging for benefits on my behalf.

Yussel was smaller than his brother Sam. Except for Mary's, all the Grossberg noses broke for the mouth about an inch and a quarter of the way down, but Yussel's nose broke at the sharpest angle, probably from a punch he got sparring with anyone who came within five feet. It was hard to spend an hour in his presence without hearing "Stop butting in" or "None of your fucking business." No one was supposed to tell Yussel what to do. Except my father, whom he worked for. Sam put twenty dollars between Yussel and starvation every week. Arguments and accusations ensued, undressing old wounds that sent Joe's voice to the border of tears. He kept quitting. Sam would worry about his younger brother and relent. At S.B.S. Trucking, Joe's presence was a life sentence for Sam.

One morning in the spring of 1968 I had an appointment with the Winston and Muss Investment Company on Fifth Avenue and Forty-ninth Street. I was meeting Lenny Holzer, the chairman of the board, about a commission for the Smith Haven Mall that was to be built in Smithtown. I was commissioned to make a large architectural construction and to choose works of other artists for the mall. I selected pieces by Jack Youngerman, Jim Dine, Bill Jennings, and others I can't remember except for the thirty-foot-high mobile by Alexander Calder. Mine was a multimedia construction called *Forty Feet of Fashion*.

I left the office excited by the prospect of keeping busy at what I enjoyed doing. Walking through the street with a happy head, I came upon a crowd of people looking down at something on the sidewalk. I stopped. It seemed too much to elbow my way through the crowd. I continued to the subway.

That afternoon in my studio my sister called and told me my father had died. His body was still at St. Clare's Hospital. I called and asked for details. "We picked him up at Fifth Avenue and Forty-ninth Street. He arrived DOA. Probable heart attack."

For years I carried around a feeling that my mother killed my father by urging him to work all the time. At the end of his life he was nothing more than an errand boy, delivering packages for B'nai Brith and a pearl-bead house in the diamond district.

My sister: "In our family there was no shame to do something for money."

Disenchanted Evening

The yearning for Jane Freilicher didn't stop. We had so many friends in common it was hard not to run into her. I rarely spoke to her in public, but I couldn't resist an occasional burning glance across a crowded loft. The electric jealousy! the strain of eavesdropping! the queries ineptly masked! Then came the blood-beating processional, leaving with the Other—to whose apartment? Before I was absolutely sure she had an Other I used to stand in a dark doorway across the street from her apartment house waiting for the lights to go on, then go off again. What more did I think I'd find out? About myself, that is. It was unoriginal exaggerated humiliation, to prove I was a sensitive soul, a sneak, a spy, and all the other attributes necessary to great art.

Spying of this sort is nothing to be ashamed of. It's not immoral. It has been given bad press. Spying is the last of the no-lose systems: whatever you discover, you come out ahead. If you learn she is sleeping with someone, at least you have the satisfaction of knowing you were right. If you find out you were wrong, well, she still loves you. I was right. Miserably right.

At my post one night, in the dark doorway, waiting for them to go into her house, I saw them coming out, cruelly intimate, huddled together against the November wind and making that heartbreaking turn around the corner, out of my sight.

I stood there for two blank minutes in the cold. I started walking. As I passed my ground-floor apartment on St. Mark's Place, I slowed down. They still had the lights on, Joe and Steven quietly wrestling on the floor, Arnold at a table, smoking a thin cigar, translating a Greek poem, Berdie with a can of soup in one hand and a can opener in the outstretched other. The window framed the scene. I stopped. They were figures in a Dutch painting of family life by Jan Steen in collaboration with Balthus. It meant nothing.

I went to my studio, to be alone, to contemplate the last lousy moments of love. I was so befuddled, so beyond thinking of any way to help myself, that I fell asleep with my clothes on. An hour or two later I woke in the dark. A window had blown open. I watched the dawn come up gray and stay gray for three whole days.

Gem

On the third of those gray days, going through with a previously made plan, I went up to the Metropolitan Museum to make a drawing based on a Titian hanging in the collection. I already had permission to do this. I took along a pad, my Mongol #1 pencils, and a single-edge Gem razor blade for sharpening. With great determination and no excuse I decided to go crosstown east to Jane's place first, not exactly the most direct route uptown to the museum, but a quick way to muck around in my misery. In her coldwater flat I found her taking a break from painting a portrait of Frank O'Hara. They were sipping and smoking. Frank was dishing a lot of Johns: John Ashbery, John Myers, John Button, John Honsbeen (out of Hollywood's *Lives of a Bengal Lancer* to the directorship of Peggy Guggenheim's museum in Venice), and Jasper Johns. Jane found everything Frank said very funny and was laughing. She had a lovable way of working her laughter up to a pitch that made her gasp and shake her wrists near her shoulders, but a bouillabaisse of French phrases and her brimming delight and a very good start on the portrait of Frank was not what I had in mind when I decided to visit her.

What did I have in mind?

Well, I was going to tell her I was doing okay, my family was fine, I was managing—as if it would please her to hear that leaving me was not the crime I wanted her to think it was—and then I'd whip out the poem I'd written about her and burst into tears on those beautiful shoulders and she would stroke my hair and tell me she still loved me. Even though the above didn't happen, my unusual silence made it look as if it was about to happen, and they talked louder and laughed louder.

Uncomfortable with making them nervous, I took my pad, pencils, and blade, and went off whistling in a not too hidden huff. I worked until the museum closed and pretty much finished the drawing.

I went back to my studio too distracted to lock the door. I looked at the dusk through the long windows. I started to cry, real tears, I put my forehead against the window and sobbed. I wasn't even thinking about Jane. There was nothing I wanted to do, nowhere I wanted to go, no one I wanted to see. Putting my hands up to wipe my eyes and cheeks, I felt the roughness of my skin. At the mirror in the bathroom I looked into my eyes. A shave was not going to improve anything. I made my way to my bed on the floor and sat down. There, as if for the first time, I saw the drawing paraphernalia, the pad, the pencil, and the single-edge razor blade I had used all afternoon. I reached for the blade. The blood at my temples began to throb. Very lightly I took a swipe at the left inner wrist where the veins are close to the skin. A little blood flowed.

Within a few seconds I had made about twenty slits. I stopped. Out loud I said, "What am I doing?"

There was no answer. I shifted the blade to my left hand and began shallow slashes on the right wrist. For symmetry? My left hand, normally shaky, was now trembling and made deeper cuts than I expected. I watched the blood come up like the sea through sand, slowly. I hadn't hit an artery. I began to slash more rapidly. I looked at the bed sheet. What a moment ago was mainly white with a few bloody spots was now a crimson expanse. I was finally frightened. In the same kind of casual slow motion, the way I had done most things that day, I reached for the phone to call Frank O'Hara.

He was home after posing for his portrait at Jane's. Twenty minutes later Frank rushed through my open door, took one look at me and the sheets, and said, "How are you feeling?"

"I think I'm all right."

"You don't feel dizzy?"

"No, I don't feel dizzy."

He ran into the kitchen for two towels and made tourniquets for my wrists. "Let's get up to Beth Israel. Now."

We took a taxi to the emergency ward, about nine blocks north of my studio.

It is possible, as many of my friends were convinced, that this halfhearted attempt at self-damage on a conscious level was only another of my many attention-getting tricks, maybe a little more melodramatic. Was it just another form of my flirting with death, like taking heroin directly into the vein with a chance of an overdose or an air bubble reaching the brain? But taking a chance with a dangerous drug is usually followed by a peaceful, numbing bliss. Or was it like the excitement I experienced darting between moving automobiles and trucks while motorcycling in the city? One mistake on a motorcycle is about all you're allowed, but the ride is full of spinal exhilaration. Perhaps I thought a spurt of blood, like a sneeze or an orgasm, would be followed by sweet repose.

I don't think I planned on dying when I reached for the razor blade. The initial slashes were only about a half inch long and just below the surface of the skin—less dangerous than a blood-brother initiation. But when I hit the veins what I was doing could have turned melodrama into real live death.

There was, and still is, a psychoanalytic notion that suicide is an unconscious attempt to punish those whose behavior the victims

261

blame for their suicide. So I was punishing Jane. Being aware of my neurotic treatment of Jane did not assuage my misery. Recently she reminded me of the misery I was inflicting on her at the time, including telling *her* to get lost. Her move on the Other must have been somewhat influenced by my being a lovable pain in the ass who had lost his lovability. Maybe that's megalomania, that the only reason Jane could want an Other was because of her difficulties with me. Why couldn't I accept the fact that Jane simply wanted Joe Hazan because he was terrific and she loved him?

After I calmed down, I began to consult Freud (required reading) on jealousy, infantile voyeurism, castration, hoping to find out what the hell motivated this self-damage. What the hell made me think Sigmund would be helpful? I was going to find out. I immediately increased my one day a week with Edith Nachmanson, a Freudian, to three or four days a week. I don't know where I got the money, but going to a psychoanalyst was the only hope I had of changing my thinking and shielding myself from future pain.

Aha!

Dr. Arnold Cooper, head of psychiatric divisions at important hospitals, is a friend I met in the late forties through Pat Hoey of chapter 10, whom he married in 1951. My second sale, a painting à la Bonnard's *Interior, Woman at a Table*, was barter for Arnie's '38 Chevy coupe, book value fifty dollars, at a time when he was earning twenty dollars a month as an intern at Bellevue. By the time Pat and Arnie separated in the sixties, their love for the painting, and its worth, inspired a novel settlement. Arnie kept the painting for ten years. Then Pat had it for the next ten. After they outlived their contractual arrangement, which covered only twenty years, Arnie bequeathed her the painting.

A calm man with a calm voice, years ago he arranged for Steven, my deranged but normal in every other way eighteen-year-old son, to be admitted to Columbia Presbyterian for a common middle-class problem, drug-induced psychosis. Last year Arnie and I talked of psychoanalysis, Freud, and neuroses.

AC: All through the late forties and fifties psychoanalysis was the dominant theme of New York intellectual society, probably throughout most of the Western world. One of the ways to think about psychoanalysis is that there is no reality except the reality each of us perceives. Psycho-analysis was a kind of deconstructionist view. It was terribly appealing, postwar, for people who had lost values. Psycho-analysis focused on one's own perceptions; it was authori-tarian. (Later it developed its own authoritarianism.) It was a sophisticated version of what people have always tried doing, to understand each other psychologically. Now you had an authority and a method for understanding people and yourself.

LR: Not only a new way to understand human experience but also a new way to putting people down.

AC: Obviously you can use this method in very aggressive ways.

LR: Psychoanalysis seemed to give such importance to sex in a person's life that it immediately had terrific interest for young people. Do you agree that psychoanalysis got a cer-tain kind of play because of the popularity of sex?

AC: Right. Psychoanalysts had a way of alluding to sex; everything was in one way or another sexual, but it wasn't exactly so permissive. It was a way of looking at and under-standing everything that went on, but it didn't necessarily invite it. And then there were subsets, offshoots of Freud like the Reichians, who if not screwing patients were cer-tainly putting their hands on them. The whole notion was: the better the orgasm the healthier you are. Everything is then improved through the quality of the orgasm. Which is not a Freudian idea. The subsets made sex the world.

LR: Since Freud brought to public awareness the problems that follow repressed sexuality, the Reichians dedicated themselves to unrepressing sex—let it happen at any given moment, never refuse it. In some circles if you refused sex you were considered sick.

AC: This was a terrific misreading of Freud. It was not what Freud had in mind at all.

LR: Dr. Cooper, the word neurotic was used so often and in so many different ways back there in the late forties and early fifties that at some point each and every dear bohemian friend of mine felt that he or she was neurotic, i.e., a mess. The dictionary defines neurotic as "an undue adherence to unrealistic ideas." How do you, as a top shrink, define neurotic?

AC: For practical purposes analysts define as neurotic life patterns, ways of relating to people, ways of seeing the world, that are maladaptive, that don't work, that get them into trouble, and that are fixed and don't change. So it doesn't make any difference that you picked the wrong partner last time, you'll pick the wrong partner the next time too.

LR: What an undue adherence to unrealistic ideas!

AC: Unrealistic doesn't quite capture it, Larry, because the ideas seem perfectly realistic at the time—except the neurotic has unconscious motives and unconscious reasons for making things work out to be less gratifying.

LR: In other words, choices the individual makes that are contrary to his interest and deliver him unhappiness.

AC: Neuroses are really ways of working out your life so that you're constantly paying debts of guilt and unhappiness. In other words, for making things work out to be self-damaging.

Now we see.

Southampton Bound

"Where do you keep your public phones, Doctor?" asked Frank.

From a pay phone hanging on the hospital wall he called Fair-field Porter, a new friend, a painter, a critic, a family man who lived in Southampton, New York. Frank told Fairfield and the entire emergency waiting room what I had tried to do to myself that after-noon. Frank took me back to the studio. He changed the sheets, we both sat on the edge of the bed and undressed, me down to my boxer shorts, him down to his skin, how he always slept. A woman I had been with for a few happy wretched years once called to ask if she could spend the evening with me and sleep over. She was unusually upset. We'd never lost contact with each other, I'd never lost my physical attraction to her. I said, "Come right over." In bed she clung to me like a frightened child. I just lay there all night stroking her shoulders and her hair, and stoically ignored my sym-pathetic hard-on. So too did Frank in bed that night, stiff prick and all, hold me and leave it at that, the little nun. We woke early to the same sad gray light. The brightest things in my studio were my white bandages. Frank went to work saying he'd keep in touch during the day and return in early evening.

Fairfield drove into the city to take me out to his house in Southampton. He found me doing what I'd been doing all day long: waiting for Jane to phone, watching the door where no Western Union messenger delivered a "Get well quick from your suicide attempt and let's have lunch real soon" telegram. Jane didn't call or send a telegram—for several reasons. One, taking thirty-five years to surface, was that she was informed by Frank that I didn't want her to call me. To think the John Keats of Grafton, Massachusetts, who wrote "In Memory of My Feelings" and a thousand avant-garde odes to insight and passion, would take me literally when I blubbered, "I never want to speak to her again!" Or did he know what he was doing?

Frank, back from work, changed my bandages and packed my valise and me into Fairfield's jeep. With Fairfield tall at the wheel, I retreated to the Hamptons. We traveled in silence. About an hour out on the road talk began, obliquely concerning my Act. Suddenly Fairfield, reserved, restrained, taciturn as a Hawthorne minister, poured out his own past sufferings to do with his wife, Anne, trying to soften my sorrow. He had been waiting a long time to air these feelings, it seemed to me. To anyone. It cheered me up. In all the years I knew him he never spoke personally in that way to me again. Nor did he mention my suicide attempt again, not even when he did his portrait of me with my wrists bandaged.

L

A

R

R

Y

I stayed with the Porters and four of their five kids for a couple of weeks, in their white-columned house on South Main Street, practically in the center of town, which I never visited as I remained in my cozy room for the entire recovery reading *Swann's Way*. From the outside the house looked to me like a slightly run-down mansion; inside, dirty dishes and food would be left on the dining room table until Fairfield finished using them as a still life—which didn't detract from the room's inherent class. The house was built in the nineteenth century, and at this point in my life, age twenty-seven —not too many years out of the Bronx—art, literature, music, architecture, anything of the nineteenth century had a romance I couldn't resist. The house had a sun porch, a fireplace in almost every room, a very expensive Swedish wood-and-coal kitchen stove from which every morning Fairfield pulled out his Irish oatmeal cooked overnight, and a specially built garbage container alongside neatly piled cords of wood waiting outside the kitchen door. Hanging casually on the living room wall was a de Kooning he'd bought when de Kooning didn't even have a gallery. It all filled me with the comfort and awe that I called class.

But more than the house and it contents, class was the fact that Fairfield lived this well without having to work for a living. His family had owned a stretch of land in downtown Chicago before it was "downtown."

It's hard to ignore one more thing that gave him class. The name Fairfield. And that was only his first name! Fairfield was not only a name I had never heard before, I was unable to imagine the world from which it sprang. For years I had to force myself not to hear it as a landscape. It wasn't a name. But he turned around when he heard it. I was still in touch with a friend I'd boxed with every day when we were twelve; he had the face of a washed-up pug and was called Mush Horowitz. I mentioned that I'd met a painter named Fairfield. "What a funny name," said Mush.

I was under the delusion that I knew something about class, reading Proust eight hours a day. Everything in his novel showed me something about me and my social surroundings. His characters' visits with each other in that stratified Parisian milieu took me back to my first summer in the Hamptons, when a band of vagabonds consisting of Nell Blaine, Jane Freilicher, Kenneth Koch, John Ashbery, and me shared a bungalow in East Hampton down

R

I

V

E

R

S

the road from Leo and Elena Castelli and their daughter, Nina. They invited us to their huge house with the circular pebble driveway, the money, the important visitors, the da Vinci expert, the long-haired dachshunds. Leo commissioned me to make a large sculpture in the center of his driveway, to greet the great and near-great in their limos and pickup trucks. Time and the ascension of Leo to king of the New York art realm did away with my lumpy female giant, except in photos. The handsome Bill de Kooning,

The commission from Leo (left)
and the final result: Elaine de Kooning (foreground)
and Martha Jackson (on ladder)
with Bonacker friends

later to become the hero of the Hamptons, then unable to afford a summer studio, was given a space in the royal couple's domain to paint to the music of Mozart, which we could hear down the road in our bungalow all day long. Kenneth Koch courted the princess Nina with his poetry like one of Proust's charmers in the salons of Faubourg St. Honoré.

That was 1951. In 1952, in Fairfield's guest room, I continued to read Proust full-time. In the house, Fairfield, Anne, and the children, unlike my screaming ménage, spoke and walked softly. I had no distraction from my fractured romance, and Proust didn't help me forget. To the matters of love and jealousy he delineated I juxtaposed my tragic romance with Jane.

Fairfield's wife was a kind woman, but I found it difficult to make contact with her. She had a quiet smile that she held in place longer than expected. Her few but nail-on-the-head remarks came across with guru brilliance. She gets my vote for canonization. Under her maiden name, Anne Channing, she wrote poetry that appeared in a socialist anthology of the thirties, among other places. Her work was delicately tinged with concern for the future of the human race. Unlike most humanitarians, she liked humans enough to invite some to live in her house. She had put her own work aside for a couple of decades to have five children and to take care of Fairfield's needs so he could be free to write and paint.

After a week Fairfield began a painting of me with my wrists bandaged. There's no way of knowing if the bandages were not a designer's idea of cloth bracelets. It's hard to think that a viewer would recognize a failed suicide in this homely young man not paying attention to his role in the portrait. I've seen this portrait in Fairfield's house and in galleries and reproductions over the years; as a painting it seems flat and rather empty, except for a lot of yellow ocher.

Sounds pretty ungrateful.

Just because Fairfield drives two hundred miles to put me up for a month, climbs up to my room to feed me and to discuss *Swann's Way*, and makes me feel important painting my portrait, and in return all I can say is there's too much yellow ocher in the painting, you call it ungrateful? I call it sitting for a portrait—the surest opportunity to rid yourself of any pretension that you prefer aesthetics over vanity.

I have my own history of responses by men and women to portraits I made of them. The fourth wife of Claude Rains once sat for a portrait, a gift from the actor. In my studio at different times for about a week, she was a delightful forty-four-year-old worldly lady, very interested in all the arts, hardly concerned with the outcome of the portrait short of a horror-house effect. When I told her I was finished—not having offered her a peek, since I never feel comfortable until I have nothing more to add or take out—she stood beside me and viewed it. There was no verbal reaction except about showing it to Claude. Next day John Myers called me from the gallery.

"Tina Rains just left."

"Did she leave any money?"

"No, she left the portrait."

"Didn't she like all that beautiful blue? And that yellow hat!"

"She hated it."

"Why?!"

"She said the face looked like her sister's."

"Call her sister."

"Don't panic, darling. Tina bought another painting of yours for the six-fifty. Isn't that divine?"

John Myers immediately unportraitized the portrait of Tina Rains by renaming it *Lady from Panama Street*, after the street in Philadelphia where she grew up (keeping the work honest). He sold it the next week for seven hundred dollars.

Fairfield

Much of Fairfield's work impressed me, his ability to create water and shoreline and sky with a few strokes, or an automobile in one stroke, or a face half lit by a nearby lamp. For a few years now he hadn't painted much. He knew de Kooning and like a lot of people admired him, but Bill's talent and legend made Fairfield think his own work was unimportant and in fact old hat. Fairfield met the new downtown horde of painters and poets, Jane et al., around the time of my self-damage. Our youthful exuberance for art and ourselves included his work. He was literate and literary and enjoyed talking and listening. We began to look at his work, and talked about it as we talked about everything else. We liked a lot of what we saw. Like every other painter's work, including our own, it had something wrong with it. All this attention lit a spark under Fairfield. At forty-eight, twenty years older than the rest of us and even a little older than de Kooning, he began taking his own painting seriously. Not only did he paint more, he moved out of Bill's orbit. We all worked on John Myers and Tibor de Nagy to give Fairfield a show at the gallery. Working for an exhibition finally pushed his work into recognized quality.

Wonderful Town

At the end of my fourth week at the Porter house I finished Proust and went back to New York. My wrists were minus their bandages, but my mind was not minus Jane or the confusion surrounding my bloody drama. But if it was theater, who did I think my audience was?

That wasn't the only drama I had a part in. At 77 St. Mark's **L** Place my boys were alive, and so was Berdie. Her Franco-American spaghetti and potato stone soup happened every day. Joe and Steven took care of lunch with a pile of baloney and Spam, a stack of thick Wonder Bread, and two containers of milk. The boys playing, **A** arguing, and scrapping led to exhaustion and finally sleep. It was mad but ordinary.

Augusta, during the four weeks I was in Southampton, eased **R** her feelings of having been abandoned by her mother and having abandoned her children by visiting the St. Mark's apartment and occasionally sleeping over. She complained to Berdie of pins sticking in her head, of feeling on the verge of a heart attack, of being **R** afraid to sleep for fear she'd wake up dead. She was unable to hide from the boys her ongoing germ phobia, her anger with me, her difficulties with her lover; her presence threw everything into a **Y** nervous spin.

In my absence sibling rivalry between Steven and Joseph had escalated to murderous proportions. A few days after I got home I placed a ladder at our rear window to give the boys access to the backyard twelve feet below, composed mostly of cement with some earth where giant sunflowers grew, often reminding me of another deranged artist. In any kind of weather the boys went up and down all day long. It was safer playing there than in the street. Berdie and **R** I could observe the mischief they were up to and easily voice our opinions to separate the combatants.

One day Steven, now seven, was coming up the ladder to confront his big brother, now twelve, for not inviting him to play with **I** the older boys. The wrangling went on for a while before I got

V

E

R

S

interested. Joe, angry, was watching Steven angrily mount the ladder. Just as Steven was in the precarious process of putting one leg over the windowsill to enter the house, Joe threw the radiator valve at him and said, "Catch." Steven did, and plummeted into the yard and lay there, still. Berdie began to wail. "He's dying, my little boy is dying! Save him!" What Joe did upset me so much I punched him in the stomach—he was only a kid, I hurt him badly. Then I went down the ladder, brought Steven up to the apartment, ran with him to my car parked up the street, didn't have my car keys, ran back to the apartment with him in my arms, handed him over to Berdie while I located the keys, which fortunately the kids hadn't hidden to keep me in the house, ran back with Steven to the car, and drove up to Bellevue. Steven remained overnight; the X-rays showed no serious damage, and he was released next morning.

Relieved that the injury wasn't serious—a friend of Joe's broke Steven's fall—I took the serious step of eliminating these fights that went on continually and wasted an astonishing amount of their time, and mine, since I was in a protracted state of anger. I called Anne Porter in Southampton and asked her what she did about her children's sibling warfare, how she kept homicidal behavior at the simple violence level. She knew her answer was not what I was really after. I wanted to separate Joe and Steven. With Fairfield's approval she volunteered to take Joseph in, offering her home and whatever her family could provide. She'd get Joe into the Southampton public school. He was packed, packaged, and shipped to the Porter house, and the brotherly buzz saw of St. Mark's Place was replaced by a normal level of loudness.

After a couple of weeks back in New York I still felt insulted and depressed. Trying to take the uncomfortable edge off unavoidable meetings, Jane would ask how things were, how the kids were, what I was working on. But I kept trying to pay her back for her "crime" and would cut my answer short with barely a look at her. Usually I talk so much that when I don't I'm asked if something is wrong. My silence didn't change anything. It was hard to keep insisting to myself that someone I'd thought so highly of for so long was a creep for leaving me. Slowly my schedule began to resemble what it was in prerejection times. Art and the quest for sex were the main entries in my book of days. A few times a month I'd take my horn and find a place to blow where there was a good chance of encountering someone who had, or knew where to procure, marijuana or maybe a little heroin.

I continued seeing Frank, even more now. He invited me and I invited him to evenings of eating, drinking, dancing, same old stuff. Sometimes, when I was too stoned to leave, I slept at his place on Forty-ninth Street, which he shared with the skinny poet James Schuyler. I answered even more calls from John Myers than before, if that's possible. To my long list of friends, almost rivaling Frank's, I added members of the Tibor de Nagy Gallery: Helen Frankenthaler, Paul Georges, even the ever unsmiling Bob Goodnough; also Al Leslie, who was going with Grace Hartigan, who almost slept with Frank O'Hara one night, until she yelped with delight, "Wait till Larry hears about this."

Kenneth Koch

Another activity I found more time for, now that my social intercourse with Jane Freilicher had ended, was enjoying Kenneth Koch, who had just returned at the end of a Fulbright year in Paris. Over six feet tall and narrow, with a raised ass, an amusing part of his silhouette, he zestfully devoured literature, women, French food, and *naturellement*, wines. When he first looked at my work, he overwhelmed me with a compliment that stood him in good grace for a month: "Larry, these are the first paintings I ever saw of a contemporary that made me feel I was in the presence of something really great." His passion to describe his feelings often gave him trouble releasing words from his mouth. He lived on Third Avenue and Seventeenth Street, near the historic home of the Bowery bums. I knew the building well. Jane had lived there a few years earlier, which made it attractive and repelling to visit Kenneth for drinks and a few private discussions. Every half hour the Third Avenue el train, about ten feet from his window, would drown us out, along with the Verdi or Billie Holiday records he had on. Occasionally Kenneth put on a rubber monkey mask, stuck his head out the window, and waved wildly at the passengers; most took no notice, but a few waved back.

Kenneth had seen action in the Pacific; as an infantryman his only fear in the jungles was that he might lose his glasses, which he did, leaving him without access to the Oscar Williams anthology of modern verse in his pocket. After graduating from Harvard, he began to hang out with us. He talked and acted gayer than our gay friends, and we knew some of the gayest. Few people believed Kenneth was arrantly straight. I believed it and knew it. He was a scion

of one of the first (Jewish) families in Cincinnati, the birthplace of homosexual dread. With his unquestioned attachment to seersucker suits and college ties, he showed a silent disdain for my longish hair and clothes that bore zoot suit traces of my jazz past. Kenneth said my "Old Testament stare of stern curiosity" unnerved him, and my very thin body accentuating the curvature of my nose gave me the appearance (he also said, to my face, instead of behind my back like a friend) of "a hawk that went through a secondhand clothing store." Well, it was true I'd sometimes come over in a suit jacket with the sleeves meticulously torn off, wearing boots when no one but Gene Autry wore boots, and a blousy orange shirt courtesy of my mother that made me look like a waiter in the Russian Tea Room. Kenneth considered my costume hopeless alongside his own wardrobe, which lock, stock, sock, and jock came off the rack at Brooks Brothers.

Over the years, one of the pleasures of my association with Kenneth was a book of his poetry called *When the Sun Tries to Go On*, for which I did the illustrations and the cover. Here's a brief selection.

> Earthworks of genuine Pierre! Molly. Champak's. Egypt.
> Esteban Vicente. Melodies'. Cow. Advance is chewing gum.
> Saith Bill de Kooning, "I turned my yoyo into a gun,
> Bang Bank! Half of the war close pinstripes.
> Timothy Tomato, Romulus Gun." "The magic of his

Cousse-cousse masterpiece," saith Pierre, "is apple blossoms'
Merchant marine gun." Ouch. The world is Ashbery
Tonight. "I am flooding you with catacombs,"
Saith Larry Rivers (more of him later on).
There is also some fools laying on their stomachs.
O show! merchant marine of Venice!
At lilac wears a beetle on its chest!
These modern masters chew up moths. How many drawers
Are in your chest? Moon Mullins' Moon Mullins
Put his feet in my Cincinnati apple blossoms. Many
Dry cigarettes have fallen into work's colors. The shop
Of geniuses has closed. Jane Freilicher
Might walk through this air like a French lilac,
Her maiden name is Niederhoffer, she tends the stove.
"O shouting shop, my basement's apple blossoms!"
There is a tiny drawer more hot than elbows,
Season. Number, favor, say. Old winter oh
Winter. The park is full of water veins and
Surly council members, or sad Creons. Sway, unsound airplanes!

Harvard Blues

In 1950 dapper Ken Koch had begun dating my eighteen-year-old
sister Joan, who was just entering Hunter College. Joanie and he
never went to bed together, he swore. As I saw it they were moving
in that direction. I brought Kenneth up to my parents' house in the
Bronx for a lunch served by my mother. I told Joan to invite Joyce,
an old friend of hers, a very pretty brunette who was beginning to
be interested in writing and writers. After lunch my mother took
me aside in the kitchen and told me not so sotto voce that it was
very foolish telling Joanie to invite such a beauty with big breasts.
My mother said, "Kenneth is a Harvard graduate, his family's well
off, and he's Jewish! Why did we give him lunch? I made borscht.
He might get confused. He might say, 'Maybe I like this one too'!"
   Kenneth says:

Mrs. Grossberg could be heard if she whispered a room
away, a talent she passed on to Larry. I too wondered why
Joyce was invited. In Larry's studio some time later the
mystery was unraveled. At the foot of Larry's bed was his
journal—open to a page entitled "Secret Observations." I
began looking through the pages, figuring that if Larry
came in I could always distract him with Auden's definition

of a friend: "Someone who, left alone with a friend's mail, reads it."

Larry's entry ran: "I'm getting really irritated about something today and I might as well talk about it. Why should Kenneth fuck my sister if I can't."

I was being psychoanalyzed then, by Dr. Rudolph Lowenstein, a very distinguished and established authority. I told him that Larry had his journal open and had written, "Why should Kenneth fuck my sister if I can't." Dr. Lowenstein smiled benignly and said—and he was a very sophisticated man—"Surely this is what you only *imagine* your friend is feeling. He did not actually write this. This is what you fear. And so you had this fantasy that you read this in your friend's diary. No sane man would expose his incestuous desires."

For a week I walked the narrow corridor between illusion and reality, reading a lot of Freud and Pirandello but never really satisfying myself that I was not nuts.

Kenneth confessed to me that he had peeked into my journal and asked if he could read more of it. I assured him that I was complimented by a writer wanting to read something I wrote, and that the diary, like my life, was an open book. He borrowed it and brought it to his next session with Dr. Lowenstein.

"My dear boy," the doctor told Kenneth when he read the entry, "first you imagine you read this item in your friend's journal, then when I suggest it was a fantasy, you write it yourself! Probably while dreaming. This is a simple case of sleep-writing."

Dr. Lowenstein was still chuckling at this indisputable proof of the wiliness of the unconscious when Kenneth left the office, never to return. Kenneth took some time out from psychoanalysis and spent a year in Paris. He was so charmed by the City of Light that for years it was hard for his friends to detour him from sharing his experiences.

In 1954 Frank O'Hara and I wrote Kenneth Koch: A Tragedy, a play usurping K.K.'s literary style to parody him and other regulars at the Cedar Tavern. Here is some of it, bringing to an end my portrait of the early, delightful, and absurd Kenneth Koch, later to become a great comic-lyric poet, top tenured Columbia professor, and writer of books teaching all kinds of people to write poetry.

(The Cedar Tavern. A day in June. Kenneth has just come from the airport, and has been repeating "Oh bag" for the past five minutes.)

KENNETH: Oh bag! June makes the head run. When I think of all the water in Greece! Hotel rooms in Saint-Germain des Prés, how I loved renting the Aspirin Suite for a month! But it's terribly continental to be back, isn't it?

BARTENDER: Beer, Kenneth?

KENNETH: I must admit my callow. Those sandy years in Cincy! My theme song. Boom. The fear of being Jewish, like a nail in your shoe, comes smelling up my dreams. Oh Lily! Oh Mother! Oh youth! Why did I ever cross the water?

BARTENDER *(disgruntled):* Well, Four-eyes? . . .

KENNETH: To run from the fags I knew at Harvard? The dread that gnaws me like a glacier? . . . Or was it the loop lips and breasts of Robin, always strumming on her old banjo? Or was it Pat Hoey's intelligence that drove me east? The little darling who visits me in the dark and left in it, those Irish eyes, . . . now married to a Man of Science? I used to think she made a mistake, like the rest of them, but travel has widened me. . . . Abroad! a wonderful state! on the rue de l'Abbaye! Climbing the Spanish Steps on your buttocks! while a gondolier you know examines a road map of Rego Park! Canaletto was good. A warm bed with a tall Swede, oh the masturbating into a fjord of it all! The mists of Greece. I mean the hot suns . . . through my glasses burning holes in my cheeks. Staring at the Parthenon a glass of orange juice and sending that darling postcard to Jane with my hand in my hat.

The village rats of Chartres. How I long for water where women wash clothes. O soap! sponge! Lysol! fingernails imprisoned in lavender underdrawers, fish, albumen! A lift from Dijon to Nice, a bearded Duke at my knee, guess what he had on his wrist: a thin blue wasp to be suffocated by your tongue. Ghiberti's gates could make one believe. . . . Europe! Daddy! . . .

DE KOONING: Yah, travel is okay, the steeples, the triptychs, it's terrific. It's like the signs I used to paint in Holland when I was a kit. Maybe inside the steeples it's dark, I don't know. But there's something about America that's farther away. Take the hotdog, for instance, it's simple and it's dumb and you eat it standing up. Cafes, talk, bah! Elaine was telling me there's this guy in New Jersey that made a lot of money, that's America for you . . .

A VOICE: Hello. I'm Mark Rothko's mother.

DE KOONING: Yah, that was the guy's name, Mark Rothko.

KENNETH: I'm not talking about money, Bill. I mean that Europe stirs the imagination . . .

DE KOONING: I only came out for a sandwich.

KENNETH: Don't you understand me? There's a past and it's all there.

PAUL BRACH: Here's your sandwich, Bill. But Kenneth, don't you realize that New York is like Carthage after it was delended, that is, destroyed? And you know Dido showed at the Stable before she got upset. Well, that's art for you, and it's all in New York.

TOM HESS: I've come to represent the American Renaissance, where is it?

JOHN MYERS: Why, my dear, haven't you heard? I have a gallery of the liveliest, most original, and above all youngest, painters in America, and for every painter there's a poet. You know we've discovered something called "the figure" that's exciting us enormously this season. I don't quite understand it myself, but it has something terribly pertinent to do with the past. It's called "Painting Divine" and includes the black laugh of surrealism, and the pile-strewn sobs of suprematism, and lots of boffing. Waldemar hates it. . . .

(A bull enters the Cedar.)

BARTENDER: What'll you have, Jackson?

JACKSON POLLOCK: Uh, Urg. Blah.

BARTENDER: Oh, the usual. Remember, no cursing.

JACKSON: Fuck you. (*Turning to Kenneth.*) My wife is a lousy lay, but you're the worst.

KENNETH: You're a bald-headed idiot, and a perfect example of what I mean. America is strong, but all it amounts to is action. You're about as necessary as an automatic salt shaker. But don't mistake me, I love your painting.

JACKSON: Shit.

KENNETH: How can we tell today? That's the tragedy, Jackson. I'm sorry I called you baldy. Were you serious about me?

MILTON RESNICK: . . . You know you never write about anything but yoyos and brassieres and factories. . . .

KENNETH: Do you think yoyo means simply yoyo? Come on, now. You wouldn't talk this way if Larry or Frank were here.

LEWITIN: Those phonies.

JACKSON: Those fags.

FRANZ KLINE: Those dope addicts.

BARTENDER: Those cheapskates.

YVONNE THOMAS: Dey are very nice, I like dem verry much when dey're drunk. . . .

MILTON: Tradition, it's like a brick wall, you built it up, it gets higher and heavier every century but yuh keep goin because yuh think there's plenty of room, and then it falls over on yuh. Why, in a hundred years nobody'll be able to do anything. And America, yuh know what America is? It's pushing that wall down. It's guys like you that're stoppin us. If I had my way I wouldn't let anybody go to Europe. Take that Brooks Brothers look off your face. Put on these dungarees. Elaine broke em in herself.

ELAINE: No, Milton. No. It was Kaldis. It was the last thing he did before he left.

CHORUS: Wahhhh! Kaldis, oh oh oh, oh Kaldis, etc.

L

A

R

R

Y

R

I

V

E

R

S

KENNETH: I don't care if Gorky broke them in!

PHILIP PAVIA: You *what!*

KENNETH: Yes, you fools. You think every time you step into an automobile you have to invent it. You think you're better than me because you haven't been to Europe. Well, I got the *Times* every day while I was away and I didn't miss a thing. Yes, man is alone in this world and it's a good thing. It's like Prévert said, "Oh, Father who art in Heaven, stay there." I'm leaving, but not before I tell you what I think of you.

AD REINHARDT: Philip, why don't you get him for a panel at the Artists Club?

KENNETH: Greatness in art isn't heavy, it's light. It strains to leave the earth but it's light. Rubens' entire production is like a balloon, it makes me feel like a lark! You small men with big paintbrushes, scaring little girls. Don't throw your lack of talent into the wind! Spread it on a page. Let it say "I love Florence!" Let it say "He is the illegitimate son of Rodin." Let it not just say, let it shout, "I am the Masaccio on the bathroom wall."

(They knock him down, drag him outside, and tar and feather him.)

The Club

For those too young to know and those too old to care, let me explain the significance of Ad Reinhardt's line to Philip Pavia at the end of the play, about using Kenneth on a symposium at the Artists Club.

The club was created in 1950 as a forum for discussions about modern art. When I first went there, I was an upstart—a young painter. The artists all seemed serious. That impressed me more than anything. They were very, very serious—in their rhetoric (aesthetic and political), their references (Barney Newman had all of ancient Greece at the end of his tongue), their clothes (a combo of corduroy and army-navy store rejects used for working-class associations). Some old-timers talked as if they had actually met the old Bolshevik Trotsky. That atmosphere still has an effect on me, who as a kid thought the boy with a copy of *Das Kapital* under his arm was the real star of the neighborhood.

The club itself was a small loft in need of a paint job, maybe two windows, located on Eighth Street between University Place and Broadway, bohemia's main street. There was a table for the symposium, which, appropriately, means "drinking together" in Greek. Everything was intimate, if not packed. Some members of the club had personal memories of Mondrian, Grosz, Léger, and the surrealists and dadaists who came to this country fleeing Europe before and during World War II. The club was trying to create an atmosphere that would resemble the commitment those refugees had to art—certainly in the way questions were asked and answered, and in what was thought to be important. At the end of each meeting a kind of unwritten manifesto was presented for the applause and catcalls of the artists. The club invited people like James Johnson Sweeney, major museum big shot, to come down and give his point of view. He was a tastemaker, an elder. There would be a question-and-answer period, with long speeches from the audience. Ad Reinhardt never gave up railing against artists with "interesting" things to say about their work, how much pain they felt, or what they went through emotionally, or how many drafts they made of a drawing, and the story behind a work of art! It was all absurd to him. Ad created undiscussable black paintings, working as hard as he could to eliminate the possibilities of rhetoric, leaving us a presence of dark brown in black. These dark works were exhibited in 1991 in a Reinhardt retrospective at MOMA, written of with a seriousness Ad would have denounced.

On certain evenings the club invited younger artists to sit around and talk and answer questions. One evening Al Leslie, Grace Hartigan, Jane Freilicher, and I were at the symposium table discussing I don't remember what, but I remember the evening made me feel that art had an intellectual as well as an emotional content. The club symposiums presented many diverse points of view, an aesthetic spectrum. And your work had a place in it! Another night I remember asking the sculptor Herbert Ferber whether he thought Renoir could be considered a modern painter. From the wooden table where he sat, he slowly removed his glasses as though this would help his hearing. The answer he gave was predictable: "Your question is absurd."

A letter to me from Frank after an evening spent at the Artists Club:

The club was of a boringness Wednesday but Grace [Hartigan] and I had fun there. Milton [Resnick] was more confident than previously but very folksy and pseudo aggressive ("What's so great about bein' aware? To hell with that."). [Ibram] Lassaw made some reference to words just being abstractions for things not present, which called forth some non-abstract words from me; after all in poems the words are all there, and they refer to each other and back, not to absent chairs tables and sentiments—"They flee from me who one time did me seek": isn't that emotion itself, not the memory of it. Harold [Rosenberg] was very funny and whispered that the only thing left for the action painters was to "paint on *cats*," a suggestion which had Grace, Elaine [de Kooning] and me disruptively laughing for several shakes of Pavia's head and finger. . . . Fairfield was clear and forceful and interesting but no one else even got off the floor except Bill de K who very much acted like you in manner and delivered a long tirade against reviewers . . . one lovely part being, "What right have you guys got to criticize a show with a few lousy lines? Why don't you write a nice essay."

At the club there were no doubts about the necessity of being modern. It was inarguable. It was so inarguable that it wasn't even mentioned. It stood behind everything that was discussed. But these people were like parents; they seemed powerful, and you got a lot from them. You couldn't really argue with them. If you weren't interested in the avant-garde, in being avant-garde yourself, no one was interested in you. Though I went my own way, which seemed to be contrary to their ideas of modernism, I still felt that the Artists Club stood for something important. After all, look at what effect their notions had on art, on how we see, on what was produced—a lot of great things, I think. Artists moved in all directions to make sure they weren't "repeating the past."

The club was a place to go Friday nights to see and be seen. No matter what the members thought of our work as painters, when they were going to have a party they would ask me and Howard Kanovitz, who painted and played trombone, to "get a band together." And we did. The variety and mixture of ages and approaches, sexual and aesthetic, that was jammed between the walls now seems incapable of explanation.

At the early Artists Club no one was commercially successful. That was meaningless. It was like belonging to a church. Not re-

Elaine de Kooning and
Howard Kanovitz

ceiving any rewards for making art somehow made the concerns even stronger. Art was not a career. Not yet.

It changed, of course, a few years later. Someone would come over and say, "Did you hear, Jackson Pollock sold a work for nine thousand dollars!" "Nine thousand dollars! Really! Who bought it?" Discussions on the virtues and problems of figurative art as opposed to abstract art began mingling with news of artists getting shows and selling their work and appearing in newspaper and magazine articles. The club didn't last very long after people started selling their work. You began to hear the word "career" used with a greater degree of reality. I remember Bill de Kooning, after he began selling his work, saying to me about being an artist, "Well, you know, it's a good living!" It sounded shocking.

Another thing about the club. The membership was composed mainly of abstract expressionists, and they considered Tom Hess "their writer." As editor in chief of *Art News* he devoted a good part of the magazine to their cause. Nowadays there doesn't seem to be a spokesman for any point of view. Do you know of one? I don't. Tom met John Ashbery, Frank O'Hara, Jimmy Schuyler, and Fairfield Porter, and brought their new and lively writing to his magazine. He would go to the club meetings. He had social and sexual relations with the artists and was invited to their downtown parties. He saw what was in the artists' studios and whatever else was going on there. In *Art News* he awarded prizes—best show of the year, second-best, best drawing show, and so on. He felt enthusiasm for what was happening and tried to stir things up. Tom thought that artists needed rewards. If they weren't selling anything, at least someone was looking. He came into the art world at a time when museum shows and collections of new work were few. He himself actually bought art and hung it on his walls, putting his money where his pen was. I wasn't always crazy about what he liked best. His interests in artists of my generation, myself included, often seemed to be about backing up his taste in the works of the previous generation, as if our work were corroborating the position he took on de Kooning, Barnett Newman, Franz Kline, et al. It didn't matter. He was still a force. It's too bad he died when he did. Aside from my missing him personally, it would have been interesting to see what he might have done as curator of American art at the Metropolitan Museum. Nothing has really challenged the power of the Museum of Modern Art, and it's possible that only the Met has the resources to do it. Now I doubt if it will ever happen. Today the art world doesn't seem to have a spokesman of Tom's kind.

Elaine de Kooning always said that if anybody was doing anything important in art, our group would be the first to know it. In the 1990s you can't talk that way; too much is happening. Fifty-seventh Street is still there, but SoHo and environs is one square mile of art biz. Everybody's eye is on the bouncing ball. Career is here, artists carving out their constituencies. This is not an accusation from a pure man, mind you. Concern with major and minor art is a hand-me-down from another time that doesn't square with the complexities of art's body politic. No art today by its appearance on the scene automatically consigns any past work to the "dustbin of history." The mad, scrambling New York art world seems like a hit-and-miss democracy responding to Milton Friedman's marketplace fantasies.

The club gave me a feeling of importance about being an artist and a part of something. The brotherhood of artists is gone. "Brotherhood of artists." It's an awful phrase, but blame Van Gogh. I no longer feel that camaraderie. Nor does anyone else. But don't think I'm dancing with tears in my eyes.

Divorce

"Larry! If I'm not free to marry, nothing will ever come of my romance with Aesop. Can we get a divorce right away?"

I was beginning to make some money. Fortune was favoring me more and more. A divorce settlement with Augusta in the future could take a healthy bite out of my mounting lucre. In her present desperation for legal action, and since I'd taken it upon myself to care for the two boys, one not mine, she'd settle for any amount of money. I had a lot to gain and a wife to lose.

A divorce those days was hard to come by. On legal grounds adultery, a respected breach of the marital contract, worked best, but you had to be caught and photographed in the act. Augusta and I took the word "act" seriously and staged a scene in which Augusta and Arnold would appear to be committing adultery.

It was no problem finding a good photographer to do the job. We asked our friend Bob Bass, who was doubly qualified: he photographed art and was recently divorced from Nell Blaine. Bass set up lights and began to take the photos. People dropped by, a few more than usual, because they heard something was going on. We resigned ourselves to having them watch, drink, quip, and opine, so long as they didn't stumble into the shot.

Well into the scene, responding to four braces of whiskey and Augusta's directed embrace, Arnold sprung an erection. Still, he continued to give a convincing performance as a startled and indignant man caught in his underwear in the flashbulb glare with another man's wife.

Roused by the applause after the last photo was taken, Arnold for an encore rolled over on Augusta and tried to fuck her. We pulled him off her glistening, embarrassed body. No one could blame him, not me, not Augusta—not her mother, who entered the apartment to find her daughter and our tenant undressed in front of a crowd. Behind Berdie came the kids. Their introduction to performance art.

The landlord came in with his own key, checking as usual on the female traffic, and as usual trying to catch us having a good time instead of working to pay off our back rent. There was a knock. One of the guests nearest the door went to see who it was.

"Larry! They're looking for a Dr. Schwartz."

"One flight up," I yelled, and went back to talk to our photographer.

Throughout the "adultery" session—I found out forty years later, interviewing them—my sons were meticulously pilfering the coats piled on the bed in the back room.

If our efforts that day didn't lead to an immediate divorce, they led to a terrific party, and a legal separation. It took another eight years to reach the next stage, a Mexican divorce, which at the behest of one woman allowed me to marry another.

Baudelaire

After fulfilling step one of my promise to Augusta, I left New York for Southampton that beautiful spring of 1953. Moving could be a geographical solution to the Jane problem, like going to Miami in 1946 for my heroin problem. Out of town, out of mind—we hope. I didn't think the birds and the trees and the lawns alone would snuff out the blazing torch I was carrying, but I expected that fewer interruptions from work and more time spent with the kids would hold my attention, and that the smoke of love's failure would finally waft away on the ocean breezes. Publicly I wouldn't let the drama fade slowly away. No, I was still interested in the image of myself as a tortured lover fleeing New York. Packing to leave for Southampton with my sons and mother-in-law, I sat right down and wrote my Jane a letter. Here is my splenetic gist of it. "Dear Jane: While I'm suffering now, I'm smart enough to know that all that happened at the end between us will pass. In the future I will certainly be

recognized as a great artist and receive the rewards for it. You will
suffer, longer and more profoundly. You and your art will end in
obscurity and you will regret your choice."

The bravura pose I imagined I struck, with its overtones of
sorrow and revenge, Jane took simply as the dismissal of her work
by a sore loser. She doesn't regret her choice. I regret the letter,
including the sentiments on loan from Baudelaire. What I said
would pass passed, including my curse. After a few years she was
about to speak to me of her defection as a great contribution to my
success—and hers.

Artist at Work

The first thing I did in Southampton, Fairfield accompanying me,
was rent from a Mr. Ralph Conklin a two-story eight-room house
for eighty-five dollars a month at 111 Toylsome Lane, down at the
end of a long, muddy driveway. Alongside the house, fortunately,
was a weathered no-doors, no-windows shed with enough space to
carry on my life as an artist. There were trees all around and above
the house, and one small lawn boxed in by tall, thick privet. The
house had dark umber shingles except where green moss grew on
them. Not long after I took up residence in this shaded grove I
began referring to the house as "my place in the country"; more apt
would have been "my slum in the trees." The wooden doors were
all chipped and changed size each season. The screen doors were
difficult to open because of the tension on the springs, which would
shut them with a smack after you managed to get inside. Most of
the rooms were ocher though originally painted white. A wide staircase stopped at a narrow hallway on the second floor, off which
were three small bedrooms.

From "Rivers Paints a Picture" by Fairfield Porter, *Art News*,
January 1954:

> In May, 1953, Rivers moved to Southampton, Long Island,
> and immediately started to work on sculpture outdoors on
> the grass, while he prepared an open garage near the house
> he had rented, for a studio. To the wall of this studio shed
> he nailed an 8-foot-high by 10-foot-wide piece of Homasote
> to hold his canvases. Skylights were set in the roof and a
> painting table was improvised out of another piece of Ho-
> masote. On top is a piece of plate glass. This combination of

something makeshift with a generally neat ingenuity char-
acterizes his style of work.

To get his hand in again, Rivers planned a large painting of his mother-in-law, whom everyone calls Berdie, to
be painted on a piece of canvas about 5 feet wide by 7 feet
high, thumbtacked to the Homasote-covered wall. He
started first with a complete pencil sketch of Berdie posing
on a wicker chair on the lawn. This was then freely transferred to the canvas without the model, by drawing with
sign-painter's charcoal. When he draws, Rivers rubs out a
great deal; about as much time is spent on erasing as making marks. Next he laid in color in thin washes. On the
work table were seven cans of turpentine and one of raw
linseed oil, in order to make sure to get his brushes clean
between colors, although he finds some dirtiness is useful
as a way of continuing and unifying colors from one area
to another. He kept pounds of rags under the table to wipe
out colors; the color that is wiped out has partly stained the
canvas already and therefore it remains under succeeding
colors. He used 1-inch to 1½-inch hardware store brushes,
¾ to ½-inch flat bristle brushes, and one ⅜-inch round
bristle brush.

Larry Rivers is thin, restless and nervous, with black
beetle-like eyes and an irrepressible manner. He likes to
entertain, to act the comedian, to make people laugh. He
has a talent for games of all kind. Mainly, he likes to try
things out. Starting as a saxophone player, a jazz musician,
his histrionic nature led him to painting when he met painters. The same trait, plus a special ability with words, a
unique idiomatic carelessness of expression, made him
write poetry. Finally he has taken to sculpture. If it is like
an actor not to know who he is, then, like an actor, and
because he likes to experiment, Rivers acts out his life in
search for a sound basis. It is as if all events in which he
participates were crucial moments in his autobiography.
Even the accidents in his life seem chosen with some
deeper plan in mind: a chance illness becomes a way of
resting. [What chance illness? A mild case of slit wrists!] His
observation, as close as it is limited, like French logic, is
directed toward his whole environment. His curiosity can
be shrewd and penetrating as well as sympathetic. Rivers

wants to remain master of the situation and he displays a **L**
certain toughness towards experience that poets often
have. To protect himself against being overwhelmed he
withdraws into art. Art gives him psychological power; it
serves as a way of finding those distinctions that appear to **A**
be the true ones in the search for his life. His self-control
stems from conscious spontaneity and constant awareness.
Rivers knows who has influenced him—among painters **R**
de Kooning and Courbet are now the most obvious—and
by accepting this and maintaining his consciousness of self
he hopes to assimilate these influences and keep his own
identity. **R**

About a year and a half after the Porter article, when the
weather forced me indoors, in one of the three small rooms off the
narrow hallway I began a painting of my mother-in-law, resplen- **Y**
dently nude, twice, on a six- by seven-foot piece of canvas. Leo
Steinberg, author of a book on the sexuality of Christ in Renaissance art, reviewed my painting, and me, for *Arts* magazine, January 1956. He accused me, I felt, of bad taste, of sadism in exhibiting
my mother-in-law's "folds of skin" and humiliating an old woman
down to her arthritic toes.

. . . the painter as superman gazing unflinchingly into the **R**
well of ugliness. What makes the model's ugliness offensive
is thus first of all a painterly failure: she is not inevitably
found in a space scooped out in one act of vision; she was
put there and we can ask why; and having been put there, **I**
why she was told to strip; and having been so told, why she
was painted with so clinical an eye for obnoxious detail
when a milder eye was in fact available for the inanimate **V**
parts of the scene. It is this lack of intrinsic aesthetic unity,
this evidence of contrivance, which makes the total absence of compassion in the rendering of "Berdie" so revolt-
ing. It remains . . . a picture in which genuine nastiness **E**
couples with false charm.

I thought I loved Berdie! I liked the way she looked! I had no
intention of shaming her; the painting of Berdie progressed natu- **R**
rally from works I had recently completed. I'd asked her how she
felt about posing in the nude for me.
"It's embarrassing, Larry."
"Berdie, no one but Rembrandt ever painted a woman your age **S**

in the nude."

"Shouldn't paintings be about beautiful things?"

"I'll make you beautiful. And maybe someone will buy it."

"I'll do anything you ask, Larry. . . . Please don't let the boys in while you paint me."

On the face of it I just tried to "render" what she looked like. But that's not the whole story. Not knowing how to keep all of the six- by seven-foot space lively, after finishing the first nude and seeing how much more canvas was free, I decided to do her again in another position. After a long period of using tints of color in my painting, no pigment, and charcoal to delineate the shapes, then swiping it all with a rag to see how much was left on the canvas, I began to yearn for a more substantial image, one less interrupted from inch to inch up and down the whole canvas. I painted an eight-and-a-half-foot canvas of Frank O'Hara in the nude, in leather boots; then Berdie dressed with my sons in the nude; then a nude of Augusta, painted in our crumbling cellar. I ended this nude series in the upstairs bedroom off the narrow hallway at the end of a wide staircase with a far-fucking-out painting of Berdie, twice.

Now that I'm two years older than Berdie was when she posed for me: Did I paint a naked sixty-three-year-old woman to prepare myself for what might face me sexually when I grew old?

Tales

I am going to devote a number of pages to telling Plain Tales of the Hamptons, around an open fire, to my children, to give them the opportunity to find out about Daddy when he came from the big city to the country, stories of his experience: about places, people, incidents, whatever will show how wise I am, and simple and strange and normal, and perhaps about things kept secret from them most of their lives.

Mr. Conklin

A few days after I paid my second month's rent, my landlord, Mr. Conklin, drove up our muddy driveway, got out of his car, and walked to me as I was kneeling on the ground chiseling the ankles of a reddish male nude sculpture.

"Hi, Mr. Conklin."

"Listen, Rivers, your rent check bounced. If that's going to be

a regular thing you can get out now."

I rose from the ground and assured him that it was an oversight and if he redeposited the check everything would be okay.

He walked over to the shed, where there was a nude drawing tacked to the wall. He looked at it and turned to me his very North European face, with a white moustache beneath a kind of snout. "Where are you from!"

"New York."

"No, I mean originally . . . what's your background?"

As if I were being forced to admit I had been jailed for child abuse, I said, "I'm Jewish." You never referred to yourself as a Jew.

"Jewish," as in "reddish" or "peckish," had the softer connotation of "sort of a Jew."

Mr. Conklin walked to his car. About to open the door, he turned to me and said, "Rivers? Is that a Jewish name?"

"Oh, it's too long a story."

He left, and I immediately drove to the National Bank of Southampton to deposit the cash.

111

One-eleven Toylsome Lane was the first house I ever lived in; it filled me with feelings that life was improving. Not that I could exist entirely on sales of my paintings; the task of becoming known for art that collectors wanted was not entirely in the hands of my dealer, John Myers, talented as he was. It was for time and fate, luck and work, to determine all that happened to me.

Between my money and Berdie's we almost met the working-class requisite of paying a quarter of our income for rent. I no longer got money under the GI Bill, having received a Bachelor of Science in teaching at NYU, but I had a GI disability pension of $220, and adding to Berdie's qualities of devotion, simplicity, and silence was her $75 monthly contribution to the eking out of our existence.

Her money came from a trust fund set aside by Walter Mirisch, producer of many Pink Panther and Billy Wilder movies (*Some Like It Hot*, among others). Walter Mirisch married into the powerful Goetz film dynasty. Berdie received her windfall because Walter at eight years old had been orphaned and sent to live with his aunt and uncle, the parents of Berdie's husband, Sydney Burger, who was Walter's age. Walter lived with them for his entire childhood. After Cousin Sydney keeled over a cutting room table in the garment center, Walter was moved to work out a monthly annuity for his widow.

Tires

We needed more money. My father helped me buy an old station wagon and go into the trucking business. I advertised in the *Southampton Press* that I was going to New York on a certain day. I would transport people's belongings, household items like paintings, furniture, a hundred hangers with and without clothes hanging on them, bowls of things, bathroom rugs, damp towels in plastic hampers, chairs and tables, and for some reason, tires, all kinds of tires. Some of my trips were as packed coming back from New York as going.

In those days the trip took three to three and a half hours; there was no Long Island Expressway. From New York you took Horace Harding Boulevard to Route 25 and went through many towns, or you took the Northern State Parkway and had the pleasure of going under the many overpasses inspired by Michelangelo's design in Florence and commissioned by the tyrant Robert Moses, czar of parkways.

On one of these trips Arnold Weinstein, who had been out for the weekend, accompanied me to New York, volunteering to help unload when we arrived. About twenty miles from the city, near Roslyn, Glen Cove, Great Neck, I felt sleepy. I asked A.W. to drive the rest of the way while I took a quick nap. His driving kept me awake. As we approached the first drop-off at the house of an artist who divided his year between New York and Hampton Bays, I expected Arnold to parallel-park in the space in front of our destination. He decided to park vertically. He mounted the sidewalk and almost did in two women minding a bunch of kids. The car finally stopped at the first step of the stoop. When the women advanced in a frenzy of maternal vengeance, looking for things to throw at us, I said, "Roll up your window, Arnold, and lock the door!" as I did the same.

"This calls for a very late delivery," A.W. agreed, and amid screaming and banging at the windows, he backed the car off the sidewalk to the safety of the busy street.

For a while this small trucking business was good for about a hundred bucks every other week. My pension, Berdie's, cheap rent, and those odd jobs kept us afloat. Later, with my trucking business in receivership, I began teaching art classes to keep baloney and beans on the table.

Berdie's Cuisine

Berdie's cooking was becoming influential in the many groups that circled the art world. There was her nouvelle boiled white chicken on Wonder Bread with Gulden's Mustard. Her spaghetti dinner, when not a can of Franco-American, was a ganglion of well-cooked Muellers noodles covered with a fresh tomato sauce just banged

out of a bottle of Heinz ketchup. She made scrumptious deep-fried lamb chops, but only when we could afford them. Her soup du jour, jour après jour, was Campbell's.

Once upon a Thanksgiving morning Anne Porter received a desperate call from Berdie. Southampton's telephone system was not set up for dialing as yet. Perfect for Berdie's continuing difficulty with the dial system! All she had to do out here was lift the receiver and tell the operator the number, or in some cases only the name, and she would be connected.

"Hello, Anne? There's this turkey. What do I do?"

Anne gave her the same recipe printed on the turkey package. Several hours later, another call from Berdie.

"Anne? There's all this cooked turkey. Now what do I do?"

"I'll be right over."

Anne examined the bird. It looked like the meat had been torn rather than sliced off the carcass. Anne tasted the stuffing and bit into something very, very bitter.

"What is this, Berdie?"

"The chestnuts! Just like you said it said in the recipe."

"What kind of chestnuts, Berdie?"

"Those kind," said Berdie, pointing to the tree out back. "Joe gave Steven a boost up the tree, and Stevie climbed right out on that big branch and threw down a lot of chestnuts, the brave little sweetheart."

"Those are horse chestnuts."

Not for human consumption, horse chestnuts are customarily cooked and mashed and served to pigs, if served at all, a local horticultural historian told me. "There ain't no eatin' chestnuts in the Hamptons. A blight did 'em in some time ago, and all that grew back were the big fellas. Bet you didn't know the chestnuts we buy round Christmas out this way are shipped in from out of state, sometimes as far away as Italy."

"Larry thought they tasted funny," said Berdie. "He thinks everything I cook tastes funny. But he enjoyed it."

Berdie the gentle soul. They don't make them like that any more. They never did.

In the hospital approaching her death she told Anne, "I feel good, I feel so good! Oy, I love everybody."

George's Place

At night, during the week, no New York guests, no energy to drive fifteen miles to Riverhead to blow my horn at a black dance hall called the Bluebird, I would spend some time at George's mixed race bar in the center of Southampton next to Town Hall. It was not only a pickup joint; all day, men sat drinking on milk crates and Coke boxes and made themselves available to be picked up for a few hours' work, everything from cleaning to skilled carpentry, even in the middle of the night. The owner, a forty-five-year-old redneck called George, tended bar. He had a straight short nose and white teeth, wore his hair slicked down, and talked through his nostrils. He had a weird easy way with his black patrons and got a big boot out of "keeping them in line." At the same time he knew the first names of all his patrons and their families. "As I live and breathe, Harold Waters, the heartthrob of the Carolinas! Drunk again!" he'd laugh a wee bit too loud. He was attracted to black women who came into the bar; putting his hand playfully on a rear end, he'd turn to the nearest white ear and say, "Nothing like a juicy black ass." Back then, there were "Negroes" and there were "colored people," but they all had black asses.

George was rezoned out of Southampton: his bar was too close to Main Street, bad business for the rich summer residents to look in and see that Southampton was after all just another American town. Undaunted, George opened a bar in Bridgehampton, seven miles away, where he catered to some familiar Southampton faces, augmented by the thriving Bridgehampton black set. He was a businessman who had affection for his customers. I alternated between liking him and thinking he was despicable. His Bridgehampton scene was now entirely black. He never untied himself from that life—Captain Ahab riding a great black whale.

Blossom

At George's Southampton bar I saw Blossom Sadowski, a frequent visitor, a talkative good-natured white woman in her late thirties. She was usually drunk, if not quite drunk, before she left for home, walking distance from the bar. She wore a plain gold ring on her finger and showed no interest in what was on my mind. There was an empty stool right next to her, which I took. It was early. A plain-looking woman wearing unfashionable glasses, she was in her nurse's uniform, probably because she came directly from her job at Southampton Hospital. I was ready to disregard her face; her figure offered little more, at least as far as I could make out under her hospital whites. She was neither big nor small. She talked a deep blue streak to everybody at the bar about who'd left town, where they went, when they were coming back from the wedding in North Carolina, and how funny they were.

I mentioned one of the names I heard her mention. We drank to him. She let me buy her the drink. I began toasting a lot of people, including President Eisenhower; soon she made me part of her discussions. The white stockings and white shoes seemed to touch on almost forgotten fantasies I'd entertained about the nurses who attended me in the Air Corps hospital before my release. I'm not sure how we decided that leaving George's was a good idea, but I remember driving to Bridgehampton, telling her I knew of an apartment above a barn that was a nice place to continue drinking.

She fell down going up the outside staircase, but we laughed; the struggle made us friendlier.

Whose place was this?

The apartment of a man I knew who had a business in the barn below. I wasn't exactly sure when he would be back from his trip to New York, but I had the key. I was supposed to deliver some books and some chairs and two tires that were still in my station wagon. I didn't attend to my trucking business right then. Once inside the apartment, we lay down on the bed. We never put on the lights; the moon lit the room, which had the shape of an attic. She was so drunk she didn't take off her uniform or her shoes. I pulled my pants down far enough. She didn't know who I was or what we were doing. With the years I had progressed to holding back on my orgasm for at least three minutes. I was at that crucial third minute when her vagina became abnormally warm. She was having a fantastic orgasm—all my doing! My legs and underwear went wet. Ah, but that was no orgasm! Blossom, I realized, was pissing! It became too much to resist. I stopped reciting piano chords to ward off my uncontrollable urge to come, and came, feeling *that* pleasure as well as the sensation I have never again experienced, being inside a woman while she was taking a nice warm leak.

Then I went out and down the stairs, picked up the stuff from my wagon, minus the tires, brought it upstairs, locked the door, went down again, and drove my wet nurse home.

Teaching

In the finished basement of Selig "Consolidated Laundry Systems of NY" Burrows and Gladys, his wife, I became my teacher Hans Hofmann. If I couldn't think of anything Hofmann taught me about art except push and pull, I never forgot the beauty and cunning of his teaching: style before content and enthusiasm before anything. I was following the advice of culture's bad boy, Ezra Pound, to a worried artist who was about to teach his first class: "Imitate your favorite teacher." It seemed to work for me.

About twelve women from twenty-eight to fifty years old, all open to me for any kind of attention, most of them Jewish, mostly interested in killing three hours on a Thursday morning. I was put in my place—between Wednesday's golf lesson and Friday's class in ethnic cooking. One or two of the women looked like they could keep their husbands home nights; for the rest, the smocks, hairstyles, and conservative carriage kept me serious about their paintings and drawings.

It was here in Great Neck that I realized all I had heard about the impossibility of teaching art was not true. I could tell them what colors to mix to make a dull green or a bright purple, or just tell them about some terrific colors, some historic, some new. I could point out the difference between painting with the wrists and swinging the elbows. I could suggest painters for them to look at who might open up the kernel of spirit I detected in their work, exhibitions at museums to whet their appetite for glory! I don't know. How do you teach a student to be someone? Do you give a course in becoming Matisse? Or a great reductionist like Mondrian? Did I want them to learn to make a Larry Rivers painting? My teaching at bottom was a fudge and I was a fake. The result was I was a hit.

Gladys Burrows found me a bigger class with better pay at the Adult Art Education Program at Great Neck High School. Now we had high ceilings, bright lights, nude models, but no coffee served by a uniformed maid. Still the students came.

One old retired candy manufacturer, Mr. Lieberman, rose to regional heights. When I came over to his easel he spoke before I spoke. "I'm painting scenes from the Bible." He told me what every inch of his canvas stood for. To mention the word "style" to him or suggest how he might better realize his ideas was futile. "Grandpa" Lieberman at eighty-one was an egomaniac with a messianic mission to forge ahead of Grandma Moses. After he graduated he was interviewed many times by the local newspapers and Newsday, and finally by the New York Times, Long Island section. In every article Grandpa Lieberman doggedly tried to destroy my career by expressing his gratitude to me for teaching him everything he knew.

On a cold wintry night, with the model asking for the heater to be brought closer to her and the students working on their small paintings I suggested should be bigger, I saw my cousin Paul behind a drawing board. For a long time, from the day he was married, Paul had been successful in his father-in-law's trunk-making business. He saw how disparate materials after six or seven steps were suddenly transformed into a black steamer trunk. I thought, How beautiful, he believes art is like that, but instead of a rectangular storage unit he can end up with pretty flowers in a vase, beautiful fruits on tablecloths, or luscious nudes like the woman in class now spreading comfortably on the divan on the model stand. His dark eyes rose and fell a few times as I walked over to greet him warmly.

"How are you, Paul?"

"Okay."

"Listen, what brings you here? When did you get interested in art?"

"Oh, my wife plays mah-jongg on Thursday nights for about three hours. So why not do something more interesting than looking at TV till she gets home?"

"Aha, I see."

"So, Irving, I mean Larry, do I have any talent?"

My cousin Paul! The same tall, handsome seventeen-year-old of my youth whose clean straight line for a nose and matinee-idol moustache evoked massive compliments from the women in my family, *in my presence*, giving me instant inferiority.

Not long ago Cousin Paul was out in Southampton, and he asked me how my autobiography was "getting along." I told him he figured big in it because I never forgot feeling put out by the compliments he received on his good looks with me standing right next to him. His wife, Ann (only a wife could get away with it), reminded me that Paul, at the time, was cross-eyed. So much for human memory.

Joseph

In 1954, at fourteen, Joseph was not a very verbal child, but he understood the workings of everything in the house that the rest of us never bothered to think of. He would look at a stuck window, squirt something, and up and down it slid. Locks that didn't work or locked you in if they did he'd examine, then leave for a minute, come back and poke around with some thin thing, and Steven would walk out of the bathroom. Clogged toilets, blown fuses, noisy fans, silenced radios—Joseph was on top of it all, when he wasn't under the car taking it apart or putting it together.

On winter mornings he would rush down naked to the living room, holding all his clothes, and dress seated on the warm grating of the forced-air system. He was tall and had a slim, beautiful figure and a synchronized lope that was pretty sexual. Painting and drawing him nude, I couldn't help observe the size of his cock and the sparse growth of his pubic hairs. I felt an occasional pang of compassion for my friends who controlled themselves. Frank asked me, hypothetically, how I would feel if he tried to "make it" with Joseph.

"I'll tell you how I would feel! Very insulted to be asked such a question by such a good friend. What kind of a bourgeois square do you think I am?" I thundered. Hadn't I firmly established my position as a thoroughgoing sexual liberal?

Connected to this is another tale, now in Joseph's own voice.

My brother Steve and I were often called upon to pose. We would hide in the house so Larry couldn't find us and ask us to pose. Whenever I posed for him I wondered one thing: Did I have to pose nude, like everyone else? On one hand I wanted to be immortalized in his paintings, but I didn't want to hang around and pose for it, but you don't say no to Larry when you know how much it meant to him.

One totally disgraceful thing almost destroyed me. It was about the painting called *Joseph*. I was fourteen and my pubic hair had just come in, very fast, but not fast enough. Here I'm standing in a cold room next to a bookcase, facing the viewer, wearing nothing but socks at a time when a fourteen-year-old is becoming aware of his body and sexuality—you don't know who you are at fourteen, let alone forty. I was skinny and felt very embarrassed about it, like a toothpick, and had what I thought was a pin head. My thinness accentuated the size of my penis, which may appear semierect but was really frozen. After six months of withering glances at the painting if I passed it in the house, I pretended I didn't see it. Larry decided to show it at a new painting space in Bob Keene's bookstore situated on Main Street in the heart of Southampton! If it was in the window the police would have taken it down sooner than they did take it down. Which would have been the end of my torture.

I often had ambivalent feelings about lounging nude in Larry's paintings, but no ambivalence about a painting featuring me in such a prominent fashion! Half of Southampton High School had parental permission, but it looked like all of them came for a viewing, just to have more detailed info to razz me. All the parents went to Keene's bookstore that week to see it, the better to fire off letters to the editor of the *Southampton Press*, and to form a committee to have this disgraceful image removed from the fair township of Southampton. The local police department, always at the ready to guard against any infraction of the moral code— pretty disgusting in those days—came in force one evening and removed the painting to a cheering parade of upstanding Hamptonians. The removal of the painting began the cooling down of the torment of Joseph Rivers by my convulsed classmates. To this day, when I see a photo of the painting, I still have a twinge of the old embarrassment, though I think back then, in my small horrified way, I enjoyed my moment of fame when the whole town was talking. For months after, Bob Keene kept that part of the wall bare except for a four-foot black censored X that marked the spot of my shame, and my fame.

I adopted Joseph two years later after many bureaucratic delays. On his birth certificate was the name Baby Burger and no mention of the father. When I signed the official adoption papers in Riverhead, Joseph burst into tears. I think I had wet eyes myself. I never knew how important it was for him to be officially Joe Rivers even if all of us knew the whole story.

A Trip to Southampton

In 1956 Bob Keene, the man who made space in his Southampton bookshop for modern art, met the tall, outspoken, full-of-artistic-promise Grace Hartigan. Grace for a while made life on the Lower East Side into a still life for her painting. Among the more memorable things she painted were fruit stands, pickle barrels, and store

Amazing Grace, 1956

windows displaying bridal gowns. Most of her men acted as if devoting themselves to her was more than enough to live for. Since I never slept with her, I'm not the best judge of why this was so. Grace was a busy actor on the scene whose rough-and-tumble ego made all our meetings and conversations anything but relaxing. Robust men seemed her favorite. Bob Keene fit the picture. So did George Spaventa, a good sculptor who made the Cedar Tavern home from dinnertime till drink and talk took him off to the land of Nod.

A few months after I moved to Southampton I began to invite artists from New York City to my house. "Paint is thicker than blood," said the Porters. Some were invited for company and some for marijuana. I invited Spaventa for both.

George's only compensation for the attention he wasn't receiving from the art world was the hot-and-heavy he was having with Grace "The Blond Ace" Hartigan. They began to visit the Hamptons together, but on many occasions he went back to the city, leaving her to pine for him during their separation. Pining took the form of painting her early masterpiece *Montauk Highway* and having a romance that ultimately ended in marriage to Bob Keene.

Spaventa heard about this romance from the cool night winds blowing in from the Hamptons. Gentle and quiet as always, he drank until the Cedar closed, by which time visions of Grace and her new lover and sand and sex crowded his floating brain. George decided to pay Grace and her bookish lover a surprise visit. Scouring the bar, borrowing money for the hundred-mile drive to Southampton from his fellow artists, who were glad to bankroll such a good cause, he climbed into a taxi and told the driver where to go and how fast to get there. Two hours later the taxi stopped outside the apartment back of Keene's bookstore.

"Keep the motor running. This won't take too long."

George banged on the door and demanded entry. Asked by big Bob Keene, naked in the doorway, what he wanted, George leaped and threw a roundhouse punch. Bob, an ex–marine sergeant, stopped the punch in midair, grabbed the looping arm, and wrapped it around George's neck. George found himself in the position of having traveled a hundred miles to give himself a half-nelson. He began to make gurgling noises. Grace pleaded with Bob not to hurt him. Bob shimmied George back to the cab, piled him into the back seat, and told the driver where to go and how fast to get there.

Some four miles from my house is a Shinnecock Indian reservation. The Shinnecock Indians have a small beautiful woods to hunt
in, full well-tended gardens, tracts of arable land, and pleasant
homes they build themselves, and they don't pay taxes. They have
a sense of their history, and once a year around Labor Day they
put on a three-day powwow attended by Indians in extraordinary
headdresses from all over the country. Thousands of Hamptonites
are more than welcome.

   In the middle of the seventeenth century the Shinnecocks from
Westhampton to East Hampton, led by Chief Wyandanch, origi-
nated a long-term policy of friendliness toward the white settler.
They taught him survival in the East End woods, where to hunt,
how to last the winter; they shared their food with him till he

Member of a hospitable tribe

learned. In return one of our own East Enders, the chivalrous Lion
Gardiner, acquired an island from Chief Wyandanch for "one large
black dog, one gun, some powder and shot, some rum and a pair of
blankets." Long Island historians give Wyandanch's hospitality
good reviews. There's a town called Wyandanch, but there's a
prime piece of private land called Gardiners Island.

   The Shinnecock Indians were known for fishing and boating.
They speared their catch at night by the light of torches on the
Hamptons' rough waters. On December 11, 1876, off Mecox Point,

the sailship *Circassian* was blown onto a sandbar in a raging tempest of blinding sleet; the rescuers hired to haul the ship off the reef were the Shinnecock seafaring braves. But the *Circassian*'s hull, bleached and weakened by the salt wind, its sails twisted and ripped by blizzard, broke in two when a second storm came up. The Shinnecocks, all the able-bodied braves in the tribe, were tossed out on the raging bay to the screeching wind's requiem. All were drowned.

After the death of so many braves, the women were forced to look outside the tribe for men. It being improbable if not impossible for them to take up with the local white men, they formed lasting relationships with the migratory black field hands who had been picking the potato and corn crops since the end of the Civil War. By the fifties, when I arrived, the local white population considered the Shinnecock Indians black, with some notable exceptions. In the United States, a child of a black parent and a white parent with the faintest features identified as African is considered black, inspiring feelings of superiority and inferiority that exist in different guises in every corner of the globe.

I met some of the interesting descendants of these Indians in George's bar; in the ensuing months we did a lot of work on my old house. We put in good hard days and had many good nights. In the great Shinnecock tradition of helping new settlers to understand the unexplored territory, the Indians showed me the ideal spot to help me survive the winter. It was called the Bluebird, a bar in Riverhead that featured live music by a good rhythm-and-blues band. It was the best dance hall in the Riverhead area, and it proved to be an enjoyable musical and social encounter. It was a little like traveling to a foreign land. The owner was a fifty-five-year-old ex-cop named Jesse Shelton, always in tight pants held up by an ancient pair of suspenders. He was big, six foot two, brown smooth skin, bald, religious, and physically powerful. On the few occasions when someone who wasn't in the band came out swinging, Jesse put his arm around the instigator's throat, walked him outside, and told him quietly, "Don't come back here. Please?" If the man came back, Jesse, cool and not in the least overbearing, came out from behind the bar with a gun pointed straight at the troublemaker's head, allowing him to leave in one piece, and peacefully, with some of his honor intact.

In the beginning I went to the Bluebird with my friends from the Shinnecock reservation. After a while I went on my own, drawn by Red Lincoln's band, which invited me to play whenever I

Blowing at the Bluebird with
Steve Smith, Margaret on piano

wanted, and by the patrons. One night, putting my horn away, I wondered if there was a woman among the few women left in the Bluebird who might be available sexually or by chance find me of some interest. I was feeling good about how I blew. The band said they enjoyed my playing and bantered warmly with me. I walked to the bar and realized I was the only white in the place. This made me feel exotic, and very nervous. Women between twenty-five and thirty-five, dressed in backcountry gingham or overalls, intermittently came up to me at the bar. What's going on? They acted flirtatious—but without a smile. They sidled up to me and demanded I buy them a drink.

There were men at the bar drinking, talking loudly and laughing, and totally tuned in to the scene between me and the women. White men have traditionally behaved horribly toward black men who show an interest in white women. Black men get a lot of shit for this, up to a stretched neck. White women associated with black men don't win any popularity prizes either. The image producing the strongest reaction is a black cock trespassing in a white vagina. As for why this is true I, like a lot of other psychiatric experts, can only offer some unprovable theories.

One of mine was expressed in an artwork, a relief called *America's Number One Problem*. On silver Mylar I show a pink cock and a burnt umber cock, leaving the viewer to determine which is longer. In fact they are both exactly the same size, as proven by a nine-inch ruler at the bottom of the work, which confronts the "size syndrome" that says black men are better in bed because they have bigger cocks than white men. Second on the list of unprovable ideas is that black men are closer to our animal beginnings on the evolutionary scale, less in control of their behavior and therefore more exciting to women. (There are even more inaccurate and improbable ideas, but I refuse to list them.) Did the black men at the Bluebird have an image of my white cock entering a black woman's vagina and find it obnoxious? Was I putting *their* women in a degrading and repulsive light? Did the white cock dangling from the body of their oppressor, me, add to the obnoxious picture? Was a lot of shit and a stretched neck in store for me? When I said earlier that I was sorry I wasn't born a Negro, I was talking about a natural advantage I would enjoy in relation to jazz. At the moment there were other reasons I was sorry I wasn't born a Negro, and I'd never meant it more.

All this was going through a brain floating in the alcohol I kept dumping into my mouth all evening long while playing. Jesse, the owner, man of God, man of peace, six-plus feet of sinew and muscle, gave me a little confidence, with his presence and his gun behind the bar, that no one was going to mess with me.

The women there were determined to get the drink they wanted and make sure I was under no illusion that they were interested in anything more. Up from the South, perhaps for the first time, I'm sure they were still careful and some even afraid of white men, except maybe one like me who wanted to fuck them. They were in an equal situation: they had something I wanted, and the decision was with them. It was more than equal. They were dominant.

"Gonna buy me a drink, mister?"

I was also in their backyard. It was put up or get out. But I felt I would be thought an instant schnook if I put up. Schnook or no, I said, "What'll you have?"

"Gin and ginger."

"What's your name?"

She waits for her drink in silence; the gin and ginger arrives, she says, "My name is Mae. . . . Thanks, now. I got to talk to my girlfriends at the end of the bar."

I bought myself another vodka, straight, and began talking to a man on my left I knew from Southampton. I felt a pull at my coattail. I turned. It was a woman in overalls.

"Don't you wanna buy *me* a drink?"

"Oh, yeah. Sure. What do you want?"

"A pink lady."

"What's your name?"

"Delia."

"I'm Larry."

"Was that you up there?"

"All night."

"Where'd you learn to play like that? You sure play good."

"What do you do?" As if the overalls she was wearing didn't tell me.

"Everything."

"Oh, I see!" Then I realized that by "everything" she meant everything migratory workers do, picking potatoes, sacking them, and hauling them into the cool barn. Still, the sexual semiotic of "everything" brightened my mood.

She gulped down the polite pink lady, held the glass up in a gesture of accomplishment, and seemed eager for another. Now I took a much closer look at her. She was about twenty-eight years old, tall and slim, not too slim. She kept her hair short, but there was enough to fashion curls right up against her face. She had on a short-sleeved T-shirt, and her breasts pushed out her overalls. Her bare arms were very dark, about the color of raw umber oil paint. I could hardly see her eyes; the natural position of her eyelids was almost down to her lower lashes. She smiled to thank me for the drink, and I saw an innocence around her beautiful Gauguinish lips. When she'd tugged on my jacket she wasn't my idea of a first choice for the evening, but as my feelings for her progressed I made up my mind that she would make an exquisite second choice. I began plotting a departure.

"I'm starving," I said, and I was.

We left the Bluebird; she invited me home for some lima beans. I think that's what she said—sometimes I couldn't understand what she was saying, between her dialect and our inebriation. We got in my station wagon; a few rights, lefts, and straight-aheads to a nameless automobile graveyard, we continued driving through the lanes of the lot until we reached her home. It was an abandoned, rusted yellow school bus without tires, standing on four cinder blocks. Since she was a seasonal worker and the season for work was summer, the missing door was in no way a problem. There was a curtain. She drew it aside, we stepped into the entrance well and up two steps into—a kitchen! She lit a candle and on a small kerosene stove began heating her pan of lima beans. A white man and a black woman in the front of the bus—smoky but smelling very good.

"I love lima beans," she said.

"So do I. It was a specialty of my mama." It really was! While waiting for the beans to reach my stage of mushiness, I got in some long hot kisses, feeling her buoyant tits under her thin T-shirt. Her skin was extraordinarily smooth. I looked over the physical plant. There didn't seem to be a flat surface long enough for the sex I couldn't stop thinking about, unless there was something more accommodating beyond the curtain that divided the kitchen from the back of the bus. She handed me a bowl of lima beans as I sat on the floor, my legs dangling in the well. The insanity of this scene was broken by blinding headlights blasting through the windshield. Was someone coming home to another bus? Delia looked very worried. The headlights passed, but her worried look remained. She got across to me that she had a boyfriend, a very big boyfriend, who worked nights. "But sometimes he come home early."

I felt such a wave of fright that I tried fucking her as she sat upright, legs out on the floor. It didn't work. I was all over her, but so clumsily she pushed me off, giving me a kiss to cool me out in case I turned into a raving rapist.

To her relief I said, "I have to get out of here. Do you want to come home with me?"

"Okay."

We fled the bus for my station wagon, but she ran back to close the curtain to the entrance. In Southampton we got into my bed and went to sleep.

We hung around together the next day. It was Sunday, and she took me to Bridgehampton, where some of her friends were playing cards in a shack under a tree at the edge of a potato field. They invited us to eat vegetables in pot liquor and offered me a pork chop sandwich. I contributed six bottles of beer. For a night and a long day I seemed to be kissing her the whole time we were together. She liked that, or behaved as if she did. Then I drove her home to her yellow bus.

L

A

R

R

Y

R

I

V

E

R

S

Crossing the Delaware

In 1953 I read *War and Peace*. Tolstoy's novel was not something I could see, not a figure or a landscape, a church or a mountainside. By meshing Napoleon's invasion of Russia with contemporary life, Tolstoy set me on a course that produced *Washington Crossing the Delaware*, a seven-by-nine-foot work, plus a dozen drawings. The size and the research were going to prove that I was a serious artist, and if the painting turned out to be terrific, a talented one. This work was going to take my style of painting, charcoal drawing and rag wiping, to a new height. The mixture of grand art and absurdity was with me from the beginning.

How did I actually picture the crossing? I knew it took place in the last days of December. I saw the moment as nerve-racking and anxious. I couldn't see getting into a very chilly river around Christmastime with thoughts of death and discomfort as an occasion for hand-on-chest heroics.

I chose to paint the crossing at the moment before it became a complex military operation. I saw large rowboats shoved here and there, men misinterpreting orders, horses slipping, sliding, and rearing, Washington shouting over the confusion in the center of all this, standing in a rocking boat, getting men, food, munitions, and spirit across a river. I had him facing the audience in tight creamy Napoleonic pants, handsome matching vest, and tall dark

boots—the same outfit as in Jacques-Louis David's *Napoleon in His* **L**
Study, which I used in my 1964 painting *The Greatest Homosexual*.

I *can* draw from imagination, but I prefer to look at visual
information based on someone else's effort, like reproductions and
photos. From these I can pick and choose and feel more confident. **A**
For the head of George I found a reproduction of a Leonardo da
Vinci drawing, *An Old Man in Hell*. He was screaming. Great. Just
what I wanted. I placed the Leonardo head on a half-invented, half- **R**
Jacques-Louis-David body. Although I knew the revolutionary
army was composed of a ragged bunch of unprofessional fighters, I
didn't know what they wore. I went to the Rogers Memorial Library
in Southampton to find out. The only things at the library that **R**
helped were illustrations in children's books, with lots of revolutionary uniforms and equipment info. I drew from them.

Feeling I had enough ammunition, I began. I tacked canvas on
a wall, which gave me the backing I needed on every inch of the **Y**
canvas to facilitate wiping some of the paint away with a rag and
digging in with the charcoal to outline the shapes. By the time I
really got into the painting, *War and Peace* had receded as a model.
Like most of my attempts at grandiose and pompous themes, this
painting after a while became more a rescue mission from failure
than a well-worked-out artistic and aesthetic progression.

Around the time of the painting and for years afterward, Sena- **R**
tor McCarthy, America's Number One Problem for intellectuals of
the fifties, was one of my recurring paranoid fantasies: I was a Jew,
and unless I could produce hard evidence to the contrary, I was a
Communist. I imagined an interrogation where I was accused of **I**
unpatriotic behavior. "It's true, I confess. I knew Alger Hiss, I met
him at a party."

MCCARTHY: Mr. Rivers, in 1955 did you perpetrate a paint- **V**
ing of Berdie Burger?

ME: Yes.

MCCARTHY: Did you use an American flag as a decorative **E**
element?

ME: Yes, I used it to cover a table.
R
MCCARTHY: Did you get the flag all dirty and messy and
gooky and yucky with wine stains?

ME: Yes sir. **S**

MCCARTHY: And food stains?

ME: No sir, I do not use food stains.

When I completed *Washington Crossing the Delaware* in 1953, I realized I had a patriotic ace in the hole and the committee could never nail me like some of the blacklisted Hollywood Jews. No sir. Despite my smoking of pot and sucking of cunt and the occasional cock, they weren't going to fry me, even if they gave my case to a Jewish judge. I could always point to my love for George and the Delaware and our revolutionary soldiers.

Until recently, art critics who wrote about *Washington Crossing the Delaware* thought it was based on the Emanuel Leutze painting hanging in the Met, that it was a parody or some kind of improvisation. It's not true; I had only seen the Leutze once or twice and had never viewed it at any length or with any passion. It was a joke I never laughed at. When I began thinking about the subject, I thought mainly about the patriotic grade school plays I sat through or participated in. I never took them seriously, even at seven or eight years old, but I enjoyed them and still have a pleasurable feeling remembering the experience.

"Does *Washington Crossing the Delaware* belong to a wave of the future?" the critic James Thrall Soby asked me in a 1953 interview in my Southampton shed.

"I don't know," says I. "I do know that Ingres was considered a reactionary neoclassic painter until Juan Gris and Picasso found him inspiring. . . . Anyway I try not to think much about these art historical shifts and developments." History's a thing of the past.

Soby, curator at the Museum of Modern Art, responsible for the biggest futurist art exhibition in America, and author of many art books, wrote:

> Rivers' picture seems to me a remarkable work, not only in the courageousness of its attempt to revitalize an outmoded theme, but in its spontaneity and fluency of technique. Unlike a lot of people, I do not see the redoing of *Washington Crossing the Delaware* as a nail in the coffin of the avant-garde. On the contrary I see Rivers as a painter who embodies the revolution in new ways of seeing.

I told Jim I needed something definite on which to hinge the mystery of art, and that definite something took the form of com-

mon references: from national myths to autos, playing cards, **L**
menus, paper money, whatever was at hand. I don't have the faith
in "self" that abstract painters need. And I didn't think then, and
don't now, that "self-expression" is much of a reason to paint.
Which self? Whose self? **A**

At a time when not making a million by the age of thirty was
not a definition of failure, I wasn't doing badly. In 1955 MOMA
purchased *Washington Crossing the Delaware* for $2,500. By ac-
quiring and displaying the painting alongside important abstrac- **R**
tionists like Kline and Guston, the museum sent conflicting signals
to those who thought it stood for modern art. What was George
doing next to Franz and Philip? Mixed signals and mixed reviews. **R**
Elaine de Kooning dubbed it "Pascin Crossing the Delaware," alluding to the style of the Jewish immigrant painter who lived in a
whorehouse. Gandy Brodie, parading in front of MOMA wearing a
sandwich board, accused the museum of ignoring his work and **Y**
implored the public to stay away; the same Gandy asked me, in
front of my painting at the museum, if corn was my favorite food.
These responses by no means depressed me. I felt a rush of importance in the company of the few abstractionists I enjoyed, personally and artistically.

Shortly after *Washington Crossing the Delaware* was finished,
Frank O'Hara wrote his ode "On First Looking at Larry Rivers' **R**
George Washington Crossing the Delaware." Kenneth Koch wrote a
Washington Crossing the Delaware in the absurdist style of Alfred
Jarry, to be presented at my son Steven's school on February 22. It
included a scene with Washington in bed saying "Good night, **I**
America" and going to sleep, to dream of cutting down his father's
cherry tree. The rehearsal room roof caved in a week before the
performance. I offered my home to the students for rehearsals, but **V**
the principal, beginning to fear the impact *Washington Crossing
the Delaware* might have on the student body, concluded over
drinks at Shippy's that they might as well just call the whole god-
damn thing off, it was all getting out of hand. So it was goodnight, **E**
America, to Kenneth Koch's play.

Meanwhile, at the Tibor de Nagy Gallery, two painters broke
into a hitherto off-limits genre: Alfred Leslie painted *Henry Ford
Standing Next to His First Model T Ford*, Harry Jackson painted **R**
Custer's Last Stand. And in the back woods of Ohio, an art teacher
named Roy Lichtenstein told me he took a breather from painting
abstractions to squiggle a small work called *Cowboys and Indians.* **S**

Two years later Jasper Johns, with the permission of history, painted an American flag.

What did I do? "Converted a banal and unpromising bit of folklore into a source of riveting artistic interest ten years before Pop Art turned its sights on popular Americana," writes Sam Hunter, the art critic.

The painting became what Frank O'Hara wrote about the painter of it: "Larry entered the scene like a demented telephone. Nobody knew whether to put it in the library, the kitchen or the toilet, but it was electric." Aside from trying to produce a visual *War and Peace*, I wanted to do something the New York art world would consider disgusting, dead, and absurd. I succeeded and was branded a rebel against the rebellious abstract expressionists, which made me a reactionary. I didn't think it was true that I was against the New. Like many younger artists, I took modern painting seriously: it should be experimental and show curiosity. The idea of Larry Rivers was born with *Washington Crossing the Delaware*.

Three Guys and a Gal

On one of Augusta's recurring tumbles with her boyfriend Aesop, from the peaks of optimism about their romance down to the valley of doubt and pessimism, she took the Long Island Rail Road out to Southampton to visit her mother, her sons, and me, her husband. In her gloomy state of mind she decided to quit her job in New York and spend a few days licking her wounds. If Augusta wasn't a woman about whom I had feelings of enduring possession, that didn't mean I had lost my early, middle, and late physical attraction for her. If I liked her because she was tall and willowy, she still had that for me to drink in. After a few days of her and only her flashing in and out of rooms in all states of robe and disrobe, and lots of conversation about the children, Mom, and what life had become for both of us, it dawned on me and later on her that away from the bleating world we could be passionate and friendly. And we were. I was a heartbeat away from no one, woman or man, and it wasn't long before our few minutes of passion ruled the nature of the day. I talked her into staying on Toylsome Lane, getting a job, contributing both body and money to our mutual well-being.

I couldn't tell what all this meant to Steve and Joe, or Berdie, for that matter, but on the surface it had the outlines of a family soap opera with a good ending coming up. We were in a state of

Mother, daughter, and son-in-law

blissful agreement. I remember buying her a very long coat, the kind that swept the floor, the kind every woman I was ever involved with had to wear one time in her life. A week after we both decided it was gorgeous, we both hated it, and both agreed she had to keep wearing it because we both agreed we were broke. She worked at the law office of Phillip Platt in a store on Main Street. On blustery November days when gray evening came early and my working approached its sixth or seventh hour, I'd go into town and pick her up and we'd ride down to the beach and sit in the car, both of us too tired to walk on sand.

Two months after Augusta became part of life on Toylsome Lane, the first figure to arrive from the bleating world was John Bernard Myers. Steven, now ten, hated John Myers. "Who wants to hear him say, 'Steven, it's past your bedtime'? That is not what a child wants to hear from a guest. After a hard day at the playground, a child wants to hear the gossip from his dad's bitchy visitors."

John was there to choose works for my show, scheduled to open just before the Christmas holiday. John thought art as gifts was smart business. Refusing to see what was going on between Augusta and me, he waited for those moments when trips to my studio might

Appraisal

begin with choosing some art and end with some "nooky," as he called it.

Unbeknownst to John Bernard Myers, the poet Frank Russell O'Hara was due on the next train, looking forward to a collaboration on some poem-paintings as well as on some sex in the studio.

On the Friday night of their arrival, after a Berdie dinner, Steven and Joseph tucked in with long telescopes at the top of the stairs, Augusta, Frank, John, and I were in the living room semi-seriously drinking (not drinking too much, just drinking too long). Augusta, because she rose early for work and was never able to compete with educated wisecrackers, went upstairs to bed without venturing a peck on my cheek; she was too intimidated to flaunt her familiarity in front of my drunken gay guests. I'm not sure who suggested the bracing walk on the beach with the dregs of a fifth of scotch, but there we were stumbling along chilled, with sand in our shoes and our hair whipped in every direction. Frank and I left John holding the bottle while we went into the dunes to urinate. Quickly we found our way home and fell onto the bed in a large closet used for extra guests. After Frank and I got rolling we heard Augusta shuffling around the ground floor, finally tugging the doorknob, shouting, "Larry, you bastard, I know you're in there!"

"We're only talking, I'll be right up."

"I have to work tomorrow."

"What time is it?"

"Five o'clock." She leaves. Frank and I go back to where we left off. Now we hear John Myers call from the dark garden, "Larry, where are you?"

A moment later John tugs the same doorknob, whispering, "Larry, are you in there?"

I was too drunk to say no. John was last heard crashing around the shed. Whatever was left for Frank left. I wanted to get up, and go up, but I fell asleep.

Augusta worked till twelve the next day, came home, didn't talk to me and my guests for the entire weekend. John and I completed a list of works for the exhibition. For Saturday night's dinner he wangled an invite to Alfonso Ossorio's. Frank and I ate at Fairfield Porter's. On Sunday we all had frankfurters and beans, and John went back to New York. Frank and I went out to the studio and worked on our collaboration, didn't finish that either. Driving him to the station for the evening train to New York, I suggested we try everything again next weekend.

After a few days the silence was broken. I convinced Augusta that nothing had happened in the closet, that I was drunk and fell asleep. Next Friday morning I told Berdie to prepare dinner for six because Frank was coming. "No," said Augusta, "keep it at five." She walked up the stairs with a calm that made me pick up the downstairs extension. I listened as she called Aesop, who said he was miserable without her; then she called Phil Platt's law office and quit, and finally phoned for a taxi. She was packed by the time it came to take her to the Southampton train station.

Animal Tales from My Son Steven

"Chappo, her son Bongo, and Tiny were our dogs on Toylsome Lane. They were always yapping when Dad practiced his horn. One day Dad told me the dogs got lost, they wandered off. Later I found out the truth. The sneak had actually taken them in the car and driven thirty-five miles away to Montauk and dumped them right out on the highway. On their own they got into a pack with other dogs and bummed around the countryside. But after a couple of weeks on the road the dogs wandered one night into Amagansett, where Larry was playing with a band at Sam Liss's Elm Tree Inn.

The dogs recognized the sound of his baritone sax, and they came in and went up to greet him. They came right up to the bandstand with a few of their newfound pals, wagging their tails and yapping hello; then they all came onto the bandstand and started jumping all over him and licking him! They loved his sound; they stayed till the gig ended that night, and Larry, overcome, took Chappo, Bongo, and Tiny back home, where they stayed on a few months listening to him practice and yapping. Larry had to get rid of them again. Bongo wound up being given to the neighbors, the Johnsons, and lived a long and prosperous life in their driveway next door to us. There were no recriminating looks. Those dogs were very stoic. Tiny was still a puppy, and the Edwardses on Dale Street were glad to raise him. For years we'd bump into them and always have to listen to a few Tiny tales; we felt as if the Edwardses were some kind of in-laws.

"Jasper Johns and Bob Rauschenberg came out to stay with us now and then, with two capuchin monkeys they were very enamored of. Berdie liked Jasper, Joe and I liked Jasper. Bob had a style so cool it seemed a little cold. Jasper seemed friendlier. The most friendly were the capuchins. During a visit to us one of the monkeys died. They buried him out back and performed a ceremony. Jasper Johns said a few words over the grave. 'Monkeys are so fragile.'

"Alfonso Ossorio and Ted Dragon visited with a gift of birds in a huge Oriental cage, intricately carved, on four legs quite high up, teakwood, very beautiful. Today an auction would bring at least ten, fifteen thousand dollars. There were cockatoos in the cage flying around screaming. Larry called Anne Porter and said he had something for her. "Oh no you don't," said Anne.

"We had one bird named Peepers that was this beautiful Indian myna bird of many colors, very gorgeous, rare. We went away for Christmas to the city and left him in the cellar. We came back and he was frozen stiff. We forgot to leave the heat on. Poor Peepers. We all liked him too. We had him stuffed. He came out looking very magic realist. Poor Peepers."

Sally

That same summer at the same Elm Tree Inn I was playing with a five-piece jazz group consisting of a New York piano player, Ed Saco, a Bonacker fisherman on drums, a Bonacker plumber on bass, Howard "The K" Kanovitz on trombone, and me on baritone. Seated at the table on the edge of the dance floor was an especially attractive female who kept popping up to dance with her redheaded girlfriend. She put a lot of energy into her intricate steps. At the end of the set I went over to their table and asked the one I liked if she was a dancer.

"Yes, I'm a dancer and I'm an actress. This is my friend Phillipa Keogh."

"And what's your name?" I said.

"Sally Hamilton."

Sally had a reserved air, lacking to my relief the sincerity of New York Jews. I was absorbed in her beauty every second I was at the table, which made me more conscious than usual of the curvature of my nose and my skinny physique covered by shabby bohemian togs. Beauty and the Beast. I talked my head off, trying to appear funny but serious, arty but plain, sexy but celibate, poor but rich, unrecognized but famous. Toward the end of the evening I asked if she'd wait till I finished playing, maybe we could go somewhere and do something together.

The gig ended at midnight. Sally had come on a bicycle. I put it in the back of my station wagon and drove with her to the Amagansett beach. We sat on the sand. There was moonlight and no wind, and the waves made a soft sound. Her laugh on the empty beach was loud and frequent. She spoke about her career as a dancer and her classes at Stella Adler's acting school. At moments she spoke softly about her life as a thing full of disheartening episodes. Along the way I found out she was a descendant of Alexander Hamilton.

"I've always admired him," I said, and kissed her, expecting a "Well, Lar, it's late, I'd like to go home now."

What followed was another kiss, a long moisture-gathering bomber that ended with her peeling off her panties and me tugging my pants and undershorts to my knees. I kept thinking sand would get into the act. If it did I didn't notice. I was immediately in love with Sally.

The next day and the next night I felt the same way. We had a beautiful walk in the moonlight and listened to the whoosh of lapping waves, then sat on the sand to talk about life and our ambitions. The evening ended with that glorious crescendo. Not bad, not bad. But more compelling was having a dancer and an actress for a girlfriend. I pictured myself, a proud number one stage-door

Johnny in a white silk scarf, picking her up at the theater to feed her and go home with her. I was impressed that someone I hoped fervently to be close to was living a strict schedule of ballet classes, drama courses, exercise, careful eating, no smoking, no drinking, leading a monastic life except for those moments when she broke her vows to be in bed with me.

At four o'clock in the afternoon I gave up playing hard-to-get and called her friend Phillipa.

"Sally left for New York."

"Do you have her number?"

"She's in the middle of moving. I don't know her new number."

"What's her old number?"

"Well, if Sally calls me I'll tell her you called."

She hung up. What's happening? She didn't ask for my number. Was our night on the beach a mistake Sally didn't care to repeat? There was only one way to find out.

On Monday: "Hello, Stanley?"

Who's Stanley?

Stanley Moss, a poet friend of mine and the young lover of stately Stella Adler.

"Stanley, listen, I met a beautiful girl in Amagansett this weekend and I want to get in touch with her. I know she studies at Stella's. Could you find out when a Sally Hamilton takes her class? By the way, she's a direct descendant of Alexander Hamilton."

"I'll call you back."

A few minutes later. "Larry, Sally Hamilton takes a class on Friday at five o'clock."

"This is Monday. What do I do?"

"I'll call you back."

A few more minutes. "Larry, Sally Hamilton works at Ernest's on Thirty-eighth and Park every day from eleven to three."

On Tuesday a little after 11:00 a.m., a menu hiding my face, I'm waiting for Sally to acknowledge my presence. On the walk over to me she doesn't make eye contact.

At my table, no smile, she says, "What are you doing here?"

"I came to see you about the other—night."

"Shhh!" Those gorgeous white teeth made me realize again how beautiful she was. "You're talking too loud." I took no offense; every person I've ever known, including the hard of hearing, says I talk too loud.

"What did I do wrong?"

She begins to walk away.

"Can I see you tonight?"

"No."

"When can I see you?"

She comes back and wipes the table, shakes her head as if it's all a little too much, and finally shines a friendly smile at me. "All right. Pick me up Friday after my class at Stella Adler's around 6:30. You can drive me out to the Hamptons."

"Great!"

"But Lar . . . please leave the restaurant now. You're making me very nervous."

I picked her up Friday at 6:25, and we drove out together.

We never lived together, but we stayed together for three years. I felt that during our romance, unlike any other woman in my life, she never slept with anyone but me—hard as it is to admit. I should have married her. She was beautiful, talented, her father was rich, her mother was good-looking, and she was a descendant of Alexander Hamilton.

Fifth Street

My trucking business and later my teaching brought me to New York often, but now, instead of turning around and going back to the Hamptons, I began to stay overnight with Sally and leave the next morning. If the ballet with Frank O'Hara came up, or gallery business with John Myers, or a jam session with Howard Kanovitz, or a party with everybody, or the desire to flatten myself with a shot of heroin, I'd stay another day—which meant another night, usually with Sally, but not always.

On Fifth Street off Avenue A was an apartment rented by a drummer I knew as Greg. At any time, I mean any time, you could knock on the door and find someone "home." Inside were four or five mattresses on the floor, four chairs, a rickety dark green card table, a dirty bathroom and lots of toilet paper, and plunked in the middle of the larger of the two rooms, an upright piano in good shape, tuned, and a proper piano bench. There was an okay set of drums. This was Greg's place, but no one was in charge of the scene. The apartment served three intertwining purposes: it was a crash pad (defined as a place to sleep on a floor, mattress, or whatever for a few hours) and a meeting place either to pick up or order heroin; and completing the trilogy was the music created by the musicians while they waited, sometimes for hours, to score. The quality of the music depended on who showed up and in what condition.

Dealers (called pushers) "fell by" like cabbies going to Idlewild Airport for action. Fat Leo was the most frequent supplier, and the most honest—a Buddha-like ex-drummer living in Coney Island with his mother, who'd heard so many of her son's Lester Young records she could la-la-la every solo.

On the mattresses people listened to the players and chatted as though in an ordinary social setting, except for falling asleep in the middle of their own sentences. I never saw a female there. "The artist has to transform himself into a visionary by a long, immense, and systematic derangement of all the senses . . . and become, at enormous personal cost, the great invalid, the great criminal, the great damned soul," as Rimbaud wrote.

Each time I visited the premises a kind of spiritual leader called tunes, set the beat, and inquired cheerfully how everyone was doing. "My name is D. Flat Major. Everyone calls me D. Flat."

Everyone was young, everyone was poor. David Amram occasionally showed up with his French horn. "I just bopped by to lay this tune on you cats for this session, Lenny Bernstein is blowing the concert version uptown. Hey, daddy, this whole cosmic scene is really groovy!"

The cosmic scene produced some terrific visuals I can still picture clearly. The nights were dramatic, fervid raised-horn blowing, glints bouncing off the instruments, nonplayers fumbling in their pockets for money, beseeching the gofer to "get back as soon as possible, man, I'm sick, I really am."

By day shafts of light in the dark apartment were soothing and the music was mellower, lulling those on the mattresses into a sweet reverie they were already in. I brought my horn each time I went, and enjoyed playing until the drug arrived. If I'd been a regular user, I could have been playing fifteen minutes after shooting up. But since I rarely "did the thing," a tiny dose of heroin sufficed to knock me on my back. So I would leave the Fifth Street apartment immediately after I scored, not wanting to be on my back on those mattresses, and go somewhere quiet. When I recovered enough to drive back to Southampton I usually needed another stretch of hours in bed to return to my normal hyper self. Berdie waited on me hands and feet. It was hard to tell if she knew I took heroin, but if she did it wouldn't have changed her feelings about me one iota; she would have thought it came with being an artist.

The Challenge

One cold, dull-looking early spring morning in 1957 out in South-ampton, a representative of Revlon Cosmetics Corporation called. How would I feel about going on a quiz show of theirs called *The $64,000 Challenge?*

"Sounds very interesting," I said, masking my excitement. It sounded terrific, and I wasn't doing much that week.

"Why don't you come see us in New York, we'll talk about it."

Face to face they checked out my looks and personality and determined my show biz value. I asked them how they happened to think of me for the quiz program; they said the Museum of Modern Art suggested me (the museum also suggested other artists, Philip Guston and Franz Kline among them). They never posed an art question, but they asked about my mother-in-law, my kids, my sax playing, just to get me to talk. They told me about the show. A week later I was given the honor of putting face, body, and art knowledge on view for forty million people. I accepted.

There was a modern art expert I'd be challenging, both of us vying for the sixty-four thou. He was a working jockey who knew art. On the show, to insure that contestants received no answers from the audience, they put us in matching soundproof booths. With earphones wrapped over my head, I heard Bert Parks, the spot-lit emcee, ask me, after a long drum roll, "Mr. Rivers, for four thousand dollars, what's the name of the Spanish painter who painted *Guernica* and whose last name begins with the letter P?"

There was music to build tension.

"Do you have the answer, Mr. Rivers?"

"Yes."

"Please give us the name."

"Picasso."

"Right for four thousand dollars!"

I began studying seriously; I thought I had a chance to win. I bought books, brought them out to Southampton, went into my studio at the beginning of the day, and pored over them. But I wasn't studying twenty-four hours a day. I painted too. Before get-ting into an art book I used to take the cover off and staple it to the wall so I could ruffle through the pages more easily. Soon I had an interesting wall full of these covers: Vuillard, Bonnard, Matisse, Picasso, etc. I made a painting of it, *The Wall*, which I sold in Southampton for $750—everything was looking up!—to the wealthy widow of a Humble Oil official.

For all my studying, most of the questions those first few weeks were easy, just part of my experience. At one point there was a tense moment. For $16,000 I was asked to identify a sculpture and the material it was made of. I said the work was by Archipenko and it was made of metal.

Wrong!

"We're sorry, Mr. Rivers, Archipenko is correct, but the sculpture is made of bronze."

There was a big groan from the audience. My heart sank. But an angel came out of the wings, a producer of the show.

"Uh, Bert, Mr. Rivers' answer is correct. The sculpture is made of bronze, but bronze is a metal."

Saved! I still had a chance for the thirty-two and the sixty-four.

Before the big question of the week, Bert Parks would devote a few moments to personal questions about myself. He asked me what kind of paintings I did.

"Well, I've painted my mother-in-law in the nude, twice."

Laughter.

"Are you a realistic painter?"

Laughter.

"Yes, I'm realistic, but I didn't paint the hairs in her nose."

Laughter.

On the streets the next day people waved hello, and some came up to say they saw me last night on TV. They didn't ask for my autograph, but they wished me luck.

It didn't take me long to realize I was in a very strong position. If I quit the quiz, they would be very unhappy. I began calling the producers for a hint as to what area the next week's question would deal with. I worked myself past the $32,000 question, and then came the big week, the final week, the $64,000 week. By today's standards I was shooting for over half a million dollars.

I switched the site of my studying entirely to the Museum of Modern Art library. Frank O'Hara, though just starting to work at the museum, got me permission. In the library a very soft-spoken man, the librarian who brought me the books I needed and took them away when I left, came over and told me he knew who I was, how much he liked my work. He was an older man. Suddenly he lowered his voice and said the panel that thought up the questions for *The $64,000 Challenge* used this library. "And I'm the one who brings out the books they ask for—to help them decide on the questions for you and the jockey!" Then this quiet but passionate librarian, standing above me, told me he'd picked up and had in his possession the notes left by the panel containing their questions and answers. He showed them to me and said the world was a commercial place and artists were the only pure people left in this society.

The most important question concerned the special signature Pierre Bonnard put to his prints. My hero! I knew all his work, stole from him, but had never looked at how he signed his prints! Bonnard never signed his full name: he drew a PB with a circle around it. The next Sunday night I went on the program, into the booth, and answered the questions correctly. So did the jockey. We each received $32,000.

Since we had no TV, all this was being watched, every week, by Berdie and the kids in a Polish bar near the Southampton railroad station. Life was looking up! We suddenly had money to add to our $1,000 in the bank, if we had that much.

I told a lot of people that if I won I'd be at the Cedar for a celebration. I went to the bar, which was jam-packed, even more than usual, and bought almost everyone there a drink. Between beer at fifteen cents and whiskey at fifty this gesture cost me a whopping $70. I took out the check for $32,000 and showed it to Franz Kline, who pulled it out of my hand and passed it to the next person, till the check made the rounds of the entire bar and the booths behind it. Miraculously it came back in one piece. It was a glorious evening, an extraordinary evening.

Once I shared the makeup room with a bright blond contestant named Joyce, who loved the glamour and glitter of TV. One day years later I was watching TV, and there was my makeup mate, Joyce Brothers, with her own program. The glamorous artist Jane Wilson also spent some time on the show answering questions that were not difficult for the M.A. in art history she was.

There was a second series, and I was chosen again for the program. This time I would call up and ask the producers more aggressively to give me the general area of the questions.

"Look, Tim, I'm going to be sick, because it's making me so nervous. I'm not sure I'll be able to show up."

"We have a policy not to inform our contestants about anything

325

specific. However . . . concentrate on Renoir."

Now that I was a star, Shirley Bernstein, sister of Lenny and a producer of the show, began looking after me.

"Larry, don't be nervous, no one is throwing curves. Take the questions in the most direct way you can."

In this new series I had reached the $8,000 level and was now going for $16,000. After a few more phone calls and threats about my state of health I began concentrating on Renoir's *Boating Party*. I studied the painting very carefully and went to the studio fully prepared to answer the questions correctly. About five minutes before I was to go on, Shirley came into the makeup room to encourage and calm me. "I'll be back in time to walk you to the stage." Now I was alone in the room in front of the mirror, and on a little shelf below it was a folder Shirley had been carrying and had left behind. I knew that the questions—and answers—were in that folder. I didn't know if it had been left purposely. If Shirley walked in as I was cheating on my exam, I'd give myself away about how badly I wanted to win. I didn't want the sister of Lenny Bernstein, whom I knew pretty well, to know this about me.

In the booth I answered all the questions correctly until I was asked the maiden name of Renoir's wife, who was in the painting. "Oh shit! Fuck!" was all I could come up with. We went off the air for a few seconds, and when we came back on I still didn't know the answer. I went back to the makeup room, Shirley put her arms around me. "I'm sorry, bubby. Get dressed, we'll go for a nice stiff drink." She went to get her coat, I washed up, I looked in the mirror and aggressively opened the fucking folder, and there were the fucking answers.

Not too many months later scandal broke out. Charles Van Doren, Columbia University professor, after winning $100,000 on another quiz show called *Twenty-One*, admitted to having been given the answers to the questions he was asked. Quiz programs came under investigation. The charge was corruption of the contest-entertainment categories. A football game on TV is a contest, two teams trying to win, the outcome not predictable. Wrestling on TV is registered under entertainment. $64,000 *Challenge* and *Twenty-One* registered themselves in the contest category. The producers of these quiz shows instinctively knew that if their programs were billed as entertainment, they wouldn't draw a fly. The producers were breaking the rules of the category and cheating the public by giving the contestants answers. I found out that the jockey art expert didn't know his ass from a Duchamp toilet seat and was fed all the answers.

I was called upon to give information, and I ran into quite a few assistant DAs who told me I would get into trouble if I didn't answer truthfully. I don't understand to this day what trouble I could have gotten into. I didn't register the program, and it was no crime to go on TV and get answers. After testimony from me, other contestants, Shirley B., Bert Parks and the producers of the show, and finally the sponsors, the DA convened a grand jury. Sitting in the witness box, I was asked by an assistant DA about certain broadcast nights. He was trying to test my art knowledge. At one point confusion arose between my first five weeks on the air and my second four weeks.

"I suggest, Mr. District Attorney, in referring to my first series you call it A and the second one B, and call each night of each series one, two, three, etc."

"Mr. Rivers," he boomed, "on the night of A-three did you answer a question on Matisse?"

The assistant DA fumbled a lot, and I began to answer facetiously, knowing they had nothing on me. At one point he asked bluntly if Shirley Bernstein had given me an answer.

"Absolutely not."

"It sounds as though you don't want to say anything against Miss Bernstein. Why are you protecting her, Mr. Rivers?"

It all sounded so absurd that I rose from the witness chair and said dramatically, "Because I love her—and I don't care if the whole world knows it!"

Through the giggles and guffaws in the courtroom I heard myself excused from further testimony. The jury members asked for my autograph and the date of my next show, or just winked. Finally, the assistant DA came over to me. "My name is Jay Goldberg. I'm engaged to your cousin Rema Hochberg."

We kissed and made up. Thus ended my show biz career.

Berdie Going

That same year, in August, for my thirty-second birthday, I gave a large afternoon party on the high grassy grounds outside my house. Inside the house Berdie was dying, but I didn't know it. I thought she was only sick—no reason not to have a party. Every so often I went to her room, where she was lying in bed, and told her who was there, who hadn't come yet, how much food and drink was being consumed, and so forth.

Bill de Kooning came, shaking everybody's hand as if they were really there to see him and his large eighty-year-old Dutch-speaking mother dressed in black. Harold (art critic) and May (social critic) Rosenberg brought me a pair of socks for a gift, Edwin Denby handed me a package of Wrigley's Spearmint chewing gum. Arnold, as he continued to do through the years, found me a cheap paperback on language. All my regular pals who were out in the Hamptons came, plus some irregulars who chipped in for a limo and sang all the way to Southampton. The best-known guest was Tennessee Williams, who was staying in a converted windmill I found for him, part of an old hotel with a golf course on the road between Southampton and Hampton Bays (it is now Long Island University at Southampton). During the party Tennessee went in to talk to Berdie and stayed with her, listening to stories of her childhood in Harlem.

A few days before the party, Berdie was taking a break from posing for a painting I was almost finished with, *The Sitter*, now in the Met. She came into the dining room with a bundle of dry laundry in her arms, walked over to me at the easel, and said, "Something happened to me, Larry, just as I was reaching up for the clothes on the line."

Except for the irises, her eyes were all red. She looked frightened and said she was "feeling funny." Laughing slightly, I told her to look in the mirror, as if she'd find it funny to see herself with such red eyes. She said, "It is funny, Larry, I never saw anything like it."

In the morning she called me into her bedroom and said a peculiar thing was happening to her vision. "I can only see half of everything. I'm looking at you and I can't see your whole face, there's a black cloud over it with a jagged edge, like a piece of you is ripped away." I called Dr. Wright. He told me if she could move to bring her to his office a couple of blocks away on South Main Street. He called me back immediately. "It sounds serious, I'm coming right over." After he examined Berdie he arranged for an ambulance to take her to Southampton Hospital.

We were living one block from the hospital, at 92 Little Plains Road, our new home. Shortly after I met Sally Hamilton I began looking for a place about an hour from New York so I'd spend less time on the road away from my painting. Instead, with Sally's approval and Jimmy Merrill's down payment, I bought an eight-room house, on the market for a cheap twelve gees. Through some "Jewing down" I bought it for $10,500, studio possibilities and all, about a stone's throw from Toylsome Lane.

The first day Berdie was in the hospital, in a ward, I went there, stayed a few minutes, and came back to the house. I did this all day long and into the evening. I became very frightened that she was going to die. I felt the awful sensation in my stomach I had as a kid when it became clear that a role I was practicing for a school play was not memorized and I would have to admit in front of the whole class and the teacher that I didn't know the part. On the street, in the house, I kept shouting, "Oh no, no!" Then I'd run back to the hospital to have a look at her.

For the first time in her saintly life, she began to display aggressive feelings. Berdie, who'd been incapable of sounding cross all her life, was now criticizing the patients and their visitors: they all talked too loud, and they were ugly! Then she said, "The nurses are mean to me. I told them not to wear perfume. Smell them." (I always asked Berdie not to wear perfume. When she switched to cologne, I told her that was no better.) Then followed a litany of warnings about "colored people" wanting to do her in, and that I should be on the lookout for them too. She had an expression on her face I'd never seen before, never: both stern and scared. I couldn't understand where all this was coming from. I had canonized Berdie before she died. Did I confer sainthood too early? Dr. Wright said she had suffered a mild stroke, probably from her very high blood pressure. Her speech was not impaired, nor her mobility, but her vision and her mind were. After three days Dr. Wright said she could go home, since the hospital could do nothing more to improve her condition; she could get better on her own at home. Or worse.

I wasn't sure how to behave toward Berdie when she came home. She ceased complaining, but her talk skipped from one subject to the next very rapidly. She sat around, we didn't let her do any housework. She was able to undress herself before bed and to dress in the morning. She went to the bathroom herself. We fed her. In the backyard our clothesline formed a wide three-sided cubicle. In this cubicle, with laundry still on the line moving in the warm breeze, I walked Berdie around and around and sang to her. Her favorite song was "Ramona," a hit of the 1920s sung by Russ Columbo, America's first crooner. She wasn't coordinated in her walking, her knees came up too high, she'd often lose her balance. She didn't comb her hair, her face was flushed, but the blood in her eyes grew less intense and some of the former white showed. I thought maybe she'd live, she didn't seem that bad.

> "Ramona, buh-buh-buh boo,
> I hear the mission bells above.
> Ramona, buh-buh-buh boo . . .
> They're ringing out our song of love,"

trying to be as Russ Columbo as I could.

The night after my party Berdie's condition, although not so hot, seemed stable. I decided to relax and go to the Bluebird and blow. Nothing too exciting happened, perhaps some drinking, but I got home early—for me. I was beginning to undress in my bedroom upstairs when I heard Berdie downstairs sounding like a whooping crane. She was having trouble breathing. I ran down to her bedroom. Steven, who slept in the cot next to her bed, was sitting up. "What's wrong with her, Dad?"

She stopped making that awful sound for a moment and asked for water. I held the glass for her as she drank. She swallowed and regained some composure. I sat on the bed holding her hand. She asked me, "Am I going to die?"

I said no, but I lost contact with her; she fell back to sleep and moaned loudly all night. In the morning, early, I heard another sound more distressing than the whooping of the night before; now it was something between a snore and an uneven gurgle. I called Dr. Wright. An ambulance came almost immediately. He arrived as they were carrying Berdie to the ambulance on a stretcher. We got in with her. Between the house and the hospital I think she died. I was holding her head as her croaking stopped. I went home, not allowed into the emergency room, where they were trying to save her. I called Augusta in New York and told her, "I think your mother's going to die, you better come out."

An hour later the hospital called. Berdie was dead. I had to make arrangements to get her body out of the hospital. Augusta arrived. We walked to the hospital and were led into a room where fifteen stretchers, the kind you see in hospital hallways, were stored. Way in the back against the wall, wrapped in a blanket and strapped, Berdie was lying dead on one of the stretchers. We stood above her, looked at her, then looked at each other and left. I cried as I put my arm around Augusta, but I cry when I hear Notre

Dame's football march. I called Schwartz's Funeral Home near my former Second Avenue studio. On Wednesday Frank O'Hara in a white rayon yarmulke made the whole congregation weep delivering a eulogy.

Berdie. I tried to fuck her. She posed for paintings that all sold, for money. She cooked for me, she raised my boys, she walked behind me and didn't talk. She dies and thirty-four years later I'm still using her—for this book. My son Joe wants to speak.

I remember Tennessee Williams spent almost the whole party with Berdie in her room, and came the next day on his own. Someone like Tennessee Williams was the thrill of her life. She didn't know much about him, but she knew he was famous. She fell in love with his southern accent, charm, and gentleness. He had an incredible ability to pay attention. His curiosity was intense.

It was hard for me to face her illness, not because I would miss her. It's not what seventeen is about, it's about starting life, women, booze and parties, having fun and running around. I didn't have any tolerance for illness. I now feel guilty about it. She was very sick and dying, and it had no meaning for me. I pushed it out of my mind. My brother was fonder of Berdie than I was. I resented that she wasn't my mother. But she raised me. She was Steven's surrogate mother, virtually all he knew; Augusta only popped in and out. At seventeen I had had a lot of trouble in school and quit. I couldn't get along there. I was going to art school. I had a 1949 Ford—I was being a kid. Her death came at a time when all of my being was devoted to being a teenager. I feel bad that I wasn't more connected to my grandmother at seventeen. When you get older you realize that time is short and you need to fix things up and talk. She had a brain tumor—a blood clot. It affected her mind. She'd call out in the middle of the night, "Sydney, help me." These cries were awful moments of pain and loneliness. Because there was no Sydney in my life, it was abstract. But when I lost my wife, Myra, I realized you can actually keep loving someone for years and years. We will remember everything when we become Berdie. Whatever ability I have to give back love comes from her.

This assessment of Joseph's was also mine.

About my own mother I was capable of a different assessment. Here, for example, is an excerpt from a 1958 lecture I gave to art students at three Florida state universities. It was published in *Art News* and read to my mother over the telephone by a good friend of hers.

> . . . my parents are from Russo-Poland. They are no more interesting than the peasants who lived and worked in the same area. During my childhood the only thing in our house resembling art was a cheap tapestry with a dark figure, a cross between a Fragonard and a Minsky stripper popular in immigrant dining rooms of the twenties and thirties; it followed us from one apartment to another. But mind you, when I took my mother to her first exhibition of paintings (Bonnard, MOMA 1948), after her having had such a profound dining room experience in art she told me which were good paintings and which were very bad in a strong voice that never showed for one moment I could have thought her an innocent but nonetheless complete idiot. So if I've inherited bad taste, talking about my mother this way, it is at least compounded with an obnoxious sense of who I am.

I blamed my mother for *my* having insulted her! Here is her letter in response to her child's words.

> Should I write dear son or foolish son? I'll start this letter by asking you how in your 34 years you haven't grown up enough to know fathers and mothers have faults and I wouldn't say I am without them but children when they grow up know that parents mean the best but I'm unlucky that you haven't past the 10 year old stage. I don't know why all of a sudden I became a peasant and an idiot. I wasn't that way when I helped you in every way. I bought you a washing machine when I didn't have one. But when you needed steam papa came every weekend in S. Hampton to work a seven day week and left me alone (And you know I'm afraid to sleep alone) And it costed $10, $15 dollars from his pocket every week. You say I told you which paintings were good and which weren't—well this "idiot" remembers an incident—that when you once had a bad write-up about a nude painting I couldn't sleep all nite worrying about you and your future—then I realized that

they were writing good or bad about you and not me, Shirley Grossberg, so I called you to tell you that and reassure you. I don't care what you call me or papa. We know what we are. But why should you have such a hate against us? You must hate yourself very much to write such things about us. Perhaps you're afraid that I am enjoying your fame and that's why you are writing about us that way. Sure I would enjoy your fame if you would be the right son. Stop and think right now and total all *you* have ever done for us. Yes, you. You are 34 years old and its time *you* started giving in life. Perhaps we haven't given *all* you wanted but we can enumerate many many things we have done for you. Truthfully can *you* find as you think one thing you have done for us? And now you are ashamed of your family. Now I want to tell you Larry we don't want to be written about. Remember when they ask about your family just say they died when you were a year old. I don't want to hear from you or know you. Even after I die don't walk behind my coffin. I don't need the indignity of my friends calling me up to tell me what my famous son says about me. This letter will make no impression on you. I'm just writing it to unburden my heart because you have none.

Your idiot mother.

She is the second from the left, a Russian schoolgirl. My mother was born Soora, later becoming Sonya, and in the United States she was Shirley.

She never knew her date of birth—something about the remoteness of where she came from and no one bothering with records. She was born somewhere between the death of Alexander III and the coronation of Nicholas II, the last czar, so it must have been 1894. She somehow knew she was older than my father, though on the basis of general deterioration he seemed at least her age. For Sonya, being older than her husband was a flaw.

She grew up with eight brothers, no sisters, in Drushkapolia, a hamlet about three hundred miles east of Warsaw. For centuries Drushkapolia kept shifting its national identity between Ukrainian, Polish, and Austrian. The Jews in the region had no identification problem. Sonya said that she found her way to New York because Communist Russia was no place for her. She cried like a White Russian at the news of the czar's death! The truth was she came to America to avoid being an old maid in Drushkapolia. Two female cousins had married Christians! A family with this sort of history reduced the matrimonial appetites of eligible Jewish hamleteers. Which explained, she thought, why she was still unmarried at twenty-five.

While she was languishing in Drushkapolian hopelessness, her brother Moishe was working his balls off in the hat business in New York by day and in a New Jersey shirt factory by night. In 1903, at seventeen, he had been shanghaied from the streets into the Russian army to fight the Japanese in Port Arthur. This was like being a black American in the Alabama militia. Basic training was all he gave "Little Father," Nicholas II. Up for his nightly outhouse urination, Moishe piled a load of firewood against the camp wall and walked over the top. In a small village nearby he found its one Jew, a friend of his father's, who hid him until he was whisked away in a cart beneath a load of hay, over the border into the town of Boratyn in Galician Austria.

There he met and wed plump, simple Brontza, who never learned to read or write in any language, who in the space of nine years delivered six sons. The live ones were Aaron and Herschel, twin monsters with pudgy, rough hands that delighted in crushing handshakes; Yankel, a Slavic Valentino and militant socialist; and the runt, Maxie. Moishe left his brood to board a ship to Le Havre, taking twenty days to get to New York, where the most adventurous of Sonya's brothers, Duvid, had worked his way up, beginning in 1907, from sleeping at the bottom of East Side stairwells to a bed in a green enameled room on Hoe Avenue in the Bronx. Moishe

arrived and moved in with brother Duvid and began to work toward
a classical immigration.
1. The man comes over. Alone.
2. Back over the water he crossed, his wife and children await
eagerly.
3. He works hard to pile up money.
4. He secures a place for all of them to live.
5. Finally, he gets them on a boat.
It wasn't until 1920 that he was able to undertake the fifth step.
Seven years hadn't dimmed the memory of Brontza's illiteracy. He
wrote his sister Sonya, about twenty-five then, asking her to guide
his family to the Golden Land; he also wrote that a friend, a distant
cousin named Sam Grossberg, was ready to marry her. After a day's
journey to Boratyn, she found her sister-in-law and her nephews,
scrubbed, enormously packed, and deranged by the excitement of
going to Papa and America.

Warsaw was a view through a train window. In Berlin they
spent the night in a railroad terminal on a bench until the train
took them to Paris. At HIAS, an organization in a warehouse set
up to facilitate the exodus of thousands of Jews from Eastern Europe, Sonya found herself and her troupe at the end of a long line.
Sonya went to the Cunard shipping office. In tears, she pointed to
her forlorn charges and their big brown pile of belongings. They
were assigned six hammocks five stories below the water, and the
next day the ship sailed.

A few days out, her nephews and sister-in-law complained that
they were starving. Mom made her way to the captain's quarters
and struck a deal. For more food, Sonya would help in the kitchen
after every meal. Scrubbing her way across the wintry Atlantic, my
mother arrived in New York in December 1920. Half a decade later
I was born to Shirley Soora Sonya Hochberg Grossberg.

L

A

R

R

Y

R

I

V

E

R

S

L

A

R

R

Y

R

I

V

E

R

S

Clarice of London

In 1960, four decades after my mother arrived, Clarice Price crossed the wintry Atlantic in a jet, coming to New York to work for me, to help with my grandmotherless twelve-year-old Steven, and to have fun. Clarice shopped for me, fed me during the day, kept clean and livable the giant duplex I rented on West Third Street, an old film studio. I was immediately attracted to her. All day long she sang songs of her native Wales. Her ordinary speech the first few months sounded like song. She had ice-blue eyes, breasts impossible to ignore, and energy to run down two flights of stairs and go two blocks to pick up any little thing my selfish heart desired.

Résumé

I hired Clarice from a photograph shown to me at the Cedar Bar by the picture-perfect girlfriend of Franz Kline, Ann Schwartly. In the crush at the bar I told Ann I needed someone to help me care for my son Steven, who came home weekends from his school in Connecticut. As I examined the passport-type snapshot, Ann, above the din, filled me in on Clarice's qualifications. She said Clarice was a rosy-cheeked, full-bodied, jolly English girl she had met in London, a favorite model of many of the artists living along the Fulham Road. To supplement her modeling income Clarice

cleaned houses, cooked, and baby-sat. And was very interested in coming to the United States.

Clarice, my future wife, arrived February 6, 1960, with two large brown satchels. Within a short while after putting them down, she adjusted Ann's version of her employment history—a version that had induced me to go to a lawyer for proper immigration papers and to send airline ticket and money.

Clarice really came from a hamlet on the river Wye in Wales. Strictly speaking, she wasn't English. She moved to London at eighteen and supported herself as a schoolteacher. She taught art, music, English, and math. She modeled for fun. She had never cleaned, cooked, or baby-sat as a job. She was willing to learn. I was more than willing to let her. New York was going to be another adventure for her and her English chum Celia, with whom she'd hitchhiked the Costa Brava of Spain and the Côte d'Azur of France. She was an irresistible twenty-two-year-old.

Except for one somnambulent quickie that first week, it took over a year for us to get together.

My girlfriend at the time was Helene Grass, a twenty-two-year-old intellectual knockout who hinted that her boyfriend before me was a famous editor of a literary journal. Will Barrett strikes again, I thought. I asked her. She denied it. I went through the masthead of every literary and political review that came out of New York.

All investigative roads led to Delmore Schwartz. I asked if it was he, remembering his taste for big, light-haired, generously proportioned types, like his wife, Elizabeth Pollet. For years after, I would gravitate toward Delmore at gatherings, hoping to hear him say something to corroborate my suspicion. He never satisfied my obsession for truth. Even as late as 1966, five years after my breakup with Helene, I made a date to meet Delmore in his residence at the Dixie Hotel, on Forty-second Street near Times Square. By this time his past life was so jumbled in his brilliant brain that nothing he said put my doubts to rest. He took the answer to his grave.

Helene Grass came from a well-to-do Jewish family in Scarsdale. She took a degree in English literature at Vassar, which gave her an excuse to dabble in bohemia with me and my art and my poet friends, John Ashbery, Kenneth Koch, Frank O'Hara, Jimmy Schuyler. She wore dark rimmed glasses. She showered every morning and every evening, had a job at Farrar, Straus, and always wore proper clothes, all of which never interfered with a not so proper sexual style.

Advice

One evening while I was taking a bath in her apartment shortly after sex, Helene, still nude, stood very close to my soapy face. With her fingers she parted her labia, pointed to her clitoris, and told me testily, "This thing here, right here, see it? Look at it! This is what you must deal with every time we do it! Understand! Am I clear, Larry?"

"Clear."

She also lectured me, with a little more charm and a little less cogency, on how to dress.

"With your rugged features you'd look quite handsome in a conventional outfit, and cleaner. Look what Brooks Brothers has done for Kenneth Koch! And John Ashbery still wears J. Press."

"What's J. Press?"

"The Brooks Brothers of Cambridge. Do it for me—darling?" And gave me a kiss full of promises.

We went uptown to Brooks Brothers. I liked some of the clothes but none of the prices. In the course of our shopping I found out that the way to overcome high prices is to have someone else pay them. Kenneth Koch bought at Brooks not only for the style; he had a charge account there footed by his old man.

Trying to alleviate Helene's distress about my clothes and mine **L** about their prices, we walked over to Guy Weill's on Madison Avenue. A collector of my work, Guy owned my *Next to the Last Confederate Soldier* painting, which he displayed in the window of his chic men's store, the British American House. Guy and I bartered wear for works. He allowed me to run up a tab of a few thousand quid against his next acquisition. For years I had a rich rackful of Daks charcoal-gray trousers, Aquascutum raincoats, Burberry blazers with Eton and Oxford coats of arms, Jaeger sweaters, and a Stetson fedora. I wore them only a few times. I always lose interest in my new purchases after a second wearing. Even today I buy things, wear them once or twice, and forget them in my closet. **R** Then, desperate for something new, I try them on and feel my original enthusiasm. After I've ventured out in them a night or two, they go back in the closet until they go out of style, when again I slip them off the hanger for an evening's wear, and forget them **Y** once more. This has not changed. As soon as I own something I begin to dislike it. But I disliked Brooks Brothers clothes *before* I put them on, Helene!

Helene's advice extended to almost every part of my life. I was so happy to have sex with her I always took her advice seriously.

> Now if that isn't love
> It'll have to do **R**
> Until the real thing comes along.

A

R

R

Y

More Advice

I

When Clarice first arrived as my au pair, Helene told her, with my grudging approval, to address me as Mr. Rivers. Helene also thought that putting Clarice in a maid's costume would start the **V** master-servant relationship on the correct foot. At first I thought it was degrading, but I didn't argue. I knew that whatever Clarice wore would not change my determination to see beneath it. As for "Mr." we got rid of that the first day. **E**

I went shopping with Clarice for her maid's outfit at S. Klein's on Union Square, a working-class department store. The occasion for me was like a Hollywood film starring dapper Adolphe Menjou **R** fitting a necklace around the throat of a young chorus girl. Clarice donned one outfit after another as I watched from a chair drawn up for me. I donned a serious employer face, offering opinions as she kept disappearing into the dressing room and coming shyly out. **S**

At first I tried having her look like an *Esquire* cartoon of a French maid, bow in hair, white doily apron with panties visible in the rear, and of course high heels. That idea faded. Clarice did have a real job to do. And her comfort counted. By the end of the afternoon there was no maid's outfit, but there were three pairs of high-heeled shoes, silk stockings to go with them, and undergarments of our mutual choosing, establishing me as the slave and Clarice as the master. I didn't know any better; Germaine Greer and Betty Friedan were still in the closet slipping out of see-through bedroom garments and jumping into housedresses to deal with the kitchen.

Eula

In the summer of 1957, in Southampton, after Berdie died, I hired Eula, a fat and funny black woman about twenty-five, from Gadsden, Alabama, accent and all, to help Steven off to school, feed him when he came home, and when Dad was out making history every night, baby-sit. Since 1953 we had been living exclusively in

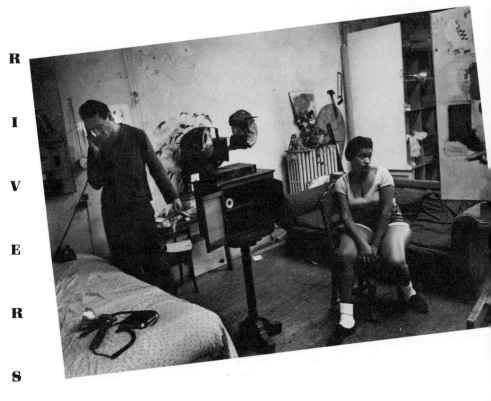

Southampton. Five years later, with Berdie dead, I decided to move back to 122 Second Avenue, which I had sublet.

Steven had been going to Southampton's public school, but rather than expose him to New York's frantic public school system, not to mention my social life, I sent him to the Cherry Lawn boarding school in Connecticut. Joe was seventeen and fending for himself—in an apartment in the West Village that he shared with four girls!? Cherry Lawn was close enough for Steven to come home to 122 Second Avenue every weekend, bringing with him all the self-sorrows of a twelve-year-old bereft of doting grandma and indulgent father.

Steven, Eula, and I stumbled through that fall, winter, and spring at 122 Second Avenue. My friend Howard Kanovitz, the artist to whom I had sublet my studio, was luckily on the verge of a Hollywood screenwriter's career, dark glasses and all, and went to California. Joe was a student at Pratt. Every so often he managed to wrest himself from his involvements to pay Dad a house call for affection and his weekly bread. Sometimes he'd work as my assistant and accompany me to the Artists Club on Eighth Street, to learn a little about art, and to meet women.

For the summer we all went back to Little Plains Road in Southampton. To this day, when I enter the house for the summer stay, no matter what thudding low point life is at, I feel a rise in spirits and expectations; when I turn the key in the fall to close the house and go back to the city, my heart actually sinks in my chest. Summer is gone and I am a year older.

Each morning, shaking off the night before, I would enter the studio to participate in the opera I am still starring in. Steven would float through for a "Good morning, Dad," ask what I thought of his black leather jacket, and split for the day to look for his gang. Joe would be underneath a 1931 Chevy roadster taking apart the engine to put it together again. Eula divided her time between cooking and cleaning and men dropping by from the community of migratory workers.

The Five Spot

In July 1958 I started to frequent a new club in Water Mill, Long Island. The Five Spot was owned by Joe and Iggie Termini, who had opened another Five Spot a few years earlier in Manhattan. Formerly a derelict bar on the Bowery run by their father, by 1957 it was a modern jazz joint featuring future greats like John Coltrane, Thelonious Monk, Elvin Jones, Ornette Coleman, and Don Cherry.

After a Leonard Bernstein concert at Carnegie Hall, my friend Lukas Foss, Lenny, and I went down to the Five Spot. I thought Len and Luke would be amazed by Ornette Coleman's compositions on a plastic sax. At one point Ornette called Lenny up to the platform to uncontrolled clapping from the sixty-five people in the club; even after the uptown applause of two thousand Lenny couldn't resist. The music starts and Lenny is playing bass fiddle! Since Ornette's music had no prearranged chords and Lenny had perfect pitch, his plucking was flawless. He walked off to an even greater ovation.

The Terminis' Bowery bum hangout evolved into a hangout for artists. Though sculptor David Smith gets credit in books for being the first known artist to walk in and stumble out of the Five Spot, Howard Kanovitz, stickler for musical and artistic truth, attributes the first abstract expressionist presence in the club to Herman Cherry, who lived in a Bowery loft across the wide street. Herman spread the news that I was playing there, and soon a social shuttle between the Cedar and the Five Spot was inaugurated.

Joe Termini thought, "If Rivers can draw half a crowd, imagine what a name could do." At my suggestion, he hired the dashing Allen Eager, lyrical exponent of the Lester Young school, whose good looks guaranteed an influx of debutantes. They were angry at him that week, and Allen's audience did not come up to our expectations. David Amram followed, playing improvisational French horn, till he wound up composing and conducting serioso stuff. After the Terminis hired Steve Lacy and a few other Caucasian epigones of Charlie Parker, Dizzy Gillespie, and Lester Young, I again offered my opinion.

"Look, Joe, jazz is black. Let's get a master."

"Who?"

"Thelonious Monk."

Monk was out of work. Through a very convoluted grapevine he heard that if he wanted it, he had a three-month gig right here in New York City. Monk brought in, among others, John Coltrane. Now the place was still downtown social, but what had been almost background music when the first group played there—unfortunately including me—began to move to the forefront. The Five Spot's reputation spread, and it began competing for New York's jazz audience. Joe seemed to take some of my advice, probably because I didn't offer it much. I made him change the lighting. Musicians should be seen as well as heard. It's better theater. He not only changed the lighting, he built a new bandstand.

Poetry and Jazz

In 1956, in such Village coffee shops as Figaro's, Rienzi's, and Cafe Wha, chess and checkers and scoring for sex or drugs mixed with an old convention that suddenly felt new—poetry reading. LeRoi Jones, Allen Ginsberg, Gregory Corso, and Jack Kerouac reported the enthusiasm of the coffee hounds that greeted their poetry, which they read mikeless, standing on a chair or table. I thought, How much more theatrical to combine the sounds of modern jazz with the sound of poetry. Before long I was producing evenings of Poetry and Jazz at the Five Spot. Producing? I rehearsed the poets and musicians for these performances. If that's producing, okay. Kenneth Koch, Arnold Weinstein, Frank O'Hara performed. Poetry reading with jazz became a weekly feature of the Five Spot.

In the spring of '58 the Termini brothers prepared to open the Water Mill Five Spot, hoping to tap the money that abounds in the

Frank O'Hara reading at another spot,
the Living Theater, with Ray Bremser, LeRoi Jones,
and Allen Ginsberg on deck

L

A

R

R

Y

R

I

V

E

R

S

Hamptons from Memorial Day to Labor Day. To the major attraction of modern jazz and the minor one of poetry performance would be added the delights of food; again I would supply writers and coordinate their readings with sounds from the musicians. Elvin Jones, the extraordinary drummer, took a personal interest in getting the Long Island club started. He lowered the Terminis' anxiety by playing for scale. He and I accompanied Joe and Iggie until we found a suitable space half a mile from the famous windmill in the center of town. In this suitable space on opening night I first laid thirsty eyes on the back of the Vassar English major Helene Grass, moving swiftly, tray in hands, dancing a kind of rhumba to avoid bumping into the tables.

Modern Romance

The night ended with Kenneth Koch telling those of us not interested in sleeping to come back to his place for a few nightcaps. Helene and I, slightly drunk, left Kenneth's party together.

Whatever part chemistry played in our romance, I never examined the chemicals. I don't remember any vows, but I remember one night early on when Helene left immediately after waitressing. That evening, from the bar, I had seen her chatting with a tallish fair-haired man at one of her tables. The man left first, she a few minutes later. She kissed me on the cheek, she'd call me tomorrow. She was tired and sleepy and wished to spend the night alone at the little farmhouse she rented. Well, she had a right to be sleepy. Besides, she had no obligation to spend every night with me. How long had I known her? A few weeks? On *my* own other nights I tried to take care of some of *my* unresolved sexual attractions. She was young, she was curious, why not? She'd told me lots of her past erotic adventures. I didn't mind. I listened with compassion. And I told you some pages ago, dear reader, with what kind of compassion I listened to my loved ones' sexual confessions.

Slowly my largess about Helene's departure dwindled to anxiety. The simple chat with the businessman she'd served was now transmogrified into a flirtatious conversation with a six-foot-two blond Adonis. Another one for the road and I decided to see for myself exactly how tired and sleepy she was!

Driven, I drove swiftly to her house on Mecox Road. Her lights were out! They could be doing it in the dark, although that was unlike her. Maybe lights out was his "bag"—some of those golden giants were shy about their fantastic bodies. I went around to the other side of the house. Her car was the only car in the yard, and I hadn't seen any cars on the road outside when I parked. She could have gone to *his* house—he left the bar first—and done it there, then come home in her own car and fallen into a blissful sleep with a throbbing vagina. All in about an hour! I put my hand on the hood of her car. It was cool. Silently I lifted the hood, the engine was still warm. But not hot. Which cooled my voyeuristic ardor. On the other hand, unable to verify infidelity, I felt relieved. I repeat,

> If that isn't love
> It'll have to do
> Until the real thing comes along.

By the end of the summer Helene was my girlfriend, and I was happy to be her boyfriend. We shared my house on Little Plains Road. And since almost everyone who is a household feature of mine ends up in some form in my work, I did many paintings that she posed for. She supplied content, I style.

Combined with some of Helene's primary sexual emanations were odd gestures of her hands and feet that had little to do with charm school influence. She constantly changed the angle of her head while listening to you speak; her eyes were wide open with the prodding of contact lenses in their primitive state of the art. Her face brimmed with expressions of enthusiasm about your point of view. She was always on the verge of interrupting you with "Yes! Yes! Yes!" to express how much she agreed with you and to add her own point.

She was a sienna-and-white being. If I'd succumbed to English romanticism, holding up a mirror to Nature, I would have produced some attractive figurative paintings, because my model was exquisitely attractive. Instead, my romance with Helene coincided with a tendency in my work to reduce all realistic details to shapes essentially abstract. At this time I liked something in the big Franz Kline black-and-white paintings, and I began incorporating his boldness in my paintings of Helene.

After the summer Helene found an apartment in New York City on Thompson Street. Fate also found me a new place, just around the corner from her, that enormous duplex on West Third Street. This former film studio of 7,500 square feet rented for $235 a month. For your average starving artist—more or less everyone I

$235 a month

knew—this was about six times the usual rent. Eula, our happy maid, in this summer of many romances, found a new man and remained in Southampton.

My proximity to Helene's apartment could have caused us some awkward moments but for some intelligent pathways to our abodes, which decreased the odds against our running into each other with a one-night standee. The subject never came up. We were two liars in love.

I decided not to send Steven back to Cherry Lawn. I couldn't take his tearful calls. With Berdie gone, I had to recognize the truth that while I'd kept him with me these past six years, nourished him, put a roof over his head and clothes on his body, I was too busy, too selfish, to be his "father." The West Third Street studio had an apartment upstairs where he could have his own room and feel the warmth he had in Southampton before Berdie died.

Until I could find someone as easy and as well-liked by Steven as Eula, Helene promised "input." She advised me to send him to a private school in the city. Forgive me, Moses, for the five days a week I sent Steven to St. Luke's parochial school! After the first year I decided that any school without Jesus and the nuns was preferable.

Helene's input also took the form of me rising first and waking Steven. That was easy. I am always the first person up no matter where I am, at home, hotels, visiting. When I open my eyes I think it's time to get up, even when I'm with someone. I feel a certain pleasant power alone in the quiet and the gray light of morning. Some mornings Helene came around the corner before going to work, spread peanut butter on a slice of bread, jammed it, threw an apple in a brown paper bag, and sent Steven off to St. Luke's with a kiss he always resisted. Except for Clarice, Steven never ever approved of my girlfriends, one-night stands, or any combination thereof.

Here is what my son, when questioned, had to say on the subject thirty years later.

SR: Your girlfriends? I hated them.

LR: Who didn't you like? In the order of dislike.

SR: Well, I didn't like Sally Hamilton because she kept calling you "Lar." I used to hate that "Lar," man, that drove me up the wall. Now and then I bump into her, she's a very sweet lady and I like her, but at the time, she was this waspy dancer who was taking my father from me, and I remember crying that you weren't spending as much time with me as with her.

Then there was Helene. I thought she had a great ass and I thought she strutted pretty good, but I was going through a very judgmental age when Berdie died, so I was fresh to her. I wouldn't even let her kiss me on the cheek. Clarice came and I allied myself with Clarice against your girlfriends. To me, they were taking you away, whereas Clarice was kind of my governess, and bringing you closer and closer, till you and she finally married. She was very sexy too. I was just hitting my pube stage, and I kept fantasizing about my future mom's big tits—which I used to try to grab whenever she was on the phone. I wouldn't leave her alone. Once, all fourteen years of me got up and said, "I'm hot for you!"

She answered, "Well, why don't you jerk off, you little clod?"

And I said, "All right, fuck you, I will."

I took my cock out right in front of her and I jerked off into the heat grating in the floor. She just looked, and laughed. It was all educational.

Opinions

At the time I never asked Steven's opinions of my girlfriends. I couldn't see how they affected his life, and I didn't need his approval. It never occurred to me that my life difficulties could be solved by finding a mother for my child. He had two mothers, Augusta and Berdie. One was not around much, the other was never out of the house. That was Berdie, and she was fine—a sweet, plump, comforting dishrag to wipe their floors with and allow the boys to muddle through their days. Neither Berdie nor I had any encumbering ambitions for them, except perhaps that they go to school and try to get something from it. But I was always open to anything resembling an interest in music on Steven's part. Twice he asked to learn an instrument. First the piano, at age nine. He had talent and no real interest. For one year I sat with him at the piano for an hour a day as he practiced. And he tried, for me, for a while. The favor he was doing me and the pain in his expression were finally too much. A few years later he tried clarinet, for four months, and that was it musically. In his late teens he led a rock band, the King Dogs, and played guitar, which he learned in the mountains near Adana in southern Turkey, at the headwaters of the hashish trade—proving that the home has its inspirational limitations.

Joseph could do anything he wanted, with my approval, like hunting with a shotgun or raising chickens and chopping off their heads with a hatchet if they missed a day laying an egg. Or making a home for three scroungy pooches. Or building anything from tree houses to automobiles.

I didn't see how any woman in my life could affect these aspects of my children's lives.

Postmodern Romance

As strong as Helene's interest in her face and body and their effect on men was her interest in the cultural activities of the day. She was gaga about modern dance. Gaga was divided between Merce Cunningham and Paul Taylor. Paul's mimimalism and its kinship with the new painting and music scene at first was more intriguing to Helene. As time went by she decided minimalism was limited. Later, when he began dancing in the usual sense of the word, filtering out of his act those stunning numbers in which, dressed in a business suit, he dropped to his knees and twisted his head to the music of a telephone ringing and announcing the time, Helene again became a Paul Taylor groupie.

No matter how unusual his choreography, Merce Cunningham always danced. Men and women in his company hopped around. When I introduced Helene to Merce, she blushed and blurted for three full minutes. Merce has a way of listening to exuberant compliments that combines surprise and calm, and has remained attractive all his professional life. He liked Helene. There were warm receptions for Merce and his dancers that Helene and I attended—which of course brought the amazing John Cage out of his Zen lair.

My one evening in that lair, quite early in the fifties, in the company of Morton Feldman and a few other "far-out" musical disciples, I ate a wooden bowlful of Cage's delicious rice mix with my fingers, sitting in a highly modified lotus position on the floor.

Later, when Cage's music went beyond international recognition, his former disciple Morty Feldman referred to the musical innovations of John Cage as "fun and games for the rich," meaning the concerts that featured a pianist in evening dress reaching into the piano to pluck the strings, slamming down the keyboard cover, shooting pistols, sounding Bronx cheers, playing slide whistles, Waring blenders, and other found sounds. I took John more seriously: his music, his noises, his silent concerto, his readings, his growing grass at an art show, his mycological scholarship—every performance, every activity, was like a sermon by Spike Jones.

Helene and I went to many of his sermons, and enjoyed them; his concerts existed in a fascinating glow that made us feel we were part of the conspiracy. Very few people, including people we knew, heard them as making music. That was part of their charm. They were admired more for their certainty of becoming the next chapter in the history of music. Today there are rock stars who proudly admit to John's influence. And here's an art star who feels the same.

Helene and I together rode the last foamy waves of the special New York avant-garde of that time. For a few years longer she and I felt good about our social connection with it. It would be ludicrous to say that avant-garde culture was the basis of our romance, but it wove itself into our days and nights. She gave me a role in her life. My proximity accelerated her sophistication. She was all of twenty-one when I met her. At twenty-one I didn't know a Bonnard from a Picasso. She met and stayed in touch with major figures of the art scene that I happened to know. I derived a lot of happiness from seeing her take these meetings and events so seriously. If I gave her the opportunity to move comfortably in these circles, her receptivity to them was a gift to me, along with her exuberance and her intelligence.

Bob and Jasper

I knew Bob Rauschenberg and Jasper Johns from the time they came to New York in the early fifties, just out of Black Mountain College, where they studied painting under lovable, huggable Franz "The Gabber" Kline. They shared a studio in the Fulton Fish Market.

Jasper kept inviting me down for my opinion of what he was working on. It took a long time for me to get around to going, and when I did I wasn't flabbergasted. After a few more visits I realized he had impressive weight in his work, gestures in his line that I recognized in the way he reached for a fork; it was in his hand, he was a natural. But he had a few snappy aesthetic diversions up his sleeve. He painted little boxes occupied by forms that alluded to Joseph Cornell and Franz Kline, and of course Marcel Duchamp. He coveted my opinion I guess because he heard about me before I heard about him. He felt a bit hurt that I didn't invite his opinions about my work. Today, along with throngs, I am a Jasper Johns admirer.

When I began seeing Helene, Bob Rauschenberg was enjoying a notoriety almost as grand as Andy Warhol's a decade later. Under the auspices of a fierce brainstorm of Billy Kluver's, a series of "Art and Technology" events, Bob played an electrified indoor tennis match. Every time the racket hit the ball you'd hear an electric boom. My exposure to John Cage's musical ideas led me to think we were meant as much to hear the event as to see it. The lighting imitated late dusk, and the space was huge and dreamy. Helene never got over it. I did. Still, I enjoyed it for what I thought it was, a theatrical piece as related, or unrelated, to his art as my playing jazz is unrelated to my painting. It was apparent that Bob was open to theater as art. After one of his booed concerts John Cage said, "It's all theater, isn't it, including the audience reaction."

Was all this driving a beautiful coffin nail further into the art of easel painting? Bob certainly gave up painting. I'm sure that if today's performance art genius Robert Wilson never saw such

Bob Rauschenberg and I discuss art.

events as "The Tennis Match," he must have ingested the whiff of it still hanging around. He knows Billy Kluver, doesn't he?

At the same time, far from dead, Jasper's easel painting of the American flag was sweeping the country. Jasper was single-handedly making art safe for the brush.

Helene won the friendship of these two boyish men. She began a cooking campaign. In the summer, as *maîtresse de maison*, she invited them for a couple of weekends. It was exciting, they were fun, they and their two pet monkeys. Bob talked an even bluer streak than I did. Jasper punctuated the meandering discussion, always from a mysterious angle. After some insoluble problem in aesthetics or gossip went on and on, I'd say, "Who knows!"

Bob, with raised glass, corroborated, "God knows!"

Jasper: "I do not."

One of those weekends when Helene, Jasper, and Bob were to come out on Saturday, Bob shows up Friday night, alone—"Hi, I felt like being by myself"—and very early in the a.m. walks into my bedroom in his shorts, martini in hand, and sits on the bed, reminding me how long we've known each other and how much we like each other. The inevitable happened: we discussed art. Later we said hello to Jasper and Helene and the monkeys as if what didn't happen didn't happen.

Art, dance, and music weren't all Helene and I got in and out of cabs for. There was the great Living Theater of Julian Beck and Judith Malina. Their productions reflected the avant-garde conceits of that period (mid-fifties to mid-sixties), one of which was to be sure their audience found something in the production annoying. The aesthetic of annoying the audience outlived its experimental stage at the Living Theater. In 1972 Abbie Hoffman showed a film on the Holocaust; when the audience in the small theater got up to leave at the end of the film they found all the exits locked. A small riot ensued; after three hours Abbie relented and unlocked the doors. He always regretted his loss of aesthetic nerve: he had planned to keep them there till the next morning.

But making it hot for the audience was only one aspect of the Living Theater's experimental strategy. Judith and Julian's productions always seemed spacious and odd. Over their dead bodies would they try a drawing-room comedy or anything reminiscent of regular theater. What went on onstage forced you to laugh and think about the subjects of sexuality, culture, and politics. In real life Julian and Judith were violent pacifists. Whatever they and their productions were, they gave you the feeling you were witnessing something important.

Composed of a hefty amount of homosexuals, the Living The- **L**
ater found little on that subject not worthy of the world's attention.
They also found worthy Jack Gelber's *The Connection*, a play about
downtown New York drug culture. A group of junkies, musicians
among them, play and listen to jazz while waiting in a disreputable **A**
East Side pad for heroin that will come and feed their addiction.
The "cosmic" Fifth Street scene I described earlier was the still life
Jack Gelber worked from for the play. After *The Connection* had **R**
been running for many months, the lead junkie had to leave the
production. I was offered his role. I guess my reputation as a sometime user of heroin and the fact that the character actually played
the saxophone were behind Judith Malina's offer. **R**

I'd always enjoyed performing. I was the neurotic artist in Rudy
Burckhardt's film *Mounting Tension*, co-starring Jane Freilicher
and John Ashbery. I also played Jack Kerouac's pal Neil Cassady in
Robert Frank and Al Leslie's *Pull My Daisy*. I had performed **Y**
in plays by Frank O'Hara, Kenneth Koch, et al. But performing in
The Connection would mean remaining in New York for the summer. My art and the lure of the Hamptons in the summer—sun

R

I

V

E

R

LR in Kenneth Koch's The Tinguely Machine Mystery, *or*
The Love Suicides at Kaluka, *Frank O'Hara's* Try! Try! *(with*
Sid Solomon), and Koch's The Election *(with Gary Goodrow)* **S**

and sea, the nearness to my sons, the pleasure of my regular pals—made me let the offer go.

The play was a great success. As a theatrical production, it introduced some very fresh ideas; one, as reported to me by Gary Goodrow, the actor who took the role offered to me, was that there was real heroin in the capsules handed out to the anxious actors waiting onstage, some of whom shot up in front of the audience. I don't think Jack Gelber foresaw such possibilities when his great and original script was in production. Actually, it gave the show a touch of realism that raises the most ancient question in the world of theater: Do you have to be a chicken to lay an egg—onstage?

All was not lost in terms of my acting career. At the end of that summer of 1960, during John Kennedy's campaign for the presidency, Kenneth Koch wrote a play called *The Election*; it took place on the stage of the Living Theater immediately after the last act of *The Connection*. Like Gelber's play, it dealt with addiction, only Koch's junkies were politicians addicted to votes. I played Lyndon Baines Johnson.

The Election opens with the author lying down "in his disorderly pad."

FRIEND: Man, I hear you've written a new play, *The Election*.

AUTHOR: Don't bug me, man. I'm waiting for the producer now.

FRIEND: The *producer*? Have you copped out, man, gone commercial? You mean you're going to *produce* one of your plays? Wow! (*Looking around at the pad.*) Is this the theater?

AUTHOR: Of course this is the theater, man. What did you think? Wait a minute. This must be the producer now. Hold it!

At this point JFK and LBJ enter. JFK is fainting with withdrawal symptoms, in desperate need of his fix. LBJ gently rebukes him.

LBJ: Come on, man. That kind of posture does not befit the President of the United States.

JFK (*pepping up a little*): Has the VOTE come in? Is it in yet? Is it over?

Shortly after LBJ, i.e., LR, speaks to the audience.

LBJ: . . . Evvybody talkin bout how unnatural and ambitious we is, jes waitin around all the time for the votes, all day long jes trying to GIT it, jes all day, and even effen you jes conneck wif one vote, man, then you is made for that day—it stand out: you say "Well, there is one vote that ole man Nixon aint gonna git," and you feel *good*, sometime like you shake all over! And, man, it's them days you doan git no vote that you is in trouble, I mean TROUBLE—and then they's all that trash you got to associate with, all that trash that doan care WHO you is or WHAT you is, they jes waiting for you to say somethin that they like or they doan like, and then they say I gonna vote for *him* or *him*—and you better sure hope that they say it's for YOU too. And sometimes you feel you aint gittin the VOTE, you jes gittin the vote OUT, for the other fellah! Then you feel all bad 'cause you doan like them and they doan like you, but you wants the VOTE. . . .

The Election of Kenneth Koch could not have been more directly inspired by *The Connection*. Exactly what was the inspiration? Kenneth's innate love of satire? The absurdity of political campaigning? Envy of the attention Jack's play received? Satire, absurdity, envy, *The Election* was a delight for both actors and audience. The inspiration for making an artwork is not very important, as disturbing as this may be to artists.

For me, inspiration for a new work is hardly ever that direct, and envy has played a larger role than I like to admit. Envy of Tolstoy's *War and Peace* led me to paint *Washington Crossing the Delaware*. And one night ten years later on the Long Island Expressway entering the Midtown Tunnel, I saw a neon billboard version of Rembrandt's *Syndics of the Drapery Guild*, supposedly representing the craftsmanship that went into the making of Dutch Masters Cigars. That billboard, combined with my recent experience painting a lot of American and French cigarette packs, stoked the fires ad infinitum for my "Dutch Masters" series, which comprises everything from an eight- by ten-inch color pencil drawing to a ten-foot 3-D version in the lobby of a corporate building.

Sometimes the motivation for a new work is simply the desire to do a large painting. I never forgot my exhilarating reaction, full of envy and inferiority and probably jealousy, to the eighteenth-

L

A

R

R

Y

and nineteenth-century historical paintings in the Louvre; nor did the size of Pollock's and Kline's large works fall on closed eyes.

One day as Helene was posing for me I thought of doing a self-portrait, not of me as I looked then, in 1960, but a giant visual narrative using photos I had of my many past lives or photos I would take on visits to my childhood haunts. Before putting one stroke to the nine- by fifteen-foot canvas, I named it *Me*—the kind of casual title I still sometimes choose for disguising seriousness.

One of the images of the past that I wanted in this extended portrait was the building and schoolyard of the grade school I attended. Helene came along with me on this sentimental but art-motivated journey. Camera in car, fairly early on a Saturday morning, we headed for good old P.S. 32, a few blocks from the site of that blow job I was forced to give Manny Schwab in the Bronx Zoo.

R

I

V

E

R

S

We parked the car and began taking photos. Doorways, doors, their enormous hinges, wrought-iron fences and gates, peaked roofs, and the long horizontal classroom windows. It's not too surprising that the building looked much smaller than it did in my childhood. It was a toy-soldier version of a dark cathedral. Going there as a kid, I assumed that image was appropriate since most of the students were Italian Catholics. The large, empty schoolyard still looked sizable in 1960. I remembered having to wait there in short pants in the middle of the winter until the teacher called us in out of the freezing cold.

After taking more shots Helene and I went back to the car and started driving down the streets surrounding the school for a last look. I noticed the hitherto entirely forgotten separate entrances for boys and girls. I slowed down to point out this relic of our Puritan history to Helene. That brought on a blare of horns from the line of cars behind us. I thought I speeded up a little, but the impatient driver behind me disagreed and gave me three more very solid blasts.

Nothing infuriates me more than someone in an automobile two or three feet behind me giving me a kick in the ass and calling me a son of a bitch by blasting his horn, letting me know no one in this world has a right to delay him. Picture what would happen to this man were he walking down a sidewalk without the protection of his car and came upon a man and woman in his way and shouted three times into their ears, "Move the fuck over."

Thirty fucking years have gone by, and I'm still passionate about that moment. I rolled down my window, stuck my head out, and screamed, "Fuck you!" My heart beating wildly, I pulled out of his way into a space at the curb. Unfortunately, as he passed me we made eye contact. He stopped his car abruptly in the middle of the street. Another chorus of klaxons. A short, stocky man about forty-five stepped out of the car. He was wearing a fedora square on his head with the small brim pushed up in front. He walked toward me. Angry as I was, he seemed angrier. Helene's advice: "Roll up the window and lock the door. Quick!" I didn't want to be a sitting duck dealing with this menace. I got out of my car. Seeing that I was a decade younger than he and a foot taller, he returned to his car, opened the front door, reached in, and now walked toward me holding a plumber's ball peen hammer. Oh no! Coming at me I see a fierce Mafioso and the *Daily News* front page showing Larry Rivers in a pool of blood, skull open, on same street where painter went to school as child.

When he reached me he raised the hammer and jiggled it as if warming up for a blow. I grabbed his hand and asked as evenly as I could, "What are you doing?"

"You shouldn't use language like that around a woman!"

With a plumber's ball peen hammer in his hand, his fundamentalism was appealing. "I'm sorry about that, friend. After all, it's only words. What are you doing with a hammer in your hand!"

Noticing that the jiggling of the hammer was only a nervous tremor, I apologized for causing a traffic jam. He won the fight and went back to his car through the crowd that had gathered.

Helene was as amazed and relieved by the outcome as I was. Laughing hysterically, glad to be alive, we put our tail pipe between our wheels and took an extended tour of the concrete hills stretching before us.

Bronx Aria

The hills and valleys of the Bronx were shaved clean in the eighteenth century as life moved north from New York Harbor. Sprouting from these bald surfaces were reds, browns, yellows, beiges, bright at first, all to become gray. Schools, stores, courts, factories, houses, low, high, narrow, fat functional sculptures throwing shadows over miles of gray gutters and sidewalks.

The hills of the Bronx really continue to exist. A few hundred yards from the Harlem River, which divides the Bronx from Manhattan, Tremont Avenue begins. Tremont (the name means "three mountains" in Italian) takes many wild turns until it descends sharply to Webster Avenue, a valley known in my time for bottling milk, baking breads, adjusting brakes, recapping tires, and the Yankee Stadium. This Webster Avenue is named for that Daniel who dominated the Senate in the 1850s, the cigar company in the 1950s, and my paintings for twenty years.

Tremont Avenue assumes more generous proportions as its commercial flanks sweep to the girders of the el about a mile from the configuration of apartment houses that resembles a vast weathered fortress with alluring walls proclaiming the benefits of Old Gold cigarettes. "Not a cough in a carload." A few steps away, the grocer, the baker, and the liquor shop dispense the essentials to these heroic-sized sculptures for living.

We pass Belmont Avenue. Belmont, "beautiful mountain." On to Crotona Avenue. Crotona was a Greek city situated high up on the coast of Calabria in southern Italy. Crotona Avenue was always an Italian neighborhood.

Onward to another reminder of my hilly beginnings, Prospect Avenue, by definition a high place for a view. The Prospect Avenue hill goes down to the house I torched on my first smoke, 2245, near the dark unrented store where a cat in the window unemotionally batted a mouse from paw to paw and the moviehouse where, hysterical, I was removed from my first film.

It was in the afternoon. I was five years old and had just been

358

fed. My mother dusted, cleaned, put away, and resolved everything she deemed worthy of a great housekeeper. She left my younger sister Goldie with Mrs. Schapiro in the next apartment. Then she took me to my first movie and sat me next to her. I'd never seen her so silent as when she beheld the silent screen, where the six-foot frantic face of a woman in a "boyish bob" arched three-foot eyebrows in mounting fear for the fates of herself and the terrified daughter she clutched to her flat bosom as they were licked by the flames that filled the screen and, so it seemed to me, the entire theater. Everything was burning. The mother's eyes went into her head. The audience took a sympathetic breath as the actors stood on the third-floor landing of the wooden stairs of the wooden house. Crowned in flames, her eyes now looking pitifully in my direction for help, the actress convinced me her life was secondary to her child's. I stood up and began crying, turned toward my mother, and in two healthy heaves deposited the lunch she had given me an hour earlier right in her lap.

On the corner of the same street as this little theater, Prospect Avenue and 180th, was a three-story house. It was one of the few wooden houses in the neighborhood, gloomy, about to fall apart, and on sale. The people who lived in it stayed home all the time (I always thought they were trying to save money) and would pull aside their curtains after you passed. I never saw anyone come through the barely functional black gate. For all I knew it was the wooden house of the actress and her child. I drove by with Helene. The house was still there.

A man is standing on a ladder trying to spell "Johnny Weissmuller" on the marquee. Gorgeous Olympic swimming champ, pal of a chimp named Cheetah, Weissmuller was Tarzan, twice on Saturday. Trapped in a cave, throwing spears into a dark gator-filled pool, taking on ol' chomp-jaws knife in teeth, bashing the chest of an enemy ape. Hours and hours of jungle.

It was 6:30, past my suppertime. I had already sat through *Tarzan the Ape Man* as well as the second feature, the Saturday chapter of the serial, the cartoons, the Fox Movietone News, and assorted short subjects, not to mention coming attractions. I moved to the last row of the moviehouse, in a dilemma. Should I leave and avoid the late-homecoming scene with my mother or stay to watch Tarzan again?

I had been at the theater since 10:00 a.m., and now tension increased as I saw evening slither through the glass doors of the lobby and adults crowd in, buying candy, waiting for their dates or mates to finish their preperformance piss. I had to be home, but I had to see the Tarzanian dagger fly once more.

As the great scene drew closer, I got out of my seat and slowly backed up the aisle to the door. My focus now was heavily on the hour, on the dark evening invading the lobby. I heard my mother. "Vhere ver you, out so late?" As her words ground through my head, the physical satisfaction I found in Tarzan's performance dwindled and disappeared. I saw through the apes to their sad gorilla costumes all plopping too slowly to the man-made jungle floor.

Helene and I drove back to Manhattan. I dropped her at her new apartment on University Place, dropped my car at my garage on West Third Street, and, as usual, dropped into my studio next door to see Clarice, the Welsh half of my sexual life. I spent a torrid twenty minutes in bed with her, got dressed, went back to Helene's. She was asleep when I arrived, looking like an angel, breathing the air of the innocent. When I got into bed she embraced me and whispered, "It was a wonderful day, honey, but I'm tired. Do you mind?"

"No."

Nothing But the Truth

My presumption about Helene and the blond giant she met at the
Five Spot, which drove me to her house that 1958 summer night to
check out the temperature of her car motor, turned out to be not
so presumptuous. It took two years to find out how warm I was. At
a Southampton fund-raising party in the summer of 1960, given by
the sixty-five-year-old granddaughter of President Grover Cleve-
land, I met a fashionable twenty-eight-year-old blonde wearing a
wide-brimmed see-through hat. She was a beautiful socialite with a
brain. Her name was Donna Marlow. As a result of a seduction
that never went anywhere, we became friends. Something in that
Upper East Side accent kept my working-class hands at my side.

One Monday evening, Helene safely tucked in New York,
Donna and I were seated on the broken couch in my living room
at 92 Little Plains Road, contemplating the fireplace.

"Why don't we make a fire?"

"I don't know if it works."

"I wonder what's behind that wall above the mantel."

"One second."

I grabbed a hammer and chisel from my studio. A foot above
the mantelpiece I ripped out a hunk of plasterboard, revealing the
brick and mortar used when the house was built in 1893. This act
was the prelude to the total destruction of the five rooms of the
ground floor of my house. With the help of some friendly Shinne-

cock Indians, carpenters, painters, and fellow drinkers, those five rooms were transformed into one clean space, from the front of the house to the rear, ninety feet long. All because Donna Marlow asked for a fire.

When the dust settled, our relationship took a decidedly odd turn.

"Do you know someone called Helene Grass?"

"Well . . . sort of."

"Do you have any influence on her?"

"What?"

"Well, this Helene and my fiancé, Milo, have been seeing each other for quite a while."

"??????"

"Oh, it's only intermittent, but—"

"Quite a while? How long?"

"They met two summers ago at the Five Spot in Water Mill. She was a waitress."

"!!!!!!"

"We're about to set the date for our marriage, and I'm running out of patience."

From the time we first met at the fund-raising party, Donna has been orchestrating this moment. She continues. The emotional pitch rises.

"Look, Larry, I know my Milo, he's eventually going to give her up; he needs me for his career. He's going to be a doctor. He and I love each other very much. Very much. Can you make it clear to Helene that what little there is between them will never go beyond a sporadic roll in the hay?"

I don't feel it now, I'm sorry to say thirty years later, but I'm sure at the time I was stung in the stomach picturing my girlfriend's powerful sexual gymnastics with someone else. And then to have it characterized as a "roll in the hay." I hate that expression. I've never thought that agrarian metaphor described anything I ever did in bed or on the ground, or for that matter in a cellar on a giant pile of coal. Should I bring up infidelity? How would Helene defend herself? She was too sophisticated to resort to the prime tenet of Reichian therapy, that it is unhealthy to reject sex at any time from anyone. (Gloria "Ginger" Brehd, companion to Stanley Gould, arch-bohemian of the fifties, sixties, seventies, and eighties, considered me so sick for not wanting to sleep with her that when I would, she wouldn't.)

Helene still came out on weekends those summers of '59 and '60 and left Monday morning on the 6:15 for New York. What was a healthy, enthusiastic young female to do the other four nights? Find out about life. Right? And what was life about? Sex. Right.

At the same time, Donna's update was a convenient disappointment. Pounds of guilt about *my* sporadic rolls in the hay with Clarice were suddenly washed away.

Perhaps Helene wanted no more from Milo than an intermittent—shall we say?—hay roll. She definitely wanted something more serious from me. On Sunday, the day after our trip to the Bronx, Helene and went out for breakfast. I still remember the bright light of eleven in the morning on University Place. Walking with the sun in our eyes, Helene asked me to marry her.

Help!

I held some very ordinary male prohibitions against marriage. Except for legalizing our ongoing affair, by now split four ways, what difference would marriage make in our life together? I would still paint all day, still feel erotic looking at attractive women; it would hardly intimidate me into remaining faithful and would have little or no effect on my interest in drugs.

Instead of putting all this before her in what would sound like serious talk preceding an important decision between lovers, I ask her, "Why do you want to get married?"

She stops walking, causing me to stop. Barely holding back tears, Helene turns to me and confesses, "Because I'm getting old!" She waits, then adds, "I'll soon be twenty-five!"

My response was silence. I needed time to think, and to be offended. On the other hand, I'd read an article in some magazine like *Glamour* or *Cosmopolitan* averring that a woman who wants to have a husband has a better chance, statistically, of remaining married than one who marries Mr. Right for love. Had Helene read that article? She didn't want me, she wanted a husband. Good for her.

"My best friend Anita has been going with Tom the same amount of time I've been going with you, and they just got engaged."

The same best friend I personally had to put in a cab whenever she visited us and with a poke from Helene put money in her hand to pay for it.

"Okay, let's get engaged!"

The color came back to her cheeks, her eyes dried.

Helene saw our engagement as the first step toward a final hookup; engagement for me meant breathing space, the first step in disengagement. I didn't want to marry Helene, and time, with good reason, would cause Helene to decide she did not want to marry me either. Not that I was sure I wanted to end what was between us. It was not hard to say I loved her. Or easy. But I was relaxed.

Engagement wouldn't change much. We'd go to art openings, plays, parties, dance, movies. Enjoy sex with each other and others. My children would remain important and worry me. I'd continue to produce art for exhibitions and commissions. Life, you fascinatin' monstah, would march on.

A few weeks later Helene told me she was planning a bridal shower—did I hear "bridal"?—just like her best friend Anita. I was not only engaged, I was in danger of being married! Probably in a double ceremony alongside her best friend Anita, whom I would have to put in cabs for the rest of my life.

Our conversation led to a baroque breakfast. We had *café au lait* and croissants and brioches at the sidewalk cafe of the venerable Brevoort Hotel. I couldn't tell what we were celebrating. Each of us felt differently about the issues, but we were happy having aired them. As if to give us something to think about besides the sensitive point we had reached between us, I told Helene that I had an exhibition scheduled in Los Angeles at the Dwan Gallery in late January, and that Virginia Dwan had invited us to stay at her glamorous home on the beach in Malibu with a white AC Bristol at our disposal. While we ate, our personal problems were secondary to our reflections on the New York light and the stark shadows thrown so early in the day, the downtown elegance of the people entering and leaving the hotel, and the familiar face of Franz or Milton or Bill or Mike passing by on the way to their studios.

After breakfast I went straight to my house on West Third Street. Steven and Clarice were there shouting and laughing, something between fight and fun. I looked in the studio. I didn't feel calm enough to deal with all the welding equipment and the sparks and the heat necessary to finish my *Iron Maiden*, the not too attractive metal sculpture I was worried about that week. One of my conditions for working is a blank mind. The marriage proposal on Ninth Street was hard to ignore.

Steven, still attending Cherry Lawn at the time, took the 4:40 back to Connecticut. Clarice went out for fresh air and pub crawling. I took a tranquilizer, i.e., I administered a shot of heroin. An hour later, flat on my back, I received a call from Helene.

"Have you been thinking about me? Us, I mean?"

I began to talk, but my speech was affected by the heroin. I was slurring my words.

"Is there anything wrong?"

"No, nodnz's wrong. I'm havin a res'."

"Have you been drinking?"

"Wha'ya saying?"

"You sound very . . . unusual . . . Larry."

She knew I had dabbled in heroin but thought it was far behind me. Was she fishing? I kept this part of me as well as I could from my "serious" friends, uptown art buyers, dealers, et al. I didn't want them to include me in their low estimate of drug users.

"Larry, why do you sound so awful?"

"Lemme call ya tomorrow."

By Monday afternoon I'd recovered and begun working on *Iron Maiden* and on my scheme for getting Helene to worry about me, leading her to worry about herself. Clarice had squeezed me fresh grapefruit juice for breakfast, which I took in bed. It was all I could get down. She told me I didn't look too good.

That's good! Suppose I spend a week or two taking heroin, running myself down, looking and sounding as though I'm coming from the lower depths. Will Helene have second thoughts about me? Everyone is full of ambiguous feelings. On Sunday morning after a beautiful day together on Saturday, Helene had seen the better side of her lover. But a sad, nonworking, unambitious Larry would move her to the other side of her ambiguity about me. That is exactly what I did! I took heroin that following week and began to find it difficult to meet her in the evenings; I was too nauseous to go out. She began visiting me at home; I was always in bed. A few weeks went by and I confessed to her that I'd been taking heroin more than I had in years and maybe I ought to go somewhere to find out why. I had no choice. It's true I was distressed about my possible future with Helene, but now I was completely unnerved by the heroin I was taking to solve the problem. Could I really call a halt the day I decided drugs were no longer necessary?

Besides, what would have been wrong with marrying Helene? She was attractive, smart, enthusiastic, and sexually exciting. But what about the Milo diversion? Sex with him once or twice, twelve or fourteen times, okay; I'm a liberal. But a run from day one concurrent with our two years together was hard to shove under any of the usual rugs! Aw, but she loved my boys, she was a good hostess, she'd eventually learn to cook, and—have I mentioned this?—she was good in bed.

A lawyer friend secured me a place high on the waiting list for the Gracie Square rehabilitation clinic, on Seventy-sixth Street and York Avenue. A week later I was a white-robed patient signed up for a three-week stint.

Gracie

My recollections of the three weeks I spent there are vague; one is of the tall, very white walls; another is of the young inmates and their troubled faces; not that there weren't men and women in their thirties, my age, with troubled faces. Each Friday evening, as I recall, the entire patient population, including myself, came shuffling in robes into an empty space filled with popular music. It looked like a gym and had a glass-covered roof. The hundred or so patients kept moving even when well inside the space, gliding as in a skating rink, minus the skates. It seemed to me that no groups formed, not even around the cheese bits and sodas. There were chaperones, I guess; none wore uniforms, but it was clear who they were and who was going to sleep at home. I was surprised there was no one in the room I knew. In New York it is rare for me, since I'm comfortable knowing everybody, to be in a room with a hundred people and fail to recognize a face. Another thing I recall from my stay at the Gracie Square rehab clinic was receiving a letter from Terry Southern with its own special gift for rehabilitating my sense of humor.

> My dear Lar, I know your time is extremely bla-bla-bla, etc. (as, indeed, is *mine!*) but don't you think here's an instance where we might sort of "pitch in" and, er, uh, well you know, *lend a hand?!?* (It's your basic 7 to 12 age-group, Lar —and, they're a heckof a lot of fun at that age, Lar!) (as a certain Mister Dumbell can attest)—if he ain't already in the dang hoosegow for heavy sod and unspeakable teeny (boy) rim! Har-har-har!! You ought to make a citizen's arrest of that durn weirdo!! Anyhoo . . . here's the ad. I think we'll want to move quick on this one, Lar—it may require

your coming here to live. What they want is sort of, well you know, mature fun-type guys to "come" in and, etc., etc.

Please let me know your view by RETURN OF POST as there are a lot of HEAVY STUDS moving in on this one.

xxx, Ter

Pasted in the middle of the letter was a news clipping headlined CUB PROGRAM IS IN TROUBLE: "The Salisbury Cub Scout program, like the Girl Scout program, is in serious trouble because of lack of adult help. . . ."

Of course I had to stop taking heroin. I got rid of the discomfort of stopping in two or three days. Five or six days later, feeling stronger, I began to get interested in what facilities existed in this clinic. Bored with reading, self-pity, therapists, checkups, and push-ups, I shuffled, robe and all, up to the art studio. It turned out to be an occupational therapy room.

I was not disappointed. I was happy to do anything requiring the use of my hands. What to make? A beaded belt? Book ends? A utensil drawer, sandals for myself? I decided to make a suede pocketbook with the large letters C and P for Clarice Price, my housekeeper, who rapidly during my incarceration was becoming my beloved housekeeper. I thought she needed me, meaning I needed her—the way people ask "Are you hungry?" because *they* are. Slowly, in the ancient manner, she had reached my heart through a satisfied stomach, not to omit a hard cock.

When it came time to leave the Gracie Square clinic, I wasn't sure where to tell the taxi driver to take me. To my studio, safe and simple with Clarice? Or to Helene's to make up my mind about whether she was interested in a future that included me? I headed downtown, flip-flopping in the taxi. At Fourteenth Street I decided to go to Helene's place. In her apartment I asked if she'd like to go with me to Los Angeles for my exhibition at the Dwan Gallery. At the opposite end of her couch, my suitcase on the floor between us observing the melodrama, she tells me, "Go to California without me, Larry, and when you get back we'll talk." My scheme to supply reasons for her not to want to marry me had worked. But success failed to calm me down. We kissed with a tear or two, mine, and I left and caught another taxi. Clarice was waiting for me at the studio.

"Would you like to go with me to Los Angeles for my exhibition at the Dwan Gallery?"

367

"Of course!"

I'm not sure if her decision wasn't as much about seeing California as about being with me, but it put an end to a three-year romance and began a fresh one going—to who knew where.

In January 1961 Clarice and I left by car for California under the brutal assumption that life was worth living.

Love and the Open Road

In a big green Chevy Impala, a map of the U.S. about to spring out of the glove compartment, a pile of cheese and crackers for uninterrupted driving, utensils and a bottle opener, Clarice and I, me driving, began to chew up the three thousand miles to Los Angeles. The only evidence of this journey is a photo of Clarice in front of the Mark Twain Hotel somewhere in Missouri, and one of me in New Mexico wearing a Pancho Villa sombrero astride a painted wooden horse. Kenneth Koch says that the past is a soft hotel with lots of rooms; some you look into and smile, others you open the door and shut it quickly. The room containing my voyage to L.A. is making me smile now. I'm enjoying Clarice on the open road.

It's twelve hours a day of driving, eating what's local for dinner, and passion in a different motel every night.

First stop, the outskirts of Detroit, to see an art connection, Gertrude Kasel, a very smart, extraordinarily sweet woman with a good-size gallery, married to an ex-rabbi, also a dealer, but he sold steel. I looked over her space, we planned a show, and Gertrude gave a dinner for us and some local artists.

In the morning Clarice and I drove to Chicago. We went to see Phyllis Lambert on the eighteenth floor of the Mies van der Rohe apartment house overlooking Lake Michigan. Phyllis was a daughter of Seagram Whiskey who got Mies to design the Seagram Building along with Philip Johnson. A few years before, I'd met her one night in New York at the Five Spot, pretending I didn't know who I was taking back to my loft. We were happy for a pleasant noncommittal year. I finally backed away—not that she clawed at me to stay—fearing no one would take my art seriously if I was married to a woman that wealthy. (Jimmy Merrill tells me his father, Charles, used to have a phone at the dinner table to call up his old flames and converse with them, giggling and dropping real tears on his cheeks. I feel a little that way sitting at this table writing about bygone affairs.) Some time after we went our friendly but separate ways Phyllis, attending the Yale School of Architecture, asked me to be her escort at the annual student ball. When I arrived she was taking a bubble bath and asked me to soap her back, and when she got out of the tub, to fetch her bathrobe.

After the ball was over we came back to her apartment. I tried to get into bed with her.

"Oh no, Larry, none of that funny stuff."

That's all right. If I was hurt by Phyllis at least I got a night's sleep. One more rejection didn't matter. I already held the world's record for sleeping with women who refused to fuck, which kept poor me and poor whoever it was wrestling all night.

Phyllis had commissioned me to do a sculpture of a plant "because all my plants die, I travel so much." So I made the stop in Chicago to see *two* old loves, Phyllis and my metal version of a rubber plant made by shaping sheet steel and steel rods with my newfound toys: an oxyacetylene torch that softened the metal for shaping, an electric welding machine that fused the metal, and a grinder that impaired my hearing. I wanted to see *Steel Plant* in Phyllis's classy environment. It was difficult to see this work as sculpture, it looked so much like the real plant. Then why can't a

LARRY RIVERS

369

plant itself be a piece of sculpture? It is. But plants keep dying. Sculpture . . . lives forever. Almost. Right, Ozymandias?

Phyllis gave Clarice and me an architectural tour of Chicago featuring the Louis Sullivan art nouveau department store, Carson Pirie Scott. Three hours later we were off to St. Louis. Clarice was singing a silly song her father taught her. All the words were meaningless, and I still remember them.

> A da kuffer, a da kuffer.
> Kista kista bomboli.
> Eeeny meeny essolini. Boff.

When we arrived in St. Louis, more Louis Sullivan architecture greeted us—in pieces. In a new complex along the Mississippi called Gaslight Square, the Crystal Palace, a bizarre and beautiful cabaret-bar-restaurant, had been constructed using doors, windows, chandeliers, grillwork, and banisters from a torn-down Sullivan building. The owners and designers of the Crystal Palace, and conceivers of Gaslight Square itself, were Jay and Fred Landesman, two natural geniuses of no particular medium. In 1950 Jay, with G. Legman, published a short story of mine called "The Addicts" in their magazine *Neurotica*.

In this midwest enclave, Clarice and I met Lenny Bruce, saw Nichols and May and the Second City troupe on stage, all shining bright and cynical. At the Crystal bar we spoke about jazz with the sculptor Ernest Trova and rubbed rumps with William Inge, who was in a soft sizzling argument with a sad bad boy named Bubber, the model for the lead character in *Picnic*. Everyone's favorite jazz impresario, Bradley Cunningham, tended bar. All this to the music of Al Cohn, Zoot Sims, et al. playing and Barbra Streisand singing jazz. Clarice's lusty Welsh laugh could be heard throughout the gigantic room. Other men looking at her as a "delectable dish," and feeling compelled to tell me pushed me closer to Clarice and made me more possessive.

Leaving St. Louis happy and with a banging headache, Clarice and I had the feeling we were at the gates of the West. We still had a few more days of burning up the cement ahead of us. We drove with serious intent through Oklahoma. Sixty miles outside of Amarillo, Texas, we stopped for a fill-up. To get the pins and needles out of our asses we got out of the car. Over the flat brown fields we saw a dark cloud moving toward us. The gas attendant told us to get back in the car pronto and roll up the windows. He ran into his office and closed his door. Now the black cloud was near us and only a few feet off the ground. We were about to experience what I remember from biblical stories—a huge swarm of huge locusts. While they seemed to be moving toward some unknown destination, thousands of them banged into the car, covering the windshield and giving us a weird close-up of tumultuous insect legs and wings. This lonely gas station was of no interest to them; they zigged out the way they zagged in. I didn't think we were in danger, but where did they come from and where did they go? Yo no se. The attendant washed our windshield, and because we'd experienced these thrilling moments together, we said goodbye in a more than usually insincere and affectionate way.

I've seen so many landscapes on the East Coast that they're like the front fender of my car. I don't see them anymore. Starting in west Texas, but more in New Mexico and Arizona, the view outside the Impala, of bone-dry scraggy landscape, purple shadows, and gorgeous mountain ridges, looked like no place I'd ever been to.

A storm came up. We turned off the radio to hear it. Now there were lightning streaks coming down a few miles ahead of us to the

L
A
R
R
Y
R
I
V
E
R
S

left and right. We were approaching Tucumcari, New Mexico, and it was getting dark. Clarice, after an especially loud bolt, screamed and dropped to the floor under the dashboard, thinking she was safer there than in her seat. I downplayed the danger to relieve her fright, but inside I wasn't sure what might happen. It was now very dark, and the lightning every few seconds illuminated the area, creating an even more dramatic scene. Clarice thought we were both going to die. I kept on going and after an hour drove out of the storm. We stopped at the next motel and spent a peaceful night in a bed that massaged you as you slept.

At 6:30 in the morning we took off and sped through mesa, canyon, valley, desert, landscape after stunning landscape, stopping only for a look at a ghost town called Zzyxx, a tourist trap at the end of a winding mountain road. Before it became a ghost, the town was dependent on a thriving copper mine. When the copper vein ran dry the mine was abandoned, and soon after so was the town. Later, money was invested to make it look like the set from the old Tom Mix cowboy film. We walked the dirt street and watched the tumbleweeds making sprays of dust. We went through a swinging double door into a bar and ordered a drink. The bartender told us business was bad, it was a slow season, we were just about the second customers for the day. The abandoned town was being reabandoned. We helped the process. We left the empty saloon without finishing our drinks.

About a hundred miles south of L.A. we hit the Pacific Coast road, which took us all the way to Malibu, "Malibu Colony" to be specific, where my dealer Virginia Dwan and her husband Vadim Kondratieff rattled around in a modest little palace. It was night. We were welcomed as the newlyweds we as yet were not. Virginia showed us to our comfortable, neat room with the softest bedding I ever put my body on. There was a fireplace with a fire already going. Well, there were two gas flames lapping painted cement that looked like white birch logs, something I'd never seen before. I was also given a studio to work in for the weeks I'd be there.

L.A. was a pop artist's dream. Fast-food drive-ins invariably had some three-dimensional image referring to what was being sold. A hamburger joint supported a giant hamburger and bun twenty feet in the air, with a figure that tall holding another burger in its palm. Not too attractive as serious sculpture, but arresting and amusing, it made you think that the idea of creating some object in a size bigger than you usually see it had some validity, and had been here

in L.A. a long time before versions of it showed up in art galleries.

At the Dwan Gallery I exhibited paintings done a year or two earlier: *Ford Truck, Cozy Cole, Jazz Drummer, Miss New Jersey, M. and Smoke.* Virginia purchased two or three of these before the show, and we had high hopes for more sales. This was the first time my work was being exhibited in California. The prices we were asking now topped the $1,000 range, some going as high as $2,000 or $3,000, a considerable rise in price for my work. But the commercial success of the exhibition was only one of the goals of a relatively new name on the scene. I don't remember the critical response; I do remember being given a big party and the use of the Kondratieffs' AC Bristol to go to it. I felt like I was driving a motorized piece of sculpture. When Clarice and I left the party, driving again up the Pacific Coast highway, I was carried away with the power of the machine. I was drunk and so was Clarice, who enjoyed the Burn-Em-Up Barns Hollywood car-racing act I was doing behind the wheel. I put on a great deal of speed. The faster we went, the louder the motor sounded. As we neared the gates to Malibu Colony our smoky trail was picked up by a state trooper who immediately sounded his siren and started his lights flashing on the roof. Over a loudspeaker I heard, "Pull over!" I went past the gate thinking I had made it safely into a haven. The trooper drove right in behind me. I rolled down the window to see what was happening.

What was happening was a long-nose pistol being pointed at my head. What did I think I was doing traveling ninety-five miles an hour? Clarice speaks up, "No, no, officer, that's not true at all. It was a hundred and ten miles an hour, I was looking at the speedometer." Between her humor, her accent, and her open bodice the trooper found it hard to look official, and instead of taking me handcuffed to the local hoosegow for drunk and reckless driving, he gave us a speeding ticket. That was one Clarice.

Another Clarice, at another party where she suspected I was interested in a girl in a slinky dress, walked down a canyon and hitched a ride back to Malibu. I showed up in the morning as she was packing to leave.

"You can't leave. You're posing for a painting I'm doing."

I saw I could lose her precious loyalty by showing so little of my own. When she was working for me in New York, Clarice made my life easier and more pleasant, and now that we were in a new arrangement, a more equal one, she continued to be more considerate of me than I was of her. There was no one else like her. I began to behave as if she meant something important to me.

But what really drew me to her was the diary she kept from her London days. I cracked her code—that is, I could tell from her entries of days and evenings, parties and bar hopping, how they ended and with whom. There was an asterisk next to many male names. Even in California I managed now and then to turn the conversation around to grilling her about these asterisked men, whom, after a while, I felt a certain affection for. My interest was out of control and served to give me a dandy erection. The open-diary tactic inspires many a man to ask for the woman's hand, meaning her cunt, in marriage, to see if she can belong to him solely.

In L.A. it began to dawn on me that it was a provincial idea to depend on one gallery, even in New York, to set the art world on fire with my work. I needed, and wanted, other people in other places to represent me. Virginia helped me widen my audience to West Coast critics, collectors, and viewers who thought N.Y. could come to L.A.

Clarice and I went back to New York via New Orleans, not for jazz but for a portrait commission I had from a Mrs. Sonny Norman, a happy liberal Jewish widow of a Jewish liberal cattleman. She was on the museum board and had important connections in the New Orleans art community. It took about a week to make a

Portrait of Joseph H. Hirshhorn, 1963
Oil and charcoal on canvas, 71 x 48″
Hirshhorn Museum and Sculpture Garden, Washington, D.C.

Dutch Masters I, 1963
Oil on canvas, 40 x 50″
Fine Arts Center, Cheekwood, Nashville, Tennessee

Dutch Masters, President's Relief, 1964
Oil and collage on canvas mounted in wooden box, 97¾ x 69¾ x 14¼″
Solomon R. Guggenheim Museum, New York, gift of Stanley and Alice Bard, 1986

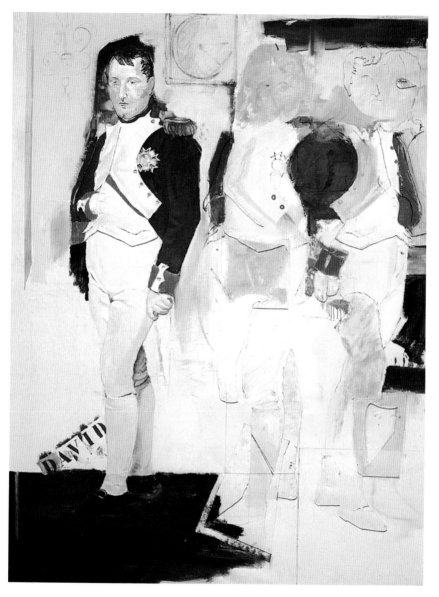

The Greatest Homosexual, 1964
Oil, collage, pencil, and colored pencil on canvas, 80 x 61″
Hirshhorn Museum and Sculpture Garden, Washington, D.C.

The History of the Russian Revolution: From Marx to Mayakovsky, 1965
Mixed media construction, 53 pieces, 14'4" x 32'5" x 18"
Hirshhorn Museum and Sculpture Garden, Washington, D.C.

Primo Levi: Periodic Table, 1988
Oil on canvas mounted on sculpted foamboard,
73 x 58½ x 4″
Collection of La Stampa, Turin

The Film Maker: Portrait of Claude Lanzmann, 1991
Oil and collage on canvas mounted on sculpted foamboard,
46¼ x 38½ x 3½"
Centre National des Arts Plastiques, Paris

Art and the Artist: Figures on a Red Wall, 1992
Pencil and colored pencil mounted on sculpted foamboard, 28 x 31½ x 2½″
Private collection

Art and the Artist: Two Profiles, 1992
Pencil and colored pencil mounted on sculpted foamboard, 19 x 26¼ x 2½″
Private collection

drawing and get a good earful of the city. Mrs. Norman was a friend of James Baldwin's, so was I. She had invited "Jimmy" down for a literary conference she was sponsoring. After the conference she gave a party for him at her suburban home. As soon as Jimmy arrived for congratulations and cocktails, Sonny motioned to her maid to pull down the shades and draw the curtains. I asked Sonny, "What's up, are we going to smoke some pot?"

"Oh, no, no, no," Mrs. Norman told me. "I think it's best the neighbors don't know I'm entertaining a Negro."

Can you call yourself a liberal and act that way? Well, just because Sonny was scared didn't mean she couldn't be a liberal. Jimmy went back to New York that evening. Next morning Clarice and I left New Orleans and left the painting. Ten years later I found out it had been put in a cardboard box under her bed and had never seen the light of day. She thought the rendering of her face showed someone seriously ugly. Twenty years later she donated it to the art museum in New Orleans. If it wasn't a good-looking face, by then at least it was younger than what she was walking around with.

Anxious to get to New York, I increased my hours at the wheel. We slept less. We stopped only in Washington. We had lunch in the National Gallery and began our tour of the museum. We came across David's *Napoleon in His Study*. I was amazed by the work, its color, its presence, everything about it. But what I went away with was the mysterious look on Napoleon's face, his pursed lips, his plump body, and the campy position of his hands, one in the crack of his vest, the other hanging with a relaxed twist. I bought a large, clear reproduction of the painting.

A few years later, as artist-in-residence at the Slade School of Fine Arts, I pulled out the reproduction of the David painting and did a painting from it that got a lot of attention, maybe because of its title, *The Greatest Homosexual*. Joe Hirshhorn offered to buy it if I changed the title. I refused. He bought it anyway. I painted another one and called it *The Second Greatest Homosexual*. A French historian saw the painting in the Hirshhorn collection and in a letter to the museum requested its removal, asking how we Americans would feel coming across a painting of George Washington, the father of *our* country, called, in effect, *The Greatest Cocksucker*. "Never, in all my years of study, have I read that Napoleon was a homosexual," wrote the professor. "I personally would hate to hear our French schoolchildren giggle if they saw such a portrait of any American historical figure." The museum was unmoved.

L

A

R

R

Y

R

I

V

E

R

S

Paris, 1961–62

Back in New York in the early spring of '61, I was preparing a show for the Tibor de Nagy Gallery when I began to hear from two European dealers asking if I'd be interested in showing at their galleries. One was Charles Gimpel of Gimpel Fils, London, wondering if I would have enough uncommitted works for a show in the middle of May '62. I was definitely interested in his interest. The other dealer was Jean Larcade in Paris, who ran Galerie Rive Droite, home of the *"nouveaux réalistes."* We decided on an exhibition to begin in April.

Clarice and I, in complicated New York again, were beginning to drift. It worried both of us. My worry was that this delicious unique female, like all the other delicious unique females in my life, was going to put herself nude beneath some other man. Clarice's fear was that Helene, beautiful and bossy, might talk me into a return engagement. There was only one way out: to marry and leave this eternally difficult city. We would find a place in Paris to live and work, and once that was done we'd go over to London to do the quick legal thing in the Chelsea town hall, then return to Paris, there to live and love and prepare for my first European one-man exhibitions. Calm at last.

In the fall Clarice and I moved to Paris, to a small studio heated by a coal stove on the Impasse Ronsin. I rented it from the pipe-puffing artist Reggie Pollack, who returned to New York City, where he came from, to seek fame and fortune. If he failed I was to give him back his studio. Before we moved into our heavenly atelier we stayed a few days at the Palais d'Orsay, a giant nineteenth-century train station transformed into a hotel. It had the longest, grandest staircase I had ever walked down, but our pillow, a hard bolster, was painful to sleep on. Clarice cried for four days straight. I was afraid to ask her why; she might say, "Maybe we're making a mistake." On the fifth day she started laughing her loud laugh. I never found out why she cried or why she began laughing.

On the other side of my painting wall in our heavenly atelier was the sculptor Brancusi's wall. He had died a few years before. Our common wall was the only one in his studio left standing when they took it brick by brick away to rebuild it outside the Pompidou center, Beaubourg. Niki de Saint-Phalle hung balloons full of paint on that wall above her sculptures of doll figures and objects, colored the sculptures by shooting holes in the balloons with a hunting rifle, and didn't warn us when she started work. It always made me jump and run to the door to see if the Algerian war had reached my street. When she used a cannon to color her sculptures, with the help of Jean Tinguely, the great "scrap contraptionist" sculptor, she was kind enough to tell us in advance.

If Matisse in the twenties looked out his window in Nice and painted some humdingers, I was going to use Paris in another way: not through my studio window—there wasn't any—but through my everyday living and keeping a sharp eye out for arresting source material. On one level Matisse is not about the beaches at Nice, or the tropical tree-lined boulevard, or the attractive spaces he both inhabited and used for paintings. He had an aesthetic in mind that selected just what he needed to give us what he has become known for: a flat, beautifully colored intelligence.

I went to L'Alliance Française to learn French. There I found source material for my "Vocabulary Lesson" series, using Clarice as a model. I frequented art supply shops on the Quai d'Orsay. The special racks set aside for amateur artists, with manuals on how to paint the figure, noses, ears, eyes, landscapes, and horses, also made for inspiring material. I painted from the hundred-franc note with the beaux arts Napoleon on it and the Arc de Triomphe, looking to me like some corny illustration of monuments that Claes Oldenburg loved to have fun with. Working in Paris was quiet, no phone calls, no unexpected visits. I produced quite a bit.

In April 1962, as planned, the Rive Droite gallery showed about fifteen of these works. Several of my large *affiches* announcing the show were posted in different parts of the city. The Rive Droite was owned and directed by Jean Larcade, a heterosexual who looked and sounded more flaming than any faggot thrown on a fire by Charles Ludlam's Ridiculous Theatrical Company. Larcade was the son of an extraordinary antique dealer—if that's what you call someone who sold the Cloisters to the Rockefellers.

Painting in Paris, I felt great certainty and exuberance about my work. At the same time, the hold of abstract art on the New York tastemakers was loosening. The work of younger painters was being looked at, written about, and finally bought. The term "pop art" made the rounds of important mouths in the art world. I first heard the expression at the Sidney Janis show of 1962; then I heard Lawrence Alloway invented it, then I heard he didn't invent it. Then I heard I invented it—not the term, the movement. In recent years I have been accused of being "the Karl Marx of the pop revolution," "the father of pop art," "the grand old man of pop art." I was considered "the first to use so-called vulgar or vernacular objects in a larger artistic context" (Sam Hunter). At my de Nagy show before I left for Paris, I showed *Camel Cigarettes, Tareytons, Lucky Strike, Webster Cigars, Buick, The Last Civil War Veteran, Playing Cards: Pair of Kings, Cedar Bar Menu*. But I never felt I was a practitioner, let alone "the grand old man," of pop. In fact, ten days before my show of paintings using popular culture, I felt an urge to complicate the exhibition's apparent message that I was hung up on everyday objects. I quickly did a copy, not a takeoff, of an Ingres painting, put it in my show, and called it *I Like Ingres— Too*.

During the opening, Bob Rauschenberg suggested that my playing card paintings were good but, "Why don't you have a whole show, a gallery full of paintings based on playing cards? You could have paintings with five cards in them showing different poker hands, straight up to the ace, or a flush, a full house, four deuces, even a lousy hand." Rauschenberg's idea forced me to admit how much more sophisticated he was than I; he knew that an exhibition could add up to more than just an accumulation of single works on display. "Originality has to be hammered home," he said. "The way you did it, Larry, it was like a passing idea."

It probably was. An ABC television producer once made a drawing of a horse for me and said, "You and I know this is a horse.

But here is what is necessary to get it over to a large audience."
Above the drawing he wrote, "This is a horse," and made an arrow
from the words to the horse.

I liked being close to, even collaborating with, other artists who
exhibited at the Rive Droite. I had admiration and affection for
these so-called *nouveaux réalistes:* Jean Tinguely, of the giant
welded sculptures that move and make sounds, was a new boyfriend
of Niki de Saint-Phalle's. He too had a studio in the Impasse, a one-
car garage with a dirt floor, junk piled up to his knees. I knew Niki,
born beautiful and French and brought up in America, from a 1956
meeting in my house in Southampton with her then husband, the
Oulipian writer Harry Mathews. Clarice and she got along infa-
mously, immediately. Clarice began a program of producing one
new French soup daily for lunch. Jean and Niki were always invited. Almost immediately after we met, Jean and I collaborated on
a work called *The Turning Friendship of America and France,* a two-
sided painting I did of French and American cigarettes, connected
to a Tinguely sculpture that turned slowly, allowing you to stand in
one place as the other side of the work automatically came into
view. And in two weeks it was shown to a milling mob at a *vernissage*
in the Musée des Arts Decoratifs of the Louvre. Jean had a bothersome quality I enjoyed, a "stick this in your pipe and smoke it"
style that reminded me of me.

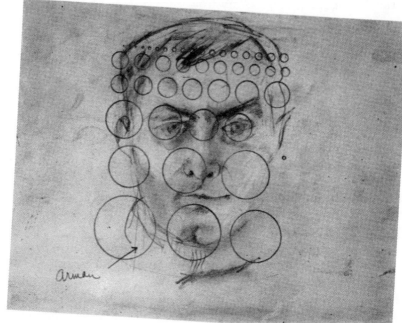

Accumulation Drawing,
Portrait of Arman

Arman also showed at the Rive Droite. He was an "accumulations" master and would arrange a hundred gas masks or knives or saws in large transparent cases, or sink five smashed violins in acrylic. Arman slept in his black leather jacket. He had a pile of wooden pegs in his studio full of notches recording his conquests. When he lost interest in accumulating sexual conquests, he gathered these pegs into one of his accumulations. He liked to dance the night away in the Carousel, a transvestite bar. One night I went along with him and spent the drunken evening dancing with Paula, a blonde from Bordeaux, elegant and serious enough in her evening gown that I remember him to this day.

Clarice and I left for London to get the marital deed done. Her parents and brother came down for the wedding from Hay on Wye in Wales. Some of the asterisked men stepped out of Clarice's diary and came to the Chelsea town hall. One of them played the role of best man. I greeted them as old friends. I feel a rush of pleasantness in public situations with the English; possibly it's the charm of English English and that they always sound considerate. We were married, took photographs, and went to a nearby pub for a short

celebration. We stayed one or two more days, during which I met
scads of her friends, almost entirely in pubs: a pub owner, a female
recluse, some artists, some pub bums, a singing Irishman with an
accent that did not come from New York, a short Indian businessman, and some children of Augustus John, Welsh painter of important people and bohemian extraordinaire (one was a retired
prizefighter, another was Caspar John, a First Sea Lord, head of
the British admiralty for NATO).

That night Liz Frink of the weighty, rough man/bird sculpture
gave Clarice and me a big London art world party. Among the small
mob invited were the poet Stephen Spender; the head of the Slade
School, painter Sir William Coldstream; the director of the Tate
Gallery, Sir John Rothenstein; the head of the Ealing School, Bill
Booker; the sculptors Lyn Chadwick and Kenneth Armitage, the
painter Joe Tilson, and the art critic David Sylvester.

I was anxious about my exhibition and wanted to return to Paris
and my studio and Clarice's soups. We took the boat train from
Victoria Station to Gare Saint-Lazare.

Clarice's dad and mum, Liz Frink,
the bride, her brother, the groom, and family friend
Harold Kaplan (foreground)

L

A

R

R

At a cocktail party given by Jean Larcade to make a little fuss over our marriage, we met Martial Raysse, another *nouveau réaliste* of the gallery, I'd say a super *nouveau réaliste*. Martial never found his way out of a plastic bottle factory. For me, his greatest triumph was an exhibition of a giant water-filled plastic pool in which he lay down fully clothed, surrounded by a bevy of plastic ducks and animal-shaped tubes, and showered himself with a hand-held douche. He had a traditional beauty that did not square with his absurdist preoccupations. He wasn't amusing himself under his hand-held douche, he was telling you, "Look around, there is more between heaven and earth to call art than you feel comfortable with."

Yves Klein

Y

R

I

V

E

R

S

And then there was Yves Klein, Yves *l'incroyable*, who stayed with me in New York before I showed in Paris. Actually, he was helpful in getting me the Rive Droite exhibition, telling Larcade I was an important American artist. Yves' most memorable work came out of a "happening" called "Blue Body Mades." He composed a "Symphonie Monotone" and hired a symphony orchestra to play the one note to an invited audience while nude females smeared themselves blue, then one by one, at Yves' direction, lay down and rolled on an enormous white canvas tacked to the floor of the stage. (If, as some claimed at the time, he did nothing for the art of painting, he certainly enlarged one's idea of a brush.) Then he cut up the canvas, each portion containing one or two of the women's surprisingly recognizable figures, and sold them according to size.

Yves was a judo black belt who belted John Myers in the stomach. John, if my selective memory serves, grabbed Yves in a dark corner at a party at my house on West Third Street and, unasked, told him two inches from his face that he was a lousy artist, that his work was always predictable, that in short Yves Klein stank. "What's so great about dipping everything you do in blue, even if it is 'international Yves Klein blue'? So what! Who cares! While Larry Rivers, my dear and great Larry, continues to dare surprise me."

John arose from the floor with a welt on his paunch that would go through the rainbow of colors for a month until it settled into international Yves Klein blue.

I asked Yves, "When you receive your judo black belt, don't you have to take an oath never to use judo unless you're in danger?"

Yves l'incroyable

"I'm sorry, I know he's your dealer, but John was so cruel! That big mouth in my face! It was *incroyable!*"

A cheer went up in the New York art world from the legion John had mistreated. John had an angry sponge inside him that liquor inflated till it crawled up his throat and out his mouth. The only force that could hold it back was his animal instinct for survival. He was charitable to the rich and lenient to the powerful. But for talent he admired, John was an unflagging groupie.

At the beginning of the summer of 1962, in Paris, Yves asked if he could cast me, face and body, cock and all, in blue plaster. On the day friendship and artistic solidarity forced me to come by his studio and be cast, he died. He was thirty-four years old.

In his own apartment, in a room full of his work, he was laid out on his sculpture *Blue Table*, dressed in the uniform of the Ancient Order of Saint Sebastian, a dark blue cape draped over one arm, like a Napoleonic naval hero. Immobilized on his own sculpture, he looked like another Yves Klein work. His chemically hardened "Blue Sponges" goose-necking from gray stone cubes were all over the floor. Above his head on the wall hung a long horizontal rectangle from his "Fire and Water" series, made with the help of a World War II flamethrower. Yves would blast fire over a plywood panel spotted and soaked with water. This produced colors ranging from black where there was no water to somber Naples yellow where there was heavy soakage. His *Blue Relief-Map of France* was angled on the fireplace mantel.

Yves felt that the color purplish Day-Glo blue was his, the way we think our nose and our arms are ours. So any object made by Yves or God, if it was drenched in Yves Klein blue, he owned, and that in itself was fantastic. In New York Yves was dismissed as an ambitious phony whose work was derivative of the new American art. Those opinions haven't done away for one moment with the zany originality of what Yves brought together in the name of art.

News from New York

Dear Kids,
Word has reached America that you have gotten married. Gosh! and Congratulations! Have you changed since the ceremony? Write me every detail. I am very interested in what people do because I am a writer. Are you becoming plumper and more kindly or slimmer and more understanding? Do you wake up at night and say, "Dear, hand me the potato"? or "Would you hand me that pineapple there on the counterpane, my beloved spouse, for I fear it is growing misty"? But then, Larry, I only write letters like this to you, since you long ago maintained that the only style I could write in was the style in which I wrote poems. This was anent a letter of mine which began something like Pineapple eagle forehead caress bumps. Oh my lost styles! . . . Life here is just as invigorating as ever, tomorrow featuring Paul Taylor and his entertainers which Jane Freilicher who saw it today said was very nice if you don't care about enjoying yourself. Please repeat this comment to John Ashbery just in case you don't like it yourself. Comment ça va? He was also threatening to sue me personally.

Chaleureusement,
Kenneth

Frank O'Hara wrote me that Clem Greenberg was threatening to sue me, *Art News*, and its editor in chief, Tom Hess, for defamation of character, because of that remark in my review of the Monet show at the Museum of Modern Art about "Clem's arrogance and inaccuracy." I wrote to Tom, suggesting that Clem, among other happy endings, should be thrown down a flight of stairs. I advised Tom to stand up to that cultural commissar and incited him to violence, suggesting that next time he saw Clem he should do something fierce.

Tom wrote back, alerting Clarice and me to his impending trip to Paris with his wife, Audrey. He said my letter filled him "with courage, hope, faith, and vertigo," and made him feel like going out and putting a boot in Clem's puss, except that Mrs. Clem had just lost a baby, which put an end to all his fantasies of aggression.

Going from dark to light, Tom said he'd spotted our becoming faces (Clarice's and mine) in *Newsweek*, "in good old Impasse Ronsin where Brancusi used to grow eggplants and tuberous begonias." His letter was full of social and artistic updates, such as Yale asking Fairfield Porter to head the art department, where Josef Albers, the previous head, "used to grow tuberous squares and other odd angles." According to Tom, John Myers thought this wasn't a good idea. I guess he was afraid that Fairfield, one of his painters, might get too busy to produce the work necessary for his next "marvelous" show.

Meanwhile, Bill de Kooning, master of the "Truss and Strut and Girder," was building a great studio and home out in East Hampton with a long, high catwalk from which he could observe "things in the middle"—his paintings, maybe. Our friend Norman Bluhm thought it would collapse, Tom told me, making Norman out as a know-it-all van der Rohe student who had already predicted the collapse of the Seagram Building.

On the literary front, Tom sent word that B. H. Friedman's new novel, *Circles*, gave a lot of space to our art world peacocks, but that our pal Mae (wife of Harold) Rosenberg would be "taking care of That for everybody" with her review. One of the characters in the book was a painter who kept saying, "Hey, how's about some more pot," and Tom wanted my opinion on whether that was realistic.

Tom reported that the Museum of Modern Art was in the market for an Ad Reinhardt painting, and even if Ad never had a good word to say about MOMA, Tom thought he should sell. Tom loved artists to contradict themselves. But Ad had taken "the coward's way out" and "gone to Hollywood" for an exhibition at the Dwan, the up-and-coming gallery where I had already shown a year or so earlier.

Tom devoted a paragraph to Nico Calas, a bright, easy-to-tease critic with a sad face, who'd gone gaga over the work of Chryssa, a sculptor of Greek descent known for her plaster, bronze, and aluminum reliefs and her introduction of neon tubing in a piece called *Times Square Sky* ("Beware of Greeks who make collages," Tom warned). Kaldis, another Greek artist, possessed of incomprehensible wit accentuated by his pre-sixties long hair and the inch-long hairs on the tip of his nose, had been sick but could now walk again, "which he usually does, right up to the telephone to chew my ear off."

Tom sent Clarice a kiss, and Audrey sent me "steel petals" as regards—a reference, I think, to a plant I made out of sheet steel and rods, which the Hesses purchased and kept in their living-room hothouse on Beekman Place. The whole letter made me feel like I hadn't left New York for a minute.

Here's part of an affectionate letter Frank O'Hara wrote from Sneedon's Landing on the Hudson.

> Bobby and I are "living together" as Tolstoy would say (or anyone else). I am very happy and would like to hear from you. I don't see that this affects our great friendship in any bad way, for after all it has survived all the other upheavals of several complicated lives and I am anxious that it survive this one.
>
> My devotion to you and your work will always be strong and important to me no matter how what happens or has happened affects your feelings for me.

On a social level, seeing the *nouveaux réalistes* every so often wasn't that funny or satisfying, given our communication problem. I saw Niki and Jean a lot although they were flying all over Europe. From time to time, I ran into Harry Mathews on his way to tasting another of the wines of France. Infrequently an evening was spent with Elizabeth de Saint-Phalle, Niki's sister, and naturally her boyfriend, the gallery dealer and small-car buff Larry Rubin. Living in Paris was about finding out how comfortably Clarice and I could live together, studying French, and painting every day, interspersed with trips to various places of interest suggested by John Ashbery, who was in Paris then and had been for years.

But life could get hilarious through the mail. Another letter from Frank:

> . . . Joe [Le Sueur], J.J. [Mitchell] and I and Kenward [Elmslie] went to dinner at Chuck Turner's, which featured

Virgil [Thomson] and Ned [Rorem] and a negro hustler **L**
named Joe who called himself Miss Dietrich, from Hollywood. It was just like John Rechy's novel. He was of course
6'2, gorgeous and ended up screwing—you guessed it—
Virgil. He liked my chest but money more. Virgil at first **A**
tried to talk him out of any fee by saying, "Well, Baby, it's
a noble thing to be a negro, but it's an ignoble thing to be
a whore, right?" To which this Harry Belafonte substitute
smiled gently and replied, "Ah don't know as ah understand **R**
quite what yuh mean." Ned was quite huffy to him since
he thinks *he's* Miss Dietrich. After we were kissing in the
kitchen the hustler opined that it was a pity I was a "poor
poet," a piece of information he picked up from that sand- **R**
bagging bastard Joe L. Anyhow, I thought you'd be interested to know how we cultural leaders who remain in New
York amuse ourselves and each other.

That's all, folks. Love to Clarice, **Y**
Frank

Three cheers for Ms. Dietrich getting his way with my cheapskate
friends.

Off to London

The show at the Rive Droite came down. John Ashbery wrote his **R**
long review for the *Herald Tribune*, with a reproduction of one of
the works in the show. I didn't walk away rich, but we sold enough
to put a respectable face on our effort. Bob Scull, a volatile Castelli
Gallery groupie, was in Paris. With a great flourish he took me to a **I**
pressed duck dinner at the Tour d'Argent restaurant and there,
literally under the table, handed me fifteen hundred American
smackers for the large "Vocabulary Lesson" of Clarice in the nude.
Jean Seberg, the hot New Wave star of Godard's *Breathless*, com- **V**
missioned me to draw her. Her husband, Romain Gary, sat through
the sittings.

Paris 1990 **E**

In June 1990 I returned to France for a show at the Beaubourg. It
was to be an exhibition of my recent three-dimensional works. I've **R**
shown my work in Paris in museums and galleries on and off for
years, not entirely to my satisfaction. The afternoon before the
opening, an official of the French cultural ministry asked me and
my French dealer to lunch. We had coffee outdoors at a big bar, **S**

just as I had done during my Paris days of 1961–62 with my good friends, among them dead Klein and Tinguely, and before that in 1950, eating in the student mess halls, drinking wine fast to return the bottle for deposit before the store closed.

The cultural official began to discuss a portrait commission, of an important living French cultural figure. This was a serious commission from the French government, but I was not too excited. To whet my competitive nature, she mentioned a few artists who had already accepted the commission, like Francis Bacon and a German painter, Baselitz, whom I had never heard of, whose name she uttered with such reverence I feigned interest. Lastly she hinted that there was a possibility of approaching, for the same project, the great—her voice lowered conspiratorially—*Jasper Johns!*

Her words had their intended effect. I thought, "This project deserves serious attention." But as we reviewed French cultural figures, none attracted me. French artistic and intellectual leadership was something of the past. Jean Tinguely hadn't helped matters; he once told me that any artist who took French culture seriously shouldn't be taken seriously. Becoming nervous about the stalled negotiations, my dealer, Pierre Nahon, suggested I paint the talented and beautiful Niki de Saint-Phalle, an artist who had de-

*Niki through the lens
of Lord Snowdon*

voted her life to color sculpture and public architecture, who exhibited at his gallery, and who had remained a close friend over the
years. The choice of subject for the commission was framed in such
heavy terms as Important and Influential. The notion that I could
have a friend who was Important and Influential reminded me of
Groucho Marx thinking there must be something wrong with any
club that wanted him as a member. Niki is a pal of mine, and to
pals I can never assign labels like Important or Influential. An artist
or poet or playwright or novelist friend can be terrific, wonderful,
tops, or deserving of more attention from the world. This commission, like most contemporary commissions, apart from the size,
gave me the freedom to choose my style and the cultural figure.

The cultural official's response to the suggestion of Niki de
Saint-Phalle was a long moment in coming. Then came a series of
mmm's, *pas mal*'s, and *peut être*'s that cast doubt on my freedom
to choose. Niki de Saint-Phalle was put on the back burner. I suggested Mendès-France, who some thirty years ago bit the dust
trying to switch the French from wine to milk.

"Defense de politicians, Larry. D'ailleurs, il est mort," said the
minister, whose name, I have not mentioned, was Alberte Grynpas
Nguyen, an Occidental married to an Oriental.

I had seen Marcel Ophuls' film *The Sorrow and the Pity*, about
French collaboration with the Nazis under the German occupation
in World War II. The portrait was to hang in the Bibliothèque de
Ville de Paris, paid for by the French government with French
money. The chance to remind everyone who passed through of the
Vichy regime should have inspired me to insist on M. Ophuls as
my choice, but his was another name placed conveniently on a
back burner that was starting to get crowded.

Tail End

I thought of Brigitte Bardot, and after a few moments she rolled off
the end of my tongue.

Brigitte Bardot represented a past idea about the French that
might still be alive but for the "sexual revolution." Love and Loving, until the fifties, was a profession in France. It sold perfume. It
brought Charles Boyer and Fifi d'Orsay to Hollywood. It was internationally envied. When I first perceived the idea of the Mistress as
a natural way of life in France, I knew I had to get there. Every
grown man had one! I was convinced no French wife begrudged

her husband this side dish! And in many instances would give him a pair of horns in homage to *Liberté, Egalité, Fraternité*. Part of this Love and Loving litany came to me through newspaper stories about manslaughter going unpunished on the grounds that it was committed under the trying condition of discovering a mate in bed with someone else. For a judge not to take this into consideration would be un-French.

When I first saw *Les Enfants du Paradis* my overwhelming emotional response seemed personal. I was affected by the beautiful Arletty, with a startling figure at the end of her youth, and by the facial gestures and bodily movements of Jean-Louis Barrault. Just when the separated lovers are going to be reunited, Barrault loses Arletty in a crowded carnival. These elements of physical beauty and passionate yearning struck something in my youthful soul, a soul searching for just such subject matter in my own life. Could I use Barrault?

But other configurations of French culture beyond that moviehouse were loading my empty urn when I started painting. Modern art was French, according to what I saw on museum and gallery walls. What I didn't see on walls I found in art books; and the first "literature" I read, at twenty-one, with a dictionary lying next to my mattress on the floor, was Balzac, Flaubert, Stendhal. And Baudelaire, the poet with the black mistress, whom I finally discovered leaning against a wall in Courbet's *Studio* painting.

For an art student like me, impressionism was not only the triumph of working outdoors over studio painting to create landscapes; it was visual information about France and French life: fields and waterways and bridges; what people wore, the parasols they carried; how they worked, how they washed, how they danced; how Toulouse-Lautrec's paintings of the "can-can" were responses to the new sensation—underwear for women, the forerunner of modern panties.

All this art came from France. Pierre Bonnard, an early favorite of mine, made paintings that gave breakfast or lying down or taking a bath or being outdoors with the family a shimmering and glorious glow. If I ate off a scrawny table in New York with five-and-dime dishes and other scrubby accoutrements and no tablecloth, it was because I was an American with an anxiety about time and didn't understand the inherent pleasantness in life, lacking what the ordinary Frenchman took as everyday fare, that life could be beautiful. Bonnard's nudes were no more important than the shape of a couch or a bed or a lawn as an area for him to display the sensuousness of color, the play of an utterly unnatural light over whatever he painted.

And the other films from France, Renoir's *Grand Illusion*, Cocteau's *Blood of a Poet*, Buñuel and Dali's *Andalusian Dog*, and the music of Milhaud and Poulenc. And anecdotes and gossip from friends who had *been there*. And those who had not but whose longing to go was so intense they lived as French a life as they could in New York, and who would talk of all this through our cheap French meal on warm days under an awning on Ninth Avenue.

Couldn't I pluck someone from the avant-garde that began with the dandyism floating around in theater pieces in the nightclubs of Paris? It wasn't long before "avant-garde" was tacked onto art, music, and dance. Acting like a political party given its charter by God, the avant-garde accepted anyone interested in joining. If you were a member, it gave you a certain stature. What you produced under this rubric may have had merit—a fur-lined teacup, a framed toilet seat—but what was more important was that the middle and upper classes find it useless, immoral, and ugly.

To Shoah

"How did you get from Brigitte Bardot to a toilet seat by Duchamp?" said La Représentative de la Culture, Alberte.

"I take it you don't like my choice of Bardot."

"Mm, uh—," she said.

My choosing BB would be like painting the resurrection of the France that no longer existed. France lost her colonies, and those that stayed in her orbit she set free. French is no longer the second language of any country. Did France explode a hydrogen bomb? Who knows, who cares?

"Brigitte Bardot would not be the subject of the painting, I guess, the subject would be the glory of France, the France I knew as an art student."

"Oh, it's a portrait of you as a young man," said La Nguyen. Discomfort entered her features. Mine projected openness to other candidates for his commission. I was silent in the realization that nothing out of contemporary France excited me. In desperation—we were running out of time—I remembered the film *Shoah*, made by Claude Lanzmann, a French Jew. I'd seen it in New York. It took two nights, four and a half hours each night, to understand his tremendous achievement. I am not going to give the film a review, except to say the portrait was to be of Claude Lanzmann or no one.

Surprisingly, Alberte tells me that what got her interested in commissioning me were my three portraits of Primo Levi, which she saw in the Marlborough Gallery in New York. The portraits were bought by *La Stampa*, the Italian newspaper Levi wrote for after returning from Auschwitz. Her voice rose in pitch, and she showed embarrassment at how emotional she suddenly became. I was convinced she was a Jew with a past connected to the Holocaust. Finally, shining in the face, she said she would get in touch with Lanzmann and perhaps if he was interested he might come to the opening of my exposition to check out my work and me. We left the empty restaurant.

It was windy outside as we walked in the same direction but to different destinations. A newspaper blew against my dealer's leg and stubbornly clung to his ankle. Reaching down to grab it and throw it away, he sees a large advertisement for a revival of *Shoah* starting that night, the night of my opening! We acted like old-fashioned séance people in touch with some other world giving us a message as we all held on to the newspaper.

The night of my opening, as requested, Claude Lanzmann showed up. I told him I agreed with all the critics and audiences that acclaimed *Shoah*, ten years in the making, a masterpiece. We got around to our common heritage. He was reticent about passing along any warm feelings about it. I asked if he spoke any Yiddish as a kid; he said no, and was not amused at all by my Yiddish words and expressions. But he submitted to my opinion of him as the greatest contemporary French cultural figure and posed for some photos right there at the opening. These photos, from which I would work to make the portrait, turned out to be too dark. When I returned to New York, the French government sent me a detailed contract offering $27,000 for the portrait. My dealer at Marlborough, Pierre Le Vai, born in Biarritz and still a French citizen, warned me not to argue with the French government. "They don't care how much you usually get for a portrait. If you squawk they'll scratch the whole idea." For the twenty-seven grand I was also expected to pay for packing, shipping, and insurance. I signed the contract, and my assistant John Duyck flew to France after Lanzmann agreed to a date for a photo session. But Lanzmann was not available on that date, nor for the next five days. John flew back.

The problem was resolved by paying a French photographer $500
for taking some shots of my hero, whose behavior by now bothered
me, but whose work was and still is a masterpiece.

Gimpel Fils

By myself I unhung the Rive Droite gallery exhibition of 1962.
Using my experience working for my father's trucking company, I
stacked, covered, and tied the paintings to the top of a rented Volkswagen. With Clarice I drove to London to the Gimpel Fils Gallery
for my English debut.

Perhaps because it was an English-speaking land, I got a better
idea of the public's reaction to my work. In Paris my show received
a few mystifying reviews accompanied by a few sales. In London,
through Charles Gimpel, I was invited to speak in the giant vortex
auditorium of the Albert Memorial Hall. The subject: Contemporary Painting and Me. I met the granddaddies of English contemporary painting and their grandchildren.

Charles Gimpel was either luckier or a better dealer than Larcade in Paris, because he sold many more of my works. As a dealer
Charles had his finger on the bouncing button, and kept it there.
His nine other fingers were spread as far as the northern regions of
Alaska. For a few weeks every year he went to live with the Eskimos,
learning their language, learning to cook seal, and bringing back to
London some of the soapstone sculpture they made. He sold the
sculpture in his gallery, enabling him to send the Eskimos much-
needed funds that they actually earned. He published a book on
soapstone sculpture.

Once a year Charles had an exhibition at his gallery for young
artists. Frank Bowling, who was a young English artist in 1962 at
the Royal College of Art, told me how inspiring it was that Gimpel
Fils, an important gallery, gave him a chance to take the first steps
in his dream of fame and fortune. Frank Bowling now shows at the
Tibor de Nagy Gallery.

During World War II Charles Gimpel was as member of the
Resistance in France. He was captured by the Germans and sent to
Auschwitz. Mostly he spared you the stories of his experience
there. If pressed, however, he rolled up his sleeve to show you the
prisoner's number tattooed on his forearm. After the war he married an exuberant Irishwoman called Kate; for many years she was
involved in anti-English activities. After Charles died and my deal-

ings with the gallery had ended, Kate gave money to needy and shipwrecked friends of mine in London, just on a phone call from me in New York City.

Charles's speech was such a pleasant thing it didn't matter what he was talking about. He took very seriously the gallery's role in the making of art. He was a nephew of the art dealer Duveen and was schooled in the philosophy that someone had to hear the tree fall in the forest for it actually to have fallen. Charles was convinced that art must make its way into public life before it could be said to exist.

I did a lot in London for the short time I spent there. Aside from museum going, street walking, art school visits, and drinking at various pubs, I also went to a few contemporary galleries. One that had a good space, clean floors, and a prosperous look, though a little darker than I thought proper for a gallery, was the Marlborough. I had heard of some of their artists but liked almost none of them.

Cherche Midi

Clarice and I night-trained it back to Paris. After one very packed year we were ready to return to the U.S., but a particular event of the very packed year propelled us immediately to this decision.

One afternoon I bumped into Bob Thompson, a New York artist friend of mine, in an art supply shop near the Grand Chaumier art school. He had found an interesting niche for himself in the boundless aesthetic painting spectrum. He made paintings with lots of figures, each done in one color, in what might be called a primitive style, but they had a strange light and always contained some anguished melodrama. When we saw each other in New York we'd find some heroin and take time out to drop out for a few hours. In Paris on the Rue Cherche Midi he lived in a long room with drapes of different lengths coming down from the ceiling and dividing the room. His paintings were all over the walls. It was like an Arabian setting. I tied up, he helped me find my vein, and zap! I instantly recognized the shot as bordering on the mortally dangerous. I made my way to a bed, but Bob knew an overdose when he saw one and used the traditional antidote of walking the near-dead around the room. A few hours later the mortal danger passed, and I thought I'd sleep off the rest of the shot at my atelier with some care from Clarice. I didn't know, as I drove home, that I'd nod off behind the wheel for a second and end up on a sidewalk. By some miracle an exceptional gendarme told me only, "Move on."

Clarice took one look and thought one thing: if we remained in Paris, I'd be out looking for Bob in a few days. She was ready to return to New York on her own. My heroin taking, even with long spaces between episodes, always frightened and depressed her: I'd die or become an addict. It was as if I was leaving her when I shot up. I compromised myself back into her good graces by pushing ahead the trip we had planned to Eastern Europe. In fact, as soon as I recovered from my OD, we left for Austria, Poland, Czechoslovakia, East Germany, West Germany, and then made it back to Paris, packed, and took a train to Cherbourg.

Via the *France* we arrived back in New York City toward the end of August 1962.

Back Home

A cocktail party was in drunken progress when Clarice and I, straight off the ship, arrived at our home on Little Plains Road in Southampton. I had given Frank O'Hara and Joe Le Sueur the use of the house when Clarice and I left for France. And they were using it. In the morning, with nothing cleared away, we were up and munching at memorable experiences that took place during the ten-month separation. Just so I wouldn't think anything in life had really changed, Frank showed me a poem he'd written recently on a quiet day. I flashed the Paris and London catalogs with John Ashbery's essay. Frank praised the writing profusely. Joe suggested "she praiseth too much." Frank and John were always neck and neck in the writing steeplechase, and until then was no declared winner. It kept things hot and funny between them for years.

After the weekend I was alone with Clarice, and we settled into what looked like tranquil country life except that we drove to New York for parties, culture, lunch, and other important things, and some extracurricular sex. Mostly we were enough for each other and spent happy days together, cooking, eating the results, painting, and fucking.

Aside from the age-old yearning to brush with nature, our decision to remain in Southampton after the summer had a practical basis. We had no place to live in New York. During a seven-week trip Clarice and I took to California and back, the landlord of my West Third Street studio demolished a space there, reducing what

was a triplex to a duplex. I stopped paying rent. I sued for a reduction of rent and lost—badly. A court order forced me to pay all the
back rent and vacate.

After that summer, our fall in Southampton stretched into winter, spring, and the end of summer of '63. We received a letter from
John Ashbery.

> It really seems an age since you were here. All has changed
> —no more Yves Klein, no more Galerie Rive Droite, Lar-
> cade has not been seen for months. . . . Yves is having a
> show of his burnt pictures at the moment. I have also man-
> aged to meet Virginia Kondratiev at last, with Martial
> Raysse, and saw a lot of Tom Hess when he was here—I'm
> afraid my capacity for three-star meals wrought havoc with
> his expense account, but he didn't seem to mind. . . .
>
> I don't want to go on with these silly details of Paris life
> especially since I know you consider Paris in the minor
> leagues and you are doubtless right. I really have missed
> you and Clarice this year, and hope that the coming season
> will see us reunited. . . .
>
> I loved the poems you sent for *Locus Solus* most of
> which I remembered very well. I am going to use huge gobs
> of them on the mag, but haven't yet gotten around to put-
> ting the issue together. Remember me to Frank.
>
> Love,
> Ashbo

Here's one of the poems John chose.

BENJAMIN F.

1. A large face.

2. A bust by Houdon.

3. Curls that lit in thunder.

4. Balls made themselves known.

5. On the deep velvet, in the marble halls
   at the fountain Lafayette kissed him on the shoulders
   He came devoid of moon, flesh, joke books,
   his turned down card was like his tight socks.

6. Philadelphia was full of smoke.
   In the forests men unbuttoned their vests.
   In a fit with picking his teeth clean
   the clerks left his house.
   He was tired.
   He turned from the long nose at his window.

7. Did he marry or invent heavy garden tools?
   Was he the stooge of honest George?
   His life inspired the masochists.
   The fields when his carriage died became empty.
   Let the thirteen vessels lie.

8. His name is like a stone.
   He was a homosexual and a thief.
   His mother died smiling.
   O bring him moons and joke books.
   He dies we die.

9. Deceit is the known quantity.

Nineteen sixty-three was also the year Joseph Hirshhorn, a man whose money helped discover uranium, commissioned me to paint

his portrait. His money satisfied his uncontrollable desire to collect art. Joe had already bought some works of mine. (By the time he died in 1981 he owned forty-five of them, bought with the help of

his adviser Abram Lerner, who became director of the Hirshhorn Museum.) Unknowingly Joe met the condition that I later adopted for portrait commissions: unless someone already owns a work of mine I refuse the commission. I want prospective collectors to have

an appreciation of what I'm up to in painting that is unrelated to their egos. I want them to realize the commissioned portrait is just another work of mine that happens to have their face in it.

I stretched a canvas, packed my paint, brushes, rags, and drove up to Joe's mansion in Greenwich, Connecticut. In a pretty small space where he did a lot of big business, even during the portrait, Joe sat with two phones on his table and answered calls as I started to work. During our breaks he walked me around the house, showed me his Picassos, Matisses, whoever amounted to anything and some who didn't. Outside we'd move among his monumental Moores, Maillols, Lipchitzes, David Smiths, Rodins, including the great *Burghers of Calais*, even the uncategorizable Sir Jacob Epsteins—just to name a few in Joe's private sculpture garden, a larger version of the great sculpture garden in the Hirshhorn Museum. I guess little guys, like Joe and Billy Rose, went for monumental sculpture.

In 1965 or 1966, Joe wanted my large piece *The History of the Russian Revolution*, thirty-five feet long, fourteen feet high, which he saw at the Jewish Museum in a 1965 retrospective. He also saw it reproduced across two pages of *Time* magazine and a few other publications. Joe bought lots of art from reproductions he saw in magazines.

To be in his collection became more exciting for every artist in it because there was talk of erecting a national museum that would house this collection in Washington, D.C. He thought this possibility deserved consideration and told me, in a taxi crossing Manhattan, that if he could have *The History of the Russian Revolution* at the right price, he would see to it that there would be a Larry Rivers Room in the museum. I don't know if I really thought it would happen, but the work Joe wanted, composed of about seventy-five different pieces, required extensive worry and expensive care, and I decided it had a better and safer future, even if in the museum's cellar, than in my studio. So, into Joe's already choked dreamboat went *The History of the Russian Revolution*, floating up the river to some art heaven. As the years went on, all the fruits of Joe's business gave his dream about a Hirshhorn Museum a chance to be realized.

But I also had a dream. In it I pictured the opening of Joe's museum, dedication ceremonies and all. I saw the president and his wife, Joe at their side, surrounded by the press, smashing a bottle of champagne against the cornerstone of the museum. Now, no matter what the American people were getting, it was still a government building costing them some $15,000,000. An institution with a Jewish name in the nation's capital, on the Mall, and the first work they see inside is a thirty-five-foot mixed-media extravaganza celebrating the Communist revolution, the birth and rise of an empire dedicated to our destruction. Joe McCarthy had been dead for quite a while, but there were still some things sacred in America. Not only would there be no room bearing my name, they would close the museum the next day!

I guess I exaggerated the possible impact of my *Russian Revolution*. If you didn't pay close attention to it, it was just another zany-looking piece of modern art. So there is a Larry Rivers Room in the Hirshhorn Museum, and it contains *The History of the Russian Revolution*, plus about ten other works at Joe's "right price." If I'm to be recognized in this drama as some kind of bohemian descendant of Michelangelo, Joe was Lorenzo de Medici in a business suit who still liked a Jewish joke.

LR and son Joe take a break from Revolution.

Aside from art projects, the question that loomed in New York was how much better would life be at the Marlborough than at the Tibor de Nagy Gallery. From the time I joined the gallery in 1962, Marlborough made no bones about what its interest in art was—profit and stature. It was never about cheering on the artist. But perhaps in 1962 I wasn't as far removed from the fatal attraction of profit and stature as I would have liked to believe. Marlborough devoted itself to sniffing out and finding buyers for the work of the granddaddies of abstract expressionism: Mark Rothko, Barnett Newman, Jackson Pollock, Franz Kline, Ad Reinhardt, Adolph Gottlieb, and Conrad Marca-Relli. One non–abstract expressionist handled by Marlborough was Francis "Bad Boy" Bacon. I liked his work. Willem de Kooning didn't join the lemming rush to Marlborough. He was crestfallen when he found that the director, Frank Lloyd, was not an English lord but only a Viennese Jew whose name was originally Levy. The prices for the work of these granddaddies were higher than mine, and their critical acclaim wider.

Frank Lloyd came to my studio about three times, once to get friendly and to look over what I was working on. The only comment I still remember was what Frank considered a compliment: that I had great technical facility for making faces, figures, and objects recognizable. He dropped by again soon after he had met a young, attractive schoolteacher from the Midwest, Susan, later to become Susan Lloyd. It was a lazy Sunday afternoon, and he wanted to amuse her with a studio visit. The third time was in Southampton; earlier that day he had been in Gottlieb's studio in East Hampton, twelve miles away, looking over Adolph's work. The fact is he didn't have much to say in an artist's studio. This was natural for Frank. He wasn't impressed by his own opinions on art, he was impressed by my sex life. Like me, he liked young women, and like me, he married one. But he listened carefully to the more professional opinions of museum directors, critics, and collectors. He had a mild myopia for paintings but a twenty-twenty eye for the painting biz. He was socially affectionate, liked gossip, loved to laugh.

Marlborough Before Me

Frank Lloyd was the son of a Viennese antique dealer. One step ahead of the goose-steppers overtaking Vienna in 1938, Frank made

his way to London. During the war he served in the British infantry. Discharged, he became a partner in a rare-book shop with Harry "Vest-Fingers" Fischer. A bookshop was too small an enterprise for the kind of pile Frank had his heart set on making. They began to hang contemporary paintings in the few spaces that books didn't crowd. Frank originally displayed the art to augment the cultural ambience of the shop and help sell books; then the art itself began to sell, and well. The inclusion of art attracted the attention of one David Somerset, future duke of Beaufort; the handsome and cultivated Englishman with connections to art money proved to be the catalyst in Marlborough's founding. Frank's pile began to grow.

In 1960 Lloyd took action on the new certainty in the art world that the center of this world, i.e., the money, was in New York. He began carefully. He bought into the Gerson Gallery on Fifty-seventh Street, dealers in solid sculpture with a roster bought from the historic Kurt Valentin Gallery that included the modern pantheonites Jacques Lipchitz, Henry Moore, David Smith, James Rosati, et al. For six or seven years Marlborough of London, operating in New York, was called Marlborough-Gerson Gallery, until Frank bought Mrs. Gerson out and dropped her name from the logo.

I'm not sure what combination of factors was responsible for my not having a show at Marlborough for the first five years I was with them. Was I so busy living, loving, painting, and worrying that I didn't think showing my work made that much difference? I had no game plan in 1962 about how to run a career. I misjudged the importance of showing in the same store with the big names connected to abstract expressionism. Not only wasn't it important, it was detrimental. Unfortunately (now I find out) the history of modern art, maybe all art, makes clear the need of showing work, like that old tree in the forest needing an audience to corroborate its fall. Marlborough, acquiring a language to go with the abstract art they were selling, seems to have had difficulty finding new rhetoric to convince themselves, other dealers, and collectors that artworks like my "Vocabulary Lesson" and "Africa" series, and my "Dutch Masters" reliefs featuring Rembrandt's *Syndics of the Drapery Guild* on a giant cigar box with cigars, were terrific paintings about to become the newest chapter in the glorious history of art.

What did sell got higher prices, but the number of sales began to fall. Those years of "Whatever Happened to Larry Rivers?" had some compensations. Being left alone, not showing every trickle that rolled off my brush and humorous brain, shielded my work from negative criticism or exaggerated compliments and allowed it to develop freely. The first five versions of "Vocabulary Lesson" had one focus—naming the features of the face and body in other languages. The sixth, out of my ordinary aversion to repetition, would expand that focus. A British group commissioned me to produce an artwork for Shakespeare's four hundredth birthday. I chose *Titus Andronicus*. Words identifying physical features in the "Vocabulary Lessons" were replaced by names identifying Shakespeare's characters. Painting the "Vocabulary Lessons," I was interested in a fresh idea of a portrait as well as my own version of the pink-and-yellow charts I'd seen in doctors' offices illustrating internal parts of the body. By the time I got to *Titus Andronicus* I was just as interested in contrasting the soft edges of my brushwork with the hard edges created by using stencils for the lettering.

I then took the whole idea of parts of the body and words into sculpture. I began sculpting and casting arms and legs, faces, breasts and knees and ankles, piercing them to hold metal letters identifying each part. During those quiet years without one one-man show creeping up on me one slow year after the other (the Tibor de Nagy Gallery gave me ten one-man shows in my ten years with them), I continued to elaborate on words and parts of the body in different ways.

Not because we were contractually related to the same gallery but because we had a common CPA, Bernard Reis, I got to know Mark Rothko. Painters showing in the same gallery, once they forget the days when they had no gallery, make no pretense of belonging to some kind of group; they represent nothing but their own work and themselves. No painter admires any living painter. The most that painters can safely admit, without endangering their own corporate structure, is "respect" for someone's work. To admit you love the work of a contemporary makes you a "sissy."

Mark Rothko was a serious-looking bespectacled fellow with a thoughtful comment a minute for any situation that came up. Once he asked me at some gathering or opening, "How are you doing? Macht a leben?" ("Are you making a living?") Not wanting to appear deprived or disgruntled about what I thought was my real complaint, namely, not getting the serious attention I thought I deserved, I said, "I'm doing okay, Mark, things are looking up. What makes you ask?"

"Well, I read about you quite a bit. People bring your name up a lot. I thought maybe with you all that glitters is not gold."

One other series of mine begun in those quiet years was "Dutch Masters." Riding as a passenger on the Long Island Expressway one night on the long bridge just before the entrance to the Midtown Tunnel, as if for the first time I saw a neon sign against the dark blue sky advertising Dutch Masters. I was so delighted by Rembrandt's *Syndics of the Drapery Guild* helping to sell stinky cigars that I began a painting on the subject. Since 1959, I had gone from Camel, Marlborough, Tareyton, and Gitanes cigarette packs to Webster cigar box covers. Yves Klein assumed that anything purplish blue was an extension of his work and belonged to him; I began to assume that all cigarettes and cigars and their packaging were ripe for my picking. The Webster cigar box had a portrait of Daniel Webster in a golden frame placed in a field of weird flowers. Terry Southern pointed out that many of the cigar box logos included flowers in hopes of carrying the buyer away to a land of sweet smells. The Dutch Masters logo didn't stoop to dealing with smells. It relied on the public to transfer their trust of sixteenth-century Flemish craftsmanship to the manufacture of cheap cigars.

Not only were these sixteenth-century garment bosses, the syndics, working on you to buy Dutch Masters cigars, but Rembrandt himself was part of the pitch, to do away with any doubt about the high quality of the stogies.

My first "Dutch Masters" painting used only the image on the inside of the cigar box cover, which was a flat, lifeless illustration of Rembrandt's painting with all the background removed as if by a razor, leaving five of the six original figures and only a slice of the table they are sitting at. Each time I painted a version of "Dutch Masters," instead of the cigar box image of Rembrandt's *Syndics* I worked from a color reproduction of the painting to make it easier to get a resemblance to the original faces and figures. I used the wall behind the men to spread on the stencil letters spelling "Dutch Masters," and below those words, on a long rectangle that I painted with one stroke of a fat brush, the word "Presidents," the particularly cheap type of Dutch Masters. I took from the cigar box logo the appropriate ratio between the names and the figures, but in order to cram more action into a smaller space, I brought the words closer to the heads of the syndics.

Over the years I've done so many paintings of these six men, although in different surroundings, that I have a story for each of them. The figure on the far left in the doge's chair is the oldest, on the verge of falling asleep; possibly he is the victim of old-fashioned senility, looking as if a minute after sitting for the portrait he leaves for home, to sit in another chair. The other men are not his friends. The standing figure holding a book with long, delicate fingers has the most intelligent but distressed face in the group and has a voice in all decisions. The center figure with the open ledger before him is obviously the leader of the group trying not to explain everything. The man next to him, a body in partial profile, has a sensuous big face, big lips, and a lot of white under the irises of his large eyes. He seems capable of aggressive pronouncements and very interested in the passing parade, especially the women in it. The last on the right, a raving dandy with a delicately trimmed moustache and a hat that seems more fashionable than the others, is elegantly holding a pair of soft gloves. The lone hatless man behind the central figure is sad, scared, and small, resigned to his position as low syndic on the totem pole.

Dutch Masters put out a new vertical package holding only five cigars. A plastic window went the length of the box to exhibit one of the cigars. This new package required a board meeting of the art directors to figure out how to fit Rembrandt's *Syndics*, a horizontal work, onto a vertical package. It was simple; they removed the old man on the left and the dandy on the right.

After about four or five brilliant uses of the Rembrandt by the Dutch Masters people, I found myself including more than the box-top logo. I began making paintings that also showed the cigars and the boxes holding them. Twenty-five years later I still find something compelling about the subject. As early as 1965, when I had done at least a dozen versions, Frank said I was the only man addicted to nicotine who didn't smoke. Each shift in the way I work is reflected in one of my many "Dutch Masters." I tried a plastic "Dutch Masters" using a vacuum form machine; when I shifted into a more pronounced use of three-dimensionality in my work, I tried it on a "Dutch Masters." Maybe one of my reasons for going back to the Rembrandt is that I never get the faces without a lot of trouble; each time I work looking at the original it's like beginning all over again, it feels like a new work. Don't get me wrong, I'm not trying to look like Rembrandt, but I love complaining to him as I paint.

Chelsea

In the fall of '63 we moved into the Chelsea Hotel on West Twenty-third, home of rock-and-roll bands and Leonard Cohen and Bob Dylan; Dylan Thomas and Thomas Wolfe; Brendan Behan, the Irish bard, singing Israeli songs with Allen Ginsberg; George Kleinsinger, composer and animal lover, who lived with snakes, lizards, beautiful women, and wackily plumed birds; a floor below the terrarium, in burnt-umber rooms, the noble Virgil Thompson, composer, deaf as the snakes above him, surrounded by picture-crowded walls; Arthur Miller typing away on his play in progress, *After the Fall*; another Arthur, Clarke, writing the novel *2001*; another Clarke, Shirley, filming her documentary *Portrait of Jason*; Andy Warhol shooting *Chelsea Girls*; Peter Brook preparing *Marat/Sade*; Ken Tynan reviewing for the *New Yorker* and reviewing nightly his marriage to Elaine Dundy; Viva, superstar; super-painters de Kooning, Alechinsky, Dine, and Arman still in his black leather jacket; pushers and users of heroin, cocaine, opium, Quaaludes, speed, mescaline, LSD, angel dust—okay enough, I'm nauseous!—and transient hookers, male and female, indistinguishable from most of the permanent residents, plying a lively trade. It all gave me the feeling the this was an ideal place to raise a family, an interesting atmosphere, comfortable and conducive to long life— remember, Virgil lived to ninety-three, John Sloane to eighty-eight, and Phineas Cole wasn't carried out of the hotel until he reached a hundred and seven. The owners, mainly Mr. Bard and Mr. Gross, were miraculously transformed by this atmosphere into martyrs and masochists: no one paid rent on time, entire bands lived and practiced in nine-by-twelve rooms, and their groupies lived in the bathroom down the hall. The front desk was a complaint bureau: people who went to bed early complained about the noisy activities of the speed-taking all-nighters, who complained of the early risers waking them on their way to work; the maids complained about doors locked to keep out the innocent. Nobody complained about Mr. Bard and Mr. Gross, who had given up complaining about anything. Everybody loved them. Dwelling in his landmark structure in a suite on the third floor were those two young marrieds, Mr. and Mrs. Larry Rivers. I painted in a studio on the ninth floor.

For my first painting in the Chelsea, Jill Johnston, *Village Voice* author of obsessive lowercase articles, came every day to pose as the Lady for *Moon Man and Moon Lady*, my only painting based on a headline—our landing on the moon. This was the same Jill

L

A

R

R

Y

R

I

V

E

R

S

who later became famous for participating in a debate with Norman Mailer at Town Hall. Michael Kernan described Jill's contribution to this legendary 1971 event, which also featured Germaine Greer and Diana Trilling, in an article in the *Washington Post* (July 19, 1980) about Donn Pennebaker's documentary *Town Bloody Hall:*

> Jill Johnston, reading one of her punning poems ("lesberated women"), spoke of the need for a "withdrawal of women to give themselves a new sense of self. . . . Until all women are lesbians, there will be no true political revolution." She ran over her 10 minutes. Mailer wouldn't let her finish: "You've read your letter; now mail it!"
>
> What's the matter?" laughed Johnston, "are you afraid of women you can't f---?"
>
> At that point two other women rushed up and embraced Johnston with some intensity. They wound up on the floor and finally left the scene entirely.

Barbara Goldsmith is a journalist and social historian (*Little Gloria . . . Happy at Last*). I knew her through Joe Hirshhorn. After buying a medium-large work of mine called *Three Weeks*, based on an artist, me, lost in Betty Weisberger's clothing closet the size of a room, Barbara stood for a portrait with "Vocabulary Lesson" tendencies. After I finished it she sent me a letter.

> Dear Larry,
>
> The terrible news of the day [Kennedy's assassination] left me in such a state of despair it prevented me from adequately thanking you for the creation of "Barbara Goldsmith—Echoes and Parts." It was a most illuminating experience for me. . . . Because it was a so called portrait, I wanted it to be me. Because it was a painting by you, I wanted it to be a great Rivers. Because of a special rapport that developed between us, I think it succeeded on both counts, for both of us.
>
> . . . I shall never again want me in a painting by you. It will be more than enough (and a lot less exhausting) just to have a Rivers. As for you, I'd steer clear of people who want portrait portraits. We want our face caught up there and that contributes very little. One ego is enough for any canvas. Most subjects are like "The Girl From Panama Street" who told you your portrait of her looked like the sister she hates.
>
> In my case, you said you'd like to remember this painting in two versions. First, with a one eyed front view and

then with the collage eye you put on for me and found acceptable enough to leave. The collage eye helped me over the face hurdle so I could see the canvas as a whole. Also, it freed the canvas for me of every trace of shock value or artifice that I thought might diminish it as a painting. However, any reason I might (and probably did) think up falls in the realm of *my* ego and only confirms what I said about great artists and people with faces. Stick to "French Money" and cigar boxes—they don't quibble about trivia.

. . . "Echoes and Parts" bears your ironic quality when in the nick of time the mind mocks the heart. "Echoes" are so romantic and "Parts" are right out of the butcher shop.

. . . Nine days of posing have given me an idea of what you give to a painting technically and emotionally. You said I was the first model who stood in a position to see you and what's going on on the canvas. Each day I became more caught up in your creative process. To watch the technical miracle of what you can produce with paint and brush gave me a fresh delight in art. To feel the emotional and intellectual rack on which you stretch to produce a canvas left me absolutely drained. You said you thought this rapport a psychological phenomena that is peculiarly modern. I don't know how the blazes I thought you did it but now I have an insight I won't forget. So you see, I've really got a lot more than six by eight feet of well stretched canvas.

Fondly,
Barbara

Foggy Days

One day in our Chelsea suite Clarice whispered in my ear, "Darling, I'm late."

"Where are you going?"

"I'm going to be a mother."

That was in February. Gwynneth Venus Rivers was born September 10, 1964. In between a few things happened.

One of the things that happened in 1964 was a return trip to England. Only a few years had passed since Clarice left her homeland. She felt an urge to see old friends (maybe old boyfriends), do some traditional pub crawling with them, and take me to their quaint lean-tos in the countryside. We did this in our gorgeous, expensive, but troubled Aston-Martin, which I got in a trade for a painting from my dealer in L.A., Virginia Dwan.

During the reign of Clarice the First she and I went to London four times: in '61 for our marriage; in '62 to show at Gimpel Fils Gallery; now, in '64, to visit her parents in Wales and so I could be artist in residence at the Slade School of Fine Arts; later, in '66, to reside in a townhouse called Toad Hall in posh Belgravia with Gwynne Rivers, two years old, Emma Rivers, four months old, Howard and Mary Kanovitz, thirty-six years old, and Cleo Kanovitz, five months old.

I wanted to be seriously reckoned with in Europe. In 1962 I had begun this process with my work, my shows, my presence, first in Paris, then London. Reports about Jasper Johns' and Robert

Rauschenberg's earlier impact in those cities set off some old anxi-eties that I was heading for the bottom of the art pile. I sought to do work and enter situations that would prevent or forestall this. But whenever I take steps to be in the right place at the right time, I quickly forget why I'm there in the first place. The Slade School in 1964 was one such place, a brown-dark one with lots of shining students. I went to the Slade almost every day to paint, on my 750 Triumph motorcycle. I even had an outfit for rainy days.

Sir William Coldstream ran the Slade School with a charming fist. We'd met in 1962 the night I spoke on art at the BBC. Sir Bill was held by many on the English art scene to be a terrific and important painter. At a time when American painting, large, busy, and avant-garde, was invading the U.K., his work, figurative and calm, was something the English could still hang on to. I liked his work but wasn't sure exactly why it was so well regarded. I liked him and knew exactly why. He was pale and good-looking, intellec-tual, and underneath his unruffled personality a pervert. I also liked him because he liked me, he liked Clarice, more important he liked my work and offered a studio at the Slade School where I could paint in eighteenth-century peace. In return I met advanced stu-dents formally once a week in class and from time to time in their studios outside. It was a time when group painting had a quiet vogue among students. One especially interesting group connected to the school was called Fine Arts, and they were already exhibiting in galleries. I was asked to pass judgment on this new approach, which seemed such an intriguing idea I didn't care much about what the work looked like. The quality of the work was in the act of collaborating.

One afternoon after finishing at the Slade I was riding my mo-torcycle over to World's End to look at the results of one of these student collaborations. I was waiting for a light to change on West-minister Bridge when another biker in an arresting outfit pulled up. We looked at each other. He smiled. I smiled and revved my motor as a signal to race him. "First light after the bridge!" I zoomed off and left him trailing all the way. Once across the long bridge, I pulled over to the curb and waited for congratulations and a chat with my newfound bike buddy. He caught up with me, got off his bike, walked toward me. Instead of admiring the power of my 750, he told me I had exceeded the speed limit. He was a policeman. What? He looked angry, more about losing the race than my break-ing the law. He gave me a ticket.

Elated by this absurd misunderstanding with a fellow biker, I continued riding in happy anticipation of seeing the work of a student who was part of a group producing art. It was more her than her work I anticipated seeing. My student, Corinthia, was a nineteen-year-old giant with blond hair down to the middle of her back, and recently arrived from Coventry. Whenever I thought about her I kept seeing her nude on a horse with her hair whipping all over her body. She had large red chapped hands with long wide fingers and dirty fingernails, probably from the paint she used. She had a long pair of orange lips and a big space between her front teeth. I liked it. I thought her figure was something I'd enjoy drawing in the nude. She treated me with respect, like a child toward an older person, even as she became aware of my interest in fucking her.

When I arrived at her basement apartment, used as a studio, there were at least eight or nine students, female and male, and a few of their dogs, and small rooms full of stretched canvas, boxes, and burlap bags. Everyone moved quickly in the narrow halls from one room to another carrying paper cups and plates, chips, peanuts, cheese. I had come in the middle of preparations for a party. For a couple of minutes she took me into a room to look at her collaboration, forty-eight inches square. She pointed out the part she had done and talked about all the things she had done that were gone over. The artists, after discussing the idea for the artwork—let's say a grid with two faces—were given fifteen minutes to paint and then had to stop and allow the next in line to proceed from that point. I liked the result. She invited me to stay for the party. She told me some teachers from the Slade might be coming, implying there'd be other old men like me. I was thirty-eight and knew what she meant.

By party time I began thinking up excuses for not meeting Clarice at 7:00 for dinner at our flat on Redcliffe Road. I thought I'd play it by ear when I got home, a thought made easier by the booze entering my veins. By 7:30 no other teachers had arrived. I was already dogging Corinthia, demanding, then begging to see her collaboration again. We entered the small space and immediately embraced, locked the door, and fell on a pile on burlap bags on the floor. As we squirmed she told me *not to stop*, no matter what she said. I promised. Everything went on its roiling rocking course, and as I was managing to get my pants down to my thighs after managing to slip her out of her jeans and underpants, with her help, she

began to tell me in a normal tone, "Please don't." I wasn't inside **L**
her yet, and what she said sounded no different than what I've
heard from women my whole life, so I continued, hardly thinking
of what she had told me a moment ago. When we were finally
connected, her voice got dramatically louder. "Please stop this!" **A**
For a moment, out of proper upbringing by all the women involved
in my sex education, I stopped. She pulled me down hard on her,
and I obeyed her admonition not to stop. I kept on not stopping. **R**
My excitement was excruciating. As she came closer to coming,
her yells got more frantic: "Stop, stop it! What are you doing!"

Wait a minute. I'm sure she was yelling, but I don't really know
whether she was coming. Note: No woman in this book has ever **R**
had an orgasm during sex with me. The truth is that I have never
been sure any woman in or out of this book has come in my presence—moans and all.

Her friends knocked loudly on the door. The Beatles record **Y**
was lowered. "Everything all right, Corinthia?"

"Go away! Leave us alone!"

We continued until we fell asleep. Up and about in a few minutes, we took a last look at the collaboration and joined the party.

Nine o'clock. I arrived at Redcliffe Road. Clarice was there,
and so was the tall, well-mannered early deconstructionist writer
Harry Mathews, estranged husband of Niki de Saint-Phalle and **R**
current boyfriend of the glamorous first editor of the *Paris Review*,
Maxine Groffsky, now a top New York literary agent. He was stopping with us on his way back to Paris after a visit to his child's
English boarding school. Before I even shook his hand: **I**

CLARICE: Where have you been, Larry?

LARRY: Oh, I had to go to the student party in the World's **V**
End. Want a drink, Harry?

HARRY: *(extending his almost empty glass):* I'll take a bit
more. **E**

CLARICE: Did you have a good time?

LARRY: It was okay. The students are so polite I ended up **R**
talking to some of the teachers who came.

CLARICE: *(reheating a meal ready at 7:00):* You didn't tell me
about a party. **S**

L

A

R

R

Y

R

I

V

E

R

S

LARRY: I didn't know about it till this afternoon.

CLARICE: Well, why didn't you phone me?

LARRY: I don't remember the number here, dear.

At this point Harry remembered a dinner date he had with friends at Finch's, Clarice's favorite haunt on the Fulham Road, around the corner. As soon as he left I maneuvered Clarice over to the bed and began kissing her and finally making love, covering completely, I thought, my evening tracks. No one could be that hot twice in one evening. Since she had given up her heavy inter-rogation more quickly than usual, I pondered whether she was not being too inquisitive to cover her own evening tracks—maybe right here at home, eh! Maybe with tall, well-mannered deconstruction-ist and assiduous Don Juan Harry Mathews. Sociosexual shifts were very common in the sixties among people in their thirties. No greater love has everybody ever had for everybody.

I was married, and it still felt like fun. I enjoyed the theatrical apparel Clarice wore, her enthusiasm for going places, to see and be seen, and her genuinely happy interpretation of the events of our lives. I loved her looks, her cooking, and that laugh. By today's fundamentalist Christian ethics and the newspapers' daily dis-pensed wisdom, some might say Clarice had a drinking problem. I

Early deconstructionist
Harry Mathews

found it enjoyable socially, and later, in the shadows of our darkened bedroom, perfect.

How was I to regard those twenty torrid minutes with Corinthia? I'll let you know when I stop thinking about her.

Changes

The child growing in Clarice's womb presented a problem for me. I wanted her to have an abortion. Maybe I didn't say it out loud, but I never went to bed with Clarice intending to make little Gwynneth. Like my son Steven's mother, she simply announced one day there was a thing growing in her womb. I did not want to worry about the life of one more creature I was responsible for. Steven, at the time a teenage dropout on the road to an illustrious substance-abuse career, affirmed my feelings—no more children! Tugging violently on his bootstraps, Steven subsequently stopped abusing himself, graduated Phi Beta Kappa from NYU School of Journalism, became a cinematographer for TV commercials (helped, of course, by older brother Joseph, also a cinematographer, for TV feature films and tabletop commercials), and is now the fervent vice-president of NABET, the cinematographers' union. Steven is married and doomed to the easy life he leads in Nyack, New York—but I couldn't know that in 1964.

From the first moment Clarice realized she was pregnant she had no doubt she was going to have her baby. Her experience as an au pair would extend to her own child. For a woman with no intention of finding a career, it would give her life the meaning everyone was busy finding. At Best and Company in New York she had already bought a ton of diapers and baby things. Clarice's determination threw a blanket over my determination to keep life and work simple. I had to paint undisturbed. (Barney Newman: "Painters paint to have something to look at.") I just shut up and, as my father did at these difficult junctures, went the route of peace at any price. In a few months I was looking forward to what this tiny creature would be like. And of course, for all I imagined could go wrong, there would also be a great deal of enjoyment—for a few years, at least. For someone who has always had fantasies of living in a whorehouse like my heroes Pascin, Lautrec, Van Gogh, and Utamaro, what am I doing with five children, adding up to 252 pairs of shoes, 1,008 boxes of cereal, hot and cold, 8,660 quarts of milk, etc., plus 23 analysts, including mine?

A

R

R

Y

R

I

V

E

R

S

By the time I left England in the summer of '64 (for Europe and North Africa) I was making a bit of a splash in London's small pond. I lectured at the ICA, a serious art institute and gallery and a forum for VIPs of the art world willing to share ideas with local artists, critics, dealers, and museum directors. My friend Frank Bowling invited me to the Reading School, where he taught, to speak to students and look at their work. In London I spoke and performed at Bill Booker's school, the Ealing, a kind of art high school. I was invited to openings, painters' studios, and gatherings.

I met Stephen Spender and through him Francis Bacon. Francis, who had seen my show at Gimpel Fils in '62 and liked it, invited Clarice and me to a party Spender was giving for him. He also invited some unsavory types, three nice young men from the slums who stole Stephen's expensive wristwatch. Francis paid a tidy sum to buy it back. I told Francis about my junkie friend Happy Bean and the heist of Murray's father's watch that I had to buy back twenty years earlier thirty-five hundred miles away in the Bronx. This didn't help his mortification, just as knowing that everyone dies does not make it more comfortable to die.

Even in busy London there are quiet nights. Ronald Allay, assistant curator to John Rothenstein at the Tate, had a wife named Anthea, an artist who cooked her ass off. They fed Clarice and me, and for this had to listen to me regale them about me, art, my art, and the New York art scene. Many a night I pulled John's head sunk in boredom out of Anthea's ginger soufflé.

A short friendship with David Hockney began at a talk I gave at another art school where he was a student with dyed blond hair. He came up to speak to me after I finished and invited me to see what he was doing. I liked it. I loved his Liverpool accent. We exchanged letters, he visited me later in Long Island. Those days he thought nothing in life was worth worrying about except his tiny drawings. I agreed, and we haven't spoken since.

The critic John Russell, who hadn't as yet moved to New York to write for the *Times* and hadn't as yet invited me for lunch, or anything, invited me for lunch at Wheeler's Fish restaurant in the heart of Soho. We were to meet at about 12:30, then take a walk through Greek Street to the studio where John Constable had lived and painted.

"If I'm late, Larry, please don't grow impatient," said John. "I'm having my hair cut, and sometimes, though rarely, there are appointment mixups."

"Oh. I could use a haircut."

"Well, then, ring up Trufits and Hill on Shaftsbury Road."

Trufits and Hill was a gigantic open space made more open by mirrored walls. White one-inch tiles covered the entire floor. There were heavy columns and long marble shelves scooped out every few feet for a sink. The only other place I had been to in London combining such grandeur and seriousness was Simpson's restaurant, where a doorknob was built to withstand a hammer attack (Italy's doorknobs were built to be opened by angels). Simpson's waiters in white tie and tails pushed elegant ebony carts laden with steaming silver tureens as if they were plumed horses drawing royal carriages, and acted as if they had the most important and interesting careers in London. This was clear from their no-nonsense servitude. Simply being there and spending all that money, you were their superior.

At the barber I was met at the door by a diplomat doubling as manager in a Groucho Marx cutaway coat with striped gray trousers, and escorted to a large black leather barber's chair. After I was seated and made comfortable, my hair was washed and, still wet, cut by a silent barber. He then put a dark brown net on my head. The female image of myself in the mirror gave me a lift. I got an even stronger sensation as I looked in the mirror into the eyes of John Russell standing behind me, also with a dark brown net on his head, and a large flowing towel à la Gainsborough draped on his shoulders. He looked strange but handsome, and without saying a word he hoped I agreed with his idea of the singularity of the scene. This was a reasonable start to our relationship, which consisted of his critically admiring my work for reasons totally different from those I wished to be admired for. He praised me for painting my friends, for instance. I wanted to be hailed as a great painter, he dubbed me a nice guy. We once walked around at an exhibition of mine in New York. Made nervous because of his bright mind, English accent, and reticent soul, I talked even more than I usually do. His advice to me, printed in a review of the show, was to keep painting my wonderful pictures, but perhaps when it came to talking about my work and art in general I would be better advised to have a glass of warm milk and go to bed.

I am indebted to John for showing me Constable's studio. It took me to the early nineteenth century in a clear warm way, the thin-legged chair drawn up to a tiny writing desk on a thin rug, the affectionate faded ocher wallpaper. It comforted me to see that in this dead room those peaceful and beautiful pictures were painted indoors miles from the actual landscapes.

Back on Greek Street he said the impressionists couldn't have happened without the work of Constable. I agreed and asked who couldn't have happened without me. He smiled—John Russell doesn't laugh. Because I was leaving London he came with me to Gower Street and my studio at the Slade. I showed him my *Greatest Homosexual*, the collage painting based on David's *Napoleon*, a conversation piece if I ever painted one. He didn't say anything. I showed him my *Lions on the Dreyfus Fund*, explaining how I saw a TV clip of a lion walking on Wall Street and leaping onto a sturdy pedestal that spelled "Dreyfus Fund," and how that work began in New York City, and how helpful was the wonderful stuffed lion in the Victoria and Albert Museum, a look-alike for the Dreyfus lion, which enabled me to sit quietly and draw from a real lion if a dead one. John and I walked silently down the dark staircase into the street, and just before we parted he said he liked very much what I was doing, especially my painting based on the David. A few years later, now writing for the *New York Times*, he bought my drawing *Bill de Kooning in My Texas Hat*. I gave it to him at half price, of course. That's something I do for poor critics.

Bumpy Trip

A trip starting in Paris, through France, Spain, and North Africa, was planned to include Jane Freilicher, her husband, Joe Hazan, Clarice, five months pregnant, me, and the Western world's greatest young poet and laugh riot, John Ashbery. By 1964 my 1952 broken heart had healed, and Joe, long no longer just a man Jane walked off with, was a good friend of mine, had been for years. My friendship with John Ashbery had continued through a changing circle of friends and was still a lively and entertaining thing. Without any trouble, sober or drunk, he'd give hilarious accounts from the back seat of his experiences of the last few days. He could also cry at the drop of a sentence he uttered. Somewhere near Poitiers as we drove one evening, tears moving down his cheeks, soon sobbing, he recited verbatim the last scene of a Jeanette MacDonald–Nelson Eddy movie where the dying Jeanette lifts her head from her pillow and tells Nelson, "I've always loved you." John was the ideal back-seat driver. He didn't know how to drive, but he knew how to read the *Guide Michelin* in French, giving us restaurants to choose from, their ratings, the kind of food, and the prices, plus historical sights and places to spend a night. Even this information was full of his world view.

"You know all the cuisine of Europe, John," said Joe. "What do you think of the Three Pigeons in Andorra?"

"Oh, it's okay if you like good food," said John.

"I like good food, but good food just doesn't like me," said Jane, who was a rare match for John.

As chauffeur I negotiated our way through the intricate system of potholes that comprised the roads of Spain. One dusty afternoon, in a rental car that lacked shock absorbers, we hit a hole with such a bang that everyone's head hit the roof, including pregnant Clarice's. I was afraid the car's sixth passenger (minus a few months) might be hurt. Everybody got on me. Jane, who had been asleep, awoke and began punching me on my back and shoulders and shouting along with everyone else.

"What do you think you're doing? I never knew you were such a terrible driver. Slow down. Don't pass that car! Let me out!"

I stopped the car and got out and stomped down the road. I was sorry it had happened but angry at the group reaction. Joe, also angry, got out of the car, jumped in behind the wheel, and sped down the road with everybody, including Clarice. In a minute he stopped, backed up, and I quietly got in the car. For the next hundred miles I apologized and sulked. Joe took over the chauffeur's job for the rest of the trip. Now it was time for everybody to take Joe to task for driving *too* carefully while I took a back seat and asked John to amuse me with tales of sex in the City of Light. Jane, unbeknownst to everybody, was pregnant too, although even she wasn't sure at the time. The rest of the trip this bump stood between everything we did.

The drive south through France and Spain finally got us to the Rock of Gibraltar. With John's salivating interest in good eating, the trip was a gourmet's journey where the landscape out the windows was only something between restaurants. On the Rock you could look across eleven miles of water and see the top of the Dark Continent. Screaming monkeys and endless tourist boutiques and sauntering soldiers, guns slung on their shoulders, is all I remember of the Rock. What a letdown! I wondered why the British had ignored the traditional Spanish claim to this hopeless gray chunk of hard matter. We took a boat, car and all, and landed in about an hour in Tangier.

In France and Spain good food was our highest priority. In Tangier our eye for ethnic information superseded, but did not do away entirely with, our interest in eating. Our hotel rooms had a good view of the blue portion of the Atlas Mountains. We stayed about a week. One day we went to the dirty camel market and took a lot of photos surrounded by a herd of those snorting beasts with bad breath. My drawings and paintings did not touch upon their discontented souls; I liked their profile. We went to see Jane Bowles in her little white home, living in bliss with her Moroccan maid, who had long hair on her legs and wore big men's shoes. Paul Bowles sat smoking an odd pipe. Mrs. Bowles asked her husband to give us a few suggestions on where to hear Moroccan street musicians. Paul kept puffing. We didn't know whether his hearing was impaired or he no longer knew where. One night we checked out a *Guide Michelin* three-star restaurant, looking for the real Morocco. Sitting on fat red cushions, we watched a belly dancer, a beautiful young boy about fourteen, shaking his hips to the music of many wind instruments in a North African dance.

Snorting beast with bad breath and tourists (LR, Jane, Clarice, John) / Young man dancing

The night before we were to leave to go to Fez, the ancient city on the crossroads to East and West Africa, I somehow got lost. I'm not sure whether I was trying to find a partner for sex or had run into some New York expatriates devoting themselves to drugs, sex, and life with the Arabs, but I returned to the hotel at 7:00 a.m., so Clarice now tells me. Fuming all night, she was about to fly back to England on the next plane to have her baby without me in London. We had decided the night before to leave early so we could arrive in Fez before dark. Jane, Joe, and John had left before I got back to the hotel. Clarice had told them she was through with me and was going back to England, so "Why don't we abandon Larry the way he's abandoned me."

Jane and Joe and John were happy finally to be out of earshot of the bickering between Clarice and me. But a few hours later, after a short faint in bed, we made up and were on our way to Fez in a wooden train packed with chickens, melons, and people. We arrived in time to join our friends as they wolfed down a sumptuous couscous.

The next day we took a tour of the city, pushing our way beneath an arch a minute through unevenly cobbled narrow streets full of goats and tiny donkeys who whipped us with their tails as they passed, almost stepping on our toes. We stopped at something that looked like a dark cave. Light filtered in from a hole in the stone ceiling. Dark men, naked except for a small covering on their groins, wet with sweat, were dumping coils of thin rope into a hot liquid pool from which rose a cloud of swift-moving smoke. It was a method of coloring. The place was a tannery. It had some features of a movie that scared me as a child, a movie about zombies in the control of an evil man.

We drove to Marrakesh to enjoy our last tourist days at a world-famous three-star hotel called the Mamounia. It was a burnt sienna city, if you can call Marrakesh a city. It was quiet, the streets extraordinarily wide. I didn't see anything except walls with foliage growing over them. In the hotel we swam in the pool and lost our interest in anything outside the hotel. We were told the great Sahara lay a few miles south. No one batted a sentence. Diana Vreeland was there, sitting at the edge of the pool. She had heard of us, probably through John Myers, and we talked with her nonstop about everything. She introduced us to her son in the water. We swam toward each other and shook hands. He was either an ambassador to Morocco or a CIA agent, I can't remember which. We

421

wore the gorgeous rich-textured towel-bathrobes loaned to us by the hotel. I was so impressed by them that I packed one in my valise when we left. This was not unusual behavior for guests at the hotel. The management had devised a system to keep the robberies to a minimum. As I was throwing my valise into the trunk of the car and saying goodbye to the parents of my friend Jean Stein, Mr. and Mrs. Jules Stein of MCA, who owned some works of mine, an Arab out of *A Thousand and One Nights* who had been hanging around my room demanded I open the valise. I did, and turned to Clarice and asked her why she'd only packed one bathrobe.

We drove back to Tangier, traveled the Costa Brava up and around to the colorful and nutty Gaudi architecture in Barcelona. I'm not sure why there are no structures in the U.S., except for the Watts Tower in L.A., that try for that look. Then I flew to Berlin for a week to oversee a piece of sculpture of mine, *The Greeks*, that was being cast in bronze at the Noack foundry. Clarice and the gang of three drove from Barcelona back to Paris, where she waited for my return from Berlin to go home. When I got back, Jane and Joe and John were flying to New York. We hugged and kissed goodbye and didn't speak for two years.

In the middle of June Clarice and I arrived in Southampton after a five-day voyage by ship. Two days out on the waters, lying down for an afternoon nap, I had a dream, the only one that ever became the basis for an artwork.

I am staying in the home of Virginia Dwan in Malibu. I open the door to my bedroom and look out the window, a storm window, at the Pacific lapping the rocky beach. When I turn to the other window, which faces the tennis court, there is no tennis court. The bust of Jim Dine, fitting perfectly into the frame of the window, blocks the view. His bald head, which I love, and his folded hairy arms, which I also love, and the grim stare of his eyes cause me to walk over to him. When I get to the window his bust is flat, as in a painting. It is only an image of Jim.

In the States, Jim and I arranged for me to make a drawing of his face, his folded arms, and his wristwatch, and then I put it in a storm window. This is one of my early three-dimensional works that hang on a wall. I'm not sure if Jim ever saw it. Because of the odd and personal basis of the work I have never sold *Jim Dine Storm Window*.

At Home

With the heat of summer in Southampton removing outer garments, the distortions of the body Clarice was moving through space became more visible and found their way as subject matter into lots of conversations. I remembered the distortions of the figure brought on by my son Steven's stay inside his mother, and I remembered that I never stopped sex with Augusta until he was four days from his way out. All that was nineteen years before this summer of '64. If I found Clarice a beautiful and inspiring creature, I think with nature slowly reducing my prowess I used her more sparingly for my selfish purposes. In common with Augusta and with most young women, Clarice imagined (correctly) that I was always interested in other women. I told her what I'd never forgotten from a lecture in Psychology 104 at NYU, that jealousy was a transference of one's own philandering, real or imagined, onto one's partner. We know what I was up to. What was she up to?

Clarice wanted photos of her in her pregnant state to send to her mother and her English friends. I took rolls of photos of this proud mother-to-be. The ones I liked best were of Clarice looking into the camera with her body in profile. These photo sessions gave

me the idea of doing an almost life-size drawing of her. Not that I had forgotten Piero della Francesca's *Pregnant Madonna* or Picasso's delightful sculpture of a pregnant woman.

That Clarice was a very talented cook was clear from the oohs and aahs of the chomping guests during her meals. She said she learned everything from the Elizabeth David cookbook, a wedding gift from Bill Booker. People naturally like to be cooked for, but there were advance rave reviews during invitations to our dinners by phone and those we proffered at cocktail parties thrown like confetti throughout the Hamptons. These dinners became so much a part of our life that we introduced variations on a theme just to keep ourselves interested. We made a few "funny" meals to contrast with Clarice's serious gourmet achievements. One was a turkey with hashish stuffing that almost did in John Ashbery, Frank O'Hara, Arthur Gold, and myself. John was the hardest hit, having stuffed himself with three giant portions. By the nature of these funny meals, we had to choose very close friends. One night we invited Howard Kanovitz, who brought his trombone and Mary Kanovitz, who brought Howard. Clarice and I toasted a few slices of white bread, laid some corn silk over them, and lightly sprinkled them with uncooked rice. On top we placed a scoop of kidney cat food. As I circled the table pouring red wine to give a semblance of familiar fare, Howard reached for his first bite.

"How is it?" I asked, already losing control.

He took another bite to fathom what he was eating. I stifled my
laughter, sounding as if I were sobbing.

Howard asked if he could venture a guess as to the ingredients.
He pulled a wad of the concoction out of his mouth and held it in
the palm of his hand, looking at it as a doctor looks into a wax-filled
ear.

"Please do, Howard," I said between hysterical sobs.

"Larry, it's dog food."

"If you don't like it don't eat it."

We continued the meal with a delicious pot roast, a large salad,
and one of Clarice's best desserts, apple crumble. At the door saying
good night, Howard asked why I'd served that disgusting dish to
him and his wife.

I apologized. "I'm sorry. I couldn't have done something like
that to anyone but a close pal like you."

"Does 'pal' mean someone you can comfortably shit on?"

Maybe. I could only commit something he, and the world,
would think degrading, with a sister of mine, or Augusta (when I
stuck my middle finger up my ass in the dark and passed it under
her nose). For whatever it may tell about me I thought it was funny
and affectionate and could only happen with someone I loved.

By late August Clarice was a week overdue and massive. Our
dinners were repaid almost in full by invitations to dinners and
parties, many of them preceded by an invitation to spend a good
part of the afternoon at the beach right below the house where we
were going to drink and eat and dance. There was always someone
with a camera on these occasions. One such was a WASP affair in
Water Mill on the sea, given by Wall Street's own Geoffrey Gates,
settling down to one woman. Chosen that sultry night to play guest
of honor was George Binky Plimpton. Geoffrey was a classic host.
Everyone who came felt liked, and a necessary ingredient for the
success of the evening. And George, a professional nice guy, was a
perfect recipient of the affection the party stirred.

I arrived in our Ford pickup with Clarice, who sat on big cushions, though she hardly ever complained about her condition.
When the dancing started, Clarice was in another part of the party.
Doing the twist to Chubby Checker was difficult, but to the music
of Ray Charles very easy. And Ray was now blowing somewhere on
the jukebox. At the end of the number Clarice found me talking to
the girl I had danced with. Seeing me continue to dance with the
same flat-stomached female, Clarice left the party and climbed

Handwritten labels on photograph: MAXINE GROFFSKY, Joe Hogan, Herbert Machiz, Roland Pease, Robert Fizdale, Dr. Frelich, Tibor de Nagy, Bob Rauschenberg, L.R., John Myers, Steven Rivers, Sandra Lee, GRACE HARTIGAN

slowly into the pickup. She had never taken a driving lesson, had never asked me to let her try driving; she simply thought it would all go well because that's what she wanted. Probably none of this went through her mind. She wanted to be out of my sight, and she didn't want to share her anger with anyone. In the pickup she turned the key in the starter. Because I'd left it in reverse the pickup lurched back into a deep patch of sand bordering the driveway. Earl McGrath, our weekend guest, seeing this all from the window upstairs, rushed down to the driveway and asked Clarice where she was going.

"I'm going to the James"—a mixed-race dance hall and cabaret about three miles from the party. "Someone there will dance with me."

"Who?"

The pickup is hopelessly mired in the sand. I try a few times to get it out and then give up. As I'm struggling, Clarice leaves and goes back to the party. Knowing nothing of this, Jeanette Seaver, a concert violinist, tells Clarice that she has to dance vigorously because jumping up and down helps in the delivery of the baby. Earl is listening and argues vigorously against this advice. After a few minutes he comes down to the driveway, where I'm still looking over the problem, and says, "Why don't we go to the James?"

Clarice's anger at me has triggered mine. "That's a good idea. Let's go."

We take Earl's car. Meanwhile Clarice gets home somehow. It's **L** late. She's upset, drunk, and full of ideas of revenge. Perfect stuff for a child about to force its way into the world, I think—anything to find fault with her.

All the doors are locked. She goes around to the back door, **A** picks up a hammer lying on the stairs, and claws into the locked screen door to get at the house door, which is unlocked. She goes to the fridge. Nothing. Opens the freezer. Frozen chickens and **R** chicken parts. She cooks it all. Earl and I arrive home from the James. Clarice's cooking always inspires me, hungry or not, to taste what she's made, so I taste and swallow and yum-yum. Clarice looks at me and leaves the kitchen and goes upstairs. Earl and I suddenly **R** hear a very loud crash and a thud. Earl runs up the stairs. Clarice is brushing her hair in the bedroom.

"Tell your friend to stop picking at my food."

"What was that noise?" **Y**

Clarice stops brushing her hair, picks up her vanity mirror with its light attachment, and throws it through the window. "You mean that noise?"

Earl runs back down the stairs and tells me Clarice has gone bonkers. The window through which she threw the missile had a screen that kept the vanity mirror and the window glass from falling to the ground. It all fell on our bed just below the window. After **R** brushing out the glass, we went to sleep at opposite ends of the bed. In the morning I woke with a pain in one eye. In the Southampton Hospital emergency ward I had the glass pieces removed and left **I** with an enormous padded bandage over my eye. Married life.

I had a good time with Clarice, and I think she did with me. I was under the impression that over and above all the things that made me an interesting type full of unexpected responses, my in- **V** clusion in Clarice's special kind of human bubble added to my growing myth. We parted in 1967 and have been married ever since.

We parted first because I went to Central Africa for seven months to make a film for NBC. Did Darwin's marriage end be- **E** cause he spent five years sailing toward the theory of evolution? No. For us seven months was too much. When I returned, we decided to stay apart. Too many things had happened, and kept happening, for us to point to this disturbing mosaic and say, "I still **R** love you, let's go on."

We saw Frank many weekends during that summer. One week- end he'd go to Morris Golde's on Water Island, the next to our **S**

427

place. Frank had begun a love affair with the curly blond J. J. Mitchell, who received mixed reviews from both his straight and gay friends. You didn't need Proust to convince you that Frank's choice of a lover didn't tell much more about him than you already knew. Clarice decided J.J. had a funny curl to his lips and an irritating giggle. Her feelings put me in the position of having to cut down on inviting Frank if his boyfriend was with him. Peace at any price, my usual stance, became a spineless stance for me to take about my closest friend. Before it became an issue Clarice and I moved back to New York. With us was our two-month-old baby, born September 10, now called Gwynne.

Frank with (counterclockwise) Steven, Clarice, Joe Le Sueur, J.J., and Bill Berkson

Living Black-and-White

Living on the second floor for two months in a studio where cock-roaches filed out of your shoes in the morning and paint hung leaflike on the walls and there was no light except for four feet near the window from which I was able to view trucks passing loudly on Twenty-second Street, Clarice and I decided the studio should serve only as a painting space, that I might have the bourgeois pleasure of going to my wife and child, in the evening after work, to the somewhat less cockroach-crowded room with designer chipped sinks, abrasive stucco walls, and constantly running hot and cold water, a home way from home, in beloved Stanley Bard's Chelsea Hotel. I began a sustained search for real estate that would provide pleasant surroundings for my art and life, wife and baby included. I could afford it.

Real estate for the artist in those days meant one thing—a loft. Jack Klein, later to become the big deal in the artist's loft explosion below Fourteenth Street that eventually played an important part in the birth of Soho, offered me a ten-year lease on a top floor loft in a building on Fourteenth Street and First Avenue.

When I moved in, Claes Oldenburg and his collaborator wife Patty were living and working on the floor below. He regretted the sequence of events that led to my acquiring the top floor, which was a better loft than his, with the best natural light in the building. It was thirty feet wide and ran from Fourteenth Street to Thirteenth and had sixteen-foot ceilings. Rent for this phenomenal space was

First daughter

$235 a month and in ten years would rise to a big $285. The space was raw. There were a few walls and a very rough floor full of splinters. So the first thing we had to do—that is, Clarice had to do, because of our little creeper—was to put a rug down everywhere but in my studio. We brought in a few tables, chairs, beds, and couches for the living part. Jack Klein, as per agreement, supplied a gas stove and a hot water heater.

While the loft was in preparation, life was getting very exciting. It was the fall of '64. We had our suite in the Chelsea, and I had the studio on Twenty-second Street to myself for painting and everything else—including sets for a play by LeRoi Jones (today Amiri Baraka).

After LeRoi's first play, *Dutchman*, in early '64, shocked people with its black-white vehemence, for which it got a lot of attention, he wrote *The Slave*, a play that takes place in the future during a bloody black uprising in which a black Army commander comes to see his former white wife. To the accompaniment of machine-gun fire, a nasty but thrilling confrontation takes place, leaving her apartment totally destroyed. LeRoi asked me if I'd be interested in doing the sets for this play and another billed for the same evening, *The Toilet*, a brutal and beautiful play. A white high school student, Karolis, writes a love letter to a black fellow student named Foots. The letter's obvious homosexuality catches up with Karolis, and he

Steven, Clarice, LeRoi, and his wife,
Hettie, in Southampton

is brutally beaten by black students in the toilet, where the entire play takes place, and left with his bloody head in one of the urinals. At the end Foots comes back to the toilet, cradles the white boy's head, and bathes his battered face. The curtain comes down on Foots's soft sobbing.

For years LeRoi and I were friends. Up to a certain point our friendship was very warm, sometimes druggy, but always full of jokes, full of unserious discussions of cultural and political affairs. His laugh was part of his speech, and I always liked seeing him. But shortly after the run of his plays, there was a Life versus Art symposium at the Village Vanguard, featuring LeRoi and Archie Shepp, the jazz saxophonist, myself, and some other white artists. The Vanguard evening began with talk about the art-lit-jazz scene. Soon things began to get wild. LeRoi told me I was making art for a bunch of uptown fags. Archie brought up the twelve million blacks in the Congo annihilated by slavery and the Belgians. I began to make an allusion to the Holocaust, trying to see just exactly what I felt about Germans. Before I finished half a paragraph, Archie pointed his finger at me and shouted, "There you go again, always bringing up the fucking Jews." He couldn't talk about *his* pain without Jews bringing up theirs! The intimidated moderator threw the ball to the audience. LeRoi's and Archie's responses to the questions amounted to: There's only one kind of white—

Whitey, who hates Negroes. Someone in the audience brought up the whites who marched for civil rights and mentioned two boys, Goodman and Schwerner, who were murdered in Mississippi, alongside a black, Chaney. LeRoi, astute and tough, said, "I can't worry about the two Jewish boys. I have my own to bury." We didn't see each other for twenty years.

As the years flamed by, I began to understand that that angry evening was LeRoi's first move toward another conception of what to do with his life. If I was painting for a lot of uptown fags, he questioned who he was writing for. He opened a black theater school in Harlem, divorced his white wife, Hettie, and devoted his life to "his people." His writing became political warfare, and he dreamed up some brilliant strategies. Amiri and I began talking again in 1984. I invited him and he came to my exhibition of *History of Matzoh: The Story of the Jews*, three large works and fifty drawings at the Jewish Museum. When his autobiography appeared, I read it and liked it and felt a great deal of empathy.

The problems connected with making the sets for his two plays were major, but minor compared with the problems connected with the director, Leo Garen, drenched in the fast pace of those years. Leo had a new idea for the set every hour. Why did he need me? For my name in the advertisement for the plays? The set for *The Slave* was to turn the stage space into the comfortable apartment of a successful female writer with bohemian tendencies. I made some pretty *moderne* stodgy pieces of furniture with my own hands—a couch, a round table stained burnt umber, and a chair composed

of different colors of thick vinyl. All that was strenuous but easy. What was difficult was how to have the room bombed every night without really destroying anything. I solved the problem by creating a giant bookcase, fifteen or sixteen feet long and eight feet high, packed fully with books. It got toppled, and on its way down to the floor hundreds of books fell. Just as the bookcase hit the ground there was an ear-shattering crash, but the bookcase actually stopped a few inches from the floor by means of an ingeniously primitive hook-and-eye arrangement. It worked!

For *The Toilet* I built a series of rectangular wooden urinals painted porcelain white, and one closed booth. I also made a fat tubular venting system running above the urinals. I then wrote some graffiti on the wall above the urinals and on the door of the booth. The actors in the play, black boys from Harlem, told LeRoi if I didn't remove the graffiti they were going to walk out. They said that the graffiti reflected a white idea of toilets in schools with mostly black students. We compromised. I removed half—their choice—of what was there.

Up Against the Wall, Bwana

I went to Africa to make a documentary and ended up with an adventure story I hadn't bargained for. What happened made me look into the conceit I had most of my life that my worship of the black deities of jazz and my never having called a Negro a nigger would be clear as the big nose on my face. So clear would this difference between myself and most Americans be that Africans would never do me any harm.

In 1967 I got involved in a film project with Pierre Gaisseau, who had done a documentary about New Guinea that I admired very much, *The Sky Above, the Mud Below*. He invited me to go to Africa to help on a documentary commissioned by NBC for its "Experiments in Television" series. Along with my son Joseph as cameraman, and Gordon Parks, Jr., as still photographer (he would later make the movie *Superfly*), we flew to Paris to gather some of Gaisseau's beautiful cameras, his sound equipment, and whatever else he thought we needed. A few days later our plane touched down in Khartoum in the Sudan before flying on to Addis Ababa, Ethiopia. The waiters who served us coffee in the airport wore endless flowing robes, bowing respectfully as they backed away from our table. This was the only place in Africa where I saw Africans with black skin.

Ethiopians are unbelievably beautiful. You see tall, thin men in sackcloth riding on the backs of small donkeys. In Asmara, the capital of Eritrea, where the Queen of Sheba held court, we filmed a hundred men in white robes leaning on stout cudgels outside a mosquelike church, wearing white yarmulkes like Jews, entering the space barefoot like Muslims, hanging crosses on their chests like Christians. Coptic Christians they were.

Two rented Opels took us across a dusty mountain range toward Gondar. Slowed by a steep slope, we spotted a man on the road carrying a shotgun, sporting a Tyrolean hat, feather and all, and holding up his hand for a lift. We stopped and squeezed him into the back of the car. He was a white man about fifty-five years old, an Italian soldier who had remained after Mussolini, with tanks and planes and heavy artillery, "conquered" the Ethiopians in white robes throwing spears in the 1935 war. He told us he fell in love with the Ethiopian people and now lived some fifteen miles down the road with his family. We all got out of our cars when we dropped him off and filed through a batch of huts to meet his young wife and a batch of his chocolate children. He had an unusual calm. I was sure it came of the ease of exchanging each wife every few years for a younger one. It took another decade for me to realize that there's no ease guaranteed by having a younger woman than last year's in your arms. He calmly waved goodbye as we headed to Gondar, the home of the Falashas, black Jews reading from the Hebrew books I used on Saturdays in the synagogue. We stayed a few days filming the Falashas, sleeping and taking our breakfast at the Hotel Lumumba, on a street busy with prostitutes

with whom I did some business. Outside of town we filmed lions **L**
herded into gated caves for Haile Selassie to enjoy once or twice a
year.

On to Kenya. Forget the animals, they're shy, they never show
up on time, if they do happen to appear by accident, they mistake **A**
your camera for a gun and they're out of there. People were different. Except for a group of black-robed Muslims who threw stones
at our autobus to stop us from filming them, most Africans just **R**
made believe we weren't there. The government of Kenya had
made it clear to its citizens that white man with camera was good
for the economy. There were wonderful days without a trace of old
Africa movies. Those were the moments I wanted to capture. The **R**
mixture of the old and new Africa thrilled me.

There are people of central Kenya who grow up wearing
weighted earrings to lengthen their lobes till they hang down almost
to the shoulder, but in Nairobi, as in cities all over the world where **Y**
people want to fit in and not be noticed for weird differences, the
long-lobed people just lift this appendage and wrap it in a coil
around the top of the ear. In Masai country, no weapons are allowed inside vendors' shacks, and one can see three or four spears
stuck in the ground outside the doorway as the men buy Coca-Cola
and Camels.

In five months of travel we picked up all sorts of footage in **R**
Ethiopia, Kenya, and Tanzania. A difference in aesthetic temper-
ament between Gaisseau and me became apparent almost immediately. He was certain that for the film to succeed we had to come
back with lots of Ye Olde Africa footage. But for this we needed **I**
official permission that officials were reluctant to give. It seemed to
them that wanting to film tribal Africa showed our lack of interest
in their country's effort to enter the modern world. I felt there was **V**
more than enough available without permission to make an outstanding film. Gaisseau spent so much time waiting in government
offices for an okay to film the life of the Masai and Turkana tribes
that I was often in charge of what to film. **E**

Back in New York, after a few penetrating looks at our footage,
we didn't see how we could possibly make a documentary from
what we had. We decided we had to return to Africa and shoot
some more. This time, to save money, we left Joe and Gordon Parks **R**
behind. There wasn't much left of the original $85,000 we'd been
given to make the film.

We landed in Lagos, Nigeria, on New Year's Eve, 1967. This **S**

435

dark and silent city with troops patrolling the streets reminded us that there was a serious civil war going on between the federal government and the Ibo people of Biafra. The one thing we found filmworthy in the city was the Yoruba, who held religious services on a beach lapped by the gentle waves of the Atlantic Ocean. They wore very colorful wrappings on their bodies and on their heads. At their church on the beach they wove their arms in the air, fell to the sand, rolled in it, and during the whole time never stopped singing. Behind the congregation two soldiers rode on horseback into the sunset. It all looked like a painting by the Dutch seascapist Jongkind. Gaisseau didn't change his mind about getting footage of Ye Olde Africa, but he broadened the notion to include old African art. And that we would find in Benin City, 150 serious miles from Lagos.

In 1898 a British colonel was murdered in Benin by a local wild man. As punishment the British burned the entire city to the ground. Benin is where the *oba* (king) had a palace and lived with sixty wives. Somewhere in his palace of many buildings many pieces of bronze sculpture were housed. When the British first saw these mysterious pieces, they had the colonial notion that the Nigerians could only have followed the casting procedure of the Portuguese, who were there early on. Scholarship nixed the notion.

We asked permission to travel to and film in Benin. It was granted. The tourist office imposed no restrictions against filming, said there would be no trouble, but refused us written consent.

Our first morning in Benin, in a cobblestone square, we stopped at the steps of a pedestal supporting a short standing figure with a broad head and pop eyes that for me had no ethnic identity. Craftily I took out the pad I'd brought along, sat on the bottom step, and began to draw, pretending I had come to Benin only as an artist. Early in our trip we learned to obfuscate our NBC television connection, which, at our expense, inspired dreams of grandeur on the part of the people we filmed. It wasn't long before ten or twelve curious kids came to watch what I was doing. No one found the drawings interesting or even asked what they were about except these kids, who began to trail us everywhere we went. A young man about twenty-six, seeing all the kids and Pierre and me walking around, asked us what the only two white men in Benin were doing here. We told him the truth: that we were here to film the palace of the *oba*, and if we could we'd like to get inside the building where the ancient Benin sculpture was stored. He acted as if he could be of some help. He was the head and only librarian of the library of Benin, called the John F. Kennedy Library—why, I never found out. He invited us to meet with the king's official sculptor.

The next day, with great enthusiasm, we went to see the grand master, Idah, a man in his late fifties in a blue-and-orange gown who did not introduce us to his four wives, the youngest a wild fourteen-year-old. He had ten servants and a beautiful house full of original seating arrangements, with plants and trees growing from the earth inside. Everywhere there were ceramic pieces, which I took to be the outtakes of the work he did for the *oba*. At the end of our visit he told us he could help us get inside the palace. I made a drawing of his face as my house gift. I don't think he liked it, but he took it.

He told us we should begin by filming the giant metal doors that were the entrance to where the sculpture was stored. He promised that at 11:00 a.m. the next day the doors would be opened for us. At 9:00 at the bronze doors we saw versions of the ceramic pieces we had seen at the sculptor's house. They were extraordinary and complicated reliefs, as extraordinary and complicated as the

Ghiberti doors of the Baptistery in Florence. At 11:00, as promised, the doors opened. What we saw inside was a disappointment, an empty walled rectangle about 50 by 150 feet. It had no floor, just raked earth. It had no roof, you could see the sky. The man who opened the doors made it clear that we should talk in hushed tones. There was no one inside. We immediately sensed that the space had some religious significance. One end of this sacred corral had a roof, and under it in the shadows we began to make out the high art of Benin sculpture. As we were discussing what to do about insufficient light, two big men in pants and shirts came into the corral and asked us to step outside for a moment.

"Can we see your permission to film, please?"

"In Lagos we were told it's okay to film here, we didn't need any papers."

"Can you come with us?"

"Can we bring our equipment?"

"Yes."

We were taken to a two-story building and introduced to the chief of police. This forty-year-old chief told us he'd spent four years in the States studying international law at Ohio State University. He was very fond of American movies, listened to Charlie Parker records, and indicated that out in Ohio he had even tried marijuana. "You know, man," he said, "if you had come to me first, this inconvenience would never have happened."

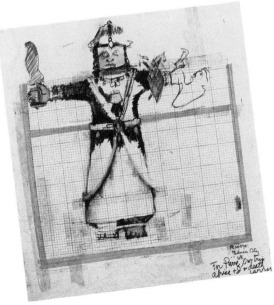

Art from the court of Benin and the hand of Rivers

"We were told in Lagos it's okay to film here."

"What's your film about?"

I told him how interesting I found Nigeria. All we wanted to do as far as Nigeria was concerned was to get footage that showed what wonderful art existed there.

"You know, Rivers, the front, where the fighting is going on, is only thirty-five miles to the east. Benin is not the safest place in the world to be. Just before the Ibos were driven out of here, they shot and killed a lot of innocent civilians. Long-haired white mercenaries were identified as being part of the death squads. . . . You're free to go back to your hotel now and free to film, but play it safe, man, check in here once a day."

We went back to our hotel. I wondered how interested I was in the high art of Benin. Gaisseau, with laid-back French bravado, said we should relax, we had spent a few days under arrest in police stations in Kenya and Uganda, and nothing had happened except we lost some time and went on to film where we left off.

Two hours later, after a very light lunch of smeared peanut butter, cheese, and crackers from a dispenser, we are rearrested and brought to a dark wooden structure with wire grates over the windows. Gaisseau and I are separated. I am put in a small room and handed a three-page questionnaire in English. Where was I born? Where are my parents from? What was my education? Was I ever, or my parents or sister or brother, a member of the Communist Party? Who did I vote for in the last two U.S. elections? Of what interest all this was to them I couldn't guess. I knew a little about Nigerian politics, and the Communist question didn't seem relevant to any of their problems, unless they wanted me to feel what visitors go through applying for a U.S. visa. Nobody answered our questions as to why we were being detained. The once or twice I was brought from my room to a basketball-player-sized man behind a desk in a very conservative pinstripe, I was told it was nothing serious and everything would be cleared up soon.

What would be cleared up soon?

They took our film and told us all they wanted to do was see what we shot. What was the real reason we were being detained? Was the chief from Ohio State worried that if our film showed Nigeria in an unattractive light the blame would fall on him? Was it for our own safety?

At about the shadow between dusk and night we were asked if we were hungry. They could get us some sandwiches, which we

L

A

R

R

Y

R

I

V

E

R

S

would have to pay for. Pierre said we'd had "sandwiches" for lunch and he preferred a good meal, if possible at a good restaurant. Sandwiches seemed okay to me, but it would be pleasant to get out of prison for a few hours. For this excursion two bulky security guards accompanied us.

Inside the restaurant, which was part of the hotel we were staying at, a Nigerian army major with a straight back and a British officer's crop firmly ensconced in his armpit is walking briskly around the room, stopping briefly at each table to say a few words to the diners. He suddenly begins to scream at a passing waiter. "You there! What are you doing? Why are you taking so blasted long? I told you I wanted to be fed quickly!"

Even as the waiter is serving, the major hits him on the head with his crop. Another waiter scrambling out of the way also receives a blow. The manager comes over. "What's wrong, sir!"

The major hits the manager over the head and walks up to us. We smell the whiskey on his breath. He's drunk. "You know, you have to treat these fuckers this way or you'll never get any damned service."

Through the top of the Dutch door of the kitchen, three curious heads poke out. They snap back in as the officer turns toward them. A second later they pop out again. He swaggers away from us and sits down with three civilians. He dominates the conversation with remarks like "Here today, gone tomorrow." The major has been at the front. Soldiers in camouflage greens are coming in and out of the restaurant. They present themselves to him, all with rifles, in an absurdly exaggerated halt, clicking their heels and saluting so hard they bend backward, almost toppling over. Finally we are served dinner. Again the major struts over to our table. "Are you enjoying your stay in Nigeria?"

We chat as pleasantly as possible in the face of such a scene. He bids us good night and walks out of the restaurant.

"What a funny guy this major is."

Pierre says he's not funny at all. We continue eating and have practically finished when the major bursts back in, lurching to our table.

"Who are you?" he demands. "What are you doing in Nigeria? You are spies."

The two security guards tell him we are in their custody, it's okay. The major attacks them with his crop. They begin to bleed. Soldiers drag them out of the restaurant. The major faces us.

"Stand up, you two. I say stand up! Let's see your identification. You think you can just walk into a country at war?"

We show him our passports. In mine is my yellow medical card. On the back of it, a few days before in Lagos, I'd drawn a map to show off to someone in a bar how well I knew where Nigeria is located.

"Aha! A map of Africa," he spits. "Nigeria! And a dot for Lagos."

I begin to feel as if I'm in a farce by Kenneth Koch.

He turns to his stunned soldiers, showing them my map. "These men are obviously spies."

Doesn't he recognize how much I love black people? "Look, Major, why are you acting this way? Fifteen minutes ago you were so friendly."

He comes closer. With his open palm he slaps me very hard, twice. "Search them," he orders.

For what? We are suddenly victims in a continuing drama of colonial history. The major calls us white men with white arrogance. Now he walks away from us, pivots dramatically, and pulls a pistol out of his holster. In a deliberately calm voice he says, "If you move I'm going to shoot you." Again, but four times the decibel level: "If you move I'll shoot you." He turns to the soldiers searching us. "Take them outside and shoot them."

Even the soldiers seem shocked. Now the major is screaming, "I told you to take them outside and shoot them. What are you waiting for?" A soldier pokes us gently in the back with his rifle. We raise our hands and start walking.

I whisper to Pierre, soon tearfully blubbering, "It's all your fault. You had to go and eat in a good restaurant!" We are marched through the lobby in front of people sitting around in many different kinds of dress. A small girl runs after us and hands me the check for our meal. I ask a soldier if it's all right to pay her. He nods approval. I pay, and we continue our march till we are finally outside.

About thirty feet from the entrance to the hotel the soldiers motion for us to stop but to keep our hands in the air. Fifteen minutes go by. I guess the soldiers want more instructions about where to do the deed, since they just stand there. A group of civilians gathers outside the hotel to see what's happening. Pierre, hands still in the air, asks a soldier, "Please let us go, we are in the custody of the police."

The soldier tells him, "Shut up, you rebel!"

Finally the major comes out, stands in front of the crowd, and shouts, "Turn around, white men, it's the major." He breaks into laughter. "Which one of you is French!"

Pierre says, "I am, sir."

"Aha! I see from your papers that you were a military man, a former paratrooper, and you live in Paris. I am now going to speak to you in perfect grammatical French." He begins to tell Pierre about the time he lived in Paris, the cafes, the wine, the cute girls.

Pierre tells him to come to Paris. We can go to all the old places together.

Are we going to get out of this? He's so unpredictable that after he gets his rocks off speaking French he might pull out his pistol and shoot us. As the Parisian reminiscence between the major and Pierre proceeds, I put my arms down and am reminded of this by a soldier poking me in the back with his gun and telling me to get them back up. Everyone is staring, no one is helping. The major now switches to English.

"Nevertheless, you are white mercenaries, aren't you? And you"—meaning me—"have long hair."

I had grown it long to appear young at heart, and here it is about to shorten my life.

"But you are free to go!"

We slowly walk to the car between our prison guards. I'm shivering. Our existential major could still easily shoot us in the back.

In two days we are flown back to Lagos but treacherously remanded once more, this time to Ikoyi Prison. More questions about our Communist background. I lose my temper. The official I address my tantrum to angrily tells me, "Sit on the floor when I talk to you. I am not your black boy."

Three days later we are released, only to be placed under hotel arrest for three more days. We give the *New York Times* reporter our story. Then I call the American embassy. They know about our case, the Nigerians have ordered us out of the country.

The next day, in an official embassy car, flags on the fenders, accompanied by the assistant American ambassador, we are driven to the airport, right onto the tarmac in front of the plane, and taken by Nigerian soldiers up the ramp to the door. We step inside, the door is latched, and we are free and alive and flying to Kinshasa, Zaire. Speaking of treachery, on the plane is a copy of the *New York Times*. If we'd remained in Lagos for one more day and this

New York Times had found its way to the desk of some official who had nothing to do, we'd have been going from prison to prison till the end of their civil war, or to the end of time.

Six months later in New York we got back our boring footage from the Nigerian embassy office at the UN. Our documentary, called *Africa and I*, was first shown on NBC TV in April 1968. In 1970 it won the Chicago Documentary Festival prize. In 1989, after Pierre Gaisseau took the only existing copy, Jean Tinguely called me from Paris to say he had just seen it on French TV.

On April 10, 1965, a large Larry Rivers retrospective opened in Brandeis University's Rose Art Museum in Waltham, Massachusetts. It was dreamed up and put together by Sam Hunter, the museum's director. It would travel to five museums, and in the fall of '65, on its third stop, it would open at the Jewish Museum in New York—where miraculously Sam Hunter was to be the new curator and would carry on the policy of exhibiting contemporary American art (Johns and Rauschenberg were shown as well). The other sites for the exhibition were the Pasadena, Detroit, and Minneapolis museums.

Sam Hunter, still at the Rose Art Museum, called to ask if I could bring a band up to Waltham for the opening night of my retrospective. He wanted to show the living connection between my art and my jazz, and if that wasn't a good enough reason, "How about just playing to make the opening nice and lively?"

Howard Kanovitz brought his trombone, Clarice brought her array of boas (I guess we got a two-day baby-sitter for Gwynne), and Niki de Saint-Phalle, also in boas, brought Jean Tinguely in a dark pegged pants suit. The rhythm section, piano, bass, and drum were local jazzbos who were pretty good. I hardly paid attention to my exhibition. We played nonstop. I made the front page of the cultural section of the local Waltham paper, circulation twenty-five hundred.

Excited as I was about a five-museum traveling exhibition, the fact that this exhibition was coming to New York in a few months throbbed harder in my head. What I thought I had accomplished in art almost seemed beside the point. Why was I given the show? Was I to believe what was written in the catalog? I'm never sure what my work is about, so, like some anxious vaudevillian, I wanted to add something to improve the act, especially as the act was moving to the big city. I had been reading Isaac Deutscher's biography of Trotsky. Deutscher considered himself a Marxist historian, and Marxist rhetoric was slightly beyond me, but I liked the clear, simply put, chronological portrayal of the events of the revolution and the men and women involved. As a boy I heard of the Russian Revolution first from my mother, a Russian—even if Jewish—who didn't get to America until almost 1921, which gave her four years of some nasty experiences. I thought I'd try something on the subject, and if it turned out to be terrific, I'd include it in

Setting up at the Jewish Museum:
I never regretted launching Sam on his career
as an art historian.

The living connection: Jazzbos, Clarice,
Sam, Don't Remember, Niki, and Tinguely

the New York exhibition. Such was the genesis of *The History of the Russian Revolution*, now hanging in the Larry Rivers Room at the Hirshhorn.

I started with an idea of storm window portraits of the grand-daddies, Marx, Engels, Lenin, Trotsky, and Stalin. To throw a Russian flavor into what was to come, I cut plywood to follow my

drawn skyline of Moscow, then expanded the skyline image to include the roofs of Leningrad. On the silhouette of these roofs I glued canvas to have a familiar surface to paint on. I had to find a way to hold the roofs up so I could attach the storm window portraits I planned. Before long it became apparent I needed a structure, a kind of foundation on which I could mount anything I wanted to include in the work. In fact I built a thirty-five-foot-long wooden grid that I could alter and still keep sturdy. It took five months, starting in the middle of April, to finish the work. I did it all alone, except for the help I got from time to time from my twenty-five-year-old adopted son Joe. I hardly got out to Southampton that hot summer of '65. I began before the 1917 revolution, with portraits of Marx and Engels, and ended with the suicide of the poet Mayakovsky, whose work and face I was introduced to by his great admirer Frank O'Hara. Writing in the Sunday *New York Times Magazine*, Grace Glueck described *The History of the Russian Revolution* as a "painting-sculpture extravaganza, . . . a giant assemblage that is at once a stage set and a play in itself."

Revolution's 70-odd canvas sections and constructions include 3D portraits, painted-over news photographs, a tangle of pipes representing Industry, cut-out wooden rifles and a real machine gun. "It's the greatest painting-sculpture mixed media of the 20th century, or the stupidest," Rivers has said. ("It looks like the Belgian Pavilion at the World's Fair," another artist's wife has countered.)

A week after the opening of the Rose retrospective, Clarice and Gwynne and I moved into the loft at 404 East Fourteenth Street. Slowly the place began to resemble some sort of a home. I always thought comfort, like good taste, was highly overrated. We divided the two-hundred-foot-long space almost equally between living and work. Deutscher's book on Trotsky might have been the inspiration for my *Russian Revolution*, but I never would have been able to think of a fourteen- by thirty-five-foot work if I didn't have a hundred-foot studio with sixteen-foot ceilings.

That summer Clarice decided to take Gwynne to our place in Southampton. I'd come out some weekends. My weeknights, after a full day of *Russian Revolution*, were about getting high and looking for sex, sometimes on a motorcycle. One night after I finished work and was turning my thoughts to the evening tasks of drugs, sex, and rock and roll, I heard a soft rapping on my front door as I was taking a bath. Standing in the doorway were two girls, the daughter of the owner of a Southampton store I patronized and her friend, both sixteen. They asked me to put them up for the night. Why not? They followed me into the bathroom, and I slipped back into the tub. In very excited tones they told me, obviously high, of the wonderful grass they'd picked up in the East Village. They lit up and turned their portable radio on full blast. They offered me a puff of the pot, holding it to my lips. Just to be nice they soaped my

Russian Revolution
at the Jewish Museum

back, both of them. Without a call or a knock on the door Claes Oldenburg appeared, shouting, "Turn the music down!" Every now and then his envy surfaced. Apparently he still thought my loft above him was rightfully his.

The girls turned the music down and off and fled to the living room. Then Claes, with his big paws around my neck, tried lifting me out of the tub.

"What the fuck are you doing?" I yelped. He stopped.

"I should be walking on *your* head instead of you walking on *mine*," he said.

"But Claes, I love your work!"

"You also love my wife!"

"I never touched your wife!"

When he left I looked for the girls. They were gone.

Lampman

Playboy magazine in its heyday, 1965, decided to commission contemporary artists to "transform the idea of the Playmate into fine
art" that would then appear in its pages. Eventually they purchased
the works for their corporate collection. My only previous contact
with *Playboy*, aside from looking at the magazine, was when I was
in Chicago having an exhibition at Bud Holland's gallery in 1960;
Hugh Hefner came to the show with an entourage and invited me
to a party in his mansion. Aside from a few abstract expressionist
paintings and some of my work, the place was furnished like a set
for an indoor King Arthur pageant. There was a pool sunk down
into a lounge where you could sit around, drink in hand, and watch
bunnies and other underwater bodies moving through the water
like sea lions in the aquarium.

Even if I had enough money to rent a studio for $235 a month,
hire an assistant, drive a car, own a house in Southampton with a
mortgage at $54.11 a month, and pay tabs in restaurants and bars
for potential sexual favors, I had no intention of looking *Playboy*'s
gift horse in the mouth. The letters and the talk surrounding the
commission sounded serious. *Playboy* was the Church, Hugh Hefner the Pope, the Playmate the Madonna, and Dali and Segal and
Warhol and Wesselmann and Rosenquist and I the Renaissance.

I didn't think *Playboy*'s nude foldout was an unspeakable offense. I chose the partially clad Playmate of the Year, Jo (Joan)

Collins. Her bold face faced the camera, and her body showed its profile. One knee and both hands were on a stool, and her naked ass was brilliantly lit. She wore a short, fashionable motorcycle jacket that concealed her breasts, drawing attention to her best feature.

I began my Playmate piece by cutting two exact Plexiglas silhouettes of a figure and face. Between them, for support and dimension according to the demands of the silhouettes, I ran a thick piece of opaque white malleable plastic. For the jacket I used vinyl. I had become interested in different materials, and shiny vinyl dazzled me. I thought it made everything look modern. I'm sure I secretly thought that if I used new material it would make me a modern artist.

After *Plexi Playmate* was photographed for the magazine, she hung around the studio quietly. One pleasure of painting and sculpture, except for Tinguely's work, is that it is silent. *Plexi Playmate* was touched frequently, commented upon, moved to differ-

ent parts of my loft, and finally ignored. Then I received a call from Sidney Janis, the smiling ex-hoofer gallery dealer, inquiring whether I would like to submit an artwork for an erotic exhibition planned for spring '66. I said certainly. All these invitations begin with some recognizable name to whet your envy glands: "Andy has already accepted and is going to exhibit a banana." A few other names were dropped, all submitting works meant to broaden the meaning of "erotic." Jim Dine offered *Green Table and Chairs* and *Artaud*, Rosenquist *Stellar Structure*, Tom Wesselmann *Seascape*. Once I said yes, my name would be used for the next call to the next artist. *Plexi Playmate* was in itself enough to expand the notion of the erotic, but for the exhibition I began making a Plexiglas-and-plastic piece that before long grew to be eight feet tall and was a lamp. It was not an ordinary lamp, it was definitely a male lamp, characterized as such by an aluminum gooseneck with a reddish purple bulb attached to it. Inside the bulb the element flickered so that the light appeared to be moving. My idea was to bring *Plexi Playmate* and this lamp into some kind of sexual conjunction.

Bob Wails was a tall black man from Philadelphia, obviously a descendant of a long line of Nigerians. He had a broad back and a broad nose, good teeth and lively orbs, and a stride hard to keep up with. I met him in the mid-sixties at a popular jazz joint called Slug's in the Far East, at Third Street and Avenue C. I was playing there with the Elvin Jones quintet. I made it clear to him one night that I was interested in obtaining some heroin. Bob Wails—to wail in jazz lingo means to be blowing very well, usually for a long time —was born Robert Brown. Always in an evening suit, he had a friendly and sincere act, with only a trace of the "man," "dig," "right on," palms-up-waiting-to-be-slapped jazz club rhetoric. He obliged me in my request, and quickly. When this request was repeated and fulfilled we'd walk back to my studio to ingest the powdered tranquilizer in a more relaxed setting. He had five tales for any one thing you began talking about.

When Bob arrived with me, Clarice, who was now pregnant with number two, retired. My loft had two entrances. The one on Fourteenth Street led up to the living quarters, and on Thirteenth Street to my studio. Clarice, in the living quarters, was unable to know if I was in the studio. I began using the Thirteenth Street entrance for late-night visitors. One night after Bob left I didn't feel so well; perhaps the heroin was bad. Clarice found me on the floor. She helped me to bed and next morning told me I'd been frothing

at the mouth. I was going too far, she said, and it was separating us. She decided to go out to Southampton and think about it all.

Bob came by more often after that and sometimes slept over. We began taking heroin more steadily. He helped me with the lamp sculpture, holding things in place, buying supplies for the piece, even shopping for food. I didn't pay him by the hour or the week; I just paid for everything, including his spending money. At the beginning we took heroin after an evening in Max's Kansas City or some jazz joint, or before going to sleep if we worked late. After a while you take heroin just to feel normal; you can even work on it, you don't feel anything you'd call high. Almost every morning Bob went out, not long after we awoke, to score. For his dangerous work —there would be grave results if he was apprehended—I bought him his share. He couldn't put a needle in his veins. He was on probation, and the marks would be bad news. He injected himself intramuscularly. Often women came by the studio for him. He wasn't a stud type, even if he looked it. He was sensitive and shy with them. The women always seemed to want him more than he wanted them, and they were always white women. One who was especially fond of him was a blond German housewife from Queens, about thirty-eight years old.

When my eight-foot lamp sculpture was almost finished and I had cut a hole in *Plexi Playmate*'s rear so asshole and vagina could be reached by the gooseneck, it struck me that having a face gave the female some personality, while the giant male lamp had no such quality. I thought that Bob Wails should be the man in the lamp. I arranged for him to go to a photographer's studio to be photographed from four sides, face, back of the head, and two profiles, looking down as if observing the object of his affection. I suggested he try to look sexy, whatever that look was. He thought he knew, and when I received the transparencies I agreed. The head of the sculpture was a nine- by six-inch plastic parallelogram, partially opaque, left open on top so the bulb inside could be cooled by air flow. I fixed the transparencies of his face in their proper place with clear plastic. The work was suddenly a black man fucking a white woman, except both pieces were such original ideas of a figure that I was never sure how it appeared to the viewer.

During this stage of the lamp sculpture, Terry Southern dropped in one evening. I love Terry. He makes you laugh even when you don't talk to him for months because he never comes to

Larry, Terry, and friends

the phone. I've told him that his being from Texas was somehow central to our friendship, which made him admit that my being from the Bronx was no slouch in the matter. Terry Southern has written the novels *Candy*, *The Magic Christian*, and the least known of his masterful works, *Flash and Filigree*. On the side, with Stanley Kubrick, he wrote the screenplay for *Dr. Strangelove* and adapted Evelyn Waugh's *Loved One* for the screen. Our collaboration was the *Donkey and the Darling*, a fairy tale for peculiar children.

Terry looked at the *Playmate* and the lamp, which now had the face of Bob Wails, and said, "That lamp fellow certainly is loving what he's into and up to, eh, Lar?" Terry suggested I call the piece *Lampman Loves It*, and I did—a normal procedure for me, to name a work before it's finished. After Terry baptized the work, Bob adopted "Lampman" for his name, and we never heard "Bob Wails" again. He became Lampman and a legend and went on to be a performance artist and had a long run at the Electric Circus on St. Mark's Place in the seventies. When he was dying of cancer, "Lampman" was the name on his medical chart.

Sidney Janis came to see the piece and seemed startled but said it looked good and he would call me in a day or two to talk over delivery date and other details. Instead he called to say that as it stood, a Negro apparently having sex of a most unusual nature with a white woman was out of the question and would cause his exhibition to be closed down "by the Irish cop on the beat who will find it disgusting and call it pornography."

"But Sidney, you invited me to show a work with no restrictions. I'm very surprised you're taking this position. I'm going to talk it over with a lawyer."

An hour later he called back to ask if he could come down next day and we'd talk. I said okay, called Harris Steinberg, a criminal lawyer and collector of my work, and asked him to be at the meeting. After his gallery closed Sidney came to the studio. Harris was already there. Little Sidney asked for a ladder, shoved it over to the piece, climbed up to the head, and said, "Larry, all you have to do is remove these transparencies. The piece is just as good if not better without them." Sidney had always shown the latest modern art: Mondrian, Klee, Picasso, contemporary art of the thirties and forties. He wrote a book called *Art of the Century*, a yellow book with a Max Ernst line drawing on the cover, which I owned and often looked at as a young artist. In the fifties he showed many of the abstract expressionists, and in '62 he had the first pop art show. Now here is Sidney, avant-garde and Jewish, on a ladder telling me to take a black face out of a work. With one demand he rid me of some of my youthful artist's ideals and smashed my image of him as an idol.

Harris called me aside. "Say goodbye to Sidney and tell him you'll have an answer for him tomorrow." With that sad scene at an end, he then told me something that superseded Sidney's objections.

"If you show this piece in public Jo Collins, the Playmate, could sue for everything you have and even garnish your future earnings. You're free to work from the photo of her in *Playboy*, but you can't add a gooseneck belonging to a black man with a bulb at the end of his cock being shoved up her ass."

I called Frank O'Hara at MOMA, where he was now a curator, and asked if he could come by for a drink to discuss a little problem of mine. I showed him *Lampman Loves It* and told him about Janis's rejection, with all the delicious details, since he, like everyone else, found idol smashing a rich subject. Drink on table beside him in my studio, arms folded, he told me not to take it all too seriously.

"I know, Larry," he said, imitating my sincerity, "there's a common erotic fantasy where everyone gets hot thinking of a black man screwing a white woman. Okay. If you present that as the theme of this piece, it's going to cut into what's really amazing about it: those blunt shapes, the use and color of industrial materials, and the wonderful idea of the two being sexually aglow. Just relax. Maybe make the female black. You're not an artist so you can see how strong a character you have and who you can stand up to. It took so long for you to get some money. Hang on to it. If you have to give it up, give it up for a more important reason."

"Frank, this piece means something to me. It makes fun of the idea of the black male as an abstract fucking machine! Why should Sidney's problem make me give it up?"

Frank reminded me that once at the Five Spot, I was playing with Mal Waldren, Billie Holiday's accompanist, and some other serious jazz musicians. We were doing poetry and jazz, but it was Kenneth's *comic* poetry the music was meant to relate to, and it occasionally had to be funny. Certain of the musicians didn't want to do funny music. "We don't want to lose our personality doing something like that," one said.

"And Larry," said Frank, "you told him, 'Look, what if you do something that's not completely you for five minutes? You think you're not going to be you when it's over?' "

Frank told me he knew a very good and good-looking black actress who would be glad to pose and could use the money. She

agreed to pose. When she arrived she immediately took off her shoes, dress, and panties and put on the short jacket I supplied. I moved a Plexiglas box into position so she could fold her arms and bend over. I then proceeded to make a life-sized side-view drawing.

She had a beautiful figure with lots of variations. With her short hair, her head had a clear silhouette.

I called Sidney Janis and told him I had an idea that would resolve our problem. "Let's both be happy! Instead of removing the

face of our black protagonist, I'll make the object of his affection black. No Irish cop will object to that, Sidney."

The real confrontation was avoided. Sidney got his way, but not the way he suggested. Now he was unnerved for other reasons. My piece was just too strange, no matter whose race was goose-necking whose. As for those thirteen lights, especially Lampman's bulb testicles . . .

Opening night of the erotic exhibition came. There was a mob. Each artist brought ten friends. No one made anything resembling a complaint about my work, or anybody's. I heard snoring. Sidney,

busy showing his Mondrians backstage, came out every so often to be congratulated for his courage.

The following day I got a call from Howard Kanovitz, who had just been to the exhibition. "Larry, why aren't the lights on?"

"I don't know, Howard." I sped up to the Janis Gallery with a supply of bulbs. When my taxi pulled up, my piece was being carried toward a truck by two men.

"Hey, you guys! That's my piece. You better wait a minute. I'm

going upstairs to find out what's happening."

Upstairs I began to threaten everybody (except Sidney, who was backstage with his Mondrians) with lawsuits and cutting poems by my friends and an exposé on hypocrisy in *Art News*. Five min-

utes later the piece was in the gallery again. I put on the lights of *Lampman Loves It* and stayed for an hour. Four people came in. They walked past it as if it were something they saw every day. The

reviews were funnier than usual. One complained that I was a wise guy who thought I would cause a stir and draw attention to myself by creating a piece featuring two men engaged in sexual intercourse. If the entire making, compromising, and showing of *Lampman Loves It* was a farce of epic proportion, this review was a beautiful ending that neither Sidney nor I ever dreamed of.

On July 20, 1966, a performance of Stravinsky's *Oedipus Rex* was given at Lincoln Center's Philharmonic Hall, with Lukas Foss, by now part of Our Gang, conducting. Lukas had asked me to design the costumes, props, and set.

Oedipus, at the end of the opera, finds out that the king he killed was his father and that in consummating his marriage to Queen Jocasta he has committed the terrible crime of incest. I placed the evening's concert performance in an amphitheater of my own devising. I took the orchestra's semicircular arrangement and built three tiers, the last of which, fifteen feet off the ground, held the percussion: timpani, xylophone, glockenspiel, the indispensable triangle, and the big brass instruments. I wanted the orchestra to play the role of the audience in my amphitheater. The formal wear of the musicians did not suit my purpose. Discreetly, through Lukas Foss, I asked them to play without their suit jackets, in shirtsleeves. They refused. But when I came personally to explain why I wanted this, I recognized the respectable-looking lead clarinetist as an old bebop cohort who used to smoke marijuana with me. He quietly arranged for the orchestra to remove their jackets for the performance, with the proviso that I remain mum about the old days.

I went on to outfit one hundred and fifty members of the Greek chorus in sleeveless underwear and dark glasses. They all stood way back on the stage behind a fence as they balanced long poles with wooden flags at the end. All kinds of spray-painted insects represented the plague besetting Thebes. I dressed King Oedipus in a purple bathrobe with a large letter O on the back, as a champion prizefighter—i.e., a strongman, in line with the original title, *Oedipus Tyrannus*. To give the costume added punch I encumbered the lead singer, Ernst Haefliger, with a padded head guard. Ernst said it impeded his hearing. I made believe I didn't hear him. The messengers bearing the incestuous tidings were motorcyclists in full 1966 regalia. I had Jocasta's costume designed by the pop, pre-punk Tiger Morse, who was fond of colored plastic. Everyone in the cast wore dark glasses. The action took place in a boxing ring without ropes and with four sets of stairs leading up to the "canvas." At the end of the opera Oedipus removes his dark glasses, sees the truth of what he has done, and blinds himself. The ring, really the platform of the piano elevator, rises slowly with the blinded Oedipus on it, revealing a ten- by fifteen-foot bank of lights, each a thousand watts, which blinds the audience into experiencing what Oedipus is going through at his last dark, brilliant moment.

Costume

In 1927 Stravinsky set music to Jean Cocteau's libretto of *Oedipus Rex*. In the important role of Narrator, which he invented for himself, Cocteau was attired in a formal evening suit. At the 1966 dress rehearsal, Igor Stravinsky and Vera, his wife, gave me a very warm three-and-a-half-second hello and took their seats as Lukas was proudly presenting my list of artistic accomplishments.

"Mr. Rivers," said Stravinsky, "I'm hoping the Narrator appears in white tie and tails, as he did in the original production."

I had gone shopping only the day before with the Narrator, Jason Robards, and outfitted him as a relaxed TV crooner, like

Perry Como, in a blue cashmere sweater, a pair of white boating shoes, and any trousers of his own, as long as they were pastel-colored.

What was I supposed to do?

Stravinsky was the biggest, most accomplished cultural star I had ever met. He was modern and jaunty and varied, and when he wrote criticism or when he was interviewed he was brilliant and nasty. He had collaborated with extraordinary men: Picasso, Nijinsky, Balanchine, Diaghilev, Auden, great conductors—you name them. And I had been added to that list. As for recognition, how could I ever have asked for more? I was flabbergasted. I was part of an evening in one of the grandest concert halls in the world, commissioned to add my visual ideas to a living master's masterpiece.

First there was awe and respect for what I was part of. Then came the acknowledgment of an honor, public approval of my past efforts, which had landed me, almost literally, in the ring with Stravinsky, Cocteau, and the Golden Age of Greece.

Getting to the visuals of the *Oedipus* production put into motion other parts of my character. Without too much exaggeration, work can be seen as physically aggressive behavior. It's not the same as going to war, but people do get out of your way when you work. I never sit when I paint. Even when I draw I stand . . . and walk. And with *Oedipus* there was enough physical labor to keep me and fifteen assistants busy.

If Cocteau could create his version of a Greek play, and Stravinsky lace it with sharp tones and snotty rhythms based on early Italian compositions, I certainly had no qualms about taking their *Oedipus* anywhere I felt would be equally lively and pleasurable, even if discordant. I was no younger than Cocteau and Stravinsky when they conceived *Oedipus*. They had the proper respect and disrespect necessary to complete this work. So did I. I was obviously in their tradition: I loved them but ignored them.

First Night

After the opera ended, Oedipus descended from his loneliness atop the boxing ring platform, and the audience of thirty-five hundred broke into applause commingled with shouts of "Bravo!" Then Lukas brought me out for my bow. In the brief and beautiful silence that followed, I was carried away, so much so that everything I had ever done in my life seemed worth doing.

As I bowed, the booing began. It got louder and louder as the audience realized that I was the individual responsible for the visual effects. It rolled on for about five minutes—a record, I believe. I kept bowing as I experienced wave upon wave of pleasurable tingling sensations. I immediately thought of John Cage at his concerts and understood at last how he got hooked on boos.

Frank and Arnold and Lampman came backstage to tell me how wonderful and interesting everything was, and that I should simply ignore the ungrateful audience.

"Exactly!" Lukas patted me on the back. "Everyone knows music crowds are notoriously conservative."

Next morning in the *New York Times* Harold C. Schoenberg felt that "the whole thing was low camp . . . patchy things hastily thrown together. . . . somehow the portly Ernst Haefliger did not look like a prizefighter." Etc. Lukas came in for some shit too, by virtue of his association with me: "Stravinsky's great score is powerful enough to withstand any sort of treatment. Lukas Foss, falling into the spirit of the occasion, did his best to destroy it. . . . If these bright boys would only keep their hands off the art works of their betters the cultural scene would be a good deal healthier."

The next day I found out that Igor and Vera were making faces when Jason appeared without white tie and tails. This, I'm afraid, was the proverbial tip of the iceberg. They didn't like much of

Lukas Foss

LARRYRIVERS

anything they saw. I was charmed by Stravinsky's control; he never asked for any changes in what I had done.

Twenty years later my East Thirteenth Street Band played on a New York rooftop at the wedding of Igor's grandson John Stravinsky. David Levy, baritone player and Parsons dean, wore pants tucked into his boots, and an academic gown with the Ph.D. collar prominent. Trumpet player Howard Brofsky was adorned in a burnoose he had picked up in Morocco. The piano player, Myron Blackman, wore no costume. He didn't have to; no matter what he wore he looked like a rabbi. Howard Kanovitz's army pants and shirt matched the color of his trombone. I wanted to be formal, so I wore a tuxedo jacket over a shirt that bore an enlarged photograph of a woodland scene, and black leather pants that had shrunk in their only trip to the cleaners, revealing the tufts of my yellow socks, which I wore inside out. The Stravinskys—John, his new bride, Dayva, and his father, Soulima, Igor's son—approved wholeheartedly of the audiovisual presentation.

Second Night

At the second *Oedipus Rex* performance, following the *Times* review, the principal singer appeared without the sparring headgear I had chosen for him. Mrs. Oedipus, the beautiful Shirley Verrett, decided she wanted to see the audience and removed her very dark glasses.

Frank O'Hara came backstage that second night, having read the *Times* review, and took me to dinner to assure me that what I had done was too fresh and unfamiliar to be appreciated immediately. He had no doubts about how beautiful it was. I felt better. He made me think it wasn't very different from other milestone moments. "The energy and enthusiasm for what you create, Larry, comes from you. Your work has never related easily to any audience. Why start worrying now?"

There's much to be said on this subject, but nothing better than what Thomas Bernhard wrote in *Wittgenstein's Nephew*.

For, faced with the least displeasure on the part of the audience, the actors who were cast in the main parts at once took sides with the audience, following the age-old tradition by which Viennese actors conspire with the audience against a play and have no compunction about stab-

bing the author in the back as soon as they sense that the
audience does not take to his play in the first few minutes,
because it does not understand it and finds both the author
and the play too difficult. It goes without saying, of course,
that actors ought to go through fire, as they say, for an
author and his play, especially if it is new and has not been
tried out before.

The End

I saw him only one more time, a few days later in the Brookhaven
hospital. He had been hit by a beach buggy on Fire Island when a
beach bus he was in had a flat and he stepped out onto the sand
waiting for the tire to be changed. Bill de Kooning and I, when we
got to the hospital, went white. Neither of us knew how badly he
had been struck. As soon as Frank felt us at his bedside, he began
a hallucinatory but not too incoherent monologue about a party
Patsy Southgate was throwing, and he listed the friends who would
be there. These last words were not so different from his letters to
me giving a fast and funny account of some party. He seemed to be
enjoying himself. In the middle of a sentence he would stop talking,
wait a moment or two, then with difficulty clear his throat and
begin again. There was no way Bill and I could join the conversation. I'm not sure Frank knew exactly who we were.

In the morning Joe Le Sueur phoned and told me that Frank
had died, that he was to be buried the next day in the cemetery in
Springs, Long Island, and that his sister had asked if I would say a
few words at the grave.

The morning of the funeral, after I spent the night with a
woman I hardly knew, Allen Ginsberg, Arnold, and I met to drive
out to Springs. As we were about to get going, a young Cuban
painter everyone knew as Carlos ran up to the car, stuck his head
in the window, and said with a grin, "Larry! Guess what! Frank
O'Hara's coming up to my studio tomorrow to look at my paintings!"

Out on the Long Island Expressway, Allen pulled out a pair of
finger cymbals and began a chant for Frank.

Hari Rama
Hari Rama
Rama Rama
Hari Hari

Arnold and I joined in. When we stopped chanting we told stories about Frank. How he had his first sexual experience at sixteen with a fifteen-year-old boy who took care of the horses in a stable Frank was hanging around, in a big pile of hay. After that he gave up on girlfriends. Allen told us that Frank was the first person he sent his manuscript of *Howl* for feedback. Arnold told us how Frank, when he first went aboard his destroyer during the war, was called Butch because of his tough-looking profile—he had a broken nose. After he got better acquainted with his shipmates, said Frank, he was called Butchie.

When we reached Springs, there were a hundred or more people standing around the small cemetery, friends and fans. Some had traveled the hundred and twenty miles from New York to be there for the funeral. Fairfield Porter and Alex Katz came from Maine, Philip Guston from Woodstock; Bill de Kooning biked in from ten blocks away; Howard and Mary Kanovitz chartered a small plane to fly them from Provincetown. The burying began, and Frank was laid to rest across from the large boulder that marks the grave of Jackson Pollock, about whom Frank had spent a year writing a book. John Ashbery read Frank's "To the Harbormaster," with frequent pauses for uncontrolled sobbing. At one point a low-flying craft completely drowned out John's voice; he never stopped reading till the poem was over. I was the next to talk and delivered the following text.

Frank was my friend. I always thought he would be the first to die among my small happy group. But I daydreamed a romantic death brought about by too much whiskey, by smoking three packs of Camels a day, by too much sex, by unhappy love affairs, by writing too many emotional poems, too many music and dance concerts, just too much living which would drain away his energy and his will to live. His real death is a shock because he was killed on the soft, safe, white sand of Long Island. This extraordinary man lay without a pillow in a bed that looked like a large crib. He was purple wherever his skin showed through the white hospital gown. He was a quarter larger than usual. Every few inches there was some sewing composed of dark blue thread. Some stitching was straight and three or four inches long, others were longer and semicircular. The lids of both eyes were bluish black. It was hard to see his beau-

tiful blue eyes which receded a little into his head. He
breathed with quick gasps. His whole body quivered. There
was a tube in one of his nostrils down to his stomach. . . .
On paper, he was improving. In the crib he looked like a
shaped wound. His leg was broken and splintered and
pierced his skin. Every rib was cracked. A third of his liver
was wiped out by the impact. What can talking about it do?
I don't know. Frank O'Hara was my best friend. At one
time or another, he was everybody's greatest and most loyal
audience. . . . His friendships were so strong he forced me
to reassess men and women I would not have bothered to
know. It is easy to deify in the presence of death. But Frank
was an extraordinary man—and everyone here knows it.
For me, Frank's death is the beginning of tragedy. My first
experience with loss. I feel lonely.

Back from the grave that night, lying in bed, I was in the middle
of a summer storm—lightning, sharp cracks, and blunt explosions.
With every flash I saw Frank's angry face lit up. I lay there thinking
I was responsible for his death. Now, calm and twenty-five years
later, I still feel responsible for his death. Frank had wanted to come
and spend the weekend with me. Clarice liked Frank very much
but didn't want to spend three days entertaining his boyfriend J.J.

So what? If she had her way this time, I'd have the right next time, out of the equality we thought should exist between us, to invite Frank and J.J. I made up some excuse to Frank to keep him and J.J. away. My homespun peace-at-any-price philosophy allows life to flow along for me, but in this instance it was where Frank's death began. Frank, who loved to spend his weekends in the summer out of the city, got himself invited instead to Morris Golde's home on Water Island, a remote part of Fire Island. On that weekend on that beach he was struck by some happy hooting youngster driving a dune buggy. To add to the villainy, his internal bleeding wasn't discovered until the next day, when it was too late.

Frank's death wasn't the end of an era. That ending had begun a few years before, for me, and probably for Frank. The lust for literature, dance, new music, not completely comprehensible plays, the uncontrollable joy and zeal and the hunt for sex, had already begun to wane. Career, the nemesis of our past, had crept up on all of us through the pressure of social and artistic identity. Frank's death put out the lightness of all I associated with him. My smartest, most exuberant audience was taken away from me, his power was gone.

No one on the immediate horizon of the sixties seemed capable of taking his place. Kenneth Koch, John Ashbery, Terry Southern, and Jane Freilicher were all talented and bright but were more sublimely self-centered than myself. Often they made me happy, and some of their work inspired me, but the personal and physical appeal Frank and I had for each other, less and less consciously expressed by the time he died, lent to all our meetings something like a whooping glow that was nonexistent with the others. I grew less interested in questions of identity. I felt an obligation to continue to amaze with my art. With Frank gone, I had to change those who monitored it. No one but Frank ever offered ideas I could seriously incorporate in my work. He was as concerned with the work of other artists as he was with his own poetry. It was his job, his calling.

The oft-thrown cocktail parties in the small railroad apartments where I either went with Frank or met him, which were like a splash in the face after a day in the studio, were disappearing. I still see a kitchen on East Ninth Street or on Second and Second with only eight or nine people stacked like a can of sardines. These parties were like Coney Island mirrors. We saw multiple images of ourselves, some delightful, some distorted, like us.

I'm reminded of an event that combines the absurd with the
incomprehensible. About three weeks before Frank was killed on
Water Island, he was visiting me out in Southampton. It was early
July. I was married to Clarice and reasonably busy with marriage
and her. Gwynne was almost two, and another child was due the
first week in August (we named her Emma Francesca). Frank,
alone with me in the house, knocked on my bedroom door late at
night, poked his head into the dark, and said, "In the mood for a
little blow job?"—which hadn't happened for years. I pondered the
question.

What was I pondering? "Why not?" I said.

When Frank died I found myself absurdly comforted by my
decision to comply. Why? So he could take one less disappointment
to the grave? I have heard people say how happy they were to have
visited with Mother a day or so before her death. What about the
visit made them happy? Conversely, after my father collapsed on
Forty-ninth Street, I kept crying because I hadn't kept an appointment we made to see each other. What difference would any of
these things have made to the disappearance of a soul? Why do we
continue to feel that what we say and what we think have some
relevance? Is it anything more than moans and groans about the
absurdity of life?

L

A

R

R

Y

R

I

V

E

R

S

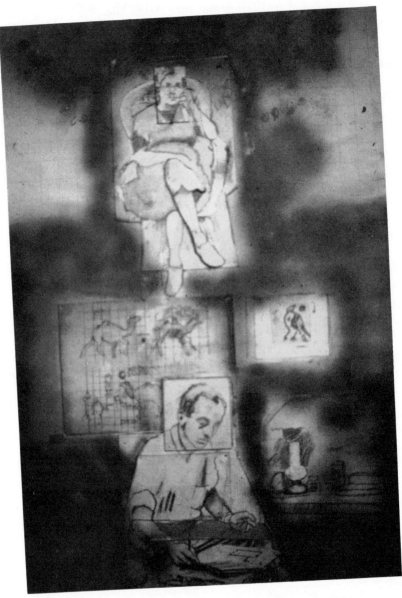

In Memory of the Dead, *1966*

CODA: LOOSE ENDS

Family

Frank's death produced no dramatic promises to myself or to anyone else. I continued to worry about painting and so I continued to paint. In the fall of 1968, Clarice moved uptown with our blond daughters, Gwynne and Emma. I spent the first night in the tenroom apartment on Central Park West with the Family and never slept over again. Clarice still lives there, scraping floors and painting walls, continuing her tradition of sumptuous dinners celebrating artists and writers, minus the singer Gwynne Rivers and the sculptor Emma Rivers, our grown daughters. She's been a close friend and an assiduous mother for these twenty-five years, and we never got divorced.

Weaning

During our amicable 1968 split, a friend of the family introduced me to a well-known Dr. Feelgood and his touted shots of vitamins and amphetamines. These shots were meant to wean me from bad, bad heroin. It worked, but in a way my friend hadn't foreseen. For obvious reasons, taking heroin intravenously was more dangerous than the intramuscular method by which I took speed, but heroin at least had the virtue of slowing down my naturally hyper soul. Speed finally got to be like shaking a hand holding a pointed rotating buzzer in its palm, from which I was unable to unlock my grip. I never felt "high," but I hardly slept for two years.

In 1969 I began to make films and videos on my own. The helping hands this required brought me in contact with young men with long hair, which I soon began to sport, "girls" in short skirts, sexual obsession, and yoga.

The first film I made after my African adventure was a documentary on breasts. As the film evolved, it grew to include the chests of Mongolian wrestlers and women of all ages, their bodies and thoughts on their bodies, and many men, including my twenty-four-year-old son Steven, wearing falsies on his hairy chest in quest of the perfect bosom. Even the milk bags and udders of cows, dogs, and sheep found their way into the film, which I called *Tits*, and which couldn't have been a redder flag to flap during the cultural wave of feminism. From my point of view *Tits* was more about absurdity and my obsessions, heightened by the shimmering energy of the speed I was taking.

The *Village Voice*, a newspaper chock-full of lines containing "fuck," "shit," "cock," "cunt," and "blow job," refused to take the ad for the film because of the title. The newspaper was an early practitioner of P(olitically) C(orrect). As a black man, H. Rap Brown could write *Die Nigger Die*, a book given respectable space and serious reviews in the dailies, but since I wasn't a woman, my use of the street expression for a woman's breasts, "tits," was tactless and unprintable. Such was the logic of the times. Without seeing the film, the movie critic Jonas Mekas, in the pages of the *Voice*, admitted that the paper was engaging in censorship but justified the censorship in terms of the "higher" claims of women's liberation. A few years later, Jonas chose to praise *Shirley*, a video movie I had done about my mother, and showed it at his own Film Forum.

Donnie

By the time Frank O'Hara took his last trip to Fire Island, my curiosity about homosexuals and life and sex among them had diminished. They were my friends, and their exotic and erotic aura continued, but only as a warm glow in my memory. I suppose time and tide played a part in the evaporation of my feelings, but fifteen-and-a-half-year-old Donnie Miller played an even bigger part, weighing in at five feet nine and a half stunning inches and one hundred and fifteen pounds, with moist green eyes and red hair.

Starting at age thirteen, she and her friend Anna would go from Forest Hills to Washington Square Park to hang around with guys and panhandle so they could buy their buddies a few six packs of Colt 45 or a bottle of Southern Comfort à la Janis Joplin. If the guys, especially the cute ones, wanted a return for their contribution, they'd allow them a free feel.

Donnie had very little experience with intercourse. She masturbated but never figured out that a man's cock could accomplish the same results (and still hasn't, so she says). Going to Washington Square Park to meet guys was adventurous. So was submitting, along with Anna, to the awkward sexual advances of boys who would line up waiting their turn on the roof of Macy's on Queens Boulevard. In high school this kind of exciting fun took the form of allowing a drama teacher to fondle her on the darkened stage of the school auditorium behind drawn curtains as students filed in for the weekly assembly.

Another exciting chapter in the life of Donnie Miller opened when she met an artist in his forties working in a city-block-long "pad" who stayed up two or three days in a row and was ravenous to see her—me. The adventure with me sometimes included my daughters, Gwynne and Emma. If they stayed over for a day, she'd help me care for them, think up places to go and things to do. Downtown, if my daughters were there, Donnie was identified as the official baby-sitter. However, uptown, at Central Park West, where the babies were living, they were being sat by a young poet, Jim Carroll. Donnie's baby-sitting title and the money she received for it were the "logical" explanation to her mother for the nights spent in New York, for a Jacques Kaplan coat and a Halston blue dress, both trades for a work of mine. The mornings after her baby-sitting, come rain or come shine, I would ride Donnie on the back of my BSA motorcycle to her den of iniquity, Crowley High.

If the special circumstances surrounding Clarice, like her being Welsh, an au pair, and an artist's model with a mellifluous voice, lent to her otherwise comely self an ambiance I found irresistible, I'd have to double the coverage of "irresistible" to cover my initial feelings for Donnie. I gave her a Sweet Sixteen party. The force of the pleasure I experienced was new, and I would lie back and allow it to roll over me. Considering our age difference, it was amazing how quickly my physical attraction and her curiosity turned us into pals. She told me everything that was happening to her, even how our sex experiences whetted her appetite for other men, which she set herself to satisfy. Whatever she told me only drew me closer to her.

After a few months we became a video team, working and acting in skits and short dramatic pieces, interviewing people on the streets of New York and other cities, on buses and beaches, on any subject we thought was potentially funny or interesting. We traveled to California (where I taught at Santa Barbara) to shoot footage for an opera, *The Artist*, presented at the Whitney Museum. This footage was part of my set for *The Artist*, based on Kenneth Koch's poem, with music by Paul Reif. We shot in the mountains, the woods, the desert, and on a rocky plateau. We ate sashimi for the first time and went back for more every day at four when we brought our still photos to the lab. Donnie learned how to edit our footage at a pretty primitive stage of video technology. I set a camera on a tripod to shoot a prescribed area, and we filmed ourselves making love for the camera. Except for my art, we reached a stage where nothing meant anything unless we shot it.

No matter what we did, no matter what or who we saw, I was always looking at and responding to what I felt was the most beautiful face and figure, so far in my life, that I could kiss and touch. Perhaps that isn't the highest form of love, but it was all I could manage. It went on for a few years, but it didn't go away quietly. Here's how it went away.

Donnie was visiting me for a long summer weekend out in Southampton, where at one time, after graduating from high school, she lived with me for six months. She packed her small hiking bag, preparing to leave for New York. I wasn't especially pleased she had somewhere else to go, but I put the best face on it and told her affectionately we'd be in touch in the next few days. Checking to see if she had all she came with, she went up to the bedroom to look around and make a last-minute telephone call. It was almost time for her to be at the train station. Upstairs I found her taking a nice, languorous shower—not that she didn't often take nice, languorous showers—but this time I saw it as the first step in the erotic adventure awaiting her in New York. By now her experiences with other men were no longer a sexual stimulant for me. I began shouting at her, putting my face in hers, acting as if it were a sadistic crime to take a shower in my house in preparation for sex somewhere else with someone else. I frightened her. She was afraid to get into the car with me. My sister had to drive her to the station. As soon as they were out of the house, I ran to the closet where she still stored some clothes, threw her favorite things on the floor, and pissed on the pile.

I thought that this vignette would be like our other explosive moments, perhaps a bit more memorable, and that we would be amused by it in just a few weeks. But my compulsion to fuck Donnie, I thought forever, kept me from seeing the shape of things. Living in Southampton, I had to make the trip to New York to see her, to hold her hands, to press her up against me, to fuck her— whatever I imagined and desired. Our extended video and still-photo collaboration had given her the confidence to work on her own. For freedom of choice and movement she had to give up her financial dependence on me. She got a job at a photo lab on Prince Street in Greenwich Village and met friends her own age, a generation with a relaxed approach to "making it." The highly audible homily in the early seventies was "doing your own thing," and Donnie set out to accomplish this.

About three days after our volatile scene she came out to Southampton to get her things. Her body and mind had already separated from me, and now her possessions were to follow. When she saw what I'd done to her clothes, which were now on the bathroom floor to facilitate the continued expression of my feelings of humiliation, she got unusually pissed off. She took the train back to New York. Just one day later she called me to ask that I come to New York for a serious talk. As I walked through the door, she handed me a straightforward divorce proceeding. She wanted $750 plus a month's rent at the Chelsea Hotel and a new Nikon camera. The long talk was cut short by her departure for a rock concert with a six-foot-two photographer friend.

Around midnight I received a call from Donnie. She was outside in the street, and could I please throw down her diaphragm? No one is that cool, but as if in a trance I obeyed. However, a few minutes after I watched her date pick up the thrown package, I called Michelle, a Southampton distraction from my deteriorating romance, and asked her to come to New York immediately.

Donnie never came home that night, but Michelle arrived by car about 2:30 in the morning. We went to sleep. At 11:00 a.m. Donnie stumbled in and was surprised to see Michelle, whom she knew. She was very calm as she watched me act affectionately toward Michelle, but she finally asked what I was going to do about her requests. For an answer, I went over to the sink, filled a large pot with water, came up behind Donnie, and poured the pot over her head. I told her that when I got angry enough at my wife Clarice for what I thought was her disturbing behavior but was really more my uncontrollable possessive nature, I announced, "I will never stick my cock in your cunt again as long as I live." Now I heatedly repeated the same promise to Donnie, and I've kept my word to both of them. As with Clarice, I never broke off communication or my financial support. To this day they receive my bounty. Donnie works harder for it.

Today Donnie is more than a girlfriend turned best friend. For the last fifteen years she's worked for me five days a week. To describe all that she does for me would require more pages than I want to write. She takes care of the biz end of my biz. I feel like poor Utrillo, married to a woman like Donnie, who took care of everything and enabled him to set up his easel every day in the narrow streets of Montmartre. Donnie makes old-fashioned Girl Fridays look as if they're lounging at a pool. She's an ace archivist, a shrewd bargainer, and a brilliant letter writer. She's impossible and unpredictable, but it's not exaggerating to say that I love her.

Reweaning

The friend of the family who was weaning me from bad heroin to worse speed now helped wean me from worse speed to fresh air. I got into the Los Angeles County Hospital because my friend's friend, head of admitting, put me at the head of the line. Three days drying out on a ward and the next ten at Hollywood and Vine at my friend's house, and I never again touched or had any further interest in the roaring rapids of speed.

History of the Present

In the very early seventies Jean de Menil, boss of the Menil Foundation, commissioned me to "make something" or "do something" about the "black experience." It came out from my sweaty fingers and clicking brain, fifteen or sixteen separate works later, as *Some American History*. I read a wide range of books on slavery in the United States, the Caribbean, and South America, some writings by ex-slaves, fat books on Frederick Douglass, jazz, Malcolm X, and other black heroes. I invited six black artists to contribute to this project; the results were mixed. It was to come to New York, but the Metropolitan Museum bombed out with their show Harlem on My Mind, a black-experience panorama, and all plans for *Some American History* were canceled for up north.

Adaptation

In 1974, browsing in my art supply shop through a section of manuals for the amateur or beginning artist, I spotted *The Coloring Book of Japan*, which contained ten or more Japanese artworks. It was a thrilling revelation to see Japanese art without color, giving me what I felt were new insights into its spirit and structure. The revelation kept me bubbling for two or three years, creating "Japanese paintings." I was using airbrush at the time. I was never able to find color reproductions of the specific works in the coloring book, but I located other works by the same artists, which enabled me to paint from a more informed base—an important part of my working process. After finishing about ten canvases with the help of two assistants and lots of stencils, one work as large as seven feet by eleven feet and shaped, I had a show of them at the Marlborough Gallery. This display first shocked, then worried, many of the individuals who owned works of mine, one so much so that a day after my exhibition opened, he put my *Lions on the Dreyfus Fund* up for auction at Park Bernet. The only result of my aesthetic twist he could imagine was a sharp drop in the market value of my work. There was some basis for his anxiety. Was I losing my way? What had happened to my rambunctious color and the popular culture subject matter? Could one of these Oriental works be recognized as a Larry Rivers (no small consideration in the art world steeplechase)? Only Picasso could flip from one way of working to another as his stockholders watched peacefully from the sidelines, secure in the knowledge that his prices would hold.

Career

By the late sixties my art had begun falling back in the expanding art world steeplechase, but I kept running. I continued to feel my passion for color, canvas, jaunty marks, and my own form of intellectual acrobatics, but I had now entered the shaky terrain of ten to one, or even higher, to win, place, or show. I refuse to ascribe these lean years to neglect by my gallery, preoccupied as it was with some higher-priced stars, or to my work becoming unfashionable as the world turned. From '62 to '67 I didn't show my work. Out of

L
A
R
R
Y
R
I
V
E
R
S

sight, out of fashion, perhaps. But what about Balthus, who hardly ever had shows and couldn't care less? Art is character. Where was mine? A gallery doesn't make a painter. Still, Marlborough backed some of my print projects, even three-dimensional multiples. I found out the hard way that plastic and Day-Glo colors for a herd of elephants or a *Dying Civil War Veteran* led naturally to "Got anything else you want to show us?" Was I interested in "new materials" as a way of sprucing up some tired subject matter?

However, one or two sour projects in my late thirties can't completely account for the diminution of the attention I had grown accustomed to. Less attention, followed by less money, began to suggest that certain abilities of mine, whether drawing, color, or arresting attitudes about art, were just myths I had invented about myself. I still had some cachet among people and organizations removed from the *au courant* center of art, but I lived as if I had had glorious former days. NBC television, backing that trip to Africa, thought I would come through for them. The Merchants Bank of New England, located on the hallowed grounds of the Boston Massacre, asked me to do two giant murals covering that event. I made what I still enjoy—a *Paul Revere Ride* and another work, a visual mixture of British soldiers shooting some complaining British-Americans who turn out to be Vietnamese and civil rights activists.

Ace

One of the French *nouveaux réalistes* I had befriended in Paris visited New York and reported on a dinner he had attended at the home of Bill Reuben, the not yet director of the Museum of Modern Art. The star guest and speaker was Clement Greenberg. A few years earlier I had done a six-foot painting called *The Daugherty Ace of Spades* that was bought by Bill Reuben, who seemed to enjoy looking at it and owning it—that is, until this dinner. My French friend, tinged by a feeling of loyalty to me, relayed that Clem told Bill he didn't like my painting and Bill should get rid of it. *The Daugherty Ace of Spades* was put up for auction at Park Bernet. A dealer I had seen around for years bought it and called me to say how happy he was to own it but that he bought it to sell it—no kidding. Calling me about this was a little unusual. I wished him luck and went on living and working.

The *Ace* was painted with wide brushes and had what I thought was the right amount of detail to be recognized as an ace of spades. Realist that I am, I avoided the more delectable range of reds, oranges, blues, and yellows of the king, queen, and jack. Let's call a spade a spade. It was black, white, and gray, perhaps with a spot of yellow. The dealer kept calling to tell me he was having difficulty selling the painting. He began to sound as if I had my nerve making such an unsalable item.

"Larry, would any of the collectors of your work be interested in acquiring the painting?"

Not only do I have to paint it, I have to get into the act of selling it? Every call from this nervous wreck substantiated a sinking sensation that my place in the art firmament was coming apart.

In 1977 the Marlborough Gallery was still absorbed in the Rothko conspiracy trial, defending itself against everything from buying cheap and selling expensive (every dealer's dream) to wasting the assets of the estate of poor Rothko, who committed suicide, to tampering with evidence. Poor Frank Lloyd, spending many years in court, ordered to pay $9,200,000 in fines and fishing full-time in the Bahamas, had no time for poor me. Ditto Lee Krasner, who walked out on the gallery.

Here comes my savior, Robert Miller, ex-manager of the Andre Emmerich Gallery, about to go out on his own and in need of a star. Backing his upbeat view of my work, Miller purchased a number of important (BIG) works and mounted a well-thought-out, well-advertised exhibition. I began to invent a brighter future. My new feeling was given a great boost by Tom Hess, slated to be the Metropolitan's curator of art, in a laudatory article for *New York* magazine. Robert Miller placed one of my *Rainbow Rembrandts* in a Japanese museum. Joe Hirshhorn, spotting a color reproduction of my other Rembrandt, used to advertise my show, bought the painting and accompanying drawing over the phone. These paintings and drawings were based on Rembrandt's *Polish Rider*. The Old Dutch Master served to lift me from the unhappy shadows of neglect, where he himself ended up at the end of his life.

Robert Miller's in-laws, Jimmy and Gretchen Johnson of the Band-Aid Johnsons, took a liking to me and my work. They began to ask me to do all sorts of art projects. Though these commissions were a bit off-center from what I was up to, I enjoyed the attention and money.

L

Two Frivolous

The *New York Times* recently reviewed a Mary McCarthy book based on her diaries, which inform us, among other things, of the many men she slept with who are now part of literary history. The reviewer found most of this interesting and lively, but essentially he felt the book failed because Mary didn't tell us what it all meant. It was not enough to gather a good part of her life, organize it intelligently, and lay it out on some pages. She had shirked the responsibility of passing judgment on herself, and that omission couldn't be ignored in the critic's final opinion.

Well, I too have failed to pass judgment on all that is written here about me. I keep writing as if what I throw into the pot, this book, can't help but make a delicious brew for the reader. I am amazed that the sum of all the parts of my story does not a clear picture of me form. So here, with natural flavors . . .

More for the Pot

One calm weekday afternoon in a spring of the early seventies, going from a sandwich shop back to my studio to pick up where I left off, I'm stopped by a young woman who says she knows me from those "nights" at the Cedar Tavern in the 1950s. Her name is Nancy Johnson, and I pretend to remember her. Her tale of woe is awful. She is dark purple beneath her eyes. She's poor, has a small child, lives in a run-down hotel on welfare, and keeps being mistreated by every boyfriend. She even shows me bruises where she's been hit. Finally she asks for money. I give her fifteen dollars, which today would be about sixty-five or seventy dollars. I wasn't the loaded artist I am now, so that was something. She walked me to my door and we parted.

A few days later, early in the morning (I'd been up all night), she rings my doorbell and wonders if I can please give her another fifteen dollars. She comes upstairs and brews me a cup of coffee. This time I hand her the money and ask if she'll let me fuck her the next time she comes. In a soft voice she says okay and goes away. She is a tall, thick woman, about thirty-two, with a sad face surrounded by long blond hair. Nothing makes her smile.

Not too many days later, she's at my studio with her child, a three-year-old girl who is a miniature version of Nancy, in unwashed face and dirty clothes. The child stumbles constantly but

A

R

R

Y

R

I

V

E

R

S

gets up each time and tries again; she never stops moving or mumbling. If Nancy and I intend joining genitals, the child presents us with a problem. We go into my bedroom. There's no window, the daylight from the living room will be enough. The child is put at the far end of the wide bed but quickly crawls over and climbs on us. Nancy gets up. "Don't worry, Larry. I'll take care of it. I've done it before." She takes her child just outside the bedroom, produces a rope she brought along, ties it around the child's stomach, and tethers her to the couch. Nancy comes back to the bed and takes her clothes off. I don't like what her breasts look like, I ask her to put her bra back on. Here, in bed, she looks bigger than her five foot ten. Her long thighs border on heavy, and she has a rolling midriff. When I look at her face, now much brighter, almost beautiful, she seems to beckon me to come closer. I kiss her stomach. All this, combined with a touching passivity, arouses me immediately. I don't think she feels much, but it doesn't seem to matter. The child is on the floor, still tied to the couch, nervously licking her hands. The rope, long enough for her to have wandered into the bedroom once or twice, causes no problem.

In the months following, I begin calling Nancy. I don't remember if I wanted to control her coming and going or whether I was really getting interested and didn't want to wait till she needed me. It was usually five or six in the morning. I go to sleep after we have sex, but now she waits till I wake up, cooks breakfast, and with the child watches me paint for hours. I'm pleased to have her in the studio; she never volunteers to talk. I hardly have anything to say to her, but my physical feeling for her deepens. I am now giving her fifty dollars for the pleasure she gives me. I still don't think very much of her except as some sad chunk of humanity that confirms my idea that life is just plain awful, but I help her and the child without hesitation. She becomes so dependent on me that I find it easy and almost pleasurable to treat her badly.

One early morning, after an entire night of drinking and talking with my pal Arnold Weinstein, Nancy comes over as planned. She and I go into a smaller bedroom, this one with two windows and no shades. The little bit of romance that accompanied our lovemaking in the low-lit bedroom is destroyed by the strong light. In this light she is not physically appealing, but it doesn't change anything much. The situation is stark. Arnold, quick to improvise, tells a *Story Theater* story to the child, who falls asleep, and with an adroit adjustment appears at the door of our sexual chamber to watch what we're doing. Except for her bra, Nancy is naked. I'm naked except for a white athletic shirt. Arnold beings to undress, getting ready to join us. Three of us are now on the narrow bed. Nancy looks more confused than usual. Why am I allowing this to happen to her? She throws herself back flat and waits. I leave the room as Arnold moves in for a groaning crescendo. They finish and come into the living room. The child is now awake and slightly frantic, yelling for her mother. I hand her to Nancy and go to sleep. Perchance to dream? Of what? Should I pass some judgment on this chapter? I'm tired, why don't *you* think about what it "means."

Ten Days

In June 1976 I received a call from the U.S. State Department's Office of Eastern European Programs, which said it was passing along an invitation from the USA (Union of Soviet Artists) to visit the USSR for ten days that September. The exact itinerary was to be worked out in conjunction with the American embassy and the artists' union. The union would also provide an interpreter and cover the cost of food, hotels, and travel within the USSR, while the State Department would provide international transportation plus fifty dollars per diem. I accepted.

In those chilly cold-war days I had to go to Washington to be "briefed." I thought that Americans officially briefed or debriefed were automatically endowed with a special class of citizenship. I was very excited. The briefing was my first step in getting a look at this insatiably discussed society, the matrix from which my mother and father emerged. During the briefing session I was told what to expect from the Russians and what they did not expect from me as an American Artist—controversial opinions about the USSR. No one in the State Department thought there was any "real" danger, but they made very few amusing remarks, except at the expense of the Russians. I think you were allowed a wife to accompany you. I took my son Steven and my video equipment, happy to have his company and his six o'clock news roving-reporter talent. I intended to come back from the trip with a lot of visual information.

Perhaps to keep alive the cloak-and-dagger dreams of the neophyte voyager going behind the Iron Curtain, we weren't allowed to fly directly to Moscow. Instead we had to fly to Stockholm and change planes there. With the switch we inherited an extraordinary-looking Swedish hostess. On the short flight to Moscow—

Steven and I were the only passengers—she kept entertaining us **L** with eye-rolling stories about the mysterious Russians.

Beneath dozens of large posters of Lenin we were met by American and Soviet officials plus the promised translator, a far cry from Greta Garbo in *Ninotchka*. She was with us all day long, and at **A** night, when we turned in, she slept a few doors down the hotel hall from us. The only "ideological" conversation we had was about Solzhenitsyn. I asked if she had read *One Day in the Life of Ivan* **R** *Denisovich* or *Cancer Ward*. She said no, not that she wasn't free to read them, but "Solzhenitsyn doesn't use the Russian language very well, and because of that he is not important here." This twenty-eight-year-old translator was called Sonja. My mother's name, I **R** enthusiastically told her! There was no response to my weak stab at solidarity in her answer: "Mmm." It took her some days to realize that Steven and I were in Russia for video or photo opportunities, **Y** with a dash of cultural exchange on the side. She began suggesting things we might find exciting to film: the enormous stadium with flags flapping and giant posters of every Soviet leader in their history, the new plastics factory, the many world visitors to beautiful Red Square.

My official role was to meet artists and lecture in each city I visited. Along with many other slides of my work and a few of some other American contemporaries, I showed my *History of the Rus-* **R** *sian Revolution*. I thought I was being courageous, contrary to the advice of the briefers in Washington. When my portrait of Trotsky appeared on the screen, I told the audience that Trotsky, a non- **I** person in their country—no photos allowed, no mention of him in any book—was the only Bolshevik leader in Moscow at the outbreak of the revolution and as head of the Red Army had played an important part in beating back the White Russian resistance. Si- **V** lence. During the question-and-answer period after the slide show, I would talk about the prejudice in America against Soviet art. Most American artists didn't take it too seriously because they knew Russian artists could only paint what was officially approved. **E**

Repairing to a back room for drinks with some artists, I was bombarded with photographs of their work, reproductions in magazines and books, all to show me how much variety existed in Soviet **R** art, the point being that Russian artists were free to do as they wished. One especially exciting moment in the art part of my trip took place in Leningrad. I was showing *America's Number One Problem*, the vacuum-form work depicting a pink cock, a black **S** cock, and a rigid ruler at the bottom. On screen this work was blown up to about eight feet high and five feet wide. I also showed a work based on a sexually explicit sixteenth-century Japanese print, where among other things ropelike sperm is trickling down from the female pubic region. The critical response from the audience sounded suspiciously like booing as two translators argued about what I really said about these works.

Steven and I flew to Uzbekistan. Riding from the airport into Tashkent, the capital of Uzbekistan, we couldn't help notice the shift from the posters of Lenin in Moscow, where he looked like a descendant of European Slavs, to the posters here in the land of Tamerlane, where Lenin was suddenly looking like a deep-thinking Mongolian with high cheekbones and slanted eyes.

Waiting for us in our hotel was the head of the local USA, Comrade Makhmoudiev, and two of his pals, all in flowing garments, hats, moustaches, and many gold teeth. All three began to sing a slow song, very close to our faces, about a beautiful river. I stopped them after about thirty seconds and asked if they would begin again out on the balcony, where there was more light, and would they mind my shooting their singing to us with my video camera. Steven held the mike up to their moustaches. They seemed to have tears in their eyes, and Sonja explained that this was an old tradition of greeting strangers in their land. I was moved by the whole thing, and to return the gesture, when they stopped I sang "You Must Have Been a Beautiful Baby," which was the only song I could think of at the moment where I remembered all the words. We drank a toast consisting of a local hundred-twenty-proof cognac and parted with plans laid out for a celebration the next day with the artists of Tashkent.

In the already hot morning we moved around town picking up footage of a carnival and some flower gardens and whatever struck our fancy. Steven tracked down some English-speaking students near a university, and we got them to pass opinions on various subjects. Just before lunch we arrived at the hotel. On the large stone entrance patio, my head turned up to the blazing sun panning the upper reaches of the building, I suddenly felt dizzy, as if I was going to pass out. I dropped to one knee and gave Steven the camera. He and Sonja helped me to our room and to a couch. I'm not sure what happened. I was worried, I closed my eyes.

In a short while a rather tall and voluptuous forty-year-old woman is standing above me. She is introduced as a doctor. She's wearing a strange-looking turban wending its way in coils up to a point and then trailing down to her neck. After some questions and answers she decides to give me a shot of something that sounds like papaverine. After more talk and translation I realize the shot has to be administered straight into my heart. This woman doesn't look like a doctor. She looks like she's about to open her black medical bag, take out a musical pipe with tiny holes, and charm the snakes that are slithering out of the bag. Steven and I go into conference and decide to take a chance on a natural recovery. But I'm still dizzy, and I don't feel up to the celebration Comrade Makhmoudiev is about to take me to. The disappointment is laying a silent bomb in the room. But nothing is going to stop the party they have prepared for me. A Russian discussion ensues, which produces a prognosis: leave me in the room with Sonja and take Steven to represent me at the celebration.

Steven is led into a large room with extraordinary mosaic walls holding a hundred or more artists, some seated on chairs, some with legs folded on the floor. On a raised platform with beautiful rugs and a microphone, Steven, in a blue jumpsuit and black-and-white-striped high-heel shoes, is profusely toasted. He can't make out what is being said, but to be polite he downs six or seven hundred-twenty-proof cognacs to whoops and cheers. Completely drunk now, he delivers a rambling rundown of the contemporary art scene in New York—not exactly his area of expertise, and all with interruptions from a translator who keeps asking Steven to repeat what he just said, which Steven can't remember.

We came back to Moscow from Tashkent and Bukhara and were met at the airport by the American cultural attaché, Marilyn Johnson. The next day at the embassy she tells me, "Tonight you are going to talk again at the Union of Soviet Artists. When you were in Leningrad, you showed *America's Number One Problem* and an erotic Japanese work of yours. You know, Larry, you're playing directly into the hands of the Russians. They think we're a very degenerate society. I wouldn't presume ever to tell you what to show—but they don't like that sort of stuff." Our attaché in Leningrad had sent along the information that there were nasty remarks and grumbling when I showed these works. I said, "Do you want me not to show these two things?" She says, "I'm too sophisticated about art to say that. You do whatever you want."

I was surprised at the Russian reaction, considering how they loved to play up any of our black-white difficulties. But from the

483

slide, I thought to myself, you can't tell that *America's Number One Problem* is a vacuum-form piece. As for the message, in a country where there were no black men to speak of, maybe the American hangup about the size of black cocks could be viewed as just a dumb joke, even if nicely painted. I began to feel as if I were a regional painter—even if my region contained 260,000,000 people. What kind of art is so-called international art?

I didn't show *America's Number One Problem*, but to prove to Marilyn Johnson that nobody, not even the American government, can shove a freedom-loving artist like me around, I flashed my pornographic Japanese work.

Dean

Pulling the reader year by year up to the older me, my gray memory moves back through the windows into the rooms at the Parsons School of Design. There, I am looking at art. I am talking to students. I am keeping a wolf from materializing at my studio door. No one knows this about me, I think, except my accountant.

It is 1974. David C. Levy, the mad dean of the Parsons School, is looking for a fresh face. He is walking six flights up a dingy stairwell to my studio to talk me into connecting myself for a few hours a week with the world of Parsons. He spends five minutes panting from the climb. Soon I learn he is the godson of David Smith, the sculptor. In fact, he is named David because his father loved David Smith. Dean Levy holds a lot of strong opinions about what's wrong with contemporary art. I can't remember all the complaints, but his exalted notion of my work, what it stands for, and what I can do for his students moves me quickly to change the subject. Now we discover that both of us are old saxophonists, lovers of the Duke, Basie, Lester Young, and Charlie Parker. I add John Coltrane, the tenor saxophonist, to the list, and here David and I part company. He wiggles his eyebrows, says, "I don't like Coltrane." I tell him I'm not sure we can work together with such a basic disagreement.

Given the 168 hours in a week, being at Parsons was an infrequent enough occurrence for me to go and come happily. Though I rarely saw student work I found exciting, mysterious, or arresting, there were enough students I found exciting, mysterious, or arresting. I became excited about something in the course of any three-hour period that featured me. It pushed my pulse and increased my verbal flow, even if I was only advising students to look at a known artist's work that bore some relationship to theirs or suggesting an exhibition for them to go to. I can look and listen to students' art problems and dream up solutions and keep them enthusiastic. I've done it, but my heart ain't in it.

The original reason for taking the position as an art prof— about $12,000 a year, which had to do with a bleak assessment of my future—couldn't have kept an eviscerated wolf from huffing and puffing down my door, behind which, oblivious to all this, were my darling daughters' mouths to feed, bodies to clothe, and heads to roof, besides expenditures for my art and amorous continuity among my impoverished sweethearts. What I found strange about myself was that when things in the "field" began to change for the better, like museum shows in Europe, laudatory feedback, and books coming out about my work and sales, I continued teaching at Parsons. It seemed worth continuing, considering the little effort I had to expend: something besides the money was taking hold.

After a while David Levy began dreaming up a wider role for me. He had an ongoing agenda that resembled nineteenth-century colonialism. Under his tenure he had opened schools all over the map and planted the Parsons flag there. In Los Angeles the Otis School of Art was on its way out. It went and came back as Parsons School West. By the mid-eighties there were Parsons Schools in Paris, Libreville in Gabon, Tokyo, Seoul, and Altos de Chavonne in the Dominican Republic, and looser connections with Puerto Rico and other outlying colonial bastions. Except for Gabon and Korea, I was a speaker at the formal openings or a guest lecturer, which afforded me all the pleasures and difficulties of a paid political jaunt. Today most of these Parsons bastions have won their freedom to disappear.

On a flight to a university in Mayaguez, Puerto Rico, David pulled out a recorder rendering a pretty good version of "Now's the Time," a Charlie Parker–Miles Davis blues classic. It was the first time I was able to ascertain his level of playing. As usual when I travel, I had brought my horn, never knowing what musical possibilities might materialize, and so we played.

The Band

During the summer season in those Parsons years, along with my friend Howard Kanovitz, the artist and trombone player, I would

Howard Kanovitz

jam almost every Thursday in Three Mile Harbor at a place called the Birches, owned by a blues-singing guitarist. I invited David and his baritone sax to join us, and he drove the sixty miles from his Fire Island home, bringing along the New School's James Joyce scholar, Myron Schwartzman (alias My Blackman), who recently wrote a terrific book on Romare Bearden. Such were the modest beginnings of a new era of blowing my horn more frequently and thinking it mattered.

But the configuration of events and people that was ultimately responsible for what's happening in music for me these days, in 1992, began with gigs at Parsons School Christmas parties, graduation parties, end-of-term parties—call it a party, we played it. Our new joy with an old toy led us to meet once a week at my loft. With Howard Brofsky, trumpet player, professor, and specialist in eighteenth-century Italian instrumental music, I began writing music to create an original book for our band. When the dust settled, we had a seven-piece group, five white, two black, three brass, four rhythm, and because we couldn't think of a name, we agreed on the East Thirteenth Street Band, for the street we used to enter my building.

Our book grew. The musical spirit was somewhere between swing and bebop and unnameable originality. Everybody's playing improved. We began to take our happy situation seriously. I built a fourteen- by ten-foot stage with three tiers in my living room to give us some added exhilaration. We bought good sound equipment and bandstands, forties style, that Howard Kanovitz and I "artfully" decorated with portraits of the players. There were no visitors allowed at our rehearsals.

Calling Jane Wrigley

We ran through an amazing amount of "chick" singers. Our choice boiled down to Phoebe Legere, a Vassar graduate with a powerful four-octave range and a fur jockstrap, who had been singing her whole life. A very beautiful and original female, she had her own punk-rock band. Old-fashioned in her attention to sexual projection while singing, she remained modern in her ability to make fun of it.

Climax

With David Levy's peculiar but widespread New York connections and my art world visibility, we started to get gigs at such disparate places as the Church of the Heavenly Rest, UJA art auctions, and the new wing of the Fine Arts Museum in Houston, Texas (for that one we were only openers for the real stars of the evening, the Count Basie Band). One or two years after we started, we often presented our music in the context of a concert, playing onstage to a seated audience, with serious introduction and hearty applause. The band even made a recording that went as far as a Fifth Avenue window in the Rizzoli bookshop. At the Brooklyn Academy of Music, Lukas Foss, their conductor, invited the East Thirteenth Street Band to be part of an evening's homage to Duke Ellington. After some of our concerts, mostly for the art departments of universities, we ran symposiums on the connection, if any, between jazz and art.

Today, having graduated to the leadership of a new group, five pieces called the Climax Band, which featured cornet player Don Cherry a few times, I continue to play and write music, along with Howard Brofsky. Considering the falling pages of the calendar, I'm wondering when I will cave in and stop. We rarely play a gig more than once a week. Sometimes even a month or two goes by. Except for Bradley's on University Place and Bourbon Street in Southampton, two "real" jazz joints, the consumers of our music are disco parties and supper clubs, but mainly organizations hooked into the art world. One of our recent gigs—and this is the last mention of the horn in my life—was under the aegis of the Guggenheim Museum, whence a program called Learning Through Art emanates. I was given an award, as was Wynton Marsalis, the trumpet player. In traditional jazz style, he sat in and jammed with us.

She's Great

My daughter Gwynne, twenty-seven, is a singer and got her start with Dad. In her engagements in uptown dinner and music clubs the Climax Band serves as her backup band. She sings jazz, but she can also swagger through the audience like a nightclub singer in an old Hollywood movie, stroking the bald heads of men and sitting in their laps. About one in three times when we work she sings with us. I'll leave off opinions of her talent, looks, and possibilities. No one believes that a father can see straight about his daughter. This assumes that fathers love their daughters (if they don't, they should), and love, we know, is blind.

So Is the Other One

Emma, twenty-five, isn't a singer, but she sings. In their middle years these sisters entertained company, by request or not, singing duets and donning instantly improvised costumes in skits they made up as they went along. That's when I loved them most, aside from when I held them.

Emma, who I thought would be a writer, given the amount of stories she handed me when she was a kid, has become a sculptor, with a one-"man" show already under her belt. She inhabits a good-size studio in Tribeca, producing figures, mostly females, in story-telling settings, sometimes autobiographical. She makes highly polished wooden tables in shapes not often seen, with post-card reproductions of Old Masters embedded in the tops. She has had, and takes, commissions for these tables, reducing the flow from my coffers.

The Final Aria

I creak and groan. With the help and sometimes hindrance of five or six art assistants, two archivists, and Donnie, I am making works in preparation for an exhibition in the spring of '93 at the Marlborough Gallery. It's a thematic show that will be called Art and the

Artist—a not too profound idea of taking a painting by some modern master like Matisse or Léger and working from it, usually on a scale two or three times bigger than the original, incorporating the face and body of the master himself, then transforming the flat work into a three-dimensional work. Is there any relationship between the looks of the master and the look of his work? Perhaps! Matisse's personal elegance equals the elegance and upperclassness of his work, and Léger's work, blunt and heavy, is not too far removed in spirit from his chunky face and body. However that may be, putting together artworks based on paintings that have been part of my life in art from the beginning affords me pleasure.

My feelings today differ from those of the past about what I'm up to as an artist. If Amy, my dog whose bark identified me for myself, is gone, my art has now taken her place. I see my making art as an obsessional or compulsive search for pleasure or satisfaction. I no longer think being an artist is such a wonderful thing, although others do. Some of my art heroes of the past have been demoted, among them Marcel Duchamp. I knew him from books, magazines, and pamphlets filled with golden tales of the avant-garde. I also knew him from the many dinners I went to in the early sixties *chez* Denise Delaney of the beautiful lisp and her husband David Hare, the sculptor. There I also saw Duchamp's wife, Tina Matisse, Henri's former daughter-in-law, who came with him, happily for me. We talked all evening. Duchamp, still handsome in his sixties, in a deep chair he rarely moved from, always looked sweet, sad, and happy. He disappointed me in the intellectual discussion department; being the dumbbell I was in those days, I expected a brilliant *mot* a minute. He didn't say much, and everything he did say sounded like a Zen joke. His *Nude Descending a Staircase* is still beautiful, but *Cracked Then Cracked Filled Glass*, or whatever its name, now seems like the work of a clever young man who believed painting had come to some kind of end and stopped making art to prove it—and, as one more tale goes, to play chess undisturbed. The effort at the end of his life to catch up to a reputation based on so little effort didn't perturb him. A frantic soul like myself couldn't help finding this kind of calm attractive. But from the production point of view, Duchamp was not a Vermeer whose brilliance has held up all these centuries on the basis of a few works.

I don't want to add my voice to the chorus of bashers of the avant-garde. It seems like hitting a grandparent who has done a lot for you. Its luminaries have left us, and left us some marvelous things to see and think about. Like my eighty-five-year-old nemesis, Clem Greenberg, at this point down the pike I too can't tell you why an artwork is good or bad, although I think I recognize good or bad when I see it.

Parts of the Body

The thrill I get looking at parts of some female in the passing parade is even stronger today than in my youth. With a weakened retina, that isn't surprising, but it lacks the earlier accompaniment of doing something about the throbbing. Now I sit back, pull on my long beard, and moan.

But I'm more upset by the countrywide issue of child abuse and its use by the threatening "sex is evil" congregation. A doctor recently told me he stopped kissing his grandchildren or patting them on their asses; even physical affection with your own child can practically get you the chair. Is petting a dog or cat animal abuse? We are physically affectionate because it makes us (and the child and the cat and the dog) feel good. All we hear or see on television talk shows is what the "sex is evil" congregation will allow: that sex ruins your life no matter where it comes from. No grown-up in the country will come out of his or her closet, go on TV, and confide what a great lay was Aunt Mary or Uncle Harry "when I was twelve years old, and how wonderful life is and continues to be, and I'm married and *happy*." It's too shameful.

Let's see. What else is shameful? Oh yes! The matter of language. According to received wisdom, rape is no longer sex against your will; it is violence. It is true today more than yesterday that what you thought was love the night before can change to rape the morning after. For myself, I must admit that the public dialogue has produced a headache and a sympathy for almost every position the issue of rape touches. Even if you have sex with a "stranger in the night" and that stranger sleeps over, from my point of view it is not incumbent on either of you to have one more go at it in the morning if you don't want to. But if you're forced to, I just ask that you give it a word that presents a clearer picture of what happened. What do you call getting someone drunk enough or high enough to allow "it"? What is sex with an employer who threatens to fire you unless you consent? Is forced fellatio or cunnilingus harassment, rape, or violence, or something else? If an eighty-six-year-old woman is robbed and then penetrated by her assailant, is "violence" a sufficient explanation of what happened? What I know for sure is that no one should be screwed against their will.

I'm not sure if during my description of my unpredictable wild heartbeat I conveyed the idea that with each episode I expected to die. The problem began in 1978, and it is now almost fourteen years that I've been thinking I face imminent death every few weeks. Being told constantly by doctors and other sufferers that these episodic malfunctions were not life-threatening didn't comfort me when the number one organ of the body seemed to be floundering around in my chest. Now it seems I'm going to have to perish for other reasons.

I recently took a new ultrasensitive blood test for the functioning of the thyroid. It showed a distinct abnormality. After a few months of daily dosages of PTU (propylthiouracil) I went from a hyper (overactive) to a hypo (underactive) thyroid and finally had it radioactive-iodined out of existence. I still have episodes of tachycardia and fibrillations, but instead of lasting six to eight hours or more, as in the past, today they last only two or three minutes and are hardly noticeable.

Okay. What Did I Do!

I married two women.

I became a father to five children. I made 3,120 artworks, 250 videos.

I accepted the call to make most of life seem absurd.

I spoke Yiddish with my family and later relearned it with Howard Kanovitz.

I limited my boundless love for Roosevelt when his gruesome policy of refusing to trade jeeps for Jews came to light.

I read Proust and Primo Levi and the other histories that came

Daria and Sam

my way. I did a triptych of Levi. Gianni Agnelli, prompted by Furio Colombo, bought it for *La Stampa*, the newspaper Levi wrote for after returning from Auschwitz. The paintings hang in Turin, city of black and white magic.

I pinned my hopes on love.

I liked Gore Vidal's snotty intelligence.

I forgave all those who left me out of major exhibitions. I criticized everybody, including Leo Castelli, but I forgave him.

I chewed on a Tampax at a party in Brooklyn. Thirty years later Whoopi Goldberg twirled one in Bob Altman's film *The Player*.

I begged for money in Paris, playing a straight soprano sax with a cup and a sign that said, "Blinded in May '68" (the uprising). I was so moved by myself I had my assistant film me.

I lived for ten years with the youthful narrative painter Daria Deshuk, a talented student I met at the Parsons School. I traveled to Paris with her in October 1984, specifically to have sex to make a child. I did it with her twice a day for five days in the Hotel Cayre on Boulevard Raspail. It worked.

I arranged for the mutilation of my son's cock, a surgery that was not necessary unless I took seriously the biblical covenant with God. I hope that when Sam grows up he won't think he needs the bit of skin and can forgive me. I'm not sure if that decision to have him circumcised made me any more Jewish than my decision ten years before to halt ingestion of the pig. I'm surprised that my talent for original thinking produced such an ordinary parent as myself, for like an ordinary parent, I complain about Sam's behavior and I love him.

I hid from the reader my conflict with and about the useful rich, toward whom I acted more democratically than I felt.

In Paris in 1962 I made a drawing of Mary McCarthy that I kept, but I still accepted her husband Jim West's embassy influence to get me a quick visa to Poland.

I scared the sous chef of the Golden Pear for serving me soft scrambled eggs hard—to save me, she swore, from the dread salmonella plague. I demanded to know why, when I ordered my soft scrambled eggs, she did not mention said plague. As I lifted my plate to show her the slab of eggs, she ran from the counter to the kitchen, fearing I was going to Frisbee her. The decibel level of my rising voice made patrons move their water glasses out of shattering distance.

What did I do? Tell me.

ACKNOWLEDGMENTS

Arnold Weinstein and I have received all kinds of help, but four people deserve special thanks. Joy Johannessen, for reducing all that was verbose and repetitive to a non-noticeable succinctness. She made many intelligent suggestions for switches of chapters and paragraphs and expressed opinions that kept me confident. She's got a large brain, a big heart, and a huge memory. I've fallen in love with her. Mike Shane, the solo trumpet player in the Johnny Morris band, for supplying me with tapes of the band's 1945 WOR radio air checks, which establish that our singer Jane Wrigley existed and that other seeming figments of my imagination were based on real life. Clarice Rivers, for putting her ability to remember dreams to the romantic part of our life in the 1960s. And Nancy Grome, for her bright industriousness in the low-paying industry of reconstructive typing and assemblage.

Grateful acknowledgment is made to the following writers and publishers for permission to reprint copyrighted material: "Two Scenes," in *Some Trees* by John Ashbery (New York: The Ecco Press, 1978). Copyright © 1956 by John Ashbery. Reprinted by permission of Georges Borchardt, Inc., for the author. Four previously unpublished letters from John Ashbery to Larry Rivers. Copyright © 1992 by John Ashbery. All rights reserved. Reprinted by permission of John Ashbery. Untitled essay from an exhibition catalogue published by Galerie Rive Droite, Paris. Copyright © 1962 by John Ashbery. Reprinted by permission of Georges Borchardt, Inc., for the author. From "Larry Rivers Paints Himself into the Canvas" by Grace Glueck, *The New York Times Magazine*, February 13, 1966. Copyright © 1966 by The New York Times Company. Reprinted by permission of The New York Times Company. Previously unpublished letter from Barbara Goldsmith to Larry Rivers. Copyright © 1992 by Barbara Goldsmith. All rights reserved. Reprinted by permission of Barbara Goldsmith. From *When the Sun Tries to Go Down* by Kenneth Koch (Los Angeles: Black Sparrow Press, 1969). Copyright © 1969 by Kenneth Koch. Reprinted by permission of Kenneth Koch. From *The Election*, in *A Change of Hearts* by Kenneth Koch (New York: Random House, 1973). Copyright © 1973 by Kenneth Koch. Reprinted by permission of Kenneth Koch. Previously unpublished letter from Kenneth Koch to Larry Rivers.

Copyright © 1992 by Kenneth Koch. All rights reserved. Reprinted by permission of Kenneth Koch. "The Day Lady Died" by Frank O'Hara, in Donald M. Allen, ed., *The New American Poetry* (New York: Grove Press, 1960). Copyright © 1959 by Frank O'Hara. Reprinted by permission of Grove Press and Maureen O'Hara Granville-Smith. Previously unpublished letters and a previously unpublished poem from Frank O'Hara to Larry Rivers. Copyright © 1992 by the estate of Frank O'Hara. All rights reserved. Reprinted by permission of Maureen O'Hara Granville-Smith. "Rivers Paints a Picture: Portrait of Berdie" by Fairfield Porter, *Art News* 52 (January 1954): 56–59. Copyright © 1954 by Fairfield Porter. Reprinted by permission of *Art News*. Previously unpublished letter from Terry Southern to Larry Rivers. Copyright © 1992 by Terry Southern. All rights reserved. Reprinted by permission of Terry Southern.

ILLUSTRATION CREDITS

p. 29   *Parts of the Body*, 1961. Bronze, 92 x 31 x 31". Museo de Arte Contemporáneo, Caracas. Photo: John Reed

p. 35   Robert Bass

p. 101   *McGovern Poster*, 1972. Silkscreen, 29¾ x 23"

p. 102   *Memory*, 1989. Oil on canvas mounted on sculpted foamboard, 76¼ x 81 x 7½". Collection of the artist

p. 106   Jack Freilicher

p. 118   *Still Life with Knoll Table*, 1946. Tempera on paper, 12 x 9". Collection of G. Stern, New York

p. 125   Nell Blaine

p. 139   *Papa a Little Later*, 1964. Pencil on paper, 18 x 18". Collection of Mr. and Mrs. Edward S. Gordon, New York

p. 145   *Mama a Little Later*, 1964. Pencil on paper, 18 x 18". Collection of Mr. and Mrs. Edward S. Gordon, New York

p. 157   *For C's 35th*, 1974. Colored pencil on paper, 14 x 17". Collection of Clarice Rivers

p. 163   Rudolph Burckhardt

p. 179   Rudolph Burckhardt

p. 183   Walt Silver

p. 191   Hans Namuth

p. 214   Living Theater Archives

p. 216   Nell Blaine

p. 223   *The Official Marriage Portrait of Earl and Camilla McGrath:* "OY," 1964. Oil on canvas, 48 x 36". Collection of Earl and Camilla McGrath. Photo on right: Camilla McGrath

p. 229   George Montgomery

p. 234   Camilla McGrath

p. 240   Courtesy of Joe Le Sueur

p. 241   Rudolph Burckhardt

p. 244   *Stones: End of All Existences*, 1957. Lithograph, 24 x 30". Collection of the artist. Photo: Walt Silver

p. 247   Jane Freilicher, *Still Life with Calendulas*, 1955. Oil on canvas, 65½ x 49½". Private collection

p. 249   *Jean Garrigue*, 1951. Pencil on paper, 23¾ x 17¾". Collection of the artist

p. 252   Walt Silver

p. 256   *The Burial*, 1952. Oil on canvas, 60 x 108". Fort Wayne Art School and Museum, Fort Wayne, Indiana

p. 266   Fairfield Porter, *Larry Rivers*, 1951. Oil on canvas, 40 x 30". Collection of Katherine Porter, Belfast, Maine

p. 268   Photo on right: Tibor de Nagy Gallery

p. 271   Hans Namuth

p. 274   *Portrait of Kenneth Koch*, 1953. Pencil, 13¾ x 16¾". Museum of Modern Art, New York

p. 291   *Augusta*, 1954. Oil on canvas, 83 x 53". Collection of the artist. Photo on right: Hans Namuth

p. 301   Walt Silver

p. 305   Hans Namuth

SET IN ELECTRA AND ITC ZAPF BOOK HEAVY
BY DIX TYPE INC., SYRACUSE, NEW YORK
PRINTED AND BOUND BY THE COURIER COMPANY,
WESTFORD, MASSACHUSETTS